lnterplay

Interplay THIRD EDITION

THE PROCESS OF INTERPERSONAL COMMUNICATION

Ronald B. Adler
Santa Barbara City College

Lawrence B. Rosenfeld
University of North Carolina
at Chapel Hill

Neil Towne
Grossmont College

Holt, Rinehart and Winston
New York   Chicago   San Francisco   Philadelphia
Montreal   Toronto   London   Sydney
Tokyo   Mexico City   Rio de Janeiro   Madrid

Cover: Pierre Auguste Renoir, *Le Moulin de la Galette*, 1876, Musée d'Orsay, Paris. Courtesy of Giraudon/Art Resource, NY.

Library of Congress Cataloging-in-Publication Data

Adler, Ronald B. (Ronald Brian), date.
 Interplay: the process of interpersonal communication.

  Bibliography: p.
  Includes index.
  1. Interpersonal communication. I. Rosenfeld, Lawrence B. II. Towne, Neil, date. III. Title.
BF637.C45A33 1986   302.2   85–17579
ISBN 0-03-002862-0

CBS COLLEGE PUBLISHING
Holt, Rinehart and Winston
The Dryden Press
Saunders College Publishing

Photo Credits

1 © Bob Adelman, Magnum. 12 © 1981 Rebecca Collette, Archive. 19 © Martine Franck, Magnum. 26 © Owen Franken, Stock Boston. 27 © Ellis Herwig, Stock Boston. 30 © Donald Dietz, Stock Boston. 33 © Slim Aarons, Photo Researchers. 43 © Joan Liftin, Archive. 50 © De Andrade, Magnum. 51 © F. B. Grunzweig, Photo Researchers. 53 © Alice Kandell, Photo Researchers. 65 © Bohdan J. Hyrnewych, Stock Boston. 72 © Joe Kelly, Archive. 79 © Charles Harbutt, Archive. 84 © Peter Southwick, Stock Boston. 93 © Eve Arnold, Magnum. 99 Courtesy of the *Hackensack Record*, New Jersey. 101 © Richard Kalvar, Magnum. 108 Copyright © 1943 James Thurber. Copyright © 1971 Helen W. Thurber and Rosemary Thurber Sauers. From *Men, Women, and Dogs*, published by Harcourt Brace Jovanovich. Copyright © Collection James Thurber, Hamish Hamilton, London. 104 © Joan Liftin, Archive. 122 (top) © J. R. Holland, Stock Boston; (bottom) © Jonathan Rawle, Stock Boston. 127 © Geoffrey Gove, Photo Researchers. 135 © Elizabeth Hamlin, Stock Boston. 147 © Richard Kalvar, Magnum. 151 © Suzanne E. Wu, Jeroboam. 161 © Bob Adelman, Magnum. 167 © Arthur Tress, Photo Researchers. 171 © Robert Foothorap, Jeroboam. 179 © Yan Lukas, Photo Researchers. 193 © Abigail Heyman, Archive. 197 © Frank Siteman, Stock Boston. 201 © Joan Liftin, Archive. 205 © Ken Reno, Jeroboam. 213 © Leonard Freed, Magnum. 216 © Mary Ellen Mark, Archive. 235 © Frank Siteman, Stock Boston. 238 © Leonard Freed, Magnum. 243 © Richard Kalvar, Magnum. 248 © Bruce Roberts, Photo Researchers. 259 © Alan Becker, Photo Reseachers. 265 © Owen Franken, Stock Boston. 275 © Dean Abramson, Stock Boston.

Acknowledgments

5 Reprinted from *The Albuquerque Tribune*, Copyright © 1982. 10 Cartoon by Hamilton reprinted by permission of Chronicle Features, San Francisco. 11 Excerpt abridged from pp. 64, 66–7 in *Dancer from the Dance* by Andrew Holleran. Copyright © 1978 by William Morrow and Company, Inc. By permission of the publisher. 13 Drawing by Stevenson; © 1983 The New Yorker Magazine, Inc. Used by permission. 22 Drawing by Saul Steinberg © 1965, Used by permission of artist and Julian Bach Literary Agency. 24 "Ziggy" cartoon by Tom Wilson. © 1973, Universal Press Syndicate. Reprinted with permission. All rights reserved. 29 "Miss Peach" cartoon by Mell Lazarus. © 1975. Used by permission of Mell Lazarus and Field Newspaper Syndicate. 37 "Garfield" cartoon by Jim Davis. © 1981. United Feature Syndicate, Inc. Used by permission. 40 Cartoon by Gahan Wilson. © 1974. Reprinted from The Register and Tribune Syndicate, Inc. 41 "Peanuts" cartoon by Charles Schulz. © 1967. United Feature Syndicate, Inc. Used by permission. 49 Cartoon by Jerry Marcus © 1979 *Redbook Magazine*. Reprinted by permission of Jerry Marcus. 54 "Coming and Going" from *The Deserted Rooster* by Ric Masten. Reprinted by permission of the poet. Sunflower Ink, Palo Colorado, Carmel, CA. 57 Cartoon by Sidney Harris. © 1984 by Sidney Harris—American Scientist Magazine. Used by Permission. 69 Excerpt from *Conversation and Communication* by J. A. M. Meerloo. © International Universities Press, Inc. Used by permission. 73 "Hagar the Horrible" by Dik Browne. © 1981 King Features, Inc. Used by permission. 75 "Cathy" cartoon by Cathy Guisewite. Copyright © 1983 Universal Press Syndicate. All rights reserved. Used by permission. 80 Used courtesy of author, Edward Sherman. 82 "Tumbleweeds" by Tom K. Ryan. © 1979 United Features Syndicate, Inc. Courtesy of News America Syndicate. 86 Excerpt from *I and Thou: Here and Now: Contributions of Gestalt Therapy*. Reprinted courtesy of the author, Claudio Naranjo. 96 Excerpt from *Zorba the Greek* by Nikos Kazantzakis. Copyright © 1953 by Simon & Schuster, Inc. renewed © 1981 by Simon & Schuster, Inc. Reprinted by permission of Simon & Schuster, Inc. 102 "Nothing" from

(continued following Index)

A good interpersonal communication text should avoid two errors. On one hand, it mustn't oversimplify the subject. Readers looking for easy prescriptions about how to achieve perfect relationships don't need to study a college text: They can find the answers they seek on the self-help racks at almost every bookseller, supermarket, airport, and drugstore. While the ideas in these books may be easy to grasp, they distort or ignore the complex factors that painstaking research has shown govern interpersonal communication.

While a good text shouldn't be too simplistic, neither should it be too complex. Students in a basic course need to get a sense of what professionals know about interpersonal communication, but they shouldn't be submerged in the minutiae of research and theorizing that is more appropriate for upper division and graduate level work.

As in past editions, our goal in this incarnation of *Interplay* is to strike a balance between simplicity and complexity, providing a useful survey of interpersonal communication for intelligent nonexperts taking their first close look at the subject. We have tried to summarize the large amount of detailed and sometimes contradictory research in a way that provides a state-of-the-art look at the field. Rather than take sides in the "theory vs. skills" debate that rages endlessly in the discipline, we have tried to show how the research on interpersonal communication suggests a number of skills that readers can use to improve the quality of their own relationships.

The third edition of *Interplay* retains all the features that made its predecessors so well received. It strives to be readable, based on the conviction that even complicated ideas can be presented in a straightforward way. Beyond clarity, *Interplay* aims to be interesting. This interest doesn't come just from the text: The following pages are sprinkled with a variety of epigrams, photos, cartoons, and poetry that illustrate some truths about interpersonal communication far more effectively than could the authors alone. Perhaps the most important feature of *Interplay* is its real-world orientation. We have made every effort to show the link between scholarship and everyday communication, so that the reader's question "So what?" will always be easy to answer.

This new edition also boasts some important changes. Most noticeably, several chapters contain new material. Chapter 4 offers new information on how language conveys power, credibility, status, and intimacy. Chapter 8 now provides a more complete and less ideological view of self-disclosure by realistically describing both the benefits *and* risks of disclosing, as well as discussing the role of "white lies" in interpersonal relationships. Information on assertiveness in Chapter 11 has been expanded at the request of many users. Throughout this new edition of *Interplay* is an extensive discussion of how gender differences affect communication. Finally, every chapter of *Interplay* has been updated to reflect current research on important topics.

Interplay's usefulness is enhanced by two companion volumes. A comprehensive instructor's manual by Jerry Allen of the University of Bridgeport will help professors fit the greatest amount of useful information into the available time. For those seeking additional methods for developing interpersonal skills, a new edition of *Toward Communication Competency* has been prepared by Susan R. Glaser and Anna Eblen. This volume offers a range of individual and group activities that parallel the structure of *Interplay*, offering advice and practice that will help readers put the ideas in this book into practice.

In a world where indifference and lack of attention to detail are all too common, we are especially grateful for the professionalism of the team that made *Interplay* possible. Anne Boynton-Trigg, Jackie Fleischer, and Lucy Rosendahl's developmental guidance; the design talents of Janet Bollow and Lou Scardino; and the editorial-production skills of Lester A. Sheinis and Nancy Myers have kept the book on target and on schedule.

We are also grateful to the reviewers whose suggestions have made *Interplay* a better book: James Biggs, Murray State University; Joan Dominick, University of Georgia; Vernon Gantt, Murray State University, Katherine Hendrix, Fresno City College; Pat Lowrance and Cindy Ross, Butler County Community College; Jerry Mayes, Murray State University; Bonnie Miley, Iowa Western Community College; Martha Moore, Murray State University; Bobby Patton, University of Kansas; and Daniel Walther, Brazosport College.

RBA
LBR
NT

Contents

**Chapter 7
Relationships 151**

**Chapter 8
Self-Disclosure 179**

Chapter 9
Emotions   205

Chapter 10
Communication Climate   235

Chapter 11
Resolving Conflicts   259

Interpersonal Process

After studying the material in this chapter

You should understand:

1. Three reasons for studying communication.
2. The needs that effective communication can satisfy.
3. The differences among linear, interactive, and transactional communication models.
4. Situational and qualitative definitions of interpersonal communication.
5. The characteristics of effective interpersonal communicators.

You should be able to:

1. Identify the important needs you attempt to satisfy by communicating.
2. Demonstrate how the transactional communication model applies to your interpersonal communication.
3. Identify when your communication is and is not qualitatively interpersonal, and describe the consequences each way.
4. Identify effective and ineffective interpersonal communicators (including yourself).

Everyone communicates. Students and professors, parents and children, employers and employees, friends, strangers, and enemies—all communicate. We have been communicating with others from the first weeks of life and will keep on doing so until we die.

Why study an activity you've done your entire life? There are three reasons. First, studying interpersonal communication will give you a new look at a familiar topic. For instance, in a few pages you will find that some people can go years—even lifetimes—without communicating in a truly interpersonal manner. In this sense, exploring human communication is rather like studying anatomy or botany—everyday objects and processes take on new meaning.

A second reason for studying the subject has to do with the staggering amount of time we spend communicating. In research at the University of Cincinnati, Rudolph Verderber and his associates (1976) measured the amount of time a sample of college students spent on various activities. The researchers found that their subjects spent an average of over 61 percent of their waking time engaged in some form of communication. Whatever the occupation, the results would not be too different.

There is a third, more compelling reason for studying interpersonal communication. To put it bluntly, none of us communicate as effectively as we could. Our friendships, jobs, and studies suffer because we fail to express ourselves well and understand others accurately. If you pause now and make a mental list of communication problems you have encountered, you'll see that, no matter how successful your relationships, there is plenty of room for improvement in your everyday life. The information that follows will help you improve your communication skill with some of the people who matter most to you.

Why we communicate

Research demonstrating the importance of communication has been around longer than you might think. Frederick II, emperor of Germany from 1196 to 1250, was called *stupor mundi*— "wonder of the world"—by his admiring subjects. Along with his administrative and military talents, Frederick was a leading scientist of his time. A medieval historian described one of his interesting, if inhumane, experiments:

> . . . He bade foster mothers and nurses to suckle the children, to bathe and wash them, but in no way to prattle with them, for he wanted to learn whether they would speak the Hebrew language, which was the oldest, or Greek, or Latin, or Arabic, or perhaps the language of their parents, of whom they had been born. But he labored in vain because all the children died. For they could not live without the petting and joyful faces and loving words of their foster mothers. (Ross and McLaughlin, 1949, p. 366)

Fortunately, contemporary researchers have found less dramatic ways to illustrate the importance of communication. In one study of isolation, subjects were paid to remain alone in a locked room. Of the five subjects, one lasted for eight days. Three held out for two days, one commenting, "Never again." The fifth subject lasted only two hours (Schachter, 1959, pp. 9–10).

You might question the value of experiments like these, arguing that solitude would be a welcome relief from the irritations of everyday life. It's true that all of us need solitude, often more than we get. On the other hand, each of us has a point beyond which we do not want to be alone. Beyond this point solitude changes from a pleasurable to a painful condition. In other words, we all need people. We all need to communicate.

l see communication as a huge umbrella that covers and affects all that goes on between human beings. Once a human being has arrived on this earth, communication is the largest single factor determining what kinds of relationships he makes with others and what happens to him in the world about him. How he manages his survival, how he develops intimacy, how productive he is, how he makes sense, how he connects with his own divinity—all are largely dependent on his communication skills.

Virginia Satir

Physical needs   Communication is so important that it is necessary for physical health. In the introduction to his excellent anthology *Bridges, Not Walls*, John Stewart (1982, p. 6) cites research showing a wide range of medical hazards that result from a lack or breakdown of close relationships. For instance:

> Socially isolated people are two to three times more likely to die prematurely than are those with strong social ties. The type of relationship doesn't seem to matter: marriage, friendship, and religious and community ties all seem to increase longevity.

> Divorced men (before age seventy) die from heart disease, cancer, and strokes at double the rate of married men. Three times as many die from hypertension; five times as many commit suicide; seven times as many die from cirrhosis of the liver; and ten times as many die from tuberculosis.

> The rate of all types of cancer is as much as five times higher for divorced men and women, compared to their single counterparts.

> Poor communication can contribute to coronary disease. One Swedish study examined 32 pairs of identical twins. One sibling in each pair had

heart disease, whereas the other was healthy. The researchers found that the obesity, smoking habits, and cholesterol levels of the healthy and sick twins did not differ significantly. Among the significant differences, however, were "poor childhood and adult interpersonal relationships," the ability to resolve conflicts, and the degree of emotional support given by others.

The likelihood of death increases when a close relative dies. In one Welsh village, citizens who had lost a close relative died within one year at a rate more than five times greater than those who had not suffered from a relative's death.

Such research demonstrates the importance of satisfying personal relationships. Remember: Not everyone needs the same amount of contact, and the quality of communication is almost certainly as important as the quantity. The important point here is that personal communication is essential for our well-being. In other words, "people who need people" aren't "the luckiest people in the world" . . . they're the *only* people!

Ego needs   Communication does more than enable us to survive. It is the *only* way we learn who we are. As you'll read in Chapter 2, our sense of identity comes from the way we interact with other people. Are we smart or stupid, attractive or ugly, skillful or inept? The answers to these questions don't come from looking in the mirror. We decide who we are based on how others react to us.

 Deprived of communication with others, we would have no sense of identity. Stewart (p. 8) dramatically illustrates this fact by citing the case of the famous "Wild Boy of Aveyron," who spent his early childhood without any apparent human contact. The boy was discovered in January 1800 while digging for vegetables in a French village garden. He showed no behaviors one would

Loneliness can contribute to heart disease

Loneliness may be hazardous to your heart, according to scientists who say single men without close friends run two or three times the risk of developing heart disease as their more sociable counterparts.

Social isolation may be as important a risk in the development of heart disease as cigarette smoking, high blood pressure, and high cholesterol, according to Leonard Syme, a professor of epidemiology at the University of California at Berkeley.

Researchers studied a randomly chosen group of 6928 residents of Alameda County, just east of San Francisco, and found that people with no friends had two to three times the death rate of people with the most friends and social contact.

The researchers also found it was not important whether a person felt lonely or isolated, or whether a socially active person was pleased with his social relationships—it was only important that he had them.

Syme said the discoveries linking social isolation and heart disease seem to apply only to men. For reasons not understood, social contact does not seem to be as important for women in lowering their chances of having heart attacks.

Albuquerque Tribune, March 5, 1982, p. C-15

---

expect in a social human. The boy could not speak, but uttered only weird cries. More significant than this absence of social skills was his lack of any identity as a human being. As author Roger Shattuck (1980, p. 37) put it, "The boy had no human sense of being in the world. He had no sense of himself as a person related to other persons." Only after the influence of a loving "mother" did the boy begin to behave—and, we can imagine, think of himself—as a human.

Like the boy of Aveyron, each of us enters the world with little or no sense of identity. We gain an idea of who we are from the way others define us. As Chapter 2 explains, the messages we receive in early childhood are the strongest, but the influence of others continues throughout life.

Social needs   Besides helping define who we are, communication is the way we relate socially with others. Psychologist William Schutz (1966) describes three types of social needs we strive to fulfill by communicating. The first is *inclusion,* the need to feel a sense of belonging to some personal relationship. Inclusion needs are sometimes satisfied by informal alliances: the friends who study together, a group of runners, or neighbors who help one another with yard work. In other cases, we get a sense of belonging from formal relationships: everything from religious congregations to a job to marriage.

A second type of social need is *control*—the need to influence others, to feel some sense of power over our world. Some types of control are obvious, such as the directions a boss or team captain gives. Much control, however, is more subtle. Experts in child development tell us that preschoolers who insist on staying up past bedtime or having a treat in the supermarket may

Man lives by affirmation even more than he lives by bread.

Victor Hugo

---

be less concerned with the issue at hand than with knowing that they have at least some ability to make things happen. Even driving a parent crazy can satisfy the need for control. This fact answers the parent's question "Why are you being so stubborn?"

The third social need is *affection*—a need to care for others and know that they care for us. Affection, of course, is critical for most of us. Being included and having power aren't satisfying if the important people in our lives don't care for us.

Practical needs We shouldn't overlook the everyday, important functions communication serves. Communication is the tool that lets us tell the hair stylist to take just a little off the sides, the doctor where it hurts, and the plumber that the broken pipe needs attention *now!* Communication is the means of learning important information in school. It is the method you use to convince a prospective employer that you're the best candidate for a job, and it is the way to persuade the boss you deserve a raise. The list of common but critical jobs performed by communicating goes on and on, and it's worth noticing that the inability to express yourself clearly and effectively in every one of the above examples can prevent you from achieving your goal.

Psychologist Abraham Maslow (1968) suggested that human needs fall into five categories, each of which must be satisfied before we concern ourselves with the next one. As you read on, think about the ways in which communication is often necessary to satisfy each need. The most basic of these needs are *physical:* sufficient air, water, food, and rest and the ability to reproduce as a species. The second of Maslow's needs

involve *safety:* protection from threats to our well-being. Beyond physical and safety concerns are the *social* needs we have mentioned already. Beyond them, Maslow suggests that each of us has *self-esteem* needs: the desire to believe that we are worthwhile, valuable people. The final category of needs involves *self-actualization:* the desire to develop our potential to the maximum, to become the best person we can be.

The communication process

So far we have used the word "communication" as if its meaning were perfectly clear. In fact, the process of communication isn't as simple as it might seem.

A linear view As recently as 40 years ago, researchers viewed communication as something one person "does" to another (Shannon and Weaver, 1949). In this view, communicating resembles giving an injection: a sender encodes ideas and feelings into some sort of message and then injects them by means of a channel (speech, writing, and so on) into a receiver (see Figure 1–1). If the message can get through any interference—termed *noise* in scientific jargon—communication has been successful.

This perspective does provide some useful information. For instance, it highlights how different channels can affect the way a receiver responds to a message. Should you say "I love you" in person? Over the phone? By renting space on a billboard? By sending flowers and a card? With a singing telegram? Each channel does have its differences.

The linear model also shows how noise can interfere with a message. Two types of noise can block communication: physical and psychological. As its name implies, some physical noise makes it hard to hear a message. Other distractions also can be physical noise: too much cigarette smoke

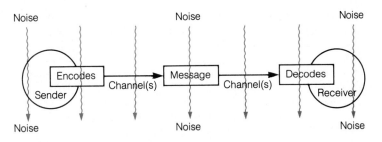

FIGURE 1–1   Linear communication model

in a crowded room might make it hard for you to pay attention to a speaker, and fatigue or illness might affect your concentration or make you less sympathetic than usual.

Psychological noise refers to forces within the sender and receiver that make them less likely to communicate effectively. For instance, a woman who hears the word "gal" might become so irritated that she has trouble listening objectively to the rest of a speaker's message. Likewise, an insecure employee might interpret a minor suggestion the boss makes as ridicule or criticism.

An interactive view   Despite its advantages, the linear model inaccurately suggests that communication flows in one direction, from sender to receiver. Although some types of messages (printed and broadcast messages, for example) do flow in a one-way, linear manner, most types of communication—especially the interpersonal variety—are two-way exchanges. To put it differently, the linear view ignores the fact that receivers *react* to messages by sending other messages of their own.

Consider, for instance, the significance of a friend's yawn as you describe your lint collection. Or imagine the blush you might see as you tell one of your raunchier jokes to a new acquaintance. Nonverbal behaviors like these show that most face-to-face communication is a two-way affair. The discernible response of a receiver to a sender's message is called *feedback*. Not all feedback is nonverbal, of course. Sometimes it is oral, as when you ask an instructor questions about an upcoming test or volunteer your opinion of a friend's new haircut. In other cases it is written, as when you answer the questions on a midterm exam or respond to a letter from a faraway friend.

When we add the element of feedback to our model, we begin to see that communication is less like giving a linguistic injection than like playing a verbal and nonverbal tennis game in which messages pass back and forth between the parties (see Figure 1–2).

A quick glance at Figure 1–2 suggests that after a period of interaction, the mental images of the sender and receiver ought to match. If they do, we can say that an act of successful communication has occurred. However, your personal experience shows that misunderstandings often occur between sender and receiver. Your constructive suggestion is taken as criticism; your friendly joke is taken as an insult; your hints are missed entirely. These sorts of misunderstandings often occur because senders and receivers occupy different environments. In communication terminology, *environment* refers not only to a physical location, but also to the personal history that each person brings to a conversation. Although they have some experiences in common, they each see the situation in a unique way. Consider just

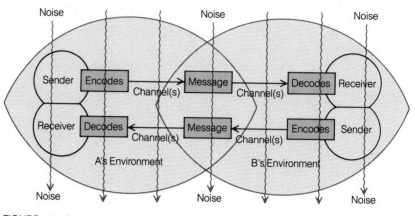

FIGURE 1–2   Interacttive communication model

some of the factors that might contribute to different environments:

A might be well rested and B exhausted;

A might be rich and B poor;

A might be rushed and B have nowhere to go;

A might have lived a long, eventful life and B might be young and inexperienced;

A might be passionately concerned with the subject and B indifferent to it.

Notice that in Figure 1–2 the environments of A and B overlap. This intersecting area represents the background and knowledge that the communicators have in common. The size of this overlap varies between two people according to the topic of communication: In some areas it might be rather large, whereas on other subjects it might be extremely small. It is impossible to acquire all the background of another person, but the kind of careful listening described in Chapter 4 can boost the environmental overlap that leads to more accurate, satisfying communication.

A transactional view   Even with the addition of feedback and environment, the model in Figure 1–2 isn't completely satisfactory. Notice that it portrays communication as a static activity, suggesting that there are discrete "acts" of

communication that begin and end at identifiable times, and that a sender's message causes some effect in a receiver. Furthermore, it suggests that at any given moment a person is either sending or receiving.

In fact, none of these characterizations is valid for most types of communication. The activity of communicating is usually not interactive, but *transactional.* A transactional perspective differs from the more simplistic ones we've already discussed in several ways.

First, a transactional model reveals that communicators usually send and receive messages simultaneously, so that the images of sender and receiver in Figure 1–2 should not be separated as if a person were doing only one or the other, but rather superimposed and redefined as "participants" (Rogers and Kincaid, 1981) (see Figure 1–3). At a given moment we are capable of receiving, decoding, and responding to another person's behavior, while at the same time that other person is receiving and responding to ours. Consider, for example, what might occur when you and a housemate negotiate how to handle household chores. As soon as you begin to hear (receive) the words sent by your partner, "I want to talk about cleaning the bathroom . . . ," you grimace and clench your jaw (sending a nonverbal

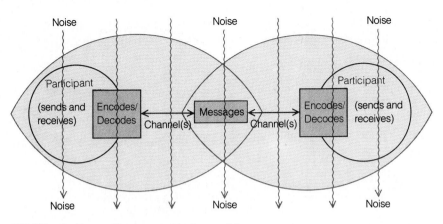

FIGURE 1–3   Transactional communication model

message of your own while receiving the verbal one). This reaction leads your partner to interrupt himself, defensively sending a new message: "Now wait a minute. . . ."

Besides illustrating the simultaneous nature of face-to-face interaction, this example shows that it's difficult to isolate a single discrete "act" of communication from the events that precede and follow it. Your partner's comment about cleaning the bathroom (and the way it was presented) probably grew from exchanges you had in the past. Likewise, the way you'll act toward one another in the future depends on the outcome of this conversation. By now you can see that a transactional model of communication should be more like a motion picture film than a gallery of still photographs. Although Figure 1–3 does a fair job of picturing the phenomenon we call communication, an animated version in which the environments, communicators, and messages constantly changed would be an even better way of capturing the process. You can also see that communication is not something that people do *to* one another, but a process in which they create a relationship by interacting *with* each other.

Now we can summarize the definition of communication we have been developing. Communication is a *continuous, transactional*

process involving *participants* who occupy different but overlapping *environments* and create a relationship by *simultaneously sending and receiving messages,* many of which are distorted by physical and psychological *noise.*

Interpersonal communication defined

So far we have talked about the communication process without specifically discussing the interpersonal variety. What is interpersonal communication? What distinguishes it from other types of interaction? There are two ways to answer this question.

A situational definition   The most obvious distinction—although not the most useful —involves the context in which the interaction occurs. We can look at how many people are involved, whether they are close to or far from one another, and how much access they have (for example, how much of one another they can see, hear, and touch, and how easy it is to offer feedback). Interpersonal communication using this approach is defined as involving a small number of communicators who are close together and who have a great deal of access to one another.

Using a situational approach, we can easily distinguish interpersonal communication from mass communication, which involves more people with greater distances between them, and with very limited access to one another. In some cases, mass communication involves feedback that takes months to process, as in the case of letters to TV stations about the most and least popular shows.

Public communication—usually consisting of a speech given before an audience—is also easily distinguished from interpersonal communication. Greater numbers of communicators at greater distances are involved in public communication, and access—especially in the form of feedback— is relatively limited, although not so much as in the case of mass communication.

Matters become a little more confusing when we compare interpersonal and small group communication. However, clear differences between these modes do exist. For example, issues such as conformity, leadership, division of labor, and decision making are much more prominent in groups, due to the greater number and complexity of interrelationships.

On the other hand, there are strong similarities between one-to-one and small group interaction. Both involve a small number of communicators who are physically close and who have great access to one another. And certainly there is a strong degree of "interpersonalness" in many group settings. Consider, for instance, a small work, study, or social group to which you've belonged. The relationships in such a group almost certainly involved elements you'll be studying in this interpersonal text: resolution of conflicts, issues of self-disclosure, the expression of feelings, changes in the emotional climate, and so on.

A qualitative definition   These topics suggest another way to define interpersonal communication, one that doesn't concern itself with the number of participants, but rather with

"If you want to talk, why don't you call up a radio talk-show?"

While his life was impeccable on the surface, he felt he was behind glass: moving through the world in a separate compartment, touching no one else. This was painful. . . . One night going home on the train to Connecticut he found himself in the air-conditioned car staring at a page of *The New Yorker* on his lap. His mind stopped. The page gleamed with a high, cold gloss in the fluorescent light: He stared at its shining surface, the pale gray pinstripe of his dark pants leg. Eventually his stop appeared. He got off in a somnambulistic daze. No one met him at the station. He felt he should call someone for help—but who?

Andrew Holleran,
Dancer from the Dance

---

the *quality* of interaction between individuals, the way they deal with one another. Gerald Miller (1978) describes this second approach as "developmental." John Stewart and Gary D'Angelo (1980, p. 63) describe the qualitative difference between developmentally interpersonal and what we might call "impersonal" communication as the contrast between personifying and objectifying others. In impersonal communication we treat others as if they were objects, or things. Consider, for example, the typical way you might respond to a gas station attendant or checkout clerk at the supermarket. Most transactions of this sort are hardly personal: Except for a ritual smile and perhaps a perfunctory "How are you doing?" we might as well be interacting with a machine. Such impersonal transactions are not cruel, nor do you need to establish a warm relationship with every person you meet. The important fact to recognize is that, from a qualitative viewpoint, not all two-person interaction is interpersonal.

Several characteristics distinguish qualitatively interpersonal relationships from impersonal ones.

A minimum of stereotyping In less personal relationships we tend to classify the other person by using labels. We fit others into neat pigeon-holes: "Anglo," "woman," "jock," and so on. Such labels may be accurate as far as they go,

but they hardly describe everything that is important about the other person. On the other hand, it's almost impossible to use one or two labels to describe someone you know well. "He's not *just* a professor," you want to say. Or "Sure, she's against abortions, but there's more. . . ."

Development of unique rules When we meet someone for the first time, we know how to behave because of the established social rules we have been taught. We shake hands, speak politely, and rely on socially accepted subjects: "How are you?" "What do you do?" "Lousy weather we've been having." The rules governing our interaction have little to do with us or the people with whom we interact; we are not responding to each other as individuals.

As we continue to interact, however, we sometimes gain more information about each other, and use that information as the basis for our communicating. As we share experiences, the rules that govern our behavior are less determined by cultural mores, and more determined by the unique features of our own relationship. This doesn't mean that we abandon rules altogether, but rather that we often create our *own* conventions, ones that are appropriate for us. For example, one pair of friends might develop a procedure for dealing with conflicts by expressing their disagreements as soon as they arise, while

another could tacitly agree to withhold a series of gripes, then clear the air periodically. In Chapter 11 we will compare such procedures; here the important point to recognize is that in both cases the individuals created their own rules.

Increased self-disclosure   A third qualitative characteristic of interpersonal relationships involves the amount of information the partners have about each other. When we meet people for the first time we have little information about them, usually no more than what others tell us and what we assume from observing what they wear and how they handle their bodies. As we talk, we gain more information in a variety of areas. The first topics we talk about are usually nonthreatening, nonintimate ones. If we continue talking, however, we may decide to discuss fewer impersonal things and to increase the number of topics we talk about. We may also choose to be more revealing of ourselves in doing so.

As we learn more about each other, and as our information becomes more intimate, the degree to which we share an interpersonal relationship increases. This new degree of intimacy and

sharing can come almost immediately, or it may grow slowly over a long period of time. In either case, we can say that the relationship becomes more interpersonal as the amount of self-disclosure increases. We'll have a great deal to say about this subject in Chapter 8.

If we accept the characteristics of minimal stereotyping, creation of unique rules, and sharing of personal information as criteria for a developmentally interpersonal relationship, then several implications follow. First, many one-to-one relationships never reach an interpersonal state. This conclusion is not surprising in itself, because establishing a close relationship takes time and effort. In fact, such relationships are not always desirable or appropriate. Some people, however, fool themselves into thinking that they have close interpersonal friendships when in fact their associations are interpersonal only in a situational context.

Another implication that follows from looking at interpersonal communication in qualitative terms is that the ability to communicate interpersonally is a skill that people possess in varying degrees. For example, some communicators are adept at recognizing nonverbal messages, listening effectively, acting supportively, and resolving conflicts in satisfying ways, whereas others have no ability or no idea how to do so. The skills you will learn by studying *Interplay* can help you become a more effective communicator.

Communication principles and misconceptions

Before exploring the elements of interpersonal communication in the following chapters, we need to take a final look at what communication is and what it isn't, at what it can and can't do.

Communication principles   From this chapter you already can draw several important conclusions about what communication is.

Communication can be intentional or unintentional   People usually plan their words carefully before they ask the boss for a raise or offer a constructive criticism. Not all communication is so deliberate, however. Sooner or later we all carelessly make a comment that would have better gone unsaid. Perhaps you lose your temper and blurt out a remark that you later regret, or maybe your private remarks are overheard by a bystander. In addition to these slips of the tongue, we unintentionally send many nonverbal messages. You might not be aware of your sour expression, impatient shifting, or sigh of boredom, but others view them regardless.

It's impossible not to communicate   These facial expressions, movements, and other nonverbal behaviors mean that although we can stop talking, we can't stop communicating. Chapter 5 introduces the multitude of ways we send messages without saying a word: through posture, gesture, distance, body orientation, and clothing, among others. For instance, does a friend's silence reflect anger, contentment, or fatigue? Whether or not these sorts of messages are understood, they do communicate constantly.

All messages have a content and a relational dimension   Virtually every verbal statement has a *content* dimension, the information it explicitly conveys: "Please pass the salt," "Not now, I'm tired," "You forgot to buy a quart of milk." In addition to this sort of obvious content, all messages also have a *relational* dimension (Watzlawick, Beavin, and Jackson, 1967, pp. 51–52). This relational component expresses how you feel about the other person: whether you like or dislike the other person, feel in control or subordinate, feel comfortable or anxious, and so on. For instance, consider how many different relational messages you could communicate by simply saying "Thanks a lot" in different ways.

Sometimes the content dimension of a message is all that matters. For example, you may not care how the directory assistance operator feels about you as long as you get the phone number you're seeking. In truly interpersonal contexts, however, the relational dimension of a message is often more important than the content under discussion. This fact explains why disputes over apparently trivial subjects become so important. In these cases we're not really arguing over whose turn it is to take out the trash or whether to play tennis or swim. Instead, we're disputing the nature of the relationship. Who's in control? How important are we to each other? Chapter 10 explores several key relational issues in detail.

Communication is irreversible   We sometimes wish that we could back up in time, erasing words or acts and replacing them with better alternatives. Unfortunately, such reversal is impossible. There are occasions when further explanation can clear up another's confusion or when an apology can mollify another's hurt feelings; but in other cases no amount of explanation can erase the impression you have created. Despite the warnings judges issue in jury trials,

"Let's just make that last remark of Don's an outtake, shall we?"
From *The New Yorker*, September 12, 1983, p. 41.

it's impossible to "unreceive" a message. Words said and deeds done are irretrievable.

Communication is unrepeatable   Because communication is an ongoing process, it is impossible to repeat the same event. The friendly smile that worked so well meeting a stranger last week might not succeed with the person you encounter tomorrow: It might feel stale and artificial to you the second time around, or it might be wrong for the new person or occasion. Even with the same person, it's impossible to re-create an event. Why? Because neither you nor the other *is* the same person. You've both lived longer. The behavior isn't original. Your feelings about one another may have changed. You need not constantly invent new ways to act around familiar people, but you should realize that the "same" words and behavior are different each time they are spoken or performed. Chapter 7 will alert you to the stages through which a relationship progresses.

Communication misconceptions   Now that we have spent some time describing what communication is, we need to identify some things it is not (McCroskey and Wheeless, 1976, pp. 3–10). Avoiding these common misconceptions can save you a great deal of personal trouble.

Meanings are in people, not words   The biggest mistake we can make is to assume that *saying* something is the same thing as *communicating* it. To use the terminology of our communication model, there's no guarantee that a receiver will decode a message in a way that matches the sender's intention. (If you doubt this proposition, list all the times you've been misunderstood in the past week.) Chapter 3 outlines the many reasons why people can interpret a statement differently from the way you intended it, and Chapter 4 describes the most common types of verbal misunderstandings and suggests ways to minimize them. Chapter 6 introduces listening skills that

help insure that the way you receive messages matches the ideas a speaker is trying to convey.

More communication is not always better
Whereas not communicating enough can cause problems, there are also situations when *too much* talking is a mistake. Sometimes excessive communication is simply unproductive, as when two people "talk a problem to death," going over the same ground again and again without making progress. There are other times when talking too much actually aggravates a problem. We've all had the experience of "talking ourselves into a hole"—making a bad situation worse by pursuing it too far. As McCroskey and Wheeless put it, "More and more negative communication merely leads to more and more negative results" (p. 5).

There are even times when *no* communication is the best course. Any good salesperson will testify that it's often best to stop talking and let the customer think about the product, and when two people are angry and hurt, they may say things they don't mean and will later regret. In such cases it's probably best to spend time cooling off, thinking about what to say and how to say it. Chapter 9 will help you decide when and how to share feelings.

Communication will not solve all problems
Sometimes even the best planned, best timed communication won't solve a problem. Imagine, for example, that you ask an instructor to explain why you received a poor grade on a project you believe deserved top marks. The professor clearly outlines the reasons why you received the low grade, and sticks to that position after listening thoughtfully to your protests. Has communication solved the problem? Hardly.

Sometimes clear communication is even the *cause* of problems. Suppose, for example, that a friend asks you for an honest opinion of the $200 outfit he has just bought. Your clear and sincere answer, "I think it makes you look fat," might do more harm than good. Deciding when and how to self-disclose isn't always easy. See Chapter 8 for suggestions.

Communication is not a natural ability   Most people assume that communication is an aptitude that people develop without the need for training—rather like breathing. Although almost everyone does manage to function passably without much formal communication training, most people operate at a level of effectiveness far below their potential. In fact, communication skills are rather like athletic ability. Even the most inept of us can learn to be more effective with training and practice.

Characteristics of effective communicators

What distinguishes effective interpersonal communicators from their less successful counterparts? Defining communication competence has been one of the leading challenges for communication researchers in the last decade. Many experts argue effectiveness varies from setting to setting (for example, Cupah and Spitzberg, 1983). You might be a successful communicator with peers but a failure with authority figures, or you might do well with members of the same sex but relate less effectively to those of the opposite sex. Despite these situational differences, scholars have searched for common denominators—characteristics that distinguish effective communication, whatever the context. Such characteristics do seem to exist.

Adaptability   Many researchers have argued that the best judges of effectiveness are the people who are engaged in communication, and not some outsider. Paul Feingold (1976) took this approach by asking more than 600 people to fill out a questionnaire consisting of items describing the communication behavior of others they knew. Some subjects were asked to pick the characteristics that described a person they thought was an effective communicator, while others identified

the characteristics of a poor communicator. The following six statements most clearly distinguished effective communicators from their less successful counterparts:

1. This person is aware of the effect of his or her communication on his or her partner.
2. This person adapts his or her communication to others.
3. This person says the right thing at the right time.
4. This person avoids using language that might be offensive to others.
5. This person reveals something about his or her feelings when he or she is talking.
6. This person is not difficult to understand.

Notice that the first four characteristics on this list all relate to adaptability. In its own way, each says that effective communicators are able to tailor messages to a particular situation. Rod Hart and others (1972, 1980) term this ability *rhetorical sensitivity.* In order to be rhetorically sensitive, a communicator needs to understand how others think and feel—a subject we will explore in Chapter 3.

The other two characteristics on the list are also important. We will focus on the fifth one, self-disclosure, in Chapter 8, and on the last one when we discuss language in Chapter 4.

Commitment and profitability   Besides highlighting the importance of rhetorical sensitivity, Hart suggested five other characteristics that promote effective communication (adapted here from Knapp, 1984, pp. 342–343). Nobody is perfect enough to exhibit these characteristics in all situations; but when they are present, the odds of a successful outcome increase.

Commitment to the other person, and to the conversation. Effective communication occurs when we talk *with*, not *at* others—when we listen to them carefully and share what we're thinking and feeling at the moment.

Communication is less successful when we stereotype others and respond in patterns and clichés.

Commitment to the message. Effective communication requires us to believe in what we say and to know what we are talking about. Phony communication is a turnoff. So are wishy-washy positions and uninformed, ignorant statements.

A desire for mutual benefit. The best communication leaves both parties as winners, each gaining from an exchange. By contrast, when communicators are self-centered or manipulative, the relationship suffers. In fact, Chapter 11 shows how both parties can wind up losers when they care only about their own welfare.

A desire to interact and to continue the relationship. Communication is most effective when people care about one another. It's not necessary to establish a deep relationship with every gas station attendant and telephone operator you encounter. Even these sorts of business transactions, however, are more satisfying when the implicit message is "I sincerely want to help you, and I hope you'll be a satisfied customer."

A desire to make the message clearly useful. Communication is effective when the message has a clear use for the listener. Sometimes this use is tangible (tips to improve your tennis game or do well on the upcoming exam). In other cases the reward is social (an enjoyable conversation or an amusing joke). Whatever the situation, the message has to be understandable before it can be of any use.

Notice that these characteristics involve two themes. The first is commitment. Good communicators *care* about the other person, about the subject, and about being understood. The second theme is profitability. Effective

communicators are interested in making the exchange produce good results.

How do you measure up against the standards of adaptability, commitment, and profitability? When you judge yourself, remember that communication skill isn't a trait that people either possess or lack. Rather, it's a state that we achieve more or less frequently. A realistic goal, then, is not to become perfect, but to boost the percentage of time when you communicate well.

Readings

Barnlund, Dean C. "A Transactional Model of Communication." In *Language Behavior: A Book of Readings in Communication*, Johnnye Akin, Alvin Goldberg, Gail Myers, and John Stewart, eds. The Hague: Mouton, 1970.

Caplan, Gerald. *Support Systems and Community Mental Health.* New York: Behavioral Publications, 1974.

Cupah, W. R., and B. H. Spitzberg. "Trait Versus State: A Comparison of Dispositional and Situational Measures of Interpersonal Communication Competence." *Western Journal of Speech Communication* 47 (1983): 364–379.

*Dance, Frank E. X. "The 'Concept' of Communication." *Journal of Communication* 20 (1970): 201–210.

Dance, Frank E. X. "Toward a Theory of Human Communication." In *Human Communication Theory: Original Essays*, Frank E. X. Dance, ed. New York: Holt, Rinehart and Winston, 1957.

Feingold, Paul. *Toward a Paradigm of Effective Communication: An Empirical Study of Perceived Communicative Effectiveness.* Doctoral dissertation, Purdue University, 1976.

*In the Readings section at the end of each chapter, items identified by an asterisk are recommended as especially useful follow-ups.

Hart, R. P., and D. M. Burks. "Rhetorical Sensitivity and Social Interaction." *Speech Monographs* 39 (1972): 75–91.

Hart, R. P., R. E. Carlson, and W. F. Eadie. "Attitudes Toward Communication and the Assessment of Rhetorical Sensitivity." *Communication Monographs* 47 (1980): 1–22.

*Holtzman, Paul D., and Donald Ecroyd. *Communication Concepts and Models.* Skokie, Ill.: National Textbook Co., 1976.

*Knapp, M. L. *Interpersonal Communication and Human Relationships.* Boston: Allyn and Bacon, 1984.

Maslow, Abraham H. *Toward a Psychology of Being.* New York: Van Nostrand Reinhold, 1968.

McCroskey, James, and Lawrence Wheeless. *Introduction to Human Communication.* Boston: Allyn and Bacon, 1976.

McQuade, W., and A. Aikman. *Stress: What It Is and What It Does to You.* New York: E. P. Dutton, 1974.

*Miller, Gerald R. "On Defining Communication: Another Stab." *Journal of Communication* 16 (1966): 88–98.

*Miller, Gerald R. "The Current Status of Theory and Research in Interpersonal Communication." *Human Communication Research* 4 (Winter 1978): 164–178.

Phillips, Gerald, and Nancy Metzger. *Intimate Communication.* Boston: Allyn and Bacon, 1976.

Rogers, E. M., and D. L. Kincaid. *Communication Networks.* New York: Free Press, 1981.

Ross, J. B., and M. M. McLaughlin, eds. *A Portable Medieval Reader.* New York: Viking Press, 1949.

Schachter, Stanley. *The Psychology of Affiliation.* Stanford, Calif.: Stanford University Press, 1959.

Schutz, William. *The Interpersonal Underworld.* Palo Alto, Calif.: Science and Behavior Books, 1966.

Shannon, Claude E., and Warren Weaver. *The Mathematical Theory of Communication.* Urbana, Ill.: University of Illinois Press, 1949.

Shattuck, Roger. *The Forbidden Experiment: The Story of the Wild Boy of Aveyron.* New York: Farrar, Straus & Giroux, 1980.

Stevens, S. S. "Introduction: A Definition of Communication." *Journal of the Acoustical Society of America* 22 (1950): 689.

*Stewart, John, ed. *Bridges, Not Walls: A Book About Interpersonal Communication,* 3d ed. Reading, Mass.: Addison-Wesley, 1982.

*Stewart, John, and Gary D'Angelo. *Together: Communicating Interpersonally.* Reading, Mass.: Addison-Wesley, 1980.

Verderber, Rudolph, Ann Elder, and Ernest Weiler. "A Study of Communication Time Usage Among College Students." Unpublished study, University of Cincinnati, 1976.

Watzlawick, P., J. Beavin, and D. D. Jackson. *Pragmatics of Human Communication.* New York: W. W. Norton, 1967.

Wenburg, John, and William Wilmot. *The Personal Communication Process.* New York: Wiley, 1973.

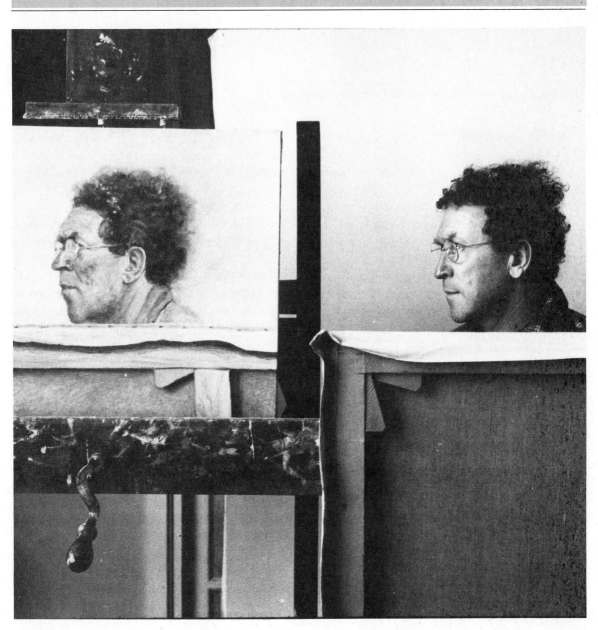

Self-Concept

Two

After studying the material in this chapter

You should understand:

1. How to define self-concept.
2. How the self-concept develops.
3. The multidimensional, subjective, resistant nature of the self-concept.
4. Some personality correlates of individuals with positive and negative self-concepts.
5. The role of self-fulfilling prophecies in shaping self-concept and influencing communication.
6. How people can change their self-concepts.

You should be able to identify:

1. The key elements of your own self-concept.
2. The most important forces that have shaped your self-concept.
3. The influence you have on shaping the self-concept of others.
4. The differences among your perceived, desired, and presenting selves.
5. The elements of your perceived self that may be inaccurately favorable or unfavorable.
6. Any self-fulfilling prophecies that you impose on yourself or on others, and that others impose on you.

Who are you?

Before reading on, take a few minutes to answer this question by trying the following simple exercise. First, make a list of the ten words or phrases that describe the most important features of who you are. Some of the items on your list might involve social roles: student, son or daughter, employee, and so on. Or you could define yourself through physical characteristics: fat, skinny, tall, short, beautiful, ugly. You might focus on your intellectual characteristics: smart, stupid, curious, inquisitive. Perhaps you can best define yourself in terms of moods, feelings, or attitudes: optimistic, critical, energetic. Or you could consider your social characteristics: outgoing, shy, defensive. You may see yourself in terms of belief systems: pacifist, Christian, vegetarian, libertarian. Finally, you could focus on particular skills (or lack of): swimmer, artist, carpenter. In any case, choose ten words or phrases that best describe you and write them down.

Next, choose the one item from your list that is the most fundamental to who you are and copy it on another sheet of paper. Then pick the second most fundamental item and record it as number two on your new list. Continue ranking the ten items until you have reorganized them all.

Now comes the most interesting part of the experience. Find a place where you won't be disturbed and close your eyes. Take a few moments to relax and then create a mental image of yourself. Try to paint a picture that not only captures your physical characteristics, but that also reflects the attitudes, aptitudes, feelings, and/or beliefs included on your list. Take plenty of time to create this image.

Now recall (or peek at) your second list, noticing the item you ranked as number ten—the one least essential to your identity. Keeping your mental image in focus, imagine that this item suddenly disappeared from your personality or physical makeup. Try to visualize how you would be dif-

ferent without that tenth item. How would it affect the way you act? The way you feel? The way others behave toward you? Was it easy to give up that item? Do you like yourself more or less without it? Take a few minutes with your eyes closed to answer these questions.

Without regaining the item you've just given up, continue your fantasy by removing item number nine. What difference does its absence make for you?

Slowly, at your own pace, continue the process by jettisoning one item at a time until you have given them all up. Notice what happens at each step of the process. After you've gone through your entire list, reclaim the items one by one until you are back to where you started.

How do you feel after trying this exercise? Most people find the experience a powerful one. They say that it clarifies how each of the items selected are fundamental to their identity. Many people say that they gain a clear picture of the parts of themselves they value and the parts with which they are unhappy.

Self-concept defined

What you've accomplished by creating this list is partially to describe your *self-concept:* a relatively stable set of perceptions you hold of yourself. One way to understand the self-concept is to imagine a special mirror that not only reflects physical features, but also allows you to view other aspects of yourself—emotional states, talents, likes, dislikes, values, roles, and so on. The reflection in that mirror would be your self-concept.

You probably recognize that the self-concept list you recorded is only a partial one. To make the description of yourself complete, you'd have to keep adding items until your list ran into hundreds of words. Take a moment now to explore some of the many parts of your self-concept simply by responding to the question "Who am I?" over and over again. Add these responses to the list you have already started.

Of course, not every item on your self-concept list is equally important. For example, the most significant part of one person's self-concept might consist of social roles, whereas for another it might be physical appearance, health, friendships, accomplishments, or skills.

Psychologists term this ranking of self-concept elements *psychological centrality*. Sometimes this centrality simply reflects the importance we attach to certain elements. For example, you probably think more about your physical attractiveness than about your left- or right-handedness. In other cases, however, centrality creates communication dilemmas. Suppose you consider yourself both honest and ambitious. What happens when you find yourself at a job interview, faced with an almost certain job offer if you only withhold one fact about your history? You have three options: You can place honesty before ambition by telling the whole truth; you can acknowledge that, at least in this situation, you're more ambitious than honest and withhold the negative information; or you can rationalize the situation in a way that leaves your concepts of both honesty and ambition intact. You might think, for example, "It's not really an important fact," or say to yourself, "That negative fact is ancient history. I'm a different person now, and telling them about the past would only confuse them." The sections of Chapter 8 that deal with white lies and the sections of Chapter 10 that deal with defensive communication and transforming negative climates describe various ways to manage this sort of dilemma and their consequences.

How the self-concept develops

Researchers generally agree that the self-concept does not exist at birth (Fitts, 1971). An infant lying in a crib has no notion of self, no notion—even if verbal language were miraculously made available—of how to answer the question at the beginning of this chapter. Consider what it would be like to have no idea of your characteristic moods, physical appearance, social traits, talents, intellectual capacity, beliefs, or important roles. If you can imagine this experience—*blankness*—you can start to understand how the world appears to someone with no sense of self. Of course, you have to take one step further and *not know* you do not have any notion of self.

Soon after birth the infant begins to differentiate among the things in the environment:

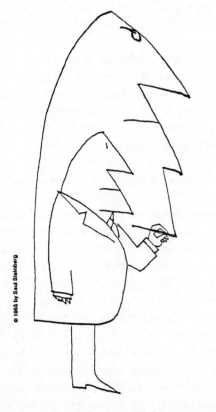

© 1965 by Saul Steinberg

From *The Catalogue.* Julian Bach Literary Agency, N.Y.: Copyright © 1965 by Saul Steinberg.

familiar and unfamiliar faces, the sounds that mean food, the noises that frighten, the cat who jumps in the crib, the sister who tickles—each becomes a separate part of the world. Recognition of distinctions in the environment probably precedes recognition of the self.

At about six or seven months the child begins to recognize "self" as distinct from surroundings. If you've ever watched children at this age you've probably marveled at how they can stare with great fascination at a foot, hand, and other body parts that float into view, almost as if they were strange objects belonging to someone else. Then the connection is made, almost as if the child were realizing, "The hand is *me,*" "The foot is *me.*" These first revelations form the child's earliest concept of self. At this early stage, the self-concept is almost exclusively physical, involving the child's basic realization of existing and of possessing certain body parts over which some control is exerted. This limited self-concept barely resembles more fully developed self-concepts older children hold.

Along with this budding sense of identity, certain behaviors develop that suggest infants are born with some social characteristics. Psychologist Jerome Kagan (1984) reports that 10 percent of children seem to be born with a biological disposition toward shyness. Babies who stop playing when a stranger enters the room, for example, are more likely than others to be reticent and introverted as adolescents. Likewise, Kagan found that another 10 percent of infants seem to be born with especially sociable dispositions. Research with twins also suggests that personality may be at least partially biologically determined (McCroskey and Richmond, 1980). Biologically identical twins are much more similar in sociability than are fraternal twins. These similarities are apparent not only in infancy, but also when the twins have grown to adulthood and have had different experiences.

Children learn what they live

If a child lives with criticism he learns to condemn.
If a child lives with hostility he learns to fight.
If a child lives with ridicule he learns to be shy.
If a child lives with shame he learns to feel guilty.
If a child lives with tolerance he learns to be patient.
If a child lives with encouragement he learns confidence.
If a child lives with praise he learns to appreciate.
If a child lives with fairness he learns justice.
If a child lives with security he learns to have faith.
If a child lives with approval he learns to like himself.
If a child lives with acceptance and friendship he learns to find love in the world.

Dorothy Law Nolte

Although children may behave more or less sociably, they do not automatically incorporate this attribute and others into their self-concepts. The self-concept is almost totally a product of social interaction. Two complementary theories describe how interaction shapes the way individuals view themselves: reflected appraisal and social comparison (Rosenberg, 1979).

Reflected appraisal Before reading on, try the following exercise. Either by yourself or aloud with a partner, recall someone you know or once knew who helped enhance your self-concept by acting in a way that made you feel accepted, worthwhile, important, appreciated, or loved. This person needn't have played a crucial role in your life, as long as the role was positive. Often one's self-concept is shaped by many tiny nudges as well as a few giant events. For instance, you might recall a childhood neighbor who took a special interest in you or a grandparent who never criticized or questioned your youthful foolishness.

After thinking about this supportive person, recall someone who acted in either a big or small way to diminish your self-esteem. Teachers, for instance, recall students who yawn in the middle of their classes. (The students may be tired, but it's difficult for teachers not to think that they are doing a poor, boring job.)

After thinking about these two types of people, you should begin to see that everyone's self-concept is shaped by those around them. To the extent that you have received supportive messages, you have learned to appreciate and value yourself. To the degree that you have received critical signals, you are likely to feel less valuable, lovable, and capable. In this sense it's possible to see that the self-concept you described in your list is a product of the messages you've received throughout your life.

The family is the first place we receive these sorts of messages. It provides us with our first feelings of adequacy and inadequacy, acceptance and rejection. Even before children can speak,

people are making evaluations of them. The earliest months of life are full of messages—the ones that shape the self-concept. The amount of time parents allow their children to cry before attending to their needs communicates nonverbally to the children over a period of time just how important they are to the parents. The parental method of handling infants speaks volumes: Do they affectionately play with the child, joggling her gently and holding her close, or do they treat her like so much baggage, changing diapers or carrying out feeding and bathing in a brusque, businesslike manner? Does the tone of voice with which they speak to the child show love and enjoyment or disappointment and irritation?

Of course, most of these messages are not intentional ones. It is rare when a parent deliberately tries to tell a child he or she is not lovable; but whether the messages are intentional or not doesn't matter—nonverbal statements play a big role in shaping a youngster's feelings of being "OK" or "not OK."

As children learn to speak and understand language, verbal messages also contribute to their developing self-concept. Close your eyes for a moment and think about messages you heard when you were being raised.

"What a beautiful child!"
"Can't you do anything right?"
"Come give me a hug."
"I don't know what to do with you!"

As you can clearly see, each of these messages implies some sort of appraisal. And because a child has no way of defining "self" other than through the eyes of surrounding adults, these evaluations have a profound influence on the developing self-concept.

In a review of self-concept literature, William Fitts (1971) focuses on parental influence on self-concept formation. Parents with healthy self-concepts tend to have children with healthy self-concepts, and parents with poor, negative, or deviant self-concepts tend to have children who view themselves in primarily negative ways. Interestingly, if one parent has a good self-concept and the other a poor self-concept, the child is most likely to choose the parent with the more positive self-concept as a model. If neither parent has a strong self-concept, it is likely that the child will seek an adult outside the family with whom to identify.

In families where one parent has a strong, positive self-concept, the child is usually provided with a secure environment in the form of love and attention. A child brought up in such an environment is able to face the world as a secure, confident person. If both parents have strong, positive self-concepts, then the effect is even more pronounced.

Later in life the self-concept continues to be shaped by how others respond to us, especially when messages come from what sociologists term "significant others"—those people whose opinions we especially value. A look at the uppers and downers you described earlier (as well as others you can remember) will show that the evaluations of a few especially important people can have long-range effects. A teacher from long ago, a special friend or relative, or perhaps a barely known acquaintance whom you respected, can all leave an influential imprint on how you view yourself. To see the importance of significant others, ask yourself how you arrived at your opinion of yourself as a student, as a person attractive to the opposite sex, as a competent worker, and you'll see that these self-evaluations were probably influenced by the way others regarded you.

What determines whether an appraisal is accepted or rejected? At least four requirements must be met for an appraisal to be regarded as important (Gergen, 1971). First of all, the person

It is thus with most of us; we are what other people say we are. We know ourselves chiefly by hearsay.

Eric Hoffer

who offers a particular appraisal must be *someone we see as competent to offer it.* Parents satisfy this requirement extremely well because as young children we perceive that our parents know so much about us—more than we know about ourselves sometimes. Second, *the evaluation must be perceived as highly personal.* The more the other person seems to know about us and adapts what is being said to fit us, the more likely we are to accept judgments from this person. In addition, the appraisal must be *reasonable in light of what we believe about ourselves.* If an appraisal is similar to one we give ourselves, we will believe it; if it is somewhat dissimilar, we will probably still accept it; but if it is completely dissimilar, we will probably reject it.

Finally, appraisals that are *consistent* and *numerous* are more persuasive than those that contradict usual appraisals or those that only occur once. As long as only a *few* students yawn in class, a teacher can safely disregard them as a reflection of teaching ability. In like manner, you could safely disregard the appraisal of the angry date who tells you in no uncertain terms what kind of person behaves as you did. Of course, when you get a second or third similar appraisal in a short time, the evaluation becomes harder to ignore.

Not only individuals but also various reference groups influence our self-concepts. A youngster who is interested in ballet and who lives in a setting where such preferences are regarded as weird will start to accept this label if there is no support from significant others. Adults who want to share their feelings but find themselves in a society that discourages such sharing might, after

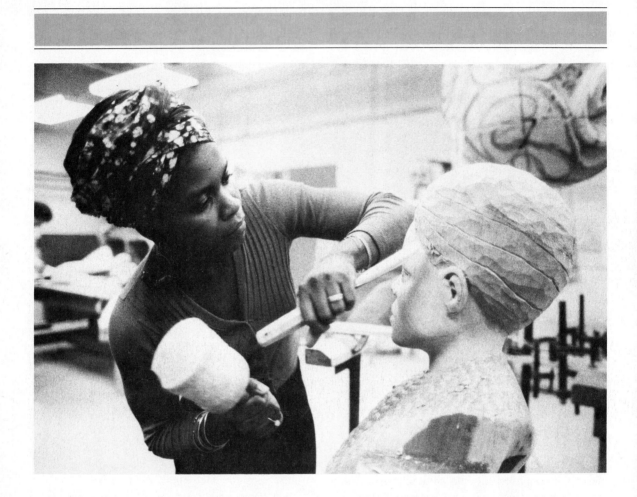

a while, think of themselves as oddballs, unless they can get some reassurance that such a desire is normal. Again, we encounter the idea of knowing ourselves through the "mirrors" of others. To a great degree, we judge ourselves by the way others see us.

You might argue that not every part of your self-concept is shaped by others, that there are certain objective facts recognizable by self-observation alone. After all, nobody needs to tell you whether you are taller than others, speak with an accent, have curly hair, and so on. These facts are obvious.

Although some features of the self are immediately apparent, the *significance* we attach to them—that is, the rank we assign them in the hierarchy of our list and the interpretation we give them—depends greatly on the opinions of others. After all, there are many of your features that are readily observable, yet you don't find them important at all because nobody has regarded them as significant.

Recently we heard a woman in her eighties describing her youth. "When I was a girl," she declared, "we didn't worry about weight. Some people were skinny and others were plump, and we pretty much accepted the bodies God gave us." In those days it's unlikely that weight would have found its way onto the self-concept list you constructed because it wasn't considered significant. Compare the modern attitude: It's seldom that you pick up a popular magazine or visit a bookstore without reading about the latest diet fads, and TV ads are filled with scenes of slender, happy people. As a result you'll rarely find a person who doesn't complain about the need to "lose a few pounds."

Obviously such concern has a lot to do with the attention paid to slimness these days. Furthermore, the interpretation of characteristics such as weight depends on the way people important to us regard them. We generally see fat as undesirable because others tell us it is. In a society where obesity is the ideal (and there are such societies), a person regarded as extremely heavy would be admired. In the same way, the fact that one is single or married, solitary or sociable, aggressive or passive, takes on meaning depending on the interpretation society attaches to those traits. Thus, the importance of a given characteristic in your self-concept reflects the significance you see others attach to it.

Social comparison   We are not totally passive recipients of environmental influence. Both consciously and unconsciously we each create our environment as well as respond to it.

In *The Concept of Self,* Kenneth Gergen (1971) describes how social comparison shapes our self-concept. Gergen explains that people have a continuing need to establish the value and correctness of their beliefs, something that is often difficult because exact standards are hard to come by. Therefore, people often look at others as a way of judging themselves. They compare their beliefs, attitudes, and behaviors with those around them in order to establish the value of their own position. Just as we determine height or size by comparison (a five-foot, seven-inch warrior would be a giant in pygmy territory), we also determine other characteristics by comparison. For instance, if you see people all around you as being generally miserable, then you might view yourself as a happy, content person; whereas, in a different environment you could wind up looking unfulfilled by comparison with others.

At first glance, social comparison theory seems rather deterministic. Besides being the product of how others see us, we are also shaped by how we measure up to others. At second glance, however, the concept of social comparison offers a way of reshaping an unsatisfying self-concept.

> **Man wishes to be confirmed in his being by man, and wishes to have a presence in the being of the other. . . . Secretly and bashfully he watches for a Yes which allows him to be and which can come to him only from one human person to another.**
>
> Martin Buber

To some degree, we're in control of who is available for comparison. It's possible to seek out people with whom we compare favorably. This technique may bring to mind a search for a community of idiots in which you could appear as a genius, but there are healthier ways of changing your standards for comparison. For instance, you might decide that it's foolish constantly to compare your athletic prowess with professionals or campus stars, your looks with movie idols, and your intelligence with only Phi Beta Kappas. Once you place yourself alongside a truly representative sample, your self-concept may improve.

On the other hand, you can use social comparison to fool yourself. For instance, suppose you wanted to think of yourself as a tremendously effective communicator (many people do), even though others disagreed with this image. You could achieve your goal by choosing a best friend who was tongue-tied. If you chose to be a big fish in a small pond, you could hang around with extremely shy or ignorant people, and thereby assure yourself of seeming a "natural" leader.

Another way of using comparison to boost self-esteem unrealistically would be to argue that those who don't approve of you have worthless opinions, whereas others who think as you do have excellent judgment. Also, you could set up standards that only you and a few other people meet and thereby argue that you are a rare individual indeed. Somewhat illogical, but when a self-concept is at stake, who worries about logic?

Characteristics of the self-concept

Now that you have a better idea of how your self-concept has developed, we can take a closer look at some of its characteristics.

The self-concept is multidimensional Just as the universe is composed of countless galaxies, each person's self-concept is a conglomeration of many beliefs. In fact, it is an oversimplification to talk about "the" self-concept as if each of us possessed only one. Morris Rosenberg (1979; Civikly, 1982) describes three ways to view this construct: (1) how we view ourselves; (2) how we would like to view ourselves; and (3) how we present ourselves to others.

The first view—we can call it the *perceived self*—is quite complex. It contains your view of your social status (including age, sex, socioeconomic standing, and occupational position), social labels (such as "jock" or "parent"), past and present membership groups (religious, political, and ethnic), and "ego extensions" (material possessions with which you identify).

The second view of self, the *desired self*, also contains a variety of elements. First there is the idealized image, which you recognize as an unobtainable fantasy. Second is the committed image, the one which you actually make efforts to obtain: degree, job, partner, and so on. Finally there is the moral image, which consists of all the messages you send about how you ought to think and act.

The third view of self, the *presenting self*, involves the ways you actually behave with others. The presenting self sometimes matches the perceived self. For instance, you might confess to the belief that you behaved admirably or made a fool of yourself last Saturday night. In other cases we present ourselves publicly in ways that more closely match the desired self, as when you know you behaved poorly but try to pass your behavior off as justified, or even virtuous ("I didn't file an income tax return because I wanted to make a statement about the unconstitutional activities of the I.R.S.!"). There are also cases in which the image you present to others falls somewhere between the perceived and ideal selves, as when you say "Well, maybe I did act a *little* unfairly . . ."

Rosenberg notes that the presenting self is important throughout life, but it undergoes the greatest changes during adolescence:

> . . . In a groping and tentative way, different selves may be rehearsed—the glamor girl, the caustic wit, the world-weary sophisticate, the dedicated revolutionary. Selves may be tried on or discarded like garments as adolescents attempt to convince others of their sophistication, cheerfulness, their allure, their intelligence. . . . When an adolescent—or anyone else—tries to achieve a certain goal, he does so not simply for the direct advantage it affords, but because it enables him to prove something about himself to himself. (pp. 48–49)

The self-concept is multidimensional in another way. It is an oversimplification to say that each of us possesses a single self-concept in the way we possess a single body. Many theorists argue that most people have flexible selves that vary from one situation to another (James, 1892; Magnussen and Endler, 1977; Mischel, 1973). You might view yourself as smart and confident in some settings, for example, and feel ignorant and insecure in others. Research shows that communication behavior does, in fact, vary across sit-

uations (Hewes and Haight, 1979). Despite this variation, many people do believe—usually mistakenly—that they have stable personalities. In one study, researchers found that there was little behavioral difference between people who defined themselves as "shy" and those who chose the label "not shy" (Zimbardo, 1977). In other words, both groups acknowledged reacting to some social situations with pounding heart, butterflies in the stomach, and blushing. Labeling made a significant difference: Whereas some subjects said "I *am* shy," their more confident counterparts—who behaved in exactly the same manner—instead chose to say "I sometimes *act* shy."

It's not hard to see that this second way of thinking leads to a much more satisfying—and in most cases a more realistic—self-appraisal. We'll have a great deal more to say about thinking and emotions in Chapter 9.

The self-concept is subjective   The way we view ourselves is often at odds with others' perceptions—and often with the observable facts. In one study (Myers, 1980), a random sample of men were asked to rank themselves on their ability to get along with others. Defying mathematical laws, all subjects—every last one—put themselves in the top half of the population. Sixty percent rated themselves in the top 10 percent of the population, and an amazing 25 percent believed they were in the top 1 percent. In the same study,

MISS PEACH   By Mell Lazarus

MISS PEACH by Mell Lazarus. Courtesy of Mell Lazarus and Field Newspaper Syndicate.

70 percent of the men ranked their leadership in the top quarter of the population, whereas only 2 percent thought they were below average. Sixty percent said they were in the top quarter for athletic abilities, whereas only 6 percent viewed themselves as below average.

There are several reasons why some people have a self-concept that others would regard as unrealistically favorable. First, a self-estimation might be based on obsolete information. Perhaps your jokes used to be well received, or your grades were high, or your work was superior, and now the facts have changed. As you'll soon read, people are reluctant to give up a familiar self-image. This principle makes especially good sense when it's possible to avoid the unpleasant truth of the present by staying in the more desirable past.

A self-concept might also be excessively favorable due to distorted feedback from others. A boss may claim to be an excellent manager because assistants pour on false praise in order to keep their jobs. A child's inflated ego may be based on the praise of doting parents.

A third reason for holding an unrealistically high self-concept is that our society demands too much of its members. Much of the conditioning we receive in our early years implies that anything less than perfection is unsatisfactory, so that admitting mistakes is often seen as a sign of weakness. Instructors who fail to admit they don't know everything about a subject are afraid they will lose face with their colleagues and students. Couples whose relationships are beset by occasional problems don't want to admit that they have failed to achieve the "ideal" relationship they've seen portrayed in fiction. Parents who don't want to say, "I'm sorry, I made a mistake," to their children are afraid they'll lose the youngsters' respect.

Once you accept such an irrational idea—that to be less than perfect is a character defect—admitting your frailties becomes difficult. Such a confession becomes the equivalent of admitting one is a failure—and failure is not an element of most people's self-concept. Rather than label themselves failures, many people engage in self-deception, insisting to themselves and to others that their behavior is more admirable than the circumstances indicate. We'll have more to say about the reasons behind such behavior and its consequences when we discuss defense mechanisms in Chapter 10.

In contrast to the cases we've just described are times when we view ourselves more *harshly* than the objective facts suggest. You may have known people, for instance, who insist that they are unattractive or incompetent in spite of your honest insistence to the contrary. In fact, you have probably experienced excessively negative self-evaluation yourself. Recall a time when you woke up with a case of the "uglies," convinced that you looked terrible. Remember how on such days you were unwilling to accept even the most sincere compliments from others, having already decided how wretched you appeared. Whereas many of us only fall into the trap of being overly critical occasionally, others constantly have an unrealistically low self-concept.

Sidney Simon (1977), in his delightful book *Vulture: A Modern Allegory on the Art of Putting Oneself Down,* describes how we diminish our self-worth. Vultures have gained their unsavory reputation for swooping down on their victims and plucking away at their flesh: not a pretty sight. The psychological vulture Simon describes is just as unappealing. It waits for a self-put-down and then uses this moment of weakness to peck away at the self-esteem of its weakened victim. These psychological vultures, of course, are subjective: They are the unnecessary creations of their own victims.

There are two types of vulture attacks, one more subtle than the other. The most obvious kind occurs whenever we engage in an overt act of self-criticism. For example, a colleague of ours has a habit of bumping into things, which is not unusual. However, her response to such events is to exaggerate and overgeneralize them by criticizing herself: "I'm such a klutz!"

The more subtle kind of vulture attack occurs when we set unrealistic limitations on ourselves. Any statement that limits your capability to think or act within the limits of your potential invites another nibble at your self-esteem. "I couldn't say

that to her!" "I could never give a speech!" "They'd never hire me for that job!" As soon as it senses such thoughts the vulture swoops down, claws extended, and carries off another chunk of self-esteem.

Simon suggests that we set ourselves up for vulture attacks in six areas: *physical* ("I'm too fat, thin, short, tall, clumsy"); *sexual* ("I'm unattractive to the opposite sex," "Nobody would want to go out with me"); *creative* ("I have no imagination," "I can't draw"); *family* ("I'm a disappointment to my parents," "I don't spend enough time with them"); *intelligence* ("I'm just dumb, I guess," "I'm no good in math"); and *relationships* ("Nobody would want me for a friend," "I'm too shy").

What are the reasons for such excessively negative self-evaluations? As with unrealistically high self-esteem, one source for an overabundance of self-put-downs is obsolete information. A string of past failures in school or with social relations can linger to haunt a communicator long after they have occurred, even though such events don't predict failure in the future. Similarly, we've known slender students who still think of themselves as fat and clear-complexioned people who still behave as if they were acne-ridden.

Distorted feedback can also create a self-image that is worse than a more objective observer would see. Having grown up around overly critical parents is one of the most common causes of a negative self-image. In other cases the remarks of cruel friends, uncaring teachers, excessively demanding employers, or even memorable strangers can have a lasting effect. As you read earlier, the impact of significant others and reference groups in forming a self-concept can be great.

A third cause for a strongly negative self-concept is again the myth of perfection, which is common in our society. From the time most of us learn to understand language we are exposed to models who appear to be perfect at whatever they do. This myth is most clear when we examine the stories commonly told to children. In these stories the hero is wise, brave, talented, and victorious, whereas the villain is totally evil and doomed to failure. This kind of model is easy for a child to understand, but it hardly paints a realistic picture of the world. Unfortunately, many parents perpetuate the myth of perfection by refusing to admit that they are ever mistaken or unfair. Children, of course, accept this perfectionist facade for a long time, not being in any position to dispute the wisdom of such powerful beings. From the behavior of the adults around them comes the clear message: "A well-adjusted, successful person has no faults."

Thus children learn that in order to gain acceptance, it's necessary to pretend to "have it all together," even though they know they haven't. Given this naive belief that everyone else is perfect and the knowledge that you aren't, it's easy to see how the self-concept would suffer. We'll have a great deal to say about perfection and other irrational ideas, both in this chapter and in Chapter 8. In the meantime, don't get the mistaken impression that we're suggesting it's wrong to aim at perfection as an *ideal.* We're only suggesting that achieving this state is usually not possible, and to expect that you should do so is a sure ticket to an unnecessarily low self-concept.

A final reason people often sell themselves short is also connected to social expectations. Curiously, the perfectionistic society to which we belong rewards those people who downplay the strengths we demand they possess (or pretend to possess). We term these people "modest" and find their behavior agreeable. On the other hand, we consider those who honestly appreciate their own strengths to be "braggarts" or "egotists," confusing them with the people who boast about accomplishments they do not possess. This convention leads most of us to talk freely about our

shortcomings while downplaying our accomplishments. It's all right to proclaim that you're miserable if you have failed to do well on a project, whereas it's considered boastful to express your pride at a job well done. It's fine to remark that you feel unattractive, but egocentric to say that you think you look good.

After a while we begin to believe the types of statements we repeatedly make. The self-putdowns are viewed as modesty and become part of our self-concept, whereas the strengths and accomplishments go unmentioned and are forgotten. In the end we see ourselves as much worse than we are.

A healthy self-concept is flexible   People change. From moment to moment we aren't the same. We wake up in the morning in a jovial mood and turn grumpy before lunch. We find ourselves fascinated by a conversational topic one moment, then suddenly lose interest. One moment's anger often gives way to forgiveness the next. Health turns to illness and back to health. Alertness becomes fatigue, hunger becomes satiation, and confusion becomes clarity.

We also change from situation to situation. You might be a relaxed conversationalist with people you know but at a loss for words with strangers. You might be patient when explaining things on the job but have no tolerance for such explanations at home. You might be a wizard at solving mathematical problems but have a terribly difficult time putting your thoughts into words. We change over long stretches of time. We grow older, learn new facts, adopt new attitudes and philosophies, set and reach new goals, and find that others change their way of thinking and acting toward us.

The self-concept also tends to change over longer periods of time. Fitts (1971) summarizes an investigation that found that the degree to which a self-concept is positive *increases with age.* Measurements of the self-concepts of people twenty, thirty, forty, fifty, sixty, and sixty-nine years old indicate that there is a steady increase in positive self-concept; generally, people feel better about themselves as they get older. Although the correlation is between self-concept and age, the real relationship is between self-concept and what happens as we get older. We gain more and more control over our lives; we gain the opportunity to structure things to ensure that we will have good feelings about ourselves.

As we change in these and many other ways, our self-concept must also change in order to stay realistic. An accurate self-portrait today would not be exactly the same as a year ago or a few months ago or even yesterday. We do not mean that you change radically from day to day. There are fundamental characteristics of your personality that will stay the same for years, perhaps for a lifetime. It is likely, however, that in other important ways you are changing—physically, intellectually, emotionally, and spiritually.

The self-concept resists change In spite of the fact that we change and that a realistic self-concept should reflect this change, the tendency to resist revision of our self-perception is strong. When confronted with facts that contradict the mental picture we hold of ourselves, we tend to dispute the facts and cling to the outmoded self-perception.

It's understandable why we're reluctant to revise a previously favorable self-concept. Some professional athletes, for instance, doggedly insist that they can be of value to the team when they are clearly past their prime. It must be tremendously difficult to give up the life of excitement, recognition, and financial rewards that comes with such a talent. Faced with such a tremendous loss, it's easy to see why the athlete would try to play one more season, insisting that the old skills are still there.

In the same way, a student who did well in earlier years but now has failed to study might be unwilling to admit that the label "good scholar" no longer applies. A previously industrious worker, citing past commendations in a personnel file, might insist on being considered a top-notch employee despite a supervisor's report of increased absences and low productivity. (Remember that the people in these and other examples aren't *lying* when they insist that they're doing well in spite of the facts to the contrary; they honestly believe that the old truths still hold, precisely because their self-concepts have been so resistant to change.)

Curiously, the tendency to cling to an outmoded self-perception also holds when the new image would be more favorable than the old one. We recall a former student whom almost anyone would have regarded as beautiful, with physical features attractive enough to appear in any glamor magazine. In spite of her appearance, this woman characterized herself as "ordinary" and "unattractive" in a class exercise. When questioned by her classmates, she described how as a child she had extremely crooked teeth, and how she had worn braces for several years in her teens to correct this problem. During this time she was often kidded by her friends, who never let her forget her "metal mouth," as she put it. Even though the braces had been off for two years, our student reported that she still saw herself as ugly, and brushed aside our compliments by insisting that we were just saying these things to be nice—she knew how she *really* looked.

Such examples illustrate the waste that occurs when we resist changing an inaccurate self-concept. Our student denied herself a much happier life by clinging to an obsolete picture of herself. In the same way, some communicators insist that they are less talented or worthy of friendship than others would suggest, creating their own needless, miserable world. These unfortunate souls probably resist changing because they aren't willing to go through the effort and disorientation that comes from redefining themselves. Whatever their reasons, it's sad to see people in such an unnecessary state of mind.

A second problem that comes from trying to perpetrate an inaccurate self-concept involves self-delusion and lack of growth. If you hold an unrealistically favorable picture of yourself, you won't see the real need for change that may exist. Instead of learning new talents, working to change a relationship, or improving your physical condition, you'll stay with the familiar and comfortable delusion that everything is all right. As time goes by, this delusion becomes more and more difficult to maintain, leading to a third problem.

To understand this third problem you need to remember that communicators who are presented with information that contradicts their self-perception have two choices: They can either accept the new data and change their perception accordingly, or they can keep their original viewpoint and in some way refute the new information. Since most communicators are reluctant to downgrade a favorable image of themselves, their tendency is to opt for refutation, either by discounting the information and rationalizing it away or by counterattacking the person who holds it. Chapter 10 describes these defensive reactions in detail, and offers alternative responses to messages that threaten an existing self-concept.

Personality correlates of the self-concept

People with positive self-concepts behave in significantly different ways from those with negative ones. Research in this area reviewed by Mary Ann Scheirer and Robert Kraut (1979) shows that there is a strong correlation between the type of self-concept a person has and the patterns of thought and action that person displays. It is unclear whether the self-concept causes these behaviors, whether the behaviors shape the self-concept, or whether the relationship is reciprocal. In any case, the link between a positive self-concept and personal adjustment is a strong one.

One element of a positive self-concept is *security*, a firm belief in the correctness of one's actions and values—a belief that is relatively immune to the judgments of others. For example, a person with a strong positive self-concept would not be terribly bothered by criticisms that career plans or personal relationships were flawed, whereas a less secure person would find such evaluations upsetting.

Along with security, the characteristic of *self-acceptance* goes hand in hand with a positive self-concept. People who accept themselves possess a number of valuable assets: the ability to change their opinions, to utilize new ideas, to accept the opinions and feelings of others, to be sensitive to others, and to engage comfortably in appropriate self-disclosure.

A third aspect of a positive self-concept is *high self-esteem*. People with high self-esteem have all these benefits: popularity, little nervousness or defensiveness, few if any feelings of inferiority, and strong feelings of security. People having high self-esteem usually do well in school, are generally happy with their lives, tend to reach out more to others, and make others feel welcome and less alienated. They seek out people with positive self-concepts more than those with negative self-concepts, and are more able to "hook into" an interpersonal relationship.

In addition, people with positive self-concepts enjoy richer vocabularies, the ability to give and take criticism comfortably, a more confident tone of voice, and an optimistic attitude toward competition.

A dramatic illustration of the effect of self-concept on communication comes from a comparison between kindergarten children with positive and negative self-concepts. Children with high self-concepts generally exhibit a number of positive characteristics: They enter new situations fearlessly, make friends easily, and experiment with new materials without hesitation. They trust their teacher, even when the teacher is a stranger, cooperate and follow rules, and largely control their own behavior. They are creative, imaginative, and free-thinking, talk freely and share experiences eagerly, are independent and need minimal direction. Most important of all, they are happy.

Kindergarten children with negative self-concepts typically demonstrate these opposite characteristics: They rarely show initiative, relying on others for direction and asking permission for almost everything. They seldom show spontaneity or enter new activities. They isolate themselves, talk very little, behave possessively with objects, make excessive demands, either withdraw or aggress, and act frustrated.

Although these behaviors refer to children about six years old, research with older children and adults finds similar patterns. Table 2–1 summarizes research describing how the level of self-esteem affects the communication behavior of adults.

Though it would be simplistic to divide the world into people with positive self-concepts and those with negative ones, the picture here is rather clear. The more positive we feel about ourselves, the more easily we will form and maintain interpersonal relationships, and the more rewarding those relationships will be.

The self-fulfilling prophecy

The self-concept is such a powerful force on the personality that it not only determines how you see yourself in the present, but can actually influence your future behavior and that of others.

TABLE 2–1 Characteristics of communicators with positive and negative self-esteem (reported by Hamachek, 1982)	
PERSONS WITH POSITIVE SELF-ESTEEM	PERSONS WITH NEGATIVE SELF-ESTEEM
1. Are likely to think well of others.	1. Are likely to disapprove of others.
2. Expect to be accepted by others.	2. Expect to be rejected by others.
3. Evaluate their own performance more favorably.	3. Evaluate their own performance less favorably.
4. Perform well when being watched: are not afraid of others' reactions.	4. Perform poorly when being watched: are sensitive to possible negative reactions.
5. Work harder for people who demand high standards of performance.	5. Work harder for undemanding, less critical people.
6. Are inclined to feel comfortable with others they view as superior in some way.	6. Feel threatened by people they view as superior in some way.
7. Are able to defend themselves against negative comments of others.	7. Have difficulty defending themselves against others' negative comments: are more easily influenced.

Such occurrences come about through a phenomenon called the self-fulfilling prophecy.

A self-fulfilling prophecy occurs when a person's expectation of an event makes the outcome more likely to happen than would otherwise have been true. Self-fulfilling prophecies occur all the time, although you might never have given them that label. For example:

1. You expected to become nervous and botch a job interview and later did so.
2. You anticipated having a good (or terrible) time at a social affair and found it met your expectations.
3. A teacher or boss explained a new task to you, saying that you probably wouldn't do well at first; you did not do well.
4. A friend described someone you were about to meet, saying that you wouldn't like the person, which turned out to be correct.

In each of these cases there is a good chance that the event happened because it was predicted. You needn't have botched the interview, the party might have been boring only because you helped make it so, you might have done better on the job if your boss hadn't

spoken up, and you might have liked the new acquaintance if your friend hadn't given you preconceptions. In other words, what helped make each event take place as it did was the expectation that it would happen exactly that way.

There are two types of self-fulfilling prophecies. The first occurs when the expectations of one person govern another's actions. The classic example is a study Robert Rosenthal and Lenore Jacobson described in their book *Pygmalion in the Classroom* (1968):

Twenty percent of the children in a certain elementary school were reported to their teachers as showing unusual potential for intellectual growth. The names of these 20 percent were drawn by means of a table of random numbers, which is to say that the names were drawn out of a hat. Eight months later these unusual or "magic" children showed significantly greater gains in IQ than did the remaining children who had not been singled out for the teachers' attention. The change in the teachers' expectations regarding the intellectual performance of these allegedly "special" children had led to an actual change in the intellectual performance of these randomly selected children.

In other words, some children may do better in school, not because they are more intelligent than their classmates, but because they learn that their teacher—a significant other—believes they can achieve.

Teachers usually convey their expectations in indirect, subtle ways. Rosenthal and DePaulo (1979) summarize the research in this area by describing four kinds of messages that label students as "special": *climate* (teachers are more supportive and confirming for certain students); *feedback* ("special" students get more positive and negative reactions than their classmates); *input* (the "special" students get more material and material of a different nature than other children); and *output* (teachers give some students more opportunities and more time to respond). The overall effect is clear: Students who are treated in a special way respond to their teachers' expectations.

To put this phenomenon in context with the self-concept, we can say that when a teacher communicates to a child the message, "I think you're bright," the child accepts that evaluation

and changes her self-concept to include that evaluation. Unfortunately, the same principle holds for students whose teachers send the message, "I think you're stupid."

This type of self-fulfilling prophecy has been shown to be a powerful force for shaping the self-concept and behavior of people in a wide range of settings outside schools. Medical patients who unknowingly use placebos—substances such as injections of sterile water or doses of sugar pills that have no curative value—often respond just as favorably to treatment as people who actually receive an active drug. The patients believe they have taken a substance that will help them feel better, and this belief actually brings about a "cure." In psychotherapy Rosenthal and Jacobson describe several studies suggesting that patients who believe they will benefit from treatment do so, regardless of the type of treatment they receive. In the same vein, when a doctor believes a patient will improve, the patient may do so precisely because of this expectation, whereas another person for whom the physician has little hope often fails to recover. Apparently

There is an old joke about a man who was asked if he could play a violin and answered, "I don't know. I've never tried." This is psychologically a very wise reply. Those who have never tried to play a violin really do not know whether they can or not. Those who say too early in life and too firmly, "No, I'm not at all musical," shut themselves off prematurely from whole areas of life that might have proved rewarding. In each of us there are unknown possibilities, undiscovered potentialities—and one big advantage of having an open self-concept rather than a rigid one is that we shall continue to expose ourselves to new experiences and therefore we shall continue to discover more and more about ourselves as we grow older.

S. I. Hayakawa

---

the patient's self-concept as being sick or well—as shaped by the doctor—plays an important role in determining the actual state of health.

In business the power of the self-fulfilling prophecy was proven as early as 1890. A new tabulating machine had just been installed at the U.S. Census Bureau in Washington, D.C. In order to use the machine, the bureau's staff had to learn a new set of skills that the machine's inventor believed to be quite difficult. He told the clerks that after some practice they could expect to punch about 550 cards per day; to process any more would jeopardize their psychological well-being. Sure enough, after two weeks the clerks were processing the anticipated number of cards, and reported feelings of stress if they attempted to move any faster.

Some time later an additional group of clerks was hired to operate the same machines. These workers knew nothing of the devices, and no one had told them about the upper limit of production. After only three days the new employees were each punching over 2000 cards per day with no ill effects. Again, the self-fulfilling prophecy seemed to be in operation. The original workers believed themselves capable of punching only 550 cards and behaved accordingly, whereas the new clerks had no limiting expectations as part of their self-concepts and so behaved more productively.

The self-fulfilling prophecy operates in families as well. If parents tell children long enough that they can't do anything right, each child's self-concept will soon incorporate this idea, and each will fail at many tasks. On the other hand, if children are told that they are capable or lovable or kind, there is a much greater chance of their behaving accordingly.

Our beliefs are so important to us that we will do anything to keep them intact. One way we protect them is by claiming that an exception to our belief is "the exception that proves the rule." For example, in our organizational consulting work, we have heard male executives argue that "women don't make good managers." When presented with evidence that sex is not a determinant of good managerial behavior, the usual response is, "Oh, sure, but those women behaved like men!"

The prophecies that others impose contribute to a person's self-concept. The statement "You'll never understand algebra" leads to the belief "I'm a mathematical idiot," and the message "We asked you to do the job because we know it will be outstanding" helps shape the belief "I'm a talented and competent person."

Once established, a person's self-concept leads to a second type of self-fulfilling prophecy—one in which the expectations we hold about ourselves influence our own behavior. Like the botched job interview and the unpleasant party mentioned at the beginning of this section, there are many times when an event that needn't occur does happen because you expect it to. In sports you've probably psyched yourself into playing either better or worse than usual; the only explanation for your unusual performance was your attitude. You've probably faced an audience at one time or another with a fearful attitude and forgotten your remarks, not because you were unprepared, but because you said to yourself, "I know I'll blow it."

Certainly you've had the experience of waking up in a cross mood and saying to yourself, "This will be a bad day." Once you decided, you acted in ways that made it come true. If you approached a class expecting to be bored, you most probably did lose interest, due partly to a lack of attention on your part. If you avoided the company of others because you expected that they had nothing to offer, your suspicions would have been confirmed—nothing exciting or new did happen to you. On the other hand, if you had approached the same day with the idea that it had the potential of being a good one, this expectation probably would also have been met. Smile at people, and they'll probably smile back. Enter a class determined to learn something, and you probably will—even if it's how not to instruct students! Approach many people with the idea that some of them will be good to know, and you'll most likely make some new friends. In such cases your attitude has a great deal to do with how you see yourself and how others will see you.

The self-fulfilling prophecy is an important force in interpersonal communication, but we don't want to suggest that it explains *all* behavior. There are certainly times when the expectation of an event's outcome won't bring about that occurrence. Believing you'll do well in a job

"If you think you can or can't you are right."

Henry Ford

interview when you're clearly not qualified for the position is unrealistic. In the same way, there will probably be people and situations you won't enjoy, no matter what your expectations. To connect the self-fulfilling prophecy with the "power of positive thinking" is an oversimplification.

In other cases your expectations will be borne out because you're a good predictor, and not because of the self-fulfilling prophecy. For example, children are not equally equipped to do well in school. In such cases it would be wrong to say that the child's performance was shaped by a parent or teacher, even though the behavior did match that which was expected. In the same way, some workers excel and others fail, some patients recover and others don't, all according to our predictions but not *because* of them.

Keeping these qualifications in mind, it's important to recognize the tremendous influence that self-fulfilling prophecies play in our lives. To a great extent we are what we believe we are. In this sense we and those around us constantly create our self-concepts and our "selves."

Changing your self-concept

You've probably begun to realize that it is possible to change an unsatisfying self-concept. In the next sections we'll discuss some methods for accomplishing such a change.

Have realistic expectations   It's extremely important to realize that some of your dissatisfaction might come from expecting too much of yourself. If you demand that you handle every act of

"YOU'RE A VERY FINE FELLOW!"

ECHO POINT

© 1974 Gahan Wilson. The Register and Tribune Syndicate, Inc.

communication perfectly, you're bound to be disappointed. Nobody is able to handle every conflict productively, to be totally relaxed and skillful in conversations, always to ask perceptive questions, or to be 100 percent helpful when others have problems. Expecting yourself to reach such unrealistic goals is to doom yourself to unhappiness at the start.

Sometimes it's easy to be hard on yourself because everyone around you seems to be handling themselves so much better than you. It's important to realize that much of what seems like confidence and skill in others is a front to hide uncertainty. They may be suffering from the same self-imposed demands of perfection that you place on yourself.

Even in cases where others definitely seem more competent than you, it's important to judge yourself in terms of your own growth, and not against the behavior of others. Rather than feeling miserable because you're not as talented as an expert, realize that you probably are a better, wiser, or more skillful person than you used to be and that this growth is a legitimate source of satisfaction. Perfection is fine as an ideal, but you're being unfair to yourself if you actually expect to reach it.

Have a realistic perception of yourself One source of a poor self-concept is inaccurate self-perception. As you've already read, such unrealistic pictures sometimes come from being overly harsh on yourself, believing that you're worse than the facts indicate. Of course, it would be foolish to deny that you could be a better person than you are, but it's also important to recognize your strengths. A periodic session of "bragging"—acknowledging the parts of yourself with which you're pleased and the ways you've grown—is often a good way to put your strengths and shortcomings into perspective.

An unrealistically poor self-concept can also come from the inaccurate feedback of others. Perhaps you are in an environment where you receive an excessive number of negative messages, many of which are undeserved, and a minimum of encouragement. We've known many housewives, for example, who have returned to college after many years spent in homemaking where they received virtually no recognition for their intellectual strengths. It's amazing that these women have the courage to come to college at all, their self-concepts are so negative; but come they do, and most are thrilled to find that they are much brighter and more competent intellectually than they suspected. In the same way, workers with overly critical supervisors, children with cruel "friends," and students with unsupportive teachers are all prone to suffering from low self-concepts due to excessively negative feedback.

If you fall into this category, it's important to put the unrealistic evaluations you receive into perspective, and then to seek out more supportive people who will acknowledge your assets as well as point out your shortcomings. Doing so is often a quick and sure boost to the self-concept.

Have the will to change   Often we say we want to change, but aren't willing to do the necessary work. In such cases the responsibility for growing rests squarely on your shoulders. Often, we maintain an unrealistic self-concept by claiming that we "can't" be the person we'd like to be, when in fact we're simply not willing to do what's required. You *can* change in many ways, if only you are willing to put out the effort.

Have the skill to change   Often trying isn't enough. There are some cases where you would change if you knew a way to do so.

First, you can seek advice—from books such as this one, the readings at the end of each chapter, and other printed sources. You can also get advice from instructors, counselors, and other experts, as well as from friends. Of course, not all the advice you receive will be useful, but if you read widely and talk to enough people, you have a good chance of learning the things you want to know.

A second method of learning how to change is to observe models—people who handle them-

> *. . . Man has a real history; having come into being, he has then through his choices to become what he is not yet, and this he cannot do unless he first chooses himself as he is now with all his finite limitations.*
>
> W. H. Auden

selves in the ways you would like to master. It's often been said that people learn more from models than in any other way, and by taking advantage of this principle you will find that the world is full of teachers who can show you how to communicate more successfully. Become a careful observer. Watch what people you admire do and say, not so that you can copy them, but so that you can adapt their behavior to fit your own personal style.

At this point you might be overwhelmed by the difficulty of changing the way you think about yourself and the way you act. Remember, we never said that this process would be an easy one (although it sometimes is). But even when change is difficult, it's possible if you are serious. You don't need to be perfect, but you *can* improve your self-concept and, as a result, your communication—*if you choose to.*

Readings

Campbell, Colin. "Our Many Versions of the Self: An Interview with M. Brewster Smith." *Psychology Today* 9 (February 1976): 74–79.

© 1967 United Feature Syndicate, Inc.

Civikly, Jean M. "Self-Concept, Significant Others, and Classroom Communication." In *Communication in the Classroom,* Larry Barker, ed. Urbana: University of Illinois Press, 1982.

*Fitts, William H. *The Self-Concept and Self-Actualization.* Nashville, Tenn.: Counselor Recordings and Tests, 1971.

*Gergen, Kenneth J. *The Concept of Self.* New York: Holt, Rinehart and Winston, 1971.

Gergen, Kenneth J. "The Healthy, Happy Human Being Wears Many Masks." *Psychology Today* 5 (May 1972): 31–35, 64–66.

Hamachek, D. *Encounters with Others.* New York: Holt, Rinehart and Winston, 1982.

Hewes, D. E., and L. Haight. "The Cross-Situational Consistency of Communicative Behaviors: A Preliminary Investigation." *Communication Research* 6 (1979): 243–270.

Insel, Paul M., and Lenore Jacobson. *What Do You Expect? An Inquiry into Self-Fulfilling Prophecies.* Menlo Park, Calif.: Cummings Publishing Co., 1975.

James, W. *Psychology: The Briefer Course.* New York: Henry Holt, 1892.

Kagan, J. *The Nature of the Child.* New York: Basic Books, 1984.

Magnussen, D., and N. Endler. *Personality at the Crossroads.* New York: John Wiley, 1977.

McCroskey, J., and V. Richmond. *The Quiet Ones: Communication Apprehension and Shyness.* Dubuque, Iowa: Gorsuch Scarisbrick, 1980.

Mischel, W. "Toward a Cognitive Social Learning Reconceptualization of Personality." *Psychological Review* 80 (1973): 252–283.

Myers, D. "The Inflated Self." *Psychology Today* 14 (May 1980): 16.

*Rosenberg, Morris. *Conceiving the Self.* New York: Basic Books, 1979.

Rosenfeld, Lawrence B. "Self-Concept and Role Behavior." In *Now That We're All Here . . . Relations in Small Groups.* Columbus, Ohio: Charles E. Merrill, 1976.

Rosenthal, Robert. "The Pygmalion Effect Lives." *Psychology Today* 7 (September 1973): 56–63.

*Rosenthal, Robert, and Bella M. DePaulo. "Expectancies, Discrepancies, and Courtesies in Nonverbal Communication." *Western Journal of Speech Communication* 43 (1979): 76–95.

Rosenthal, Robert, and Lenore Jacobson. *Pygmalion in the Classroom.* New York: Holt, Rinehart and Winston, 1968.

Rubin, Z. "Does Personality Really Change After Twenty?" *Psychology Today* 15 (May 1981): 18–27.

Samuels, Shirley C. *Enhancing Self-Concept in Early Childhood: Theory and Practice.* New York: Human Sciences Press, 1977.

Scheirer, Mary Ann, and Robert E. Kraut. "Increasing Educational Achievement via Self-Concept Change." *Review of Educational Research* 49 (Winter 1979): 131–150.

Simon, Sidney B. *Vulture: A Modern Allegory on the Art of Putting Oneself Down.* Niles, Ill.: Argus Communications, 1977.

Snyder, M. "Self-Fulfilling Stereotypes." *Psychology Today* 16 (July 1982): 60–68.

Snyder, Mark, E. D. Tanke, and Ellen Bersheid. "Social Perception and Interpersonal Behavior: On the Self-Fulfilling Nature of Social Stereotypes." *Journal of Personality and Social Psychology* 35 (1977): 656–666.

Survant, A. "Building Positive Self-Concepts." *Instructor* 81 (1972): 94—95.

Videbeck, R. "Self-Conception and the Reaction of Others." *Sociometry* 23 (1960): 351–359.

Zimbardo, P. *Shyness.* Reading, Mass.: Addison-Wesley, 1977.

Perception

After studying the material in this chapter

You should understand:

1. How the processes of selection, organization, and interpretation operate in human perception.

2. How physiological factors influence interpersonal perception.

3. How cultural factors influence interpersonal perception.

4. How social roles influence interpersonal perception.

5. How the self-concept influences interpersonal perception.

6. Common psychological factors that distort interpersonal perception.

7. The nature of interpersonal empathy.

You should be able to:

1. Describe the physiological, cultural, social, and psychological influences that have shaped your perception of important people and events.

2. Describe your interpersonal conflicts from the other parties' points of view, showing how and why those parties view that event so differently.

"Look at it my way . . . "

"Put yourself in my shoes . . . "

"If you really knew how I felt . . . "

"YOU DON'T UNDERSTAND ME!"

Such statements reflect one of the most common barriers to effective, satisfying communication. We talk to (or at) one another until we're hoarse and exhausted; yet we still don't understand each other . . . not really. We're left feeling isolated and alone, despairing that our words don't seem able to convey the depth and complexity of what we think and feel. Something more seems necessary.

We've often fantasized about what that "something more" might be. Sometimes our image of the ideal understanding-promoter takes the shape of a device with two chairs. The users would seat themselves and place electrically connected metallic caps on their heads. When the switch was thrown, each person would instantly experience the other's world. Each would see through the other's eyes, possess the other's memories, and in all other ways know how it felt to be the other person.

You can imagine how misunderstandings would disappear and tolerance would increase once everyone used this invention. It's hard to harbor dislike once you've been inside someone's skin.

Our miracle chair doesn't exist, so this chapter will have to attempt the same goal. We'll show you the many ways in which each of us experiences the world uniquely, and try to help you transcend the narrow viewpoint that each of us usually occupies.

The perception process

Before we begin looking at the specific factors that shape our beliefs, we need to take a look at how the perception process operates. The first point to realize is that we do not take notice of every stimulus that is available to us. William James made this point poetically when he said, "To the infant the world is just a big blooming, buzzing confusion." Newborn children certainly are overwhelmed with an overload of new sensations, and they spend the first years of life learning which stimuli are meaningful and important.

Even as adults we are faced with more stimuli than we can manage. It would be impossible to focus on every word, noise, sight, or other sensation, so we find ways of screening out stimuli that seem unimportant. The perception process occurs in three steps.

Selection Because we are exposed to more input than we can possibly manage, the first step in perceiving is to select data to which we will attend. There are several factors that cause us to notice some messages and ignore others.

Stimuli that are *intense* often attract our attention. Something (or someone) that is louder, larger, or brighter stands out. This attraction explains why—other things being equal—we're more likely to remember extremely tall or short people, and why someone who laughs or talks loudly attracts more attention (not always favorable) than do quiet people.

Stimuli that are *repetitious* also attract attention. Just as a quiet but steadily dripping faucet can dominate your awareness, messages we hear again and again become noticeable.

Attention also is related to *contrast* or *change* in stimulation. Unchanging things or people become less and less noteworthy, until some change reminds us of them. This principle explains why we sometimes come to take wonderful people for granted, and why we only appreciate them when they stop being so wonderful or go away.

For the most part we do not see first and then define; we define first and then see.

Walter Lippmann

A final factor that influences selection involves *motives.* Just as a hungry person looks for a restaurant or a tardy one glances at clocks, someone looking for romance notices potential partners.

Organization   After selecting information from the environment, we must arrange those data in some meaningful way. Many messages are ambiguous; you can organize them in more than one manner. For instance, consider the picture of the boxes in Figure 3–1. How many ways can you view the figure? Most people have a hard time finding more than one perspective. (There are four.) If you can't find all of them, turn to Figure 3–3 on page 48 for some help.

We can see the principle of alternative organizing patterns in human interaction. Young children usually don't classify people according to their skin color. They are just as likely to identify a black person, for example, as being tall, wearing glasses, or being a certain age. As they become more socialized, however, they learn that one common organizing principle in today's society is race, and their perceptions of others change. Do you organize according to age, education, occupation, physical attractiveness, or some other scheme? Imagine how different your relationships would be if you used different criteria for organizing.

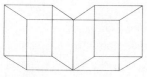

FIGURE 3–1

Many interpersonal disputes arise from the different ways people organize a series of events. Watzlawick, Beavin, and Jackson (1967, p. 56) term this process *punctuation,* and illustrate it by describing a running quarrel between a husband and wife. The husband accuses the wife of being a nag, while she complains that he is withdrawing from her. Figure 3–2 describes this cycle.

Notice that the order in which each partner punctuates this cycle affects how the dispute looks. The husband begins by blaming the wife: "I withdraw because you nag." The wife organizes the situation differently, starting with the husband: "I nag because you withdraw." Once the cycle gets rolling, it is impossible to say which accusation is accurate. The answer depends on how the sequence is punctuated.

Interpretation   After organization, the third step in perception is interpretation. Consider the husband-wife quarrel we just discussed. Suppose the wife suggests that they get away for a weekend vacation. If the husband interprets his wife's idea as more nagging ("You never pay attention to me"), the fight will continue. If he views it as a romantic break from the past, his reaction is likely to be positive. It wasn't the event itself that shaped the outcome, but the way the husband interpreted it.

Interpretation plays a role in virtually every interpersonal act. Is the person who smiles at you across a crowded room interested in romance or simply being polite? Is a friend's kidding a sign of affection or irritation? Should you take an invitation to "drop by anytime" literally or not?

There are several factors that cause us to interpret an event one way or another. The first is *past experience.* What meanings have similar events held? If, for instance, you've been gouged by landlords in the past, you might be skeptical about an apartment manager's assurances that careful housekeeping will assure the refund of your cleaning deposit.

Assumptions about human behavior also influence interpretations. "People do as little work as possible." "In spite of their mistakes, people generally do the best they can." Such beliefs shape the way you interpret another's actions.

Expectations are a third factor that shapes our interpretations. If you imagine your boss is unhappy with you, you'll probably feel threatened by a request to "see me in my office Monday morning." On the other hand, if you imagine that your work will be rewarded, your weekend will be filled with pleasant anticipation.

Knowledge of others affects the way we interpret their actions. If you know a friend has just been jilted by a lover or fired from a job, you'll interpret his aloof behavior differently than if you were unaware of what happened. If you know an instructor is rude to all students, then you won't be likely to take such remarks personally.

Finally, *personal moods* affect interpretations. When you're feeling insecure, the world is a different place than when you're confident. The same goes for happiness and sadness or any other opposing emotions. The way we feel determines how we'll interpret events.

Influences on perception

How we select, organize, and interpret data about others is influenced by a variety of factors. Some of our perceptual judgments are affected by physiology, others by cultural and social forces, and still others by psychological factors.

Physiological influences   Visit a large camera store and you'll be confronted by an impressive array of equipment: everything from

l strive automatically to bring the world into harmony with my own nature.

George Bernard Shaw

cheap pocket models to sophisticated systems including lenses, filters, tripods, and timers. Some cameras can photograph miniature items at close range, and others can capture distant objects clearly. With the right film, it's even possible to take pictures of objects invisible to the unaided eye. There's only one world "out there," but different equipment allows us to see different parts of it. In the same way, each person's perceptual equipment gives a different image of the world. Sometimes these pictures are so unlike that it seems as if we're not talking about the same events at all.

The senses   The differences in how each of us sees, hears, tastes, touches, and smells stimuli

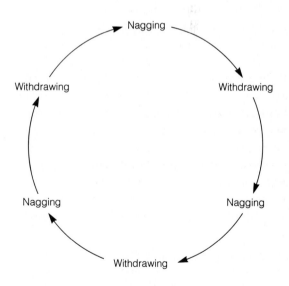

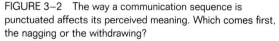

FIGURE 3–2   The way a communication sequence is punctuated affects its perceived meaning. Which comes first, the nagging or the withdrawing?

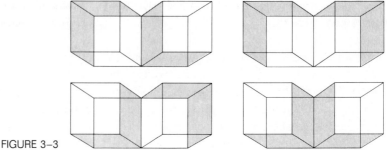

FIGURE 3–3

can affect interpersonal relationships. Consider the following everyday situations:

"Turn down that radio! It's going to make me go deaf."

"It's not too loud. If I turn it down, it will be impossible to hear it."

"It's freezing in here."

"Are you kidding? We'll suffocate if you turn up the heat!"

"Why don't you pass that truck? The highway is clear for half a mile."

"I can't see that far, and I'm not going to get us killed."

These disputes aren't just over matters of opinion. The sensory data we receive is different. Differences in vision and hearing are the easiest to recognize, but other gaps exist as well. Evidence exists that identical foods taste different to various individuals (Bartoshuk, 1980). Odors that please some people repel others (Moncrieff, 1966). Likewise, temperature variations that leave some of us uncomfortable are inconsequential to others. Remembering these differences won't eliminate them, but it will make it easier to remember that the other person's preferences aren't crazy, just different.

Age   One reason older people view the world differently than younger ones is because of a greater scope and number of experiences. There are also developmental differences that shape perceptions. Swiss psychologist Jean Piaget (1952) described a series of stages that children pass through on their way to adulthood. According to Piaget, younger children are incapable of performing mental feats that are natural to the rest of us. Until they approach the age of seven, for example, they aren't able to take another person's point of view. This fact helps explain why youngsters often seem egocentric, selfish, and uncooperative. A parent's exasperated plea, "Can't you see I'm too tired to play?" just won't make sense to a four-year-old full of energy, who imagines that everyone else must feel the same.

Health   Recall the last time you came down with a cold, flu, or some other ailment. Do you remember how different you felt? You probably had much less energy. It's likely that you felt less sociable, and that your thinking was slower than usual. These kinds of changes have a strong impact on how you relate to others. It's good to realize that someone else may be behaving differently because of illness. In the same way, it's important to let others know when you feel ill, so they can give you the understanding you need.

Fatigue   Just as being ill can affect your relationships, so can being overly tired. Again it's important to recognize the fact that you or someone else may behave differently when fatigued.

Trying to deal with important issues at such a time can get you into trouble.

Hunger   People often get grumpy when they haven't eaten and sleepy after stuffing themselves. A number of physiological changes occur as we eat and become hungry again. Trying to conduct important business at the wrong time in this cycle can lead to problems.

Biological cycles   Are you a "morning person" or a "night person"? Most of us can answer this question pretty easily, and there's a good physiological reason behind our answer. Each of us is in a daily cycle in which all sorts of changes constantly occur, including body temperature, sexual drive, alertness, tolerance to stress, and mood (Luce, 1971). Most of these changes are due to hormonal cycles. For instance, adrenal hormones, which affect feelings of stress, are secreted at higher rates during some hours. In the same man-

ner, the male and female sex hormones enter our systems at variable rates. We often aren't conscious of these changes, but they surely govern the way we relate toward each other. Once we're aware that our own daily cycles and those of others govern our feelings and behavior, it becomes possible to run our lives so that we deal with important issues at the most effective times.

For some women, the menstrual cycle plays an important role in shaping feelings and thus affects communication. Women aren't the only ones whose communication is affected by periodic changes in mood. Men, too, go through recognizable mood cycles, even though they aren't marked by obvious physical changes. Although they may not be aware of it, many men seem to go through biologically regulated periods of good spirits followed by equally predictable times of depression (Ramey, 1972). The average length of this cycle is about five weeks, although in some cases it's as short as sixteen days or as long as

"This is nothing. When I was your age the snow was so deep it came up to my chin!"

two months. However long it may be, this cycle of ups and downs is quite regular.

Although neither men nor women can change these emotional cycles, simply learning to expect them can be a big help in improving communication. When you understand that a bad mood is predictable from physiological causes, you can plan for it. You'll know that every few weeks your patience will be shorter, and you'll be less likely to blame your bad moods on innocent bystanders. The people around you can also learn to expect your periodic lows. If they can attribute them to biology, maybe they won't get angry at you.

Cultural influences   In addition to physiology, culture plays a major role in shaping our perceptions of the world. Every culture has its own world view, its own way of looking at the world. At times it's easy to forget that people everywhere don't see things the way we do. When we remember these differing cultural perspectives, they can be a great way of learning more about both ourselves and others.

The most obvious cross-cultural problems arise out of poor translation from one language to another. Some examples:

- Chevrolet was baffled when its Nova model did not sell well in Latin American countries. Officials from General Motors finally realized the problem: In Spanish, *no va* means "does not go."
- One airline lost customers when it promoted the "rendezvous lounges" on its planes flying Brazilian routes. In Portuguese, a *rendezvous* is a place to have sex.
- McDonald's Corporation was chagrined to learn that in French-Canadian slang "big macs" are large breasts (Armao, 1981).

Nonverbal behaviors, too, differ from one part of the world to another. In many cultures, the American "O.K." sign made by touching the thumb and forefinger is an obscene gesture. To a woman it is a proposition for sex, and to a man it is an accusation of homosexuality (Harrison, 1972). It's easy to imagine the problems that could result from an unsuspecting American's innocent gesture.

The range of cultural differences is wide. In Middle Eastern countries, personal odors play an important role in interpersonal relationships. Arabs consistently breathe on people when they talk. As anthropologist Edward Hall (1969, p. 160) explains:

To smell one's friend is not only nice, but desirable, for to deny him your breath is to act ashamed. Americans, on the other hand, trained as they are not to breathe in people's faces, automatically communicate shame in trying to be polite. Who would expect that when our highest diplomats are putting on their best manners they are also communicating shame? Yet this is what occurs constantly, because diplomacy is not only "eyeball to eyeball" but breath to breath.

The gap between cultures often extends beyond dissimilar norms, extending to a wide range of different experiences and feelings. One of the clearest examples of these differing perceptions is the gap between white and black people in the United States. Even to people of good will it seems that there's a barrier that makes understanding difficult; there just seem to be too many different experiences that separate us.

John Howard Griffin (1959) found one way to bridge the gulf that separates whites and blacks. Realizing the impossibility of truly understanding the black experience by reading and talking about it, he went one step further: Through a series of treatments that included doses of skin-darkening drugs, he transformed himself into a black man— or at least a man with black skin. Then he traveled through the southern United States to get in touch with what it truly meant to be black in America. He was treated like a black, and eventually, to his own surprise, came to find himself responding to white people's demands as if he were one. The insults, the prejudice, sickened him.

This experiment took place in the Deep South of 1959, and times have certainly changed since then. To what extent is the world still a different place to contemporary whites and blacks? How about other groups—Hispanics, Orientals, Native Americans, old people, and women? Do you ever find yourself prejudging or being prejudged before getting acquainted with someone from a different sector of society?

Perhaps by sharing the personal experiences of others in your group you can gain a more per-

sonal insight into how people from different co-cultures view life in your community, not only in terms of discrimination, but also in terms of values, behavioral norms, and political and economic issues. How would life be different if you were of a different race or religion, social or economic class? See if you can imagine.

Total role reversals aren't likely to happen, but it's possible to create experiences that give a good picture of another's perspective. The story of one Iowa schoolteacher and her class illustrates the point. Shortly after Martin Luther King's assassination in 1968, Jane Elliott wanted to make sure her third-graders never became prone to the sickness that caused such events. How could she do it? Everyone in the small town of Riceville was white, and most of her eight-year-olds had never really known blacks. How could she bring home to them the nature of prejudice?

Her solution was to divide the class into two groups, one containing all the children with blue eyes, and the other made up of the brown-eyed students. Then for the next few days she treated the brown-eyes as better people. They all sat in the front of the room, had second helpings at lunch, got five extra minutes of recess, and received extra praise for their work from Mrs. Elliott. At the same time, the blue-eyes were the butt of both subtle and obvious discrimination. Besides the back-row seats, skimpy meals, and other such practices, the blue-eyes never received praise for their schoolwork from Elliott, who seemed to find something wrong with every-thing they did. "What can you expect from a blue-eyed person?" was her attitude. The level of the blue-eyed children's schoolwork dropped almost immediately.

At first the children treated the experiment as a game; but shortly they changed from cooperative, thoughtful people into small but very prejudiced bigots. Classmates who had always been best friends stopped playing with each other and even quit walking to school together.

After the level of intolerance had grown pain-fully high, Elliott changed the rules. Now the blue-eyed people were on top, and the brown-eyes were inferior. Soon the tables were turned, with children who had only days before been the object of discrimination now being bigots themselves.

Seeing things from the other person's point of view was all that was needed for the students to recognize what was happening. Selecting, organizing, and interpreting things from one per-spective, adopting one particular role, limited the

information available. The result was conflict. The perception process requires an understanding of how perception affects all the participants' behavior and not simply your own.

Social influences   Almost from the time we are born, each of us is indirectly taught a whole set of roles we're expected to play. In one sense this collection of prescribed parts is necessary because it enables a society to function smoothly and provides the security that comes from know-ing what's expected of you. In another way, having roles defined in advance can lead to wide gaps in understanding. When roles become unquestioned and rigid, people tend to see the world from their own viewpoint, having no experiences to show them how other people view it. Naturally, in such a situation communication suffers.

Sex roles   In every society one of the most important factors in determining roles is sex. How should a woman act? What kinds of behavior define being a man? Until recently most of us never questioned the answers our society gave to these questions. Boys are made of "snips and snails and puppy-dog tails" and grow up to be the breadwinners of families; little girls are "sugar and spice and everything nice," and their mothers are irrational, intuitive, and temperamental. Not every-one fits into these patterns, but in the past the patterns became well established, and most peo-ple never questioned them.

Research on male and female behavior in small group settings supports some of these stereo-types. As a group males appear more confident, dominant, achievement-oriented, and task-oriented than females, and females are more accommodating and social-oriented than males. In an analysis of male and female democratic lead-ers, Rosenfeld and Fowler (1976) found that the personality variables that characterize democratic male leaders include being forceful, intellectually superior, analytical of self and others, and utilitarian. Democratic females were characterized as open-minded, helpful, affectionate, accepting of blame, and desirous of stability and unity.

In a follow-up study, Fowler and Rosenfeld (1979) observed the behavior of male and female democratic leaders. They found the communicative behavior of female democratic leaders to be predominantly socioemotional, expressing more friendly acts and agreement than male democratic leaders. The communicative behavior of male democratic leaders was concentrated in the task areas. For example, the male leaders offered more suggestions than female leaders, disagreed more, and performed more unfriendly acts.

These findings support the stereotyped sex roles ascribed to males and females in our society. Males often behave in independent, aggressive, competitive, risk-taking, and task-oriented ways, whereas females tend to be more noncompetitive, dependent, empathic, passive, fragile, interpersonally oriented, expressive, and cooperative.

These stereotyped sex-role descriptions are also supported by research in the area of nonverbal communication, summarized by Rosenthal and DePaulo (1979) and LaFrance and Mayo (1979). Compared to men, for example, women are more supportive in conversations, laugh more at others' jokes, argue less, interrupt less, smile more, are visually more attentive, look more pleasant, and intrude less on others' personal space. The general conclusion that Rosenthal and DePaulo arrived at from these findings was that "women are more polite in the nonverbal aspects of their social interactions than are men. They are more guarded in reading those cues that senders may be trying to hide but more open in the expression of their own affective states. . . . Perhaps women in our culture have been taught that there may be social hazards to knowing too much about others' feelings" (p. 95).

What accounts for these differences? In an earlier time most people would have automatically assumed that physical differences between men and women cause them to think and act in distinct ways. More recently, however, social scientists and laypersons have recognized that human behavior—male and female—is also influenced by *psychological* differences, brought about by the social environment in which each of us lives. One needn't be a social scientist to realize that the ways in which boys and girls are socialized differ in many ways. Boys are discouraged from behaving in "feminine" ways: playing with dolls, dressing up (except for a brief stint as Spiderman or

I have noticed
that men
somewhere around forty
tend to come in from the field
with a sigh
and removing their coat in the hall
call into the kitchen
   you were right
   grace
   it ain't out there
   just like you've always said
and she
with the children gone at last
breathless
puts her hat on her head
   the hell it ain't
coming and going
they pass
in the doorway

Ric Masten

---

the Incredible Hulk on Halloween). They're reinforced for playing in competitive sports. Girls, on
the other hand, find that adults are more willing to
accept cuddles, tears, and other overt emotional
expressions from them. They don't receive much
approval for assertive or aggressive acts.

J. M. Bardwick and E. Douvan (1971) point out
another way in which the two sexes are socialized
differently. They explain that male role behavior is
more narrowly defined than female role behavior
(young girls may behave in a moderately masculine way as well as acting feminine, whereas
young boys are firmly discouraged from behaving
any way but extremely masculine), creating a situation in which males receive more punishment
than females. Because early relationships for girls
are rewarding, they tend toward being people- or
relationship-oriented when they get older, and
because early relationships for boys are generally
punishing, they tend to seek satisfaction outside
relationships with other people, and so become
object-oriented as opposed to people-oriented.

The combination of social expectations, physiological differences, and personal characteristics led Sandra Bem (1974), one of the first
researchers in the area of sociosexual behavior,
to expand the traditional male-female dichotomy
to two separate dimensions. She reasoned that
masculinity and femininity are not opposite poles
of a single continuum, but rather two separate
sets of behavior. With this view, an individual can
be masculine, feminine, or exhibit both types of
characteristics. The male-female dichotomy, then,
is replaced with four psychological sex-types,
including masculine, feminine, androgynous (masculine and feminine), and undifferentiated (neither
masculine nor feminine). Combining the four
psychological sex-types with the traditional
physiological sex-types, we arrive at the eight categories listed in Table 3–1.

TABLE 3–1 Bem's sex types

	MALE	FEMALE
MASCULINE	Masculine males	Masculine females
FEMININE	Feminine males	Feminine females
ANDROGYNOUS	Androgynous males	Androgynous females
UNDIFFERENTIATED	Undifferentiated males	Undifferentiated females

In a series of studies designed to test whether psychological sex was a better predictor of behavior than anatomical sex, Bem (1974, 1975, 1976; Bem and Lenney, 1976) observed the responses of psychological sex-types to a variety of situations that called for independence, nurturance, and performance on sex-typed and non-sex-typed tasks. She found that only androgynous subjects (those who rate high on both masculine and feminine traits) display a high level of masculine independence as well as a high level of feminine nurturance. In general, research by Bem and others supports the conclusion that androgynous individuals are less restricted in their behaviors and are better able to adapt to situations that require characteristics presumed of men *or* women. This flexibility, this sex-role transcendence, may be the hallmark of mental health.

Masculine males and feminine females, the sex-typed individuals who most likely come to mind when we think of the words "male" and "female," experience more personality development problems, more marital problems, and more problem-solving difficulties than do androgynous males and females. Traditional sex-role stereotypes describe masculine males and feminine females fairly well.

What does this discussion of sexual stereotypes and attitudes have to do with perception and communication? A great deal. Each one of the eight psychological sex-types, including the stereotyped masculine males and feminine females, perceives interpersonal relationships differently. For example, masculine males probably see their interpersonal relationships as opportunities for competitive interaction, as opportunities to win something. Feminine females probably see their interpersonal relationships as opportunities to be nurturing, to express their feelings and emotions. Androgynous males and females, on the other hand, probably differ little in their perceptions of their interpersonal relationships.

Washing and ironing and cooking meals for me (yum yum)
Cleaning and sewing, she's busy as a bee (buzz buzz)
I want to help her in every single way
Because I love my mommy every day.

Working, he's working, he works so hard for us (work work)
Though he is tired he never makes a fuss (nay nay)
I want to help him in every single way
Because I love my daddy every day.

Preschool Song (overheard in 1979)

Androgynous individuals probably see their relationships as opportunities to behave in a variety of ways, depending on the nature of the relationships themselves, the context in which a particular relationship takes place, and the myriad other variables affecting what might constitute appropriate behavior. These variables are usually ignored by the sex-typed masculine males and feminine females, who have a smaller repertoire of behavior.

Occupational roles The kind of work we do also governs our view of the world. Imagine five people taking a walk through the park. One, a botanist, is fascinated by the variety of trees and plants. The zoologist is on the lookout for interesting animals. The third, a meteorologist, keeps an eye on the sky, noticing changes in the weather. The fourth, a psychologist, is totally unaware of the goings-on of nature, concentrating instead on the interaction among the people in the park. The fifth, a pickpocket, quickly takes advantage of the others' absorption to collect their wallets. There are two lessons in this little story. The first, of course, is to watch your wallet carefully. The second is that our occupational roles frequently govern our perceptions.

Even within the same occupational setting, the different roles of participants can affect their experience. Consider a typical college classroom, for example: the experiences of the instructor and students are often quite dissimilar. Having dedicated a large part of their lives to their work, most professors see their subject matter—whether French literature, physics, or speech communication—as vitally important. Students who are taking the course to satisfy a general education requirement may view the subject as one of many obstacles standing between them and a degree, or as a chance to meet new people.

Another difference centers on the amount of knowledge people possess. To an instructor who has taught the course many times, the material probably seems extremely simple; but to students encountering it for the first time, it may seem strange and confusing. Toward the end of a semester or quarter the instructor might be pressing onward hurriedly to cover all the course material, while the students are fatigued from their studies and ready to move more slowly. We don't need to spell out the interpersonal strains and stresses that come from such differing perceptions.

Even within occupational roles the different interests and personalities of each person can lead to differing perceptions. For example, focusing on college classes, Ringwald, Mann, Rosenwein, and McKeachie (1971) found that passive students see the class as an extension of their home, a place to listen to "Mom or Dad" and do little thinking. Anxious, dependent students probably see the class as a place to look foolish, to lose part of their self-esteem. Independent students probably see it as a place to do well, to achieve important things. Attention-seekers see the class as a place to have some fun. Silent students find class a frustrating place, in which they are torn between the desire to be accepted and the fear of being rejected.

The attitudes of instructors also govern their

picture of a classroom. A teacher who takes on the role of expert probably sees the classroom as a place to display wisdom, to show off. Formal authorities most likely see the classroom as a place to play judge and jury, to represent the authority of the school, to wield power. Socializing agents see their students as children and see themselves as helpful fathers and mothers. Facilitators may see the classroom as a place to support egos, to help. Teachers who enact the role of ego ideal probably see the classroom as a place to obtain self-glorification, to be loved and admired. Other instructors see themselves as partners with their students in the learning process, cooperatively working with students whom they respect in the process of sharing new material. How would you characterize your instructors? What role do you play as a student?

The most dramatic illustration of how occupational roles shape perception occurred in 1971. Stanford psychologist Philip Zimbardo (1971) recruited a group of middle-class, well-educated young men, all white except for one Oriental. He randomly chose eleven to serve as "guards" in a mock prison set up in the basement of Stanford's psychology building. He issued the guards uniforms, handcuffs, whistles, and billy clubs. The remaining ten subjects became "prisoners" and were placed in rooms with metal bars, bucket toilets, and cots.

Zimbardo let the guards establish their own rules for the experiment. The rules were tough: no talking during meals and rest periods and after lights out. They took head counts at 2:30 A.M. Troublemakers received short rations.

Faced with these conditions, the prisoners began to resist. Some barricaded their doors with beds. Others went on hunger strikes. Several ripped off their identifying number tags. The guards reacted to the rebellion by clamping down hard on protesters. Some turned sadistic, physically and verbally abusing the prisoners. They threw prisoners into solitary confinement. Others

"Sure it's beautiful, but I can't help thinking about all the interstellar dust out there."
American Scientist, Nov.–Dec. 1984, p. 581.

forced prisoners to call each other names and clean out toilets with their bare hands.

Within a short time the experiment had become reality for both prisoners and guards. Several inmates experienced stomach cramps and lapsed into uncontrollable weeping. Others suffered from headaches, and one broke out in a head-to-toe rash after his request for early "parole" was denied by the guards.

The experiment was scheduled to go on for two weeks, but after six days Zimbardo realized that what had started as a simulation had become too intense. "I knew by then that they were thinking like prisoners and not like people," he said. "If we were able to demonstrate that pathological behavior could be produced in so short a time, think of what damage is being done in 'real' prisons. . . . "

This dramatic exercise, in which twenty-one well-educated, middle-class citizens turned almost overnight into sadistic bullies and demoralized victims, tells us that how we think is a function of our roles in society. It seems that *what* we are is determined largely by the society's designation of *who* we are.

Self-concept   A final factor that influences perception is the self-concept. Extensive research shows that a person with positive self-esteem is likely to think well of others, whereas someone with negative self-esteem is likely to have a poor opinion of others (see, for example, Baron, 1974). Your own experience may bear out this fact: Persons with negative self-esteem are often cynical and quick to ascribe the worst possible motives to others, whereas those who feel good about themselves are disposed to think favorably about the people they encounter. As one writer put it, "What we find 'out there' is what we put there with our unconscious projections. When we think we are looking out a window, it may be, more often than we realize, that we are really gazing into a looking glass."

Besides distorting the facts about others, our self-concepts also lead us to distorted views of ourselves. We already hinted at this fact when we explained in Chapter 2 that the self-concept is not objective. "It wasn't my fault," you might be tempted to say, knowing deep inside that you were responsible. "I look horrible," you might think as you look into the mirror, despite the fact that everyone around you sincerely insists you look terrific.

Distortions like these usually revolve around the desire to maintain a self-concept that has been threatened. Recall that in Chapter 2 we described the tendency to maintain a presenting self-image, which is often an idealized form of the person we privately believe ourselves to be. If you want to view yourself as a good student or musician, for example, then an instructor who gives you a poor grade or a critic who doesn't appreciate your music *must* be wrong, and you'll find evidence to show it. If you want to think of yourself as a good worker or parent, then you'll find expla-

nations for the problems in your job or family that shift the responsibility away from you. Of course, the same principle works for people with excessively negative self-images: They'll go out of their way to explain any information that's favorable to them in terms that show they really are incompetent or undesirable.

Common mistakes in perception

Physiology, social and cultural roles, and self-concept aren't the only factors that affect our perceptions of others. A large body of research has revealed several tendencies that often distort the judgments we make (see Hamachek, 1982, pp. 29–30).

We are influenced by the obvious   The error of being influenced by what is most obvious is understandable. As you read earlier, we select stimuli from our environment that are noticeable: intense, repetitious, unusual, or otherwise attention-grabbing. The problem is that the most obvious factor is not necessarily the only cause—or the most significant one—of an event. For example:

- When two children (or adults, for that matter) fight, it may be a mistake to blame the one who lashes out first. Perhaps the other one was at least equally responsible, teasing or refusing to cooperate.
- You might complain about an acquaintance whose malicious gossiping or arguing has become a bother, forgetting that by putting up with that kind of behavior you have been at least partially responsible.
- You might blame an unhappy working situation on the boss, overlooking other factors beyond her control such as a change in the economy, the policy of higher management, or demands of customers or other workers.

These examples show that it is important to take time to gather all the facts.

We cling to first impressions   Labeling people according to our first impressions is an inevitable part of the perception process. These labels are a way of making interpretations. "She seems cheerful." "He seems sincere." "They sound awfully conceited."

If they're accurate, impressions can be useful ways of deciding how to respond best to people in the future. Problems arise, however, when the labels we attach are inaccurate; for once we form an opinion of someone, we tend to hang onto it and make any conflicting information fit our image.

Suppose, for instance, you mention the name of your new neighbor to a friend. "Oh, I know him," your friend replies. "He seems nice at first, but it's all an act." Perhaps this appraisal is off-base. The neighbor may have changed since your friend knew him, or perhaps your friend's judgment is simply unfair. Whether the judgment is accurate or not, once you accept your friend's evaluation, it will probably influence the way you respond to the neighbor. You'll look for examples of the insincerity you've heard about . . . and you'll probably find them. Even if the neighbor were a saint, you would be likely to interpret his behavior in ways that fit your expectations. "He *seems* nice," you might think, "but it's probably just a front." Of course, this sort of suspicion can create a self-fulfilling prophecy, transforming a genuinely nice person into an undesirable neighbor.

Given the almost unavoidable tendency to form first impressions, the best advice we can give is to keep an open mind and be willing to change your opinion as events prove you mistaken.

We assume others are like us   People commonly imagine others possess the same attitudes and motives that they do. For example, research shows that people with negative self-esteem

The belief that one's own view of reality is the only reality is the most dangerous of all delusions.

Paul Watzlawick

---

imagine that others view them unfavorably, whereas people who like themselves imagine that others like them, too (King, 1979, p. 152). The frequently mistaken assumption that others' views are similar to our own applies in a wide range of situations. For example:

- You've heard a slightly raunchy joke that you found funny. You might assume that it won't offend a friend. It does.
- You've been bothered by an instructor's tendency to get off the subject during lectures. If you were a professor, you'd want to know if anything you were doing was creating problems for your students; so you decide that your instructor will probably be grateful for some constructive criticism. Unfortunately, you're wrong.
- You lost your temper with a friend a week ago and said some things you regret. In fact, if someone said those things to you, you would consider the relationship was finished. Imagining that your friend feels the same way, you avoid making contact. In fact, your friend feels that he was partly responsible and has avoided you because he thinks you're the one who wants to end things.

These examples show that others don't always think or feel the way we do and that assuming similarities can lead to problems. How can you find out the other person's real position? Sometimes by asking directly, sometimes by checking with others, and sometimes by making an educated guess after you've thought the matter out. All these alternatives are better than simply assuming everyone would react the way you do.

The test of a first-rate intelligence is the ability to hold two opposed ideas in mind at the same time and still retain the ability to function.

F. Scott Fitzgerald

We favor negative impressions   What do you think about Harvey? He's handsome, hard-working, intelligent, and honest. He's also conceited.

Did the last quality make a difference in your evaluation? If it did, you're not alone. Research shows that when people are aware of both the positive and negative characteristics of another, they tend to be more influenced by the undesirable traits. In one study, for example, researchers found that job interviewers were likely to reject candidates who revealed negative information even when the total amount of information was highly positive (Regan and Totten, 1975).

Sometimes this attitude makes sense. If the negative quality clearly outweighs any positive ones, you'd be foolish to ignore it. A surgeon with shaky hands and a teacher who hates children, for example, would be unsuitable for their jobs, whatever their other virtues. But much of the time it's a bad idea to pay excessive attention to negative qualities and overlook good ones. Some people make this mistake when screening potential friends or dates. They find some who are too outgoing or too reserved, others who aren't intelligent enough, and still others who have a strange sense of humor. Of course, it's important to find people you truly enjoy, but expecting perfection can leave you lonely.

We blame innocent victims   The blame we assign for misfortune depends on who the victim is. When others suffer, we often blame the problem on their personal qualities. On the other hand, when we're the victims, we find explanations outside ourselves. Consider a few examples:

- When *they* botch a job, we think they weren't listening well or trying hard enough; when *we* make the mistake, the problem was unclear directions or not enough time.
- When *he* lashes out angrily, we say he's being moody or too sensitive; when *we* blow off steam, it's because of the pressure we've been under.
- When *she* gets caught speeding, we say she should have been more careful; when *we* get the ticket, we deny we were driving too fast or say, "Everybody does it."

There are at least two explanations for this kind of behavior. Because most of us want other people to approve of us, we defend ourselves by finding explanations for our own problems that make us look good. Basically we're saying, "It's not *my* fault." Also, putting others down can be a cheap way to boost our own self-esteem; we are stating, in effect, "I'm better than they are."

We don't always commit the kind of perceptual errors described in this section. Sometimes, for instance, people *are* responsible for their misfortunes, and our problems are not our fault. Likewise, the most obvious interpretation of a situation may be the correct one. Nonetheless, a large amount of research has proven again and again that our perceptions of others are often distorted in these ways. The moral, then, is clear: don't assume that your first judgment of a person is accurate.

Empathy in interpersonal relationships

The perceptual errors in the preceeding section show how difficult it is to understand another person's position, yet we could argue that this sort of understanding is the most important goal of communication.

Empathy defined The ability to understand others completely is called *empathy*. The term "empathy" is derived from two Greek words (έn + πάqos) that mean "feeling in(side)" (King, 1979, p. 152). These words suggest that empathy involves more than just intellectually understanding another person: It requires you to *experience* the other's perception. When you empathize, you comprehend another's reasons for acting, experience the other's emotions. In effect, you feel as the other does, at least temporarily.

Empathy is quite different from sympathy. The roots for sympathy (σύn + páqos) mean "feeling with." As this definition implies, when you feel sympathetic, you stand beside the other person, feeling compassion. Despite your concern, sympathy doesn't involve the degree of understanding that empathy does. When you sympathize, it is still the other's confusion, joy, or pain. When you empathize, the experience becomes your own, at least for the moment.

The importance of empathy The impact of truly empathizing with another person is powerful. Actor Dustin Hoffman learned this fact when he played the role of a female in the movie *Tootsie*. During the film's production Hoffman participated in several screen tests to assess his progress. Leslie Bennetts (1983) of the *New York Times* news service described Hoffman's experience.

> . . . At one screen test, he—as Dorothy Michaels, the soap opera star he plays in the film—was improvising in front of the camera when he was asked whether he thought he would ever have children.
>
> In her soft Southern voice, Dorothy said no, she said she thought she wouldn't be having children. Her interrogator persisted: Why not? "I think it's a little late in the day for that," said Dorothy—and, suddenly overwhelmed, she burst into tears.

> "I felt so terrible that I would never have that experience," says Hoffman, his voice still filled with wonderment. . . . "I've been acting . . . nearly 30 years . . . and I've never had a moment like that before in my life." (p. 17E)

The role had a powerful impact on Hoffman, opening the way for intensive self-examination. He began to explore the issues raised by the film: What does it mean to be a woman? What barriers do our gender and attractiveness create?

His experiences as Dorothy Michaels gave Hoffman other insights. In altering his physical experience, Hoffman had to come to grips with the fact that, though he might convincingly portray a woman, he could never turn himself into a pretty one. "The next step was outrage over how he was treated by men; while Hoffman freely admits that he, as a man, has been guilty of the same sin, he was devastated that his homeliness as a woman rendered him next to invisible to many men" (p. 17E).

As Dorothy, Hoffman encountered men who would meet "her," say hello, and "immediately start looking over my shoulder trying to find an attractive woman! I could feel that number printed on me, that I was a four, or maybe a six. And I would get very hostile: I wanted to get even with them. But I also realized I wouldn't ask myself out: If I looked the way I looked as Dorothy, I wouldn't come up to myself at a party" (p. 19E).

Few of us have the chance to experience another person's point of view so completely, but less dramatic shifts of perspective can make a profound difference in how we feel about others. In one study (Regan and Totten, 1975), college students were asked to list their impression of people either shown in a videotaped discussion or described in a short story. Half of the students were instructed to empathize with the person as much as possible, and the other half were not given any instructions about empathizing. The results were impressive: The students who did not practice empathy were prone to explain the person's behavior in terms of personality characteristics. For example, they might have explained a cruel statement by saying the speaker was mean, or they might have attributed a divorce to the partners' lack of understanding. The empathic students, on the other hand, were more aware of possible elements in the situation that might have contributed to the reaction. For instance, they might have explained a person's unkind behavior in terms of job pressures or personal difficulties instead of simply labeling that person as mean. In other words, practicing empathy seems to make people more tolerant.

You might argue here: "Why should I be more tolerant? Maybe behavior I disapprove of *is* due to the other person's personality defects and not just to outside factors. Maybe people are selfish, lazy, or stupid much of the time." Perhaps they are, but research clearly shows that we are much more charitable when finding explanations for our own behavior. When explaining our actions, we are quick to suggest situational causes: "I was tired." "She started it." "The instructions weren't clear." In other words, we often excuse ourselves by saying, "It wasn't my fault!" As we've already said, we're less forgiving when we judge others. Becoming more empathic can help even the score, enabling us to treat others at least as kindly as we treat ourselves.

Requirements for empathy   Empathy may be valuable, but it isn't always easy. In fact, research shows that it's hardest to empathize with people who are different from us radically: in age, sex, socioeconomic status, intelligence, and so forth (Cronkhite, 1976, p. 82). In order to make the kind of perceptual leaps we are talking about, you need to develop several skills and attitudes.

Open-mindedness   Perhaps the most important characteristic of an empathic person is the ability and disposition to be open-minded—to set aside for the moment beliefs, attitudes, and values and consider those of the other person. Open-mindedness is especially difficult when the other person's position is radically different from your own. The temptation is to think (and sometimes say), "That's crazy!" "How can you believe that?" or "I'd do it this way. . . . "

Being open-minded is often difficult because people confuse *understanding* another's position with *accepting* it. They are quite different matters. To understand why a friend disagrees with you, for example, doesn't mean you have to give up your position and accept hers.

Imagination   Being open-minded often isn't enough to allow empathy. You also need enough imagination to be able to picture another person's background and thoughts. A happily married or single person needs imagination to empathize with the problems of a friend considering divorce. A young person needs it to empathize with a parent facing retirement. A teacher needs it to understand the problems facing students, just as students can't be empathic without having enough imagination to get an idea of how their instructor feels.

Commitment   Because empathizing is often difficult, a third necessary quality is the sincere desire to understand the other person. Listening to unfamiliar, often confusing information takes time and isn't always fun. If you aim to be empathic, be willing to face the challenge.

Readings

*Alpern, Mathew, Merle Lawrence, and David Wolsk. *Sensory Processes.* Belmont, Calif.: Brooks/Cole, 1967.

Alsbrook, Larry. "Marital Communication and Sexism." *Social Casework* 57 (1976): 517–522.

Armao, R. "Worst Blunders: Firms Laugh Through Tears." *American Business* (January 1981): 11.

*Baird, John E., Jr. "Sex Differences in Group Communication: A Review of Relevant Research." *Quarterly Journal of Speech* 62 (1976): 179–192.

Bardwick, J. M., and E. Douvan. "Ambivalence: The Socialization of Women." In *Women in Sexist Society,* V. Gornick and B. Moran, eds. New York: Basic Books, 1971.

Baron, P. "Self-Esteem, Ingratiation, and Evaluation of Unknown Others." *Journal of Personality and Social Psychology* 30 (1974): 104–109.

Bartoshuk, L. "Separate Worlds of Taste." *Psychology Today* 14 (September 1980): 48–63.

Bem, Sandra L. "Sex Role Adaptability: One Consequence of Psychological Androgyny." *Journal of Personality and Social Psychology* 31 (1975): 634–643.

*Bem, Sandra L. "Probing the Promise of Androgyny." In *Beyond Sex-Role Stereotypes: Readings Toward a Psychology of Androgyny,* A. G. Kaplan and J. P. Bean, eds. Boston: Little, Brown, 1976.

Bem, Sandra L. "The Measurement of Psychological Androgyny." *Journal of Consulting and Clinical Psychology* 42 (1974): 155–162.

Bem, Sandra L., and E. Lenney. "Sex-Typing and the Avoidance of Cross-Sex Behavior." *Journal of Personality and Social Psychology* 33 (1976): 48–54.

Bennetts, L. "Hoffman: Role as Woman Shattering." *Chapel Hill Newspaper* (January 16, 1983): 17E, 19E.

Cline, M. "The Influence of Social Context on the Perception of Faces." *Journal of Personality* 25 (1956): 142–158.

*Condon, John, and F. S. Yousef. *Introduction to Intercultural Communication.* Indianapolis: Bobbs-Merrill, 1975.

Cronkhite, G. *Communication and Awareness.* Menlo Park, Calif.: Cummings, 1976.

Fowler, Gene D., and Lawrence B. Rosenfeld. "Sex Differences and Democratic Leadership Behavior." *Southern Speech Communication Journal* 45 (1979): 69–78.

Greenblatt, Lynda, James E. Hasenauer, and Vicki S. Freimuth. "Psychological Sex Type and Androgyny in the Study of Communication Variables: Self-Disclosure and Communication Apprehension." *Human Communication Research* 6 (1981): 117–129.

*Griffin, John Howard. *Black Like Me.* Boston: Houghton Mifflin, 1959.

Hall, E. T. *The Hidden Dimension.* New York: Doubleday Anchor, 1969.

Hamachek, D. E. *Encounters with Others: Interpersonal Relationships and You.* New York: Holt, Rinehart and Winston, 1982.

Harrison, R. "Nonverbal Behavior: An Approach to Human Communication," in *Approaches to Human Communication,* R. Budd and B. Ruben, eds. New York: Spartan Books, 1972.

Horn, J. "Conversation Breakdowns: As Different as Black and White." *Psychology Today* 8 (May 1974): 30.

King, R. G. *Fundamentals of Human Communication.* New York: Macmillan, 1979.

*LaFrance, Marianne, and Clara Mayo. "A Review of Nonverbal Behaviors of Women and Men." *Western Journal of Speech Communication* 43 (1979): 96–107.

Leathers, Dale G. "The Tactile and Olfactory Communication Systems." In *Nonverbal Communication Systems.* Boston: Allyn and Bacon, 1976.

Luce, Gay Gaer. *Body Time.* New York: Pantheon Books, 1971.

Montcrieff, R. W. *Odour Preferences.* New York: Wiley, 1966.

Montgomery, Charles L., and Michael Burgoon. "An Experimental Study of the Interactive Effects of Sex and Androgyny on Attitude Change." *Communication Monographs* 44 (1977): 130–135.

Piaget, J. *The Origins of Intelligence in Children.* New York: International Universities Press, 1952.

*Ramey, Estelle. "Men's Cycles." *Ms.* (Spring 1972): 10–14.

Regan, D. T., and J. Totten. "Empathy and Attribution: Turning Observers into Actors." *Journal of Personality and Social Psychology* 35 (1975): 850–856.

Ringwald, Barbara, Richard D. Mann, Robert Rosenwein, and Wilbert J. McKeachie. "Conflict and Style in the College Classroom." *Psychology Today* 4 (1971): 45–47, 76, 78–79.

Rosenfeld, Lawrence B., and Jean M. Civikly. "Senses." In *With Words Unspoken: The Nonverbal Experience.* New York: Holt, Rinehart and Winston, 1976.

*Rosenfeld, Lawrence B., Jean M. Civikly, and Jane R. Herron. "Anatomical Sex, Psychological Sex, and Self-Disclosure." In *Self-Disclosure,* Gordon J. Chelune, ed. San Francisco: Jossey-Bass, 1979.

Rosenfeld, Lawrence B., and Gene D. Fowler. "Personality, Sex, and Leadership Style." *Communication Monographs* 43 (1976): 320–324.

*Rosenthal, Robert, and Bella M. DePaulo. "Expectancies, Discrepancies, and Courtesies in Nonverbal Communication." *Western Journal of Speech Communication* 43 (1979): 76–95.

*Schneider, David J., Albert H. Hastrof, and Phoebe C. Ellsworth. *Person Perception,* 2d ed. Reading, Mass.: Addison-Wesley, 1979.

Schneider, R. A. "The Sense of Smell and Human Sexuality." *Medical Aspects of Human Sexuality* 5 (1971): 156–168.

Segall, M. H., D. T. Campbell, and M. J. Herskovits. *The Influence of Culture on Visual Perception.* Indianapolis: Bobbs-Merrill, 1966.

Trenholm, Sarah, and Toby Rose. "The Compliant Communicator: Teacher Perceptions of Appropriate Classroom Behavior." *Western Journal of Speech Communication* 45 (1981): 13–26.

Tyler, Leona. *The Psychology of Human Differences.* New York: Appleton-Century-Crofts, 1965.

Watzlawick, P., J. Beavin, and D. D. Jackson. *Pragmatics of Human Communication.* New York: W. W. Norton, 1967.

Wilentz, Joan S. *The Senses of Man.* New York: Thomas Y. Crowell, 1968.

Zimbardo, Philip G. *The Psychological Power and Pathology of Imprisonment.* Statement prepared for the U.S. House of Representatives Committee on the Judiciary, Subcommittee No. 3, Robert Kastemeyer, Chairman. Unpublished manuscript, Stanford University, 1971.

Language

After studying the material in this chapter

You should understand:

1. The symbolic nature of language.
2. That language is rule-governed.
3. That meanings are in people, not words.
4. The consequences of using various types of troublesome language.
5. The ways in which entire languages, and the choice of terminology and structure within a language, shape attitudes.
6. The ways in which language reflects the attitudes of a speaker.
7. The differences between male and female speech.
8. The relationship between language use and sex-roles.

You should be able to:

1. Recognize cases in which you have ascribed meanings to words instead of people.
2. Identify the kinds of troublesome language described in this chapter and suggest more effective alternatives.
3. Clarify your personal problems, goals, appreciative messages, complaints, and requests with behavioral descriptions.
4. Identify the way your language makes others see your credibility, status, and power.
5. Describe how linguistic messages have contributed to your present degree of self-esteem.
6. Notice how your language reflects your own sense of power, attraction to others, interest in topics, intimacy, and responsibility.
7. Identify the male or female characteristics of your speech.

ach one of us is alone in the world. He is shut in a tower of brass and can communicate with his fellows only by signs, and the signs have no common value, so that their sense is vague and uncertain. We seek pitifully to convey to others the treasures of our heart, but they have not the power to accept them, and so we go lonely, side by side but not together, unable to know our fellows and unknown by them. We are like people living in a country whose language they know so little that with all manner of beautiful and profound things to say, they are condemned to the banalities of the conversation manual. Their brain is seething with ideas and they can only tell you that the umbrella of the gardener's aunt is in the house.

W. Somerset Maugham
The Moon and Sixpence

The nature of language

As Maugham suggests in the discouraging passage above, language is an imperfect vessel to convey ideas. In everyday life we alternate between the sad realization that others rarely grasp what we think and feel, and the unconscious assumption that, because *we* know what we're talking about, others automatically understand us.

In this chapter we will explore the relationship between words and ideas. We will describe some important characteristics of language, and show how these characteristics affect our day-to-day communication. We will outline several types of troublesome language and show how to replace them with more effective kinds of speech. Finally, we will look at the power language has to shape and reflect our attitudes toward others.

Language is symbolic As you first read in Chapter 1, words are arbitrary symbols that have no meaning in themselves. The word "five," for example, is a kind of code that represents the number of fingers on your hand only because we agree that it does. As Bateson and Jackson (1964, p. 271) point out, "There is nothing

particularly five-like in the number 'five.'" To a speaker of French, the symbol "cinq" would convey the same meaning; to a computer, the same value would be represented by the electronically coded symbol "00110101."

Despite the fact that symbols are arbitrary, people often act as if they had some meaning in themselves. S. I. Hayakawa (1964, p. 27) points out the vague sense we often have that foreign languages are rather odd, and that the speakers really ought to call things by their "right" names. Hayakawa illustrates the mistaken belief that words are inherently connected to the things they label by describing the little boy who was reported to have said, "Pigs are called pigs because they are such dirty animals."

Language is rule-governed The only reason symbol-laden languages work at all is because people agree on how to use them. The linguistic agreements that make communication possible can be codified in rules. Languages contain two types of rules. *Syntactic* rules govern the way symbols can be arranged. For example, in English, syntactic rules require every word to contain at least one vowel, and prohibit sentences such as "Have you the cookies brought?," which would

"I don't know what you mean by 'glory,' " Alice said.

Humpty Dumpty smiled contemptuously. "Of course you don't—till I tell you. I meant 'there's a nice knock-down argument for you!' "

"But 'glory' doesn't mean 'a nice knock-down argument,' " Alice objected.

"When I use a word," Humpty Dumpty said, in a rather scornful tone, "it means just what I choose it to mean—neither more nor less."

"The question is," said Alice, "whether you can make words mean so many different things."

"The question is," said Humpty Dumpty, "which is to be master—that's all."

Lewis Carroll
Through the Looking Glass

---

be a perfectly acceptable arrangement in German. Although most of us aren't able to describe the syntactic rules that govern our language, it's easy to recognize their existence by noticing how odd a statement that violates them appears.

Semantic rules also govern our use of language. Whereas syntax deals with structure, semantics governs meaning. Semantic rules reflect the ways in which speakers of a language respond to a particular symbol. Semantic rules are what make it possible for us to agree that "bikes" are for riding and "books" are for reading; and they help us know whom we will encounter when we use rooms marked "men" and "women." Without semantic rules, communication would be impossible: each of us would use symbols in unique ways, unintelligible to others.

Meanings are in people, not in words   If the semantic rules of language were more precise, and if everyone followed those rules, we would suffer from fewer misunderstandings. You respond to a "while you were out" note and spend a full day trying to reach Barbara, only to find you called the wrong Barbara. You have an hour-long argument about "feminism" with a friend, only to discover that you were using the term in very different ways.

These problems occur because people attach different meanings to the same word or words. Ogden and Richards (1923) illustrated this point graphically in their well-known "triangle of meaning" (see Figure 4–1). This model shows that there is only an indirect relationship—indicated by a broken line—between a word and the thing or idea it claims to represent.*

*Some of these "things," or referents, do not exist in the physical world. For instance, some referents are mythical (such as unicorns), some are no longer tangible (such as the deceased Mr. Smith), and others are abstract ideas (such as "love").

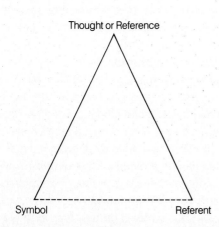

FIGURE 4–1   Ogden and Richards' triangle of meaning

• • • "**I** love you" [is] a statement that can be expressed in so many varied ways. It may be a stage song, repeated daily without any meaning, or a barely audible murmur, full of surrender. Sometimes it means: *I desire you* or *I want you sexually.* It may mean: *I hope you love me* or *I hope that I will be able to love you.* Often it means: *It may be that a love relationship can develop between us* or even *I hate you.* Often it is a wish for emotional exchange: *I want your admiration in exchange for mine* or *I give my love in exchange for some passion* or *I want to feel cozy and at home with you* or *I admire some of your qualities:* A declaration of love is mostly a request: *I desire you* or *I want you to gratify me,* or *I want your protection* or *I want to be intimate with you* or *I want to exploit your loveliness.*

Sometimes it is the need for security and tenderness, for parental treatment. It may mean: *My self-love goes out to you.* But it may also express submissiveness: *Please take me as I am,* or *I feel guilty about you, I want, through you, to correct the mistakes I have made in human relations.* It may be self-sacrifice and a masochistic wish for dependency. However, it may also be a full affirmation of the other, taking the responsibility for mutual exchange of feelings. It may be a weak feeling of friendliness, it may be the scarcely even whispered expression of ecstasy. *"I love you,"*—wish, desire, submission, conquest; it is never the word itself that tells the real meaning here.

J. A. M. Meerloo
Conversation and Communication

Overcoming troublesome language

After reading this far, you may be thinking that effective communication is hopeless. If no two people speak the same language, what hope is there for understanding one another fully? The semantic barriers that block understanding are certainly great, but they can be overcome to a great extent. By recognizing the kinds of problems we face when using language, you can speak and listen in ways that boost the odds of communicating accurately.

Equivocal language   The most obvious semantic misunderstandings involve equivocal language—words that have more than one commonly accepted definition. Some equivocal misunderstandings are trivial. Recently we ate dinner at a Mexican restaurant and ordered a "tostada with beans." Instead of being served a beef tostada with beans on the side, we were surprised to see the waiter bring us a plate containing a tostada *filled* with beans. As with most equivocal misunderstandings, hindsight showed that the phrase "tostada with beans" has two equally correct meanings.

Other equivocal misunderstandings can be more serious. A nurse gave one of her patients a scare when she told him that he "wouldn't be needing" his robe, books, and shaving materials any more. The patient became quiet and moody. When the nurse inquired about the odd behavior, she discovered that the poor man had interpreted her statement to mean he was going to die soon. In fact, the nurse meant he would be going home shortly.

The problems crop up when we start talking about other types of deviant behavior. We say of a person who drinks too much that he "is" an alcoholic, and we say of people who think bizarre thoughts that they "are" schizophrenic. This person is a drug addict and that person is a homosexual. Others are sadomasochists, pedophiliacs, juvenile delinquents. The English language is constructed in such a way that we speak of people *being* (certain things) when all we know is that they *do* certain things . . .

That kind of identity is a myth. Admittedly, if a person believes the myth, the chances rise that he will assume the appropriate, narrowly defined role. Believing that one is an addict, an alcoholic, a schizophrenic, or a homosexual can result in relinquishing the search for change and becoming imprisoned in the role.

Edward Sagarian

Some equivocal misunderstandings can go on for a lifetime. Consider the word "love." J. A. Lee (1973) points out that people commonly use that term in six very different ways: *eros* (romantic love), *ludus* (game-playing love), *storge* (friendship love), *mania* (possessive, dependent love), *pragma* (logical love), and *agape* (all-giving, selfless love). Imagine the conflicts that would occur between a couple who sincerely pledged their love to one another, each with a different kind of love in mind. "If you really love me, why are you acting like this?" we can imagine them asking one another—never realizing that they each view the relationship differently.

Vigilance is the best way to avoid equivocal misunderstandings. Whenever you face a term that has the remotest chance of being interpreted in more than one way, take the time to clarify its meaning: "I hate that idea. Well, I don't really *hate* it, but there are a couple of reasons why I think it won't work. . . ."

Static evaluation   "Mark is a nervous guy." "Karen is short-tempered." "You can always count on Wes." Statements that contain or imply the word "is" lead to the mistaken assumption that people are consistent and unchanging—

clearly an incorrect belief. Instead of labeling Mark as permanently and totally nervous, it would probably be more accurate to outline the situations in which he behaves nervously. The same goes for Karen, Wes, and the rest of us: we are more changeable than the way static, everyday language describes us.

Edward Sagarian (1976) writes about an unconscious language habit that imposes a static view of others. Why is it, he asks, that we say "he *has* a cold," but say "he *is* a convict" or homosexual, slow learner, or any other set of behaviors that are also not necessarily permanent? Sagarian argues that such linguistic labeling leads us to typecast others, and in some cases forces them to perpetuate behaviors that could be changed.

Describing John as "boring" (you can substitute "friendly," "immature," or many other adjectives) is less correct than saying, "The John I encountered yesterday seemed to me to be. . . . " The second type of statement describes the way someone behaved at one point; the first categorizes him as if he had always been that way.

Alfred Korzybski (1933) suggested the linguistic device of dating to reduce static evaluation. He suggested adding a subscript whenever appropri-

ate to show the transitory nature of many objects and behaviors. For example, a teacher might write as an evaluation of a student: "Susan$_{May\ 12}$ had difficulty cooperating with her classmates."
Although the actual device of subscripting is awkward in writing and impractical in conversation, the idea it represents can still be used. Instead of saying, "You are self-centered!" a more accurate statement might be, "You've certainly been self-centered for the last few weeks." (Even the amended statement has its problems, some of which we'll discuss in this chapter and some in Chapter 10.)

Fact-inference confusion   We can make statements about things we observe as well as about things we do not observe. The problem is that the grammar of our language does not distinguish between the two. "She is driving a Mercedes" is *grammatically* equivalent to "She is seething with rage"; yet the first sentence is a matter of fact, whereas the second is inferential. We can directly observe the car and her driving it, but we cannot directly observe her seething rage. Any statement we make about rage is based on a few observations and conclusions we draw from them.

Arguments often result when we label our inferences as facts:

A: Why are you mad at me?
B: I'm not mad at you. Why have you been so insecure lately?
A: I'm not insecure. It's just that you've been so critical.
B: What do you mean, "critical"? I haven't been critical. . . .

Instead of trying to read the other person's mind, a far better course is to identify the observable behaviors (facts) that have caught your attention and to describe the interpretations (inferences) that you have drawn from them. After describing this train of thought, ask the other person to comment on the accuracy of your interpretation:

> "When you didn't return my phone call (fact), I got the idea that you're mad at me (inference). Are you?" (question)

> "You've been asking me whether I still love you a lot lately (fact), and that makes me think you're feeling insecure (inference). Is that right?" (question)

Emotive words   Emotive terms seem to describe something but really announce the speaker's attitude towards it. If you approve of a friend's roundabout approach to a difficult subject you might call her "tactful"; if you don't like it, you might accuse her of "beating around the bush." Whether the approach is good or bad is more a matter of opinion than of fact, although this difference is obscured by emotive language.

You can appreciate how emotive words are really editorial statements when you consider these examples:

IF YOU APPROVE, SAY	IF YOU DISAPPROVE, SAY
thrifty	cheap
traditional	old-fashioned
extrovert	loudmouth
cautious	coward
progressive	radical
information	propaganda
military victory	massacre
eccentric	crazy

Bertrand Russell, the philosopher, provided a good method for seeing how emotive words work: "conjugating irregular verbs." First, examine an action or personality trait, and then show how it can be viewed either favorably or unfavorably, according to the label people give it. For example:

I'm casual.
You're a little careless.
He's a slob.

Or try this one:

> I read love stories.
> You read erotic literature.
> She reads pornography.

Or:

> I'm thrifty.
> You're money-conscious.
> He's a tightwad.

Now perform a few conjugations with the following statements:

> I'm tactful.
> I'm conservative.
> I'm quiet.
> I'm relaxed.
> My child is high-spirited.
> I have a lot of pride.

The best way to avoid arguments involving emotive words is to describe the person, thing, or idea you are discussing in neutral terms, and to label your opinions as such. Instead of saying "I wish you'd quit making those sexist remarks," say "I really don't like it when you call us 'girls' instead of 'women.'" Not only are nonemotive statements more accurate; they have a much better chance of being well received by others.

Relative words   Relative words gain their meaning by comparison. For example, do you attend a large or small school? This depends on what you compare it to. Alongside a campus such as the University of Michigan, with over 30,000 students, your school may look small; but compared with a smaller institution, it might seem quite large. Relative words such as "fast" and "slow," "smart" and "stupid," "short" and "long," are clearly defined only through comparison.

Using relative terms without explaining them can lead to communication problems. Have you ever responded to someone's question about the weather by saying it was warm, only to find out the person thought it was cold? Have you followed a friend's advice and gone to a "cheap" restaurant, only to find that it was twice as expensive as you expected? Have classes you heard were "easy" turned out to be hard? The problem in each case resulted from failing to link the relative word to a more measurable term.

Euphemisms Euphemisms (from the Greek word meaning "to use words of good omen") are pleasant terms substituted for blunt ones. Euphemisms soften the impact of information that might be unpleasant. Unfortunately, this pulling of linguistic punches often obscures the accuracy of a message.

There are certainly cases where tactless honesty can be brutal: "What do I think of your new hair style? I think it's ugly!" or "How do I feel about the relationship? I can hardly wait to get away from you!" At the same time, being too indirect can leave others wondering where you stand: "What an original haircut," or "We could grow closer than we are now." When choosing how to broach difficult subjects, the challenge is to be as kind as possible without sacrificing either your integrity or the clarity of your message. (The guidelines for self-disclosure outlined in Chapter 8 will help you.)

Overly abstract language High-level abstractions are convenient ways of generalizing about similarities among several objects, people, ideas, or events. Figure 4–2 is an "abstraction ladder" that shows how to describe the same phenomenon at various levels of abstraction.

We use higher-level abstractions all the time. For instance, rather than saying "Thanks for washing the dishes," "Thanks for vacuuming the rug," "Thanks for making the bed," it's easier to say "Thanks for cleaning up." In everyday situa-

tions like this, abstractions are a useful kind of verbal shorthand; but in other cases, problems arise when we speak too generally.

Overly abstract language causes four types of problems. The first is stereotyping. Imagine someone who has had one bad experience and, as a result, blames an entire group: "Marriage counselors are worthless," "Californians are all flaky," or "Men are no good." Overly abstract expressions like these can cause people to *think* in generalities, ignoring uniqueness. As you learned in Chapter 2, expecting people to act a certain way can become a self-fulfilling prophecy. If you expect the worst of people, you have a good chance of getting it.

Besides narrowing your own options, excessively abstract language can also confuse others.

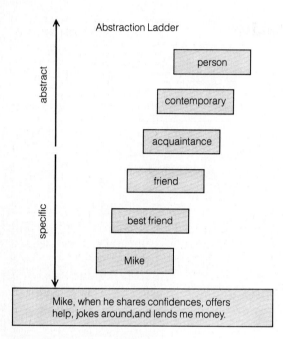

FIGURE 4–2   Abstraction ladder

A: Don't be stupid. All I'm saying is that we're in a rut. We should be living more exciting lives.
B: Well, I don't know what you want.

Overly abstract language also leads to confusing directions:

Professor: I hope you'll do a thorough job on this paper.
Student: When you say thorough, how long should it be?
P: Long enough to cover the topic thoroughly.
S: How many sources should I look at when I'm researching it?
P: You should use several—enough to show me that you've really explored the subject.
S: And what style should I use to write it?
P: One that's scholarly but not too formal.
S: Arrgh!!!

Even appreciation can suffer from being expressed in overly abstract terms. Psychologists have established that behaviors that are reinforced will recur with increased frequency. Your statements of appreciation will encourage others to keep acting in ways you like; but if they don't know just what it is that you appreciate, the chances of that behavior being repeated are lessened. There's a big difference between "I appreciate your being so nice" and "I appreciate the way you spent time talking to me when I was upset."

Overly abstract language can leave you unclear even about your own thoughts. At one time or another we've all felt dissatisfied with ourselves and others. Often these dissatisfactions show up as thoughts such as "I've got to get better organized" or "She's been acting strangely lately." Sometimes abstract statements such as these are shorthand for specific behaviors that we can identify easily; but in other cases we'd have a hard time explaining what we'd have to do to get organized or what the strange behavior is. With-

Telling the hair stylist "not too short" or "more casual" might produce the look you want, or it might lead to an unpleasant surprise.

Overly abstract explanations can cause problems of a more serious nature. Imagine the frustration that could come from these vague complaints:

A: We never do anything that's fun anymore.
B: What do you mean?
A: We used to do lots of unusual things, but now it's the same old stuff, over and over.
B: But last week we went on that camping trip, and tomorrow we're going to that party where we'll meet all sorts of new people. Those are new things.
A: That's not what I mean. I'm talking about *really* unusual stuff.
B: *(becoming confused and a little impatient)* Like what? Taking hard drugs or going over Niagara Falls in a barrel?

out clear ideas of these concepts it's hard to begin changing matters. Instead, the tendency is to go around in mental circles, feeling vaguely dissatisfied without knowing exactly what is wrong or how to improve it.

You can make your language—and your thinking—less abstract and more clear by learning to make *behavioral descriptions* of your problems, goals, appreciations, complaints, and requests. We use the word *behavioral* because descriptions of this sort move down the abstraction ladder to describe the specific, observable objects and actions about which we're thinking. Table 4–1 shows how behavioral descriptions are much more clear and effective than vague, abstract statements. Notice that most good behavioral descriptions answer three questions:

1. *Who is involved?* Be as specific as possible when you answer this question. Instead of saying "I want to feel more comfortable around members of the opposite sex," say "I want to feel more comfortable around members of the opposite sex *whom I'd like to date*." Rather than saying "I'd like to talk more comfortably with authority figures," say "I'd like to talk more comfortably with *my boss* and *my professors*."

2. *In what circumstances does the behavior occur?* You can identify the circumstances by answering several questions. In what places does the behavior occur? Does it occur at any particular times? When you are discussing particular subjects? Is there anything special about you when it occurs: are you tired, embarrassed, busy? Do you feel good or bad about your physical appearance? Is there any common trait shared by the other person or people involved? Are you friendly or hostile, straightforward or manipulative, nervous or confident? In other words, if the behavior you're describing doesn't occur all the time (and few do), you need to pin down what circumstances set this situation apart from other ones.

cathy   **by Cathy Guisewite**

3. *What behaviors are involved?* While terms such as "more cooperative" and "helpful" might sound like concrete descriptions of behavior, they are usually too vague to do a clear job of explaining what's on your mind. Behaviors must be *observable*, ideally both to you and to others. For instance, moving down the abstraction ladder from the relatively vague term "helpful," you might come to behaviors such as "does the dishes every other day," "volunteers to help me with my studies," or "fixes dinner once or twice a week without being asked." It's easy to see that terms like these are easier for both you and others to understand than are more vague abstractions.

There is one exception to the rule that behaviors should be observable, and that involves

TABLE 4–1 Abstract and behavioral descriptions

	ABSTRACT DESCRIPTION	BEHAVIORAL DESCRIPTION			REMARKS
		Who is involved	*In what circumstances*	*Specific behaviors*	
PROBLEM	I'm no good at meeting strangers.	People I'd like to date.	At parties and in school.	I think, "They'd never want to date me." Also, I don't originate conversations.	Behavioral description more clearly identifies thoughts and behaviors to change.
GOAL	I'd like to be more assertive.	Telephone and door-to-door solicitors.	When I don't want the product or can't afford it.	Instead of apologizing, I want to keep saying "I'm not interested" until they go away.	Behavioral description clearly outlines how to act; abstract description doesn't.
APPRECIATION	"You've been a great boss."	(no clarification necessary)	When I've needed to change my schedule because of school exams or assignments.	"You've rearranged my hours cheerfully."	Give both abstract and behavioral descriptions for best results.
COMPLAINT	"I don't like some of the instructors around here."	Professors A and B.	In class when students ask questions the professors think are stupid.	They either answer in a sarcastic voice (you might demonstrate), or accuse us of not studying hard enough.	If talking to A or B, use only behavioral description. With others, use both abstract and behavioral descriptions.
REQUEST	"Quit bothering me!"	You and your friends, X and Y.	When I'm studying for exams.	"Instead of asking me over and over to party with you, I wish you'd accept my comment that I need to study tonight."	Behavioral description will reduce defensiveness and make it clear that you don't *always* want to be left alone.

the internal processes of thoughts and emotions. For instance, in describing what happens to you when a friend has kept you waiting for a long time, you might say "My stomach felt like it was in knots—I was really worried. I kept thinking that you had forgotten and that I wasn't important enough to you for you to remember our date."

What you're doing when offering such a description is to make unobservable events clearer.

You can get a clearer idea of the value of behavioral descriptions by looking at the examples in Table 4–1. Notice how much more clearly they explain the speaker's thought than do the vague terms.

Language shapes our world

Language not only clarifies or obscures meaning. In some cases the language we use actually shapes our attitudes—even our entire view of the world.

Cultural perspective   Anthropologists have long known that the culture people live in shapes their perceptions of reality. Some social scientists believe that cultural perspective is at least partially shaped by the language the members of that culture speak. Benjamin Lee Whorf and Edward Sapir (Whorf, 1956) asserted this idea in their writings.

After spending several years with various North American Indian cultures, Whorf found that their patterns of thinking were shaped by the language they spoke. For example, Nootka, a language spoken on Vancouver Island, contains no distinction between nouns and verbs. The Indians who speak Nootka view the entire world as being constantly in process. Whereas English speakers see something as fixed or constant (noun), Nootka speakers view it as constantly changing. Therefore the Nootka speaker might label a "fire" as a "burning," or a house as a "house-ing." In this sense our language operates much like a snapshot camera, whereas Nootka works more like a moving-picture camera.

What does this difference have to do with communication? Because of the static, unchanging nature of our grammar, we often regard people and things as never changing. Someone who spoke a more process-oriented language would view people quite differently, assuming their changeable nature. Some cultures, for example, allow their members to change names whenever they wish. We can speculate that this practice might make it easier to see that others change over time, and in the same way it might make it

easier for individuals to escape the inhibiting effects of an obsolete self-concept.

The Sapir-Whorf hypothesis has never been conclusively proved or disproved. Some critics point out that it is possible to conceive of flux even in static languages like English. Supporters of the hypothesis respond that although it is *possible* to conceptualize an idea in different languages, some languages make it easier to follow a certain thought pattern than others.

A look at more familiar languages also shows how the linguistic world we inhabit can subtly shape our attitudes. English-speaking parents often label the mischievous pranks of their children as "bad," implying that there is something immoral about acting wild. "Be good!" they are inclined to say. On the other hand, French adults are more likely to say "*Sois sage!*"—"Be wise." The linguistic implication is that misbehaving is an act of foolishness. Swedes would correct the same action with the words "*Var snell!*"—"Be friendly, be kind." By contrast, German adults use the command "*Sei Artig!*"—literally "Be of your own kind"—in other words, get back in step, conform to your role as a child (Sinclair, 1954).

Impression formation   It isn't necessary to study German, Swedish, French, or Nootka to see how language shapes perception. Research shows that how speakers of English express a message—perhaps more than the message itself—shapes the way others regard them.

Credibility   Scholarly speaking is a good example of how speech style influences perception. We refer to what has been called the Dr. Fox hypothesis (Cory, 1980): "An apparently legitimate speaker who utters an unintelligible message will be judged competent by an audience in the speaker's area of apparent expertise." The Dr. Fox hypothesis got its name from one Dr.

Myron L. Fox, who delivered a talk followed by a half-hour discussion on "Mathematical Game Theory as Applied to Physical Education." The audience included psychiatrists, psychologists, social workers, and educators. Questionnaires collected after the session revealed that these educated listeners found the lecture clear and stimulating.

Despite his warm reception by this learned audience, Fox was a complete fraud. He was a professional actor whom researchers had coached to deliver a lecture of double-talk—a patchwork of information from a *Scientific American* article mixed with jokes, non sequiturs, contradictory statements, and meaningless references to unrelated topics. When wrapped in a linguistic package of high-level professional jargon, however, the meaningless gobbledygook was judged as important information. In other words, Fox's credibility came more from his style of speaking than from the ideas he expressed.

The same principle seems to hold for academic writing (Armstrong, 1980). A group of 32 management professors rated material according to its complexity rather than its content. When a message about consumer behavior was loaded with unnecessary words and long, complex sentences, the academics rated it highly. When the same message was translated into more readable English, with shorter words and clearer sentences, the professors judged the same research as less competent.

Status   In the stage classic *My Fair Lady* Professor Henry Higgins transformed Eliza Doolittle from a lowly flower girl into a high-society woman by replacing her Cockney accent with an upper-crust speaking style. The power of speech to influence status is a real-life fact. In 1971 British researcher Howard Giles conducted experiments that conclusively demonstrated (if any proof was necessary) that in Britain, judgments of attractiveness and status are strongly influenced by style of speech. Other research by social psychologists in North America shows that the same principle applies in the New World (see Giles and Poseland, 1975).

Power   Communication researchers have identified a number of language patterns that add to or detract from a speaker's power to influence others. In a study of courtroom speech, Bonnie Erickson and her colleagues (1978) identified several "powerless" speech mannerisms (see Table 4–2). Experimental subjects who heard testimony containing these powerless forms judged the speakers less credible and the positions they advocated less acceptable than when the same testimony was presented without the powerless elements. Interestingly, further research showed that plaintiffs and defendants who use powerful language are sometimes viewed by experimental jurors as being more blameworthy—probably because they appear to have more control over their lives than less powerful speakers, whom

TABLE 4–2 Examples of powerless language	
HEDGES	"I'm *kinda* disappointed ..." "*I think* we should ..." "*I guess* I'd like to ..."
HESITATIONS	"*Uh*, can I have a minute of your time?" "*Well*, we could try this idea ..." "I wish you would—*er*—try to be on time."
INTENSIFIERS	"I *really do* think that ..." "I'm not *very* hungry"
POLITE FORMS	"Excuse me, *sir* ..."
TAG QUESTIONS	"It's about time we got started, *isn't it?*" "*Don't you think* we should give it another try?"
DISCLAIMERS	"*I probably shouldn't say this, but* ..." "*I'm not really sure, but* ..."

juries would be inclined to see as victims (Bradac, Hemphill, and Tardy, 1981). Bradac and Mulac (1984b) conclude that outside the jury setting, people who use the powerless language forms in Table 4–2 are perceived as powerless and ineffective.

Self-esteem   The words we use to describe people's roles or functions in society can also shape the way they feel about themselves. Much of people's self-esteem is derived from the impor-

tance they feel their work has, a perception which often comes from the titles of their roles. For example, a theater owner had trouble keeping ushers working for more than a week or two. The ushers tired quickly of their work, which consisted mostly of taking tickets, selling popcorn, and showing people to their seats. Then, with only one change, the personnel problems ended. The manager simply "promoted" all the ushers to the "new" position of "assistant manager." Believe it or not, the new title was sufficient to make the employees happy. The new name encouraged

STRAIGHT, *strāt, adj.* direct, unbent, even; adjusted; honest, candid, forthright, true, reliable, veracious; clear, accurate, trustworthy; heterosexual. (From the *Thesaurus of Synonyms and Antonyms,* and *Webster's New Collegiate Dictionary*)

We are constantly being compared and contrasted; gay sensibilities versus straight sensibilities; gay lifestyles versus straight lifestyles; gay audiences versus straight audiences; gay press versus straight press; and here at the Greater Gotham Business Council, gay businesses versus straight businesses.

If *they* are *straight,* then what, really, are *we?*

The *Thesaurus of Synonyms and Antonyms* lists the following as antonyms for the word *straight:* crooked, curved, unreliable, confused, false, ambitious, evasive. It lists the following as synonyms for the word *crooked:* twisted, dishonest, distorted, deformed, warped, corrupt.

If *they* are *straight,* are *we,* therefore, all of the above?

I've considered using the word *heterosexuals* when referring to *them,* but I find it too long and too clinical. *Heteros* or *hets* is short and easy to say, but opens us up to being called *homos.*

The ad for the Oscar Wilde Memorial Bookstore in New York City says, "Think Straight, Be Gay," a sentiment with which I am in full agreement. But if we *think,* and therefore we *are,* what does that make *them?* Queers?

Breeders gets right to the point, and of course we can always use the Yiddish word my grandfather used when he referred to non-Jews: *yenim,* "the others." This, however, can get confusing: sexual preferences and religious beliefs get mixed.

May I suggest, then, when the subject comes up that we refer to those with different sexual preferences in a term that *does not* reflect negatively on *us.* Instead of calling them *straights,* I propose that we call them *non-gays.*

Edward Sherman

---

them to think more highly of themselves and to take new pride in their work.

The significance of words in shaping our self-concept goes beyond job titles. Racist and sexist language greatly affects the self-concepts of the people discriminated against (Pearson, 1985). An article in the *New York Times Magazine* by Casey Miller and Kate Swift (1972) points out some of the aspects of our language that discriminate against women, suggesting women are of lower status than men. Miller and Swift write that, except for words referring to females by definition, such as "mother" and "actress," English

defines many nonsexual concepts as male. The underlying assumption is that people in general are men. Also, words associated with males have positive connotations, such as "aggressive," "confident," "forceful," "strong," and "tough"; whereas words related to females are fewer and often have less positive connotations, such as "fickle," "frivolous," "jolly," and "timid" (Heilbrun, 1976).

Differences in definitions of the terms "woman" and "man" in the *Oxford English Dictionary* indicate discriminatory treatment. The definition of "woman" is an adult female being, a female servant, a lady-love or mistress, and a wife. "Man" is defined as a human being, the human creature regarded abstractly, an adult male endowed with manly qualities, and a person of importance or position (O'Donnell, 1973).

Sexism even extends to the language of the deaf (Pearson, 1985). American Sign Language divides the head into two areas: above the center is used to represent words such as "he," "him," "father," and so on; whereas below the center is used to represent "she," "her," and "mother." In general, the area closest to the brain is used for masculine referents and the area closest to the mouth is used for feminine referents. For example, an intelligent woman is signed as "thinks like a man," a secretary is "a girl who writes," and the president is a "respected man." In general, sign language portrays women as expressive and men as rational.

Any language expressing stereotyped sexual attitudes or assuming the superiority of one sex over another is sexist, so adding feminine endings to nonsexual words, such as "poetess" for female poet, is as sexist as "separate but equal" is racist.

Whereas sexist language usually defines the world as made up of superior men and inferior women, racist language usually defines it as composed of superior whites and other inferior racial groups. Words and images associated with "white" are usually positive, whether it's the hero-cowboy in white clothing or connotations of white as "pure," "clean," "honorable," "innocent," "bright," and "shiny." The words and images associated with black are often negative, a concept that reaches from the clothes of the villain-cowboy to connotations such as "decay," "dirt," "smudge," "dismal," "wicked," "unwashed," and "sinister."

To the extent that our language is both sexist and racist, our view of the world is affected. For example, men are given more opportunity than women to see themselves as "good," and in the same way whites are given more opportunity than blacks. Language shapes the self-concepts of those it labels in such a way that members of the linguistically slighted group see themselves as inferior.

Many linguistic changes beginning in the late 1960s aimed at teaching speakers and writers a new vocabulary in order to change the destructive connotations that accompany many of our words. For example, "black is beautiful" is an effort to reduce perceived status differences among blacks and whites.

Changes in writing style were also designed to counter the sexual prejudices inherent in language, particularly eliminating the constant use of "he" and introducing various methods either to eliminate reference to a particular sex, or to make reference to both sexes (Miller and Swift, 1972). Words that use "man" generically to refer to humanity at large often pose problems, but only to the unimaginative. Consider the following substitutions: "mankind" may be replaced with "humanity," "human beings," "human race," and "people"; "man-made" may be replaced with "artificial," "manufactured," and "synthetic"; "manpower" may be replaced with "labor," "workers," and "workforce"; and "manhood" may be replaced with "adulthood."

"Congressmen" are "members of Congress."

"Firemen" are "fire fighters."

"Chairmen" are "presiding officers," "leaders," and "chairs."

"Foremen" are "supervisors."

"Policemen" and "policewomen" are both "police officers."

"Stewardesses" and "stewards" are both "flight attendants."

Throughout this book we have used a number of techniques for avoiding sexist language: switching to the sexually neutral plural (they);

occasionally using the passive voice to eliminate sexed pronouns; carefully balancing individual masculine and feminine pronouns in illustrative material; and even doing total rewrites to delete conceptual sexual bias.

Language reflects our attitudes

Besides shaping perceptions, language often reflects the attitudes of a speaker. Feelings of attraction, control, commitment, responsibility—all these and more are reflected in the way we speak.

Power   We already saw how the use of certain language lessens a speaker's ability to influence others (see Table 4–2). The use of "powerful" or "powerless" language also reflects the speaker's own sense of control over others. Notice the difference in the perceived control in the following examples:

"Excuse me, sir. I hate to say this, but I . . . uh . . . I guess I won't be able to turn in the assignment on time. I had a personal emergency and . . . well . . . it was just impossible to finish it by today. I'll have it in your mailbox on Monday, okay?"

"I won't be able to turn in the assignment on time. I had a personal emergency and it was impossible to finish it by today. I'll have it in your mailbox on Monday."

Whether or not the professor finds the excuse acceptable, it's clear that the second speaker feels confident, whereas the first one is apologetic and uncertain. The first statement is a classic example of what has come to be called "one-down" communication.

Some relationships are characterized by what social scientists term *complementary* communication, in which one partner uses consistently powerful language, while the other responds with powerless speech. A demanding boss and compliant employees or the stereotypically tyrannical husband and submissive wife are examples of complementary relationships. In other relationships, called *symmetrical,* the power is distributed more evenly between the partners: Both may use equally powerful or powerless speech. The locus of power isn't constant: As relationships pass through different stages, the distribution of power shifts, and so do the speech patterns of the partners (Fisher and Drecksel, 1983). You can test this principle for yourself. Recall situations where you were feeling especially vulnerable, uncertain, confused, or powerless. Did your language include the characteristics listed in Table 4–2? Did these characteristics disappear when you felt more safe, confident, or powerful? What factors led to these changes? The subject being discussed? Your feelings about yourself at the moment? The way the other person was treating you?

Simply counting the number of powerful or powerless statements won't always reveal who has the most control in a relationship. Social rules often mask the real distribution of power. A boss who wants to be pleasant might say to a secretary, "Would you mind retyping this letter?" In truth, both boss and secretary know this is an order and not a request, but the questioning form makes the medicine less bitter (Bradac, 1983, p. 155). Therefore, a knowledge of the context and the personalities of two speakers is necessary before it's safe to make any assumptions about who controls whom.

Attraction and interest   Social customs discourage us from expressing like or dislike in many situations. Only a clod would respond to the question "What do you think of the cake I baked for you?" by saying "It's terrible." Bashful or cautious suitors might not admit their attraction to a potential partner. Even when people are reluctant to speak out candidly, the language they use can suggest their degree of interest and attraction toward a person, an object, or an idea. Morton Wiener and Albert Mehrabian (1968) outline a number of linguistic clues that reveal these attitudes.

Demonstrative pronoun choice   Although several pronouns can correctly refer to a person, some are more positive than others. Consider the difference between saying, "These people want our help" and the equally accurate, "Those peo-

ple want our help." Most people would probably conclude that the first speaker is more sympathetic than the second. In the same way, speakers sound more positive when they say, "Here's Tom" than if they say, "There's Tom." The difference in such cases is one of grammatical *distance*. People generally suggest attraction by indicating closeness and dislike by linguistically removing themselves from the object of their conversation.

Sequential placement   Another way to signify attitude is to place positive items earlier in a sequence. For example, notice the difference between discussing "Jack and Jill" and referring to "Jill and Jack." Likewise, consider how people respond to questions about courses they are taking or friends they intend to invite to an upcoming party. In many cases the first person or subject mentioned is more important or better liked than subsequent ones. (Of course, sequential placement isn't always significant. You may put "toilet bowl cleaner" at the top of your shopping list simply because it's closer to the market door than champagne.) Wiener and Mehrabian point out an interesting example of the sequencing principle that often occurs in psychotherapy, where the patient mentions a certain subject first, not because it is most important, but because it's the easiest one to discuss. Even here the same principle applies: Positive subjects often precede negative ones.

Negation   People usually express liking in a direct, positive manner while they use more indirect, negative language with less favorable subjects. Imagine, for instance, that you ask a friend's opinion about a book, movie, or restaurant. Consider the difference between the responses, "It was good" and "It wasn't bad." In the same way, the positive "I'd like to get together with you" may be a stronger indication of liking than the more negative "Why don't we get together?"

Duration   The length of time people spend discussing a person or subject can also be a strong indicator of attraction either to the subject or to the person with whom they're talking. If you ask a new acquaintance about work and receive the brief response, "I'm a brain surgeon" with nothing more, you would probably suspect either that the subject was a sensitive one or that this person wasn't interested in you. Of course, there may be other reasons for short answers, such as preoccupation, but one good yardstick for measuring liking is the time others spend communicating with us.

Intimacy   Beyond simple interest and liking, language can also reflect the degree of intimacy between two partners. The most obvious indications are terms of affection or endearment. In romantic relationships, labels such as "honey" or "babe" suggest a new degree of intimacy. Even nonromantic friends often begin to use special labels for one another as their relationship becomes stronger: "Okay, buddy"; "See you later, amigo." Friends, lovers, and family members also create "personal idioms" that are unique to their relationship (Hopper, Knapp, and Scott, 1981). The pet names children often use for their grandparents are a clear example. J. Berrisford Worthington may be the terror of the board room, but to his loving grandchildren he's "Baba." At a party you might introduce an old friend as "Barbara," but to your circle of friends she's "Babs."

The language partners use when problems arise also reveals their degree of intimacy. Research shows that partners who are strongly committed to a relationship tend to use emotional appeals and personal rejection when arguing their case, whereas less intimate couples tend to rely on more logical arguments (Fitzpatrick and Winke, 1979). Partners also use linguistic devices to smooth over disputes (Krueger, 1982). One such device is blaming the problem on forces external to the self and the relationship: "I know I've been touchy lately. It's nothing you've done: Work has been frantic lately." Other cohesiveness-building devices in conversation include balanced turn-taking, frequent topic shifting, and frequent interrupting during mutual affirmation:

"You've sure been a good sport about . . . "

"I know you don't want to be selfish, and . . . "

"I'm glad you're so understanding. I wish I could . . . "

Responsibility   Besides indicating liking or interest, language can also reflect a speaker's unconscious willingness to take responsibility for statements, as the following categories show.

The "it" statement   Notice the difference between the sentences of each set:

"It bothers me when you're late."
"I'm worried when you're late."

"It's nice to see you."
"I'm glad to see you."

"It's a boring class."
"I'm bored in the class."

"It" statements externalize the subject of the conversation. The subject is neither the person talking nor the one listening, but some "it" that is never really identified. Whenever people hear the word "it" used this way, they should ask themselves what "it" refers to. They inevitably find that the speaker uses "it" to avoid clearly identifying to whom the thought or feeling belongs.

The "you" statement   The word "you" also allows the speaker to disown comments that might be difficult to express:

"You get frightened" instead of "I get frightened . . . "

"You wonder . . . " instead of "I wonder . . . "

"You start to think . . . " instead of "I'm starting to think . . . "

The "we" statement   The word "we" can sometimes bring people together by pointing out their common beliefs. But in other cases the word becomes a device for diffusing the speaker's responsibility, a device that refers to a nebulous collection of people that doesn't really exist. Like "it" and "you," "we" often really means "I." "We all believe . . . " means "I believe . . . ," and "We ought to . . . " means "I want to. . . . " (You might notice that this text uses a lot of "we's." Do you find your beliefs included enough to think the word is justified?)

Questions   In the manner of "you" statements, questions often pass responsibility to the other person. They can also be used as a form of flattery ("Where did you get that lovely tie?"), or as a replacement of "I" statements (the most common). Some therapists argue that there are very few *real* questions; most questions hide some statement that the person does not want to make, possibly out of fear.

"my hand is doing this movement . . . "

    "Is *it* doing the movement?"

    "I am moving my hand like this . . . and now the thought comes to me that . . . "

    "The thought 'comes' to you?"

    "I have the thought."

    "You *have it*?"

    "*I think*. Yes. I think that I use 'it' very much, and I am glad that by noticing it I can bring it all back to me."

    "Bring it back?"

    "*Bring myself back.* I feel thankful for this."

    "*This*?"

    "Your idea about the 'it.' "

    "My idea?"

    "I feel thankful towards you."

Claudio Naranjo

"What are we having for dinner?" may hide the statement, "I want to eat out," or "I want to get a pizza."

"How many textbooks are assigned in that class?" may hide the statement, "I'm afraid to get into a class with too much reading."

"Are you doing anything tonight?" can be a less risky way of saying, "I want to go out with you tonight."

"Do you love me?" safely replaces the statement, "I love you," which may be too embarrassing, too intimate, or too threatening for the person to state directly.

The "but" statement   Statements that take the form X-but-Y can be quite confusing. A closer look at this construction explains why. "But" has the effect of canceling the thought that precedes it:

"You're a really swell person, but I think we ought to stop seeing each other."

"You've done good work for us, but we're going to have to let you go."

"This paper has some good ideas, but I'm giving it a grade of D because it's late."

These "buts" often mask the speaker's real meaning behind more-pleasant-sounding ideas. A more accurate and less confusing way of expressing complex ideas is to replace "but" with "and." In this way you can express a mixture of attitudes without eliminating any of them.

Male and female language differences

So far we have discussed linguistic patterns as if they were identical for both sexes. In many cases, however, there are significant differences between the way men and women speak.

Content   While there is much variation within each gender, on the average men and women discuss a surprisingly different range of topics. Adelaide Haas and Mark Sherman (1982a, 1982b; Sherman and Haas, 1984) surveyed women and men ranging in age from 17 to 80, asking the range of topics each discussed with friends of the same sex. Certain subjects were common to both sexes: work, movies, and television proved to be frequent topics for both groups. Both men and women reserved discussions of sex and sexuality for members of the same gender. The differences between men and women were more striking than the similarities. Female friends spent much more time discussing personal and domestic subjects: relationship problems, family, health and reproductive matters, weight, food, and clothing. Women also reported discussing other women frequently. Men, on the other hand, spent less time talking about other men. They were more likely to discuss music, current events, and sports.

These differences can lead to frustration when men and women try to converse with one another. Sherman and Haas report that "trivial" is the word often used by both men and women to describe topics discussed by the opposite sex. "I want to talk about important things," a woman might say, "like how we're getting along. All he wants to do is talk about the news or what we'll do this weekend."

Structure   Just as significant as the topics they discuss are the differences in the structure of male and female speech. A large body of research (summarized by Berryman and Wilcox, 1980; Lakoff, 1975; and Pearson, 1985) describes the ways in which men and women use language differently. Women, for example, are more likely to speak in a grammatically correct manner. They ask more questions, use more tag questions (questions added or "tagged on" to the end of a statement, such as, "Let's go to the movies tonight, *okay*?"), use more intensifying adverbs and adjectives, choose more words implying emotions, make more self-references, utter a higher number of incomplete assertions, and generally talk more than males. Men are more likely to use obscene expressions and expletives.

Differences between male and female speech aren't quite as radical as these findings suggest. Shimanoff (1983) found males and females talk about the same amount, and Martin and Craig (1983) found both sexes use the same number of qualifiers when talking to males, yet differ when talking to females (males decrease their qualifiers while women increase theirs).

Purpose   Men and women use language for different purposes. Men value talks with friends for their freedom, playfulness, and camaraderie. When Sherman and Haas asked them what they liked best about their all-male talk, the most frequent answer was its ease. A common theme was appreciation of the practical value of conversation: new ways to solve problems about cars, taxes, and other everyday matters. Some men also mentioned enjoying the humor and rapid pace that characterized their all-male conversations.

Women, on the other hand, looked for very different kinds of satisfaction when talking with their friends. The most common theme mentioned was a feeling of empathy or understanding— "To know you're not alone," as some put it, or "The feeling of sharing and being understood without a sexual connotation." Whereas men commonly described same-sex conversations as something they *liked*, females characterized their woman-to-woman talks as a kind of contact they *needed*.

The greater frequency of female conversations reflects their importance. Nearly 50 percent of the women surveyed said they called friends at least once a week just to talk, whereas less than half as many men did so. In fact, 40 percent of the men surveyed reported that they never called another man just to chat.

Sex roles   Most people intuitively recognize the difference between characteristically male and female speech patterns. In one study Cynthia onsider the marriage of a man who has had most of his conversations with other men, to a woman who has had most of hers with other women. . . . He is used to fast-paced conversations that typically stay on the surface with respect to emotions, that often enable him to get practical tips or offer them to others and that are usually pragmatic or fun. She is used to conversations that, while practical and fun too, are also a major source of emotional support, self-understanding and the understanding of others. Becoming intimate with a man, the woman may finally start expressing her concerns to him as she might to a close friend. But she may find, to her dismay, that his responses are all wrong. Instead of making her feel better, he makes her feel worse. The problem is that he tends to be direct and practical, whereas what she wants more than anything else is an empathetic listener. Used to years of such responses from close friends, a woman is likely to be surprised and angered by her husband's immediate "Here's what ya do. . . . "

Mark Sherman and Adelaide Haas

Berryman and James Wilcox (1980) asked students to evaluate statements allegedly made by one group member in a discussion. Actually, there were two different transcripts, each created by the researchers. Although the content of the message was the same in both cases, one transcript reflected linguistic features associated with female sex-typed behavior, whereas the other was characteristic of male language. The "female" message, for example, contained eight intensifiers, six questions, four phrases implying feeling or emotion, and was 384 words long. The "male" version contained no intensifiers, no questions, no phrases implying feeling or emotion, two obscenities, four instances of slang, five instances of incorrect grammar, and was 338 words long.

Subjects were asked to guess the sex of the speaker. Approximately 80 percent of the subjects described the stereotypically male version as having been delivered by a man, while roughly 55 percent guessed that the "female" version was spoken by a woman. Whether subjects identified the speaker as a man or a

woman, they saw the source of the "male" message as being more masculine, more commanding, and less accommodating than the source of the "female" message. The authors attribute the impression of lesser command for the "female" version to the use of questions and incomplete assertions. They speculate that the absence of questions and unfinished sentences as well as the inclusion of obscenities probably contribute to the perception of the male sex-typical speaker as more commanding.

With few exceptions, the bulk of research on male–female language differences supports the stereotypic view that characterizes women as submissive, affected by social pressure, and responsive to the needs of others—all of which makes it logical to associate deferential language usage (such as tag questions and qualifiers) with women. Liska, Mechling, and Stathas (1981) tested perceptions of deferential language style and found that men and women agreed that the style had less power and more personal warmth, and that they both associated it with femininity. Burgoon, Dillard, and Doran (1983) reported complementary findings related to other expectations: males and females expect males to use verbally aggressive strategies and females to use more prosocial strategies.

What happens to language when sex roles and work roles combine? Is the sex role the more important influence, or the work role? Baird and Bradley (1979) looked at male and female supervisors in organizations to see whether female managers enact a "male" role. Employees in several different organizations rated their male and female managers with respect to the content and style of their verbal behavior. Female managers were rated as providing more information, putting more emphasis on happy interpersonal relationships, and being more encouraging, receptive to new ideas, concerned, and attentive. Male managers were rated as being more dominant, direct, and quick to challenge. The researchers concluded that "male and female managers [exerted] leadership in their own distinct fashions. . . . Females didn't slip into the 'male' role" (p. 108). They also argued that females may be superior managers because their verbal communication promotes more job satisfaction.

Research shows that language reflects not only the speaker's biological sex (male or female), but also a masculine or feminine psychological orientation. Donald Ellis and Linda McCallister (1980) used the Bem Sex-Role Inventory described in Chapter 3 (see pages 54–55) to identify subjects of each sex as one of the following sex-types: masculine, feminine, or androgynous. Then they observed the language behavior of these subjects in group discussions to determine whether each psychological sex-type used a characteristic language pattern.

The results showed that language does, in fact, reflect psychological sex-type. One area in which this distinction became apparent was relational control. Whenever individuals interact, their messages have implications for how the power in their relationship will be distributed. Messages can express dominance ("one-up"), submissiveness ("one-down"), or equivalence (mutual identification). Ellis and McCallister found that the masculine sex-type subjects used significantly more dominance language than either feminine or androgynous group members. Feminine members expressed slightly more submissive behaviors and more equivalence behaviors than the androgynous group members, and their submissiveness and equivalence were much greater than the masculine subjects'.

The patterns of interaction between members of the same psychological sex-type were also revealing. Masculine subjects engaged in a pattern that the authors described as "competitive symmetry": A masculine sex-type would respond to another member's bid for control with a counter-attempt to dominate the relationship, resulting in an almost continuous series of "one-up" interactions. Feminine sex-type subjects responded to another's bid for control unpredictably, using dominance, submission, and equivalence behaviors in an almost random fashion. Androgynous individuals behaved in a more predictable pattern: They most frequently met another's bid for dominance with a symmetrical attempt at control, but then moved quickly toward an equivalent relationship, some-times acting deferentially during a transitional stage. Ellis and McCallister characterize this approach as more workable and efficient than either the sex-typically masculine or feminine styles.

As you read the foregoing information, it's important to realize that "masculinity" and "femininity" are culturally recognized sex roles, not necessarily gender-related. For instance, at one time or another we have classified some speakers as "feminine men" or "masculine women." It is tempting to quarrel with Bem's use of the terms "masculine" and "feminine," arguing that these terms perpetuate stereotyping. Whatever descriptors you use, the overriding point remains: Language reflects a speaker's attitudes.

Language reflects attitudes. Language shapes attitudes. Language can clarify or obscure. Symbols stand for ideas, but not always the same ones. Our brief look at language shows that words and things aren't related in the straight forward way that we might assume. Because it's so difficult to understand each other's ideas through words, it's tempting to look for better alternatives. As you'll see in the next chapter, other ways of communicating do exist, but often we're faced with no other choice but to carry on with our often inadequate means of verbal expression. The best we can do is to proceed with caution, trying our best to understand one another and always realizing that the task is a difficult one.

Readings

Alexander, Hubert G. *Meaning in Language.* Glenview, Ill.: Scott, Foresman, 1969.

Armstrong, J. Scott. "Unintelligible Management Research and Academic Prestige." *Interfaces* 10 (1980): 80–86.

Baird, John E., Jr., and Patricia Hayes Bradley. "Styles of Management and Communication." *Communication Monographs* 46 (1979): 101–111.

Bateson, G., and D. D. Jackson. "Some Varieties of Pathogenic Organization." *Disorders of Communication* 42 (Research Publications: Association for Research in Nervous and Mental Disease, 1964): 270–283.

Berger, C. R., and J. A. Bradac. *Language and Social Knowledge: The Social Psychology of Language.* London: Edward Arnold, 1982.

*Berryman, Cynthia L., and James R. Wilcox. "Attitudes Toward Male and Female Speech: Experiments on the Effects of Sex-Typical Language." *Western Journal of Speech Communication* 44 (1980): 50–59.

*Bradac, J. J. "The Language of Lovers, Flowers, and Friends: Communicating in Social and Personal Relationships." *Journal of Language and Social Psychology* 2 (1983): 141–162.

Bradac, J. J., M. R. Hemphill, and C. H. Tardy. "Language Style on Trial: Effects of 'Powerful' and 'Powerless' Speech upon Judgments of Victims and Villains." *Western Journal of Speech Communication* 45 (Fall 1981): 327–341.

Bradac, J. J., and A. Mulac. "Attributional Consequences of Powerful and Powerless Speech Styles in a Crisis-Intervention Context." *Journal of Language and Social Psychology* 3 (1984a): 1–19.

Bradac, J. J., and A. Mulac. "A Molecular View of Powerful and Powerless Speech Styles: Attributional Consequences of Specific Language Features and Communicator Intentions. *Communication Monographs* 51 (1984b): 307–319.

Burgoon, Michael, James P. Dillard, and Noel E. Doran. "Friendly or Unfriendly Persuasion: The Effects of Violations of Expectations by Males and Females." *Human Communication Research* 10 (1983): 283–294.

Chase, Stuart. *The Tyranny of Words.* New York: Harvest Books, 1938.

Clark, Virginia P., Paul A. Eschholz, and Alfred F. Rosa, eds. *Language: Introductory Readings*, 2d ed. New York: St. Martin's Press, 1977.

*Condon, John C. *Semantics and Communication*, 2d ed. New York: Macmillan, 1975.

Cook, Robert E. "Pin Cherry Perceptions." *Natural History* 90 (November 1981): 97–102.

Cory, C. T., ed. "Bafflegab Pays." *Psychology Today* 13 (May 1980): 12.

Davis, Ossie. "The English Language Is My Enemy." In *Language: Concepts and Processes,* Joseph A. DeVito, ed. Englewood Cliffs, N.J.: Prentice-Hall, 1973.

DeVito, Joseph A., ed. *Language: Concepts and Processes.* Englewood Cliffs, N.J.: Prentice-Hall, 1973.

Donohue, William A. "Development of a Model of Rule Use in Negotiation Interaction." *Communication Monographs* 48 (1981): 106–120.

*Donohue, William A., Donald P. Cushman, and Robert E. Nofsinger, Jr. "Creating and Confronting Social Order: A Comparison of Rules Perspectives." *Western Journal of Speech Communication* 44 (1980): 5–19.

*Eakins, Barbara Westrook, and R. Gene Eakins. *Sex Differences in Human Communication.* Boston: Houghton Mifflin, 1978.

Ellis, Donald G., and Linda McCallister. "Relational Control Sequences in Sex-Typed and Androgynous Groups." *Western Journal of Speech Communication* 44 (1980): 35–49.

Erickson, B., E. A. Lind, B. C. Johnson, and W. M. O'Barr. "Speech Style and Impression Formation in a Court Setting: The Effects of 'Powerful' and 'Powerless' Speech." *Journal of Experimental Social Psychology* 14 (1978): 266–279.

Fisher, B. A., and G. L. Drecksel. "A Cyclical Model of Developing Relationships: A Study of Relational Control Interaction." *Communication Monographs* 50 (1983): 66–78.

Fitzpatrick, M. A., and J. Winke. "You Always Hurt the One You Love: Strategies and Tactics in Interpersonal Conflict." *Communication Quarterly* 27 (1979): 3–16.

Francis, W. Nelson. "Word-Making: Some Sources of New Words." In *Language: Introductory Readings,* 2d ed., Virginia P. Clark, Paul A. Eschholz, and Alfred F. Rosa, eds. New York: St. Martin's Press, 1977.

Giles, H., and P. F. Poseland. *Speech Style and Social Evaluation.* New York: Academic Press, 1975.

Haas, A., and M. A. Sherman. "Conversational Topic as a Function of Role and Gender." *Psychological Reports* 51 (1982a): 453–454.

Haas, A., and M. A. Sherman. "Reported Topics of Conversation Among Same-Sex Adults." *Communication Quarterly* 30 (1982b): 332–342.

*Hayakawa, S. I. *Language in Thought and Action.* New York: Harcourt Brace Jovanovich, 1964.

Hayakawa, S. I. *The Use and Misuse of Language.* Greenwich, Conn.: Fawcett Books, 1962.

Heilbrun, A. B. "Measurement of Masculine and Feminine Sex Role Identities as Independent Dimensions." *Journal of Consulting and Clinical Psychology* 44 (1976): 183–190.

Hogan, Patricia. "A Woman Is Not a Girl and Other Lessons in Corporate Speech." *Business and Society Review* 14 (1975): 34–38.

Hopper, R., M. L. Knapp, and L. Scott. "Couples' Personal Idioms: Exploring Intimate Talk." *Journal of Communication* 31 (1981): 23–33.

Korzybski, Alfred. *Science and Sanity.* Lancaster, Penn.: Science Press, 1933.

Krueger, D. "Marital Decision Making: A Language-Action Analysis." *Quarterly Journal of Speech* 68 (1982): 273–287.

Lakoff, Robin. *Language and Woman's Place.* New York: Harper Colophon Books, 1975.

Lee, J. A. *The Colors of Love: Exploration of the Ways of Loving.* Don Mills, Ontario: New Press, 1973.

Liska, Jo, Elizabeth Walker Mechling, and Susan Stathas. "Differences in Subjects' Perceptions and Believability Between Users of Deferential and Nondeferential Language." *Communication Quarterly* 29 (1981): 40–48.

Markel, Norman N., Joseph F. Long, and Thomas J. Saine. "Sex Effects in Conversational Interaction: Another Look at Male Dominance." *Human Communication Research* 2 (1976): 356–364.

Martin, Judith N., and Robert T. Craig. "Selected Linguistic Sex Differences During Initial Social Interaction of Same-Sex and Mixed-Sex Dyads." *Western Journal of Speech Communication* 47 (1983): 16–28.

McLaughlin, Margaret L., Michael J. Cody, Marjorie L. Kane, and Carl S. Robey. "Sex Differences in Story Receipt and Story Sequencing Behaviors in Dyadic Conversations." *Human Communication Research* 7 (1981): 99–116.

Miller, Casey, and Kate Swift. "One Small Step for Genkind." *New York Times Magazine* (April 16, 1972). Reprinted in *Language: Concepts and Processes,* Joseph A. DeVito, ed. Englewood Cliffs, N.J.: Prentice-Hall, 1973.

Miller, Casey, and Kate Swift. *Words and Women.* Garden City, N.Y.: Anchor Press, 1976.

Mulac, Anthony, and Torborg Louisa Candell. "Differences in Perceptions Created by Syntactic-Semantic Productions of Male and Female Speakers." *Communication Monographs* 47 (1980): 111–118.

*Newman, Edwin. *A Civil Tongue.* Indianapolis: Bobbs-Merrill, 1976.

O'Donnell, H. S. "Sexism in Language." *Elementary English* 50 (1973): 1067–1072.

Ogden, C. K., and I. A. Richards. *The Meaning of Meaning.* New York: Harcourt, Brace, 1923.

*Pearson, J. C. *Gender and Communication.* Dubuque, Iowa: Wm. C. Brown, 1985.

Rich, Andrea L. *Interracial Communication.* New York: Harper & Row, 1974.

Ritchie-Key, Mary. *Male/Female Language.* Metuchen, N.J.: Scarecrow Press, 1975.

Rosenfeld, Lawrence B. "The Confrontation Policies of S. I. Hayakawa: A Case Study in Coercive Semantics." *Today's Speech* 18 (1970): 18–22.

Sagarian, Edward. "The High Cost of Wearing a Label." *Psychology Today* (March 1976): 25–27.

Sherman, M. A., and A. Haas. "Man to Man, Woman to Woman." *Psychology Today* 17 (June 1984): 72–73.

Shimanoff, Susan B. "The Role of Gender in Linguistic References to Emotive States." *Communication Quarterly* 30 (1983): 174–179.

Sinclair, L., ed. "A Word in Your Ear," in *Ways of Mankind.* Boston: Beacon Press, 1954, pp. 28–29.

Whorf, Benjamin Lee. *Language, Thought and Reality,* John B. Carroll, ed. Cambridge, Mass.: M.I.T. Press, 1956.

Wiener, Morton, and Albert Mehrabian. *A Language Within Language: Immediacy, a Channel in Verbal Communication.* New York: Appleton-Century-Crofts, 1968.

*Wood, Barbara S. *Children and Communication: Verbal and Nonverbal Language Development.* Englewood Cliffs, N.J.: Prentice-Hall, 1976.

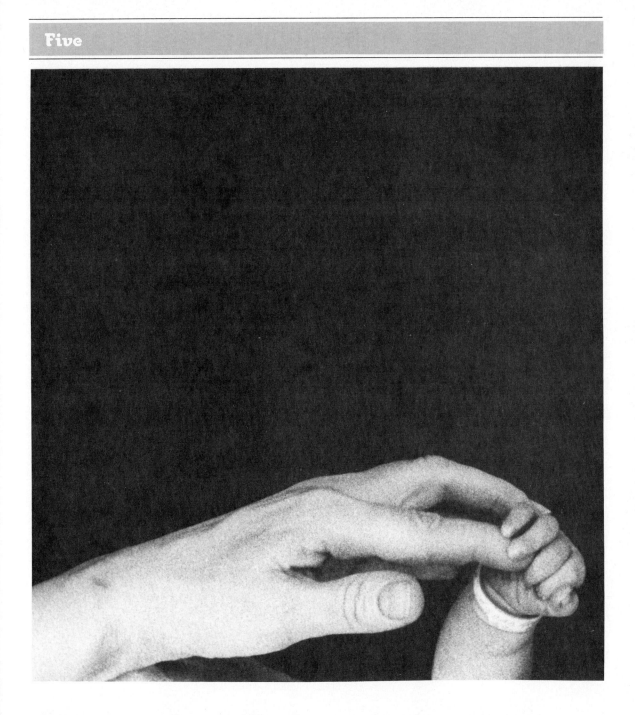

Nonverbal Communication

Five

After studying the material in this chapter

You should understand:

1. The five distinguishing characteristics of nonverbal communication.
2. The functions that nonverbal communication can serve.
3. The various types of nonverbal communication.

You should be able to:

1. Describe your nonverbal behavior in any situation.
2. Realize when you see nonverbal behavior that repeats, substitutes for, complements, accents, regulates, or contradicts a verbal message.
3. Analyze the emotional messages in examples of your own nonverbal behavior.
4. Share your interpretation of another's nonverbal behavior appropriately.

People don't always say what they mean . . . but their body gestures and movements tell the truth!

Will he ask you out? Is she encouraging you? Know what is really happening by understanding the secret language of body signals. You can:
  Improve your sex life . . .
  Pick up your social life . . .
  Better your business life . . .

Read Body Language *so that you can penetrate the personal secrets, both of intimates and total strangers . . .*

  Does her body say that she's a loose woman?
  Does her body say that she's a phony?
  Does her body say that she's a manipulator?
  Does her body say that she's lonely?

Unless you've been trapped in a lead mine or doing fieldwork in the Amazon Basin, claims like these are probably familiar to you. Almost every drugstore, supermarket, and airport bookrack has its share of "body language" paperbacks. They promise that, for only a few dollars and a fifth grade reading ability, you can learn secrets that will change you from a fumbling social failure into a self-assured mindreader who can uncover a person's deepest secrets at a glance.

Although such promises may sell lots of books, they are almost always exaggerations. Don't misunderstand: There *is* a scientific body of knowledge about nonverbal communication, and it *has* provided many fascinating and valuable clues to human behavior. That's what this chapter is about. It's unlikely the next few pages will turn you instantly into a rich, sexy, charming communication superstar, but don't go away. Even without glamorous promises, a quick look at some facts about nonverbal communication shows that it's an important and valuable field to study.

Nonverbal communication defined

If *non* means "not" and *verbal* means "with words," then it seems logical that *nonverbal communication* would involve "communication without words." This definition is an over-simplification, however: It fails to distinguish between *vocal* communication (by mouth) and *verbal* communication (with words). As Table 5–1 shows, some nonverbal messages have a vocal element, whereas others do not. A better definition of nonverbal communication is "messages expressed by nonlinguistic means."

These nonlinguistic messages are important because what we *do* often conveys more meaning than what we *say*. Albert Mehrabian (1972), a psychologist working in the area of nonverbal behavior, claims that 93 percent of the emotional impact of a message comes from a nonverbal source, whereas only a paltry 7 percent is verbal.

TABLE 5–1 Types of communication		
	VOCAL COMMUNICATION	NONVOCAL COMMUNICATION
VERBAL COMMUNICATION	Spoken words	Written words
NONVERBAL COMMUNICATON	Tone of voice, sighs, screams, vocal qualities (loudness, pitch, and so on)	Gestures, movement, appearance, facial expression, and so on

Adapted from John Stewart and Gary D'Angelo, *Together: Communicating Interpersonally*, 2d ed. (Reading, Mass.: Addison-Wesley, 1980), p. 22.

"Come on, Zorba," I cried, "teach me to dance!"
Zorba leaped to his feet, his face sparkling . . .

"Watch my feet, boss," he enjoined me. "Watch!"

He put out his foot, touched the ground lightly with his toes, then pointed the other foot; the steps were mingled violently, joyously, the ground reverberated like a drum.

He shook me by the shoulder.

"Now then, my boy," he said. "Both together!"

We threw ourselves into the dance. Zorba instructed me, corrected me gravely, patiently, and with great gentleness. I grew bold and felt my heart on the wing like a bird.

"Bravo! You're a wonder!" cried Zorba, clapping his hands to mark the beat. "Bravo, youngster! To hell with paper and ink! To hell with goods and profits! To hell with mines and workmen and monasteries! And now that you, my boy, can dance as well and have learnt my language, what shan't we be able to tell each other!"

He pounded on the pebbles with his bare feet and clapped his hands.

"Boss," he said. "I've dozens of things to say to you. I've never loved anyone as much before. I've hundreds of things to say, but my tongue just can't manage them. So I'll dance them for you!"

Nikos Kazantzakis
Zorba the Greek

Anthropologist Ray Birdwhistell (1970) describes a 65–35 percent split between actions and words. Although we must not generalize too much from these figures (Hegstrom, 1979), the point remains: Nonverbal communication contributes a great deal to sharing meanings.

You might ask how this idea can be true. At first glance it seems as if meanings come from words. To answer this question, imagine that you've just arrived in a foreign country in which the inhabitants speak a language you don't understand. Visualize yourself on a crowded street, filled with many types of people, from the very rich to the quite poor. In spite of these differences in wealth, there seems to be little social friction, with one exception. On one corner two people seem close to a fight. One man—he seems to be a shopkeeper—is furious at a customer, who seems to be complaining about an item he has just bought. Two police officers stroll by and obviously notice the commotion, but walk on unconcerned. Most of the pedestrians are in a great hurry, rushing off to who-knows-where . . . all except one couple. They are oblivious to everything but each other, obviously in love.

In spite of the fact that you've never been here before, you feel comfortable because everyone seems friendly and polite. Shoppers murmur apologetically when they bump into you on the crowded sidewalks, and many people smile when your eyes meet theirs. In fact, you notice that one attractive stranger seems *very* friendly, and quite interested in you. In spite of the fact that you've been warned to watch out for shady characters, you know there's no danger here. "Why not?" you think. "It's a vacation." You smile back and both of you walk toward each other. . . .

Aside from being a pleasant daydream, this little experiment should have proved that it's possible to communicate without using words. With no knowledge of the language, you were able to make a number of assumptions about what was going on in that foreign country. You obtained a picture of the economic status of some of its inhabitants, observed some conflicts and speculated about their nature, noticed something about the law enforcement policy, formed impressions about the pace of life, and became acquainted with courtship practices. How did you do all this work? You tuned into the many nonverbal channels available: facial expressions, clothing, postures, gestures, vocal tones, and more. Of course, you don't have to travel abroad to recognize nonverbal messages, for they're present all the time. Because we're such a vocal society, we often ignore the other channels through which we all communicate; but they're always there.

Characteristics of nonverbal communication

The many types of nonverbal communication share some characteristics. Some of these characteristics are similar to verbal, linguistic means of communication; others are different.

Nonverbal communication exists   Our fantasy trip to the foreign country demonstrated that nonverbal messages exist. Even without talking, it's possible to get an idea about how others are feeling. In fact, you can often learn

Writer (to movie producer Sam Goldwyn): Mr. Goldwyn, I'm telling you a sensational story. I'm only asking for your opinion, and you fall asleep.

Goldwyn: Isn't sleeping an opinion?

---

more about others by noticing what they do rather than what they say. Sometimes you might suspect people seem friendly, sometimes distant, sometimes tense, excited, bored, amused, or depressed. The point is that without any formal experience you can recognize and to some degree interpret messages that other people send nonverbally. In this chapter we want to sharpen the skills you already have, to give you a better grasp of the vocabulary of nonverbal language, and to show you how this understanding can help you know yourself and others better.

It's impossible not to communicate   The fact that communication without words does take place brings us to the second important feature of nonverbal communication. To understand what we mean here, think back to a recent time you spent with another person. Suppose we asked you not to communicate any messages at all while with your partner. What would you have done? Closed your eyes? Withdrawn into a ball? Left the room? You can probably see that even these behaviors communicate messages that mean you're avoiding contact.

Take a minute and try *not* communicating. Find a partner and spend some time trying not to disclose any messages to each other. What happened?

The impossibility of not communicating is extremely significant because it means that each of us is a kind of transmitter that cannot be shut off. No matter what we do, we send out messages that say something about ourselves. If, for instance, someone were observing you now, what nonverbal clues would they get about how you're feeling? Are you sitting forward or reclining back? Is your posture tense or relaxed? Are your eyes wide open, or do they keep closing? What does your facial expression communicate now? Can you make your face expressionless? Don't people with expressionless faces communicate something to you?

The fact that we are all constantly sending nonverbal clues is important because it means that we have a constant source of information available about ourselves and others. If you can tune into these signals, you'll be more aware of how others feel and think, and you'll be able to respond better to their behavior.

Nonverbal messages are relational As you read in Chapter 1, relational messages deal with the feelings of the parties for one another and their attitudes toward the topic under discussion. Nonverbal behavior is especially well suited to convey these relational messages. It is less effective at conveying thoughts or ideas. Recall the fantasy you just completed. Think about the different messages you sent and received. Most were probably relational, dealing with how you *felt* rather than what you *thought*.

You can test this assertion another way. Here's a list that contains both thoughts and feelings. Try to express each item nonverbally, and see which ones come most easily:

1. You're tired.
2. You're in favor of capital punishment.
3. You're attracted to another person in the group.
4. You think marijuana should be legalized.
5. You're angry at someone in the room.

This experience shows that, short of charades, thoughts don't lend themselves to nonverbal expression, but feelings obviously do.

Nonverbal communication is ambiguous
Some words of caution before introducing you to a fourth feature of nonverbal communication: A great deal of ambiguity surrounds nonverbal behavior. To understand what we mean, consider: How would you interpret silence from your companion during an evening together? Consider all the possible meanings of this nonverbal behavior: warmth, anger, preoccupation, boredom, nervousness, thoughtfulness . . . the possibilities are many.

Not all nonverbal behavior is equally ambiguous (Druckmann et al., 1982, p. 52). Positive emotions (happiness, love, surprise, and interest) are easier to identify than negative feelings (fear, sadness, anger, and disgust). Even apparently unambiguous emotions can be misinterpreted, however, as the photo on page 99 indicates. What do you imagine the couple is feeling? Grief? Anguish? Agony? After making a guess, check your skill by reading the accompanying caption.

Government authorities are often aware of the hazards of misinterpreting ambiguous nonverbal messages. White House experts recently updated the Washington–Moscow hot line that enables the United States and Soviet governments to communicate in times of crisis. Despite the available technology, experts rejected the idea of adding video and voice links because "in a crisis situation, we wouldn't want to leave room for mistaken interpretations or impressions that might be drawn from facial expressions or voice patterns" (Newsweek, 1984).

The same kind of caution is wise when responding to nonverbal cues in more personal situations. Rather than jumping to conclusions about the meaning of a sigh, smile, slammed door, or yawn, it's far better to consider such messages as clues to be checked out: "When you yawned, I got the idea you might be tired of me. Is that right?" Popular advice on the subject notwithstanding, it's usually *not* possible to read a person like a book.

This couple has just learned that they won $1 million in the New Jersey state lottery.

Nonverbal communication is culture-bound

The significance of many nonverbal behaviors varies from one culture to another (Blonston, 1985). The "A-Okay" gesture made by joining thumb and forefinger to form a circle is a cheery affirmation to most Americans, but it has less positive meanings in other parts of the world (Ekman, Friesen, and Baer, 1984). In France and Belgium it means "You're worth zero." In Greece and Turkey it is a vulgar sexual invitation, usually meant as an insult. In parts of southern Italy it translates as "asshole." Given this sort of cross-cultural ambiguity, it's easy to imagine how an innocent tourist might wind up in serious trouble.

Less obvious cross-cultural differences can damage relationships without the parties ever recognizing exactly what has gone wrong. Edward Hall (1969) points out that, whereas Americans are comfortable conducting business at a distance of roughly four feet, people from the Middle East stand much closer. It is easy to visualize the awkward advance and retreat pattern that might occur when two diplomats or businesspeople from these cultures meet. The Middle Easterner would probably keep moving forward to close the gap that feels so wide, while the American would continually back away. Both would feel uncomfortable, probably without knowing why.

Like distance, patterns of eye contact vary around the world (Kleinke et al., 1976; Watson, 1970). A direct gaze is considered appropriate for speakers in Latin America, the Arab world, and southern Europe. On the other hand, Asians, Indians, Pakistanis, and northern Europeans gaze at a listener peripherally or not at all. In either case, deviations from the norm are likely to make a listener uncomfortable.

Functions of nonverbal communication

Although this chapter deals with nonverbal communication, don't get the idea that our words and actions are unrelated. Quite the opposite is true: Verbal and nonverbal communication are interconnected, although not always in the same way. Let's take a look at the various relationships between our words and other types of expression (Knapp, 1978).

Repeating   First, nonverbal behavior can *repeat* a verbal message. If someone asked you for directions to the nearest drugstore, you could say, "Go north about two blocks," and then repeat your instructions nonverbally by pointing north. This kind of repetition is especially useful when we're describing an idea with a visual dimension, such as size, shape, or direction.

Substituting   Nonverbal messages may also *substitute* for verbal ones. For example, instead of saying, "Go north about two blocks," you could point north and add, "about two blocks." The usefulness of substitution goes far beyond simply describing physical ideas. For instance, the more you know someone, the easier it is to use nonverbal expressions as a kind of shorthand to substitute for words. When you see a familiar friend wearing a certain facial expression, it isn't necessary to ask, "What kind of day did you have?" In the same way, experience has probably shown you that certain kinds of looks, gestures,

and other clues say far better than words, "I'm angry at you," or "I feel great."

Some nonverbal behaviors—called *emblems*—are culturally understood substitutes for verbal expressions. Nodding the head up and down is an accepted way of saying "yes" in most cultures. Likewise, a side-to-side head shake is a nonverbal way of saying "no," and a shrug of the shoulders is commonly understood as meaning "I don't know" or "I'm not sure." Remember, however, that some emblems—like the "A-Okay" sign we mentioned earlier—vary from one culture to another, and other nonverbal signs can be ambiguous even within a single culture. A wink, for example, might mean something entirely different to the person on the receiving end than it does to the winker.

Because of this potential ambiguity, it's often dangerous to substitute unspoken messages. Even with the people you know best, there's room for misunderstanding, and the potential for jumping to wrong conclusions increases the less you know the other person. Remember our warning: Nonverbal communication is ambiguous.

Complementing and accenting   Whereas nonverbal emblems convey meaning independent of words, *illustrators* are behaviors that complement or reinforce verbal statements, but have no meaning of their own. Snapping your fingers, running your fingers through your hair, or pounding one fist into the other can accompany a positive statement in one instance and a negative one in others: Their meaning only comes from the context in which they arise.

Emblems are used consciously; you roll your eyes and circle your finger around one ear to signal "He's crazy." Illustrators are usually unconscious (Ekman, Friesen, and Baer, 1984). We rarely plan the smiles and frowns, sighs and laughs, and all the other nonverbal behaviors that so richly complement and accent our words.

Regulating   Nonverbal behaviors sometimes help control verbal interaction. The best example of this sort of regulation is the wide array of turn-taking signals in everyday conversation (Duncan 1972, 1974; Duncan and Fiske, 1979). Research has shown that three nonverbal signals indicate a speaker has finished talking and is ready to yield to a listener: (1) changes in vocal intonation—a rising or falling in pitch at the end of a clause; (2) a drawl on the last syllable or the stressed syllable in a clause; (3) a drop in vocal pitch or loudness when speaking a common expression, such as "you know." You can see how these regulators work by observing almost any conversation.

Eye contact is another way of regulating verbal communication. Lack of visual contact is one way to signal turn-taking, or even to exclude an unwanted party from a conversation. Speakers make surprisingly little eye contact during a conversation, but they commonly focus on another person when coming to the end of their turn. Children (and some socially insensitive adults) have not learned all the subtle signals indicating this sort of turn-taking. Through a rough series of trial and error (*very* rough in some

I suppose it was something you said
That caused me to tighten
And pull away.
And when you asked,
"What is it?"
I, of course, said,
"Nothing."

Whenever I say, "Nothing,"
You may be very certain there is something.
The something is a cold, hard lump of Nothing.

Lois Wyse

---

homes), children finally learn how to "read" other people well enough to avoid interrupting behaviors.

Contradicting   Finally, and often most significantly, nonverbal behavior can often *contradict* the spoken word. If you said "Go north about two blocks" and pointed south, your nonverbal message would contradict what you said.

Although sending such incompatible messages might sound foolish at first, there are times when we deliberately do just that. One frequent use of double messages (as they're often called) is to send a message politely but clearly that might be difficult to handle if it were expressed in words. For instance, think of a time when you became bored with a conversation while your companion kept rambling on. At such a time the most straightforward statement would be, "I'm tired of talking to you and want to go meet someone else." Although it might feel good to be so direct, this kind of honesty is impolite for anyone over five years of age.

Instead of being blunt, people frequently rely on nonverbal methods of sending the same message. While nodding politely and murmuring "uh-huh" and "No kidding?" at the appropriate times, you can signal a desire to leave by looking around

the room, turning slightly away from the speaker, or even making a point of yawning. In most cases such clues are enough to end the conversation without the awkwardness of expressing outright what's going on.

Courtship is one area in which double messages abound. Even in these liberated times the answer "no" to a romantic proposition may mean "yes." Of course, it may also really mean an emphatic "no." The success of many relationships has depended on the ability of one partner to figure out—mostly using nonverbal messages—when a double message is being sent, and when to take the words at face value.

Deception is perhaps the most interesting type of double message. Signals of deception (often called *leakage*) can occur in every type of nonverbal behavior. Some nonverbal channels are more revealing than others, however. Facial expressions are less revealing than body clues, probably because deceivers pay more attention to controlling their faces (Ekman and Friesen, 1969). Even more useful is the voice, which offers a rich variety of leakage clues (DePaulo, Zuckerman, and Rosenthal, 1980; Greene, O'Hair, Cody, and Yen, 1985; Mehrabian, 1971). In one experiment subjects who were encouraged to be deceitful made more speech errors, spoke for shorter periods of time, and had a lower rate of speech than others who were encouraged to express themselves honestly. Another study (Streeter et al., 1977) revealed that the vocal frequency of a liar's voice tends to be higher than that of a truth-teller. These sorts of cues aren't necessarily direct signals of lying itself; rather, they may reflect the anxiety that some liars feel. Table 5–2 outlines the conditions under which liars are most likely to betray themselves through nonverbal leakage.

As we discuss the different kinds of nonverbal communication, we'll point out a number of ways in which people contradict themselves by either conscious or unconscious behaviors. Therefore, by the end of this chapter you should have a better idea of how others feel, even when they can't or won't tell you with their words.

Types of nonverbal communication

So far we've talked about the characteristics of nonverbal communication and the ways unspoken messages relate to our use of words. Now it's time to look at the many types of nonverbal communication.

Face and eyes   The face and eyes are probably the most noticeable parts of the body. However, the nonverbal messages from the face and eyes are not the easiest to read. The face is a tremendously complicated channel of expression to interpret for three reasons.

First, it's hard to describe the number and kind of expressions commonly produced by the face and eyes. For example, researchers have found that there are at least eight distinguishable positions of the eyebrows and forehead, eight more of the eyes and lids, and ten for the lower face (Ekman and Friesen, 1975). When you

Fie, fie upon her!
There's language in her eyes, her cheek, her lip.
Nay, her foot speaks; her wanton spirits look out at
  every joint and motive in her body.

William Shakespeare
Troilus and Cressida

multiply this complexity by the number of emotions we experience, you can see why it would be almost impossible to compile a dictionary of facial expressions and their corresponding emotions.

Facial expressions can also be difficult to read because they change with incredible speed. For example, slow-motion films have shown expressions fleeting across a subject's face in as short a time as one-fifth of a second. Also, it seems that different emotions show most clearly in different parts of the face: happiness and surprise in the eyes and lower face; anger in the lower face, brows, and forehead; fear and sadness in the eyes; and disgust in the lower face.

Finally, most people are reasonably successful at disguising or censoring undesired messages (O'Hair, Cody, and McLaughlin, 1981). In spite of

TABLE 5–2 Circumstances in which a deceiver leaks nonverbal cues to deception

LEAKAGE MOST LIKELY	LEAKAGE LEAST LIKELY
Wants to hide emotions being experienced at the moment.	Wants to hide information unrelated to emotions.
Feels strongly about the information being hidden.	Has no strong feelings about the information being hidden.
Feels apprehensive about the deception.	Feels confident about the deception.
Feels guilty about being deceptive.	Experiences little guilt about the deception.
Gets little enjoyment from being deceptive.	Enjoys the deception.
Needs to construct the message carefully while delivering it.	Knows the deceptive message well and has rehearsed it.

Based on material from "Mistakes When Deceiving" by Paul Ekman, in *The Clever Hans Phenomenon: Communication with Horses, Whales, Apes, and People,* Thomas A. Sebeok and Robert Rosenthal, eds. (New York; New York Academy of Sciences, 1981), pp. 269–278.

this censoring, the rapid speed at which expressions can change, and the inability of senders to see their own faces and make sure they send the desired messages, means that each of us does convey a great deal of "true" information, whether we want to or not.

Two prominent researchers in this area, Paul Ekman and Wallace Friesen (1975), talk about three ways in which we falsify messages by controlling our facial expression. First, sometimes we hide a lack of feeling by *simulating*. For example, suppose someone tells you that a friend

you know only casually was in a minor auto accident. You may not be particularly concerned by this news, but you feign an expression of upset because you feel the situation calls for it. The real feeling you had was closer to indifference, but you created the upset expression to meet the demands of the social situation.

At other times we avoid expressing an undesired emotion by *neutralizing* our expression. For example, suppose the doorbell chimes just as you get into the shower. You have to shut off the water, dry yourself, jump into a robe, and rush to the door before the person who rang walks off—all in about twenty seconds. Your expression as you race to the door is probably one of anger, or at least irritation. Just as you open the door you neutralize the expression, toning it down, covering the expression of the real feeling.

A third technique of falsifying involves *masking* a true emotion with one seemingly more appropriate. Boring classes may result in half-closed eyes, frequent yawns, and a dull, glazed-over expression, but they also give rise to a common mask for boredom: an "interested" face, one with wide-open eyes, a brow wrinkled to convey thought, and the expression of other more situation-appropriate responses.

The eyes themselves can send several kinds of messages. Gazes and glances are usually signals of the looker's interest. The *type* of interest can vary, however. Sometimes looking is a conversational turn-taking signal that says, "I'm finished talking. Now it's your turn." Gazing also is a good indicator of liking (Druckman et al., 1982, pp. 77–79). Sometimes eye contact *reflects* liking that already exists, and at other time it actually *creates* or *increases* liking—hence the expression, "making eyes." Paradoxically, there are courtship games in which the players deliberately hide their liking by avoiding one another's eyes.

In other situations eye contact indicates interest, but not attraction or approval. A teacher who glares at a rowdy student or a police officer who "keeps an eye on" a suspect are both signaling their interest with their eyes.

Several studies show that a high degree of eye contact can influence verbal responses. In interviews where the questioner gazed intently while asking questions, subjects made more self-references and revealed more intimate information (Snow, 1972; Ellsworth and Ross, 1976). These findings have practical implications for information-seekers of all types: If you want to get

The face is the mirror of the mind, and eyes without speaking confess the secrets of the heart.

St. Jerome

the most out of your conversation, keep your gaze focused on the other person.

Even the pupils of our eyes communicate. E. H. Hess and J. M. Polt (1960) measured the amount of pupil dilation while showing men and women various pictures. The results of the experiment were interesting: The pupils grow larger in proportion to the degree of interest a person has in an object. For example, men's pupils grew about 18 percent larger when looking at pictures of a naked woman, and the rate of dilation for women looking at a naked man's picture was 20 percent. The greatest increase in pupil size occurred when women looked at a picture of a mother and infant. A good salesperson can increase profits by being aware of pupil dilation. As Edward Hall (1969) describes, he was once in a Middle East bazaar, where an Arab merchant insisted that a customer looking at his jewelry buy a certain piece to which the shopper hadn't been paying much attention. The vendor had been watching the pupils of the buyer's eyes and had known what the buyer really wanted.

Posture   Another way we communicate nonverbally is through our posture. To test this, stop reading for a moment and notice how you're sitting. What does your position say nonverbally about how you feel? Are there any other people near you now? What messages do you get from their present posture? By paying attention to the postures of those around you, as well as to your own, you'll find another channel of nonverbal communication that can furnish information con-

He was so uncomfortable through all these discussions and inquisitions (he didn't know what to do or where or how to look; no matter how much we joshed and chuckled to put him at ease, he was never at ease. His doubtful smile was always forced and wavering as he strained to joke back cordially with us and asked questions and gave answers to ours in a profound and abortive effort to understand just what in the world it was we had grown so determined to teach him, and why) I suppose he really wanted to give up and cry: when I look back now and recall his delicate, furrowed expression, his lowered, obliging voice, it seems evident (now) that he had come awfully close to tears, but he would not (because we did not want him to) let them flow: he masked it well (but I know him better now): he flashed his doubtful smile often at us instead, from one to the other of us, as we harangued and excoriated him affably and he groped undecidedly, with knitted brow, to catch on to and hold what we felt we had explained so fluently.

Joseph Heller
Something Happened

cerning how people feel about themselves and others.

The English language indicates the deep links between posture and communication. English is full of expressions that tie emotional states with body postures:

"I won't take this lying down!"
"He can't stand on his own two feet."
"She has to carry a heavy burden."
"Take a load off your back."
"You're all wrapped up in yourself."
"Don't be so uptight!"

Such phrases show an awareness of posture, even if it's often unconscious. The main reason we miss most posture messages is that they aren't too obvious. It's seldom that people who feel weighed down by a problem hunch over dramatically. When we're bored, we usually don't lean back and slump enough to embarrass the person with whom we're bored. In interpreting posture, then, the key is to look for small changes that might be shadows of the way people feel.

Psychologist Albert Mehrabian (1972) has found that other postural keys to feelings are

tension and relaxation. He says that we take relaxed postures in nonthreatening situations and tighten up when threatened. We can tell a good deal about how others feel simply by watching how tense or loose they seem to be. For example, he suggests that watching tenseness is a way of detecting status differences: the lower-status person is generally the more rigid and tense-appearing, whereas the one with higher status is more relaxed. Often we picture a "chat" with the boss (or professor or judge) this way. We sit ramrod straight while our "superior" leans back in a chair.

The same principle applies to social situations. Often you'll see someone laughing and talking as if perfectly at home, with a posture that shouts nervousness. Some people never relax, and their posture shows it.

Gestures   We use our entire body to communicate through postures, but we also express feelings with just one body part through gesturing. Like other forms of nonverbal communication, gestures can either reinforce or contradict a speaker's words. We've all seen the reinforcing power of certain body movements. For instance, imagine the gestures that would accompany the following statements:

"What can I do about it?"
"I can't stand it anymore!"
"Now let me tell you something!"
"Easy now. It'll be all right."

It was easy to envision what gestures should accompany each message, wasn't it? You can see what an important role these movements play by imagining a speaker expressing the same words without gesturing. Somehow the speaker would seem less involved or sincere. In fact, an absence of gestures is usually a good indication that the speaker may be feeling unenthusiastic about the subject being discussed.

Gestures can produce a wide range of reactions in receivers (Druckmann et al., 1982, pp. 71–72). In many situations, the right kinds of gesturing can increase persuasiveness. Increasing hand and arm movements, a leaning forward, fidgeting less, and keeping limbs open all make a speaker more effective at influencing others. Even more interesting is the fact that persuasiveness increases when one person mirrors another's movements. When persuader and audience are reasonably similar, reciprocating the other person's gestures has a positive effect, whereas acting in a contrary manner is likely to have the opposite result.

People who gesture appropriately often create other impressions that differ from their less expressive counterparts: They are rated as being more warm, casual, agreeable, and energetic. They are also viewed as more enthusiastic, considerate, approachable, and likable. On the other hand, less expressive people are viewed as more logical, cold, and analytic. Not only are they less persuasive, they are viewed as less likable in general.

Some kinds of gestures offer revealing clues about deception (Ekman and Friesen, 1974). Deceivers tend to display more hand-shrug

"Don't pounce."

New Yorker, October 3, 1983, p. 42.

James Thurber.

emblems, use fewer illustrators to punctuate and emphasize their points, and engage in more face-play than truth-tellers. In other words, liars do more fiddling that is unrelated to a message, and they are likely to use more gestures that complement their verbal message.

As with almost any nonverbal behavior, the context in which gestures occur can make all the difference in the results they produce. Animated movements that will be well received in a cooperative social setting might seem like signals of aggression or attempts at domination in a more competitive setting. Fidgeting that might suggest deviousness in a bargaining session could be appropriate when you offer a nervous apology in a personal situation. In any case, trying to manufacture insincere, artificial gestures (or any other nonverbal behaviors) will probably backfire. A more useful goal is to recognize the behaviors you find yourself spontaneously delivering, and to consider how they reflect the attitudes you already feel. Impression management has its uses, but it is a tricky skill.

Touch   Besides being the earliest means we have of making contact with others, touching is essential to our healthy development (Jones and Yarbrough, 1985). During the nineteenth and early twentieth centuries a large percentage of children born every year died from a disease then called *marasmus*, which translated from Greek means "wasting away." In some orphanages the mortality rate was nearly 100 percent, but even children in the most "progressive" homes, hospitals, and other institutions died regularly from the ailment (Halliday, 1948). When researchers finally tracked down the causes of this disease, they found that the infants suffered from lack of physical contact with parents or nurses, rather than from lack of nutrition, medical care, or other factors. The infants hadn't been touched enough, and died as a result. From this knowledge came the practice of "mothering" children in institutions—picking the baby up, carrying it around, and handling it several times each day. At one hospital that began this practice, the death rate of infants fell from between 30 and 35 percent to below 10 percent (Bakwin, 1949).

As children develop, their need for being touched continues. In his excellent book *Touching: The Human Significance of the Skin* (1971), Ashley Montagu describes research suggesting that allergies, eczema, and other health problems are in part caused by a person's lack of mother-contact while an infant. Although Montagu says that these problems develop early in life, he also cites cases where adults suffering from conditions as diverse as asthma and schizophrenia have been successfully treated by psychiatric therapy that uses extensive physical contact.

Touch seems to increase a child's mental functioning as well as physical health. L. J. Yarrow (1963) conducted surveys showing that babies who have been given plenty of physical stimulation by their mothers have significantly higher IQs than those receiving less contact.

Touch also plays a large part in how we respond to others and to our environment. (See Willis and Hamm, 1980, for a review of research on this subject.) For example, touch increases self-disclosure, verbalization of psychiatric patients, and the preference children have for their counselors. Touch also increases compliance. In a study by Chris Kleinke (1977), subjects were approached by a female confederate who requested the return of a dime left in the phone booth from which they had just emerged. When the request was accompanied by a light touch on the subject's arm, the probability that the subject would return the dime increased significantly. In a similar experiment (Willis and Hamm, 1980), subjects were asked by a male or female confederate to sign a petition or complete a rating scale. Again, subjects were more likely to cooperate when they were touched lightly on the arm. In the rating scale variation of the study, the results were especially dramatic: 70 percent of those who were touched complied, whereas only 40 percent of the untouched subjects were willing to cooperate (indicating a predisposition not to comply).

Touch can communicate many messages. Jones and Yarbrough (1985) catalogued twelve different kinds of touches, including "positive,"

Why have hands? They are, from time to time, useful. This has been, in many cases, established. They are mankind's only really trustworthy vocabulary, the nerves and muscles of the spirit made manifest.

Kenneth Patchen

"playful," "control," and "ritualistic." Some types of touch indicate varying degrees of aggression. Others signify types of relationship (Heslin and Alper, 1983):

> functional/professional (dental exam, haircut)
>
> social/polite (handshake)
>
> friendship/warmth (clap on back, Spanish *abrazo*)
>
> love/intimacy (holding hands, hugs)
>
> sexual arousal (some kisses, strokes)

You might object to the examples following each of these categories, saying that some nonverbal behaviors occur in several types of relationships. A kiss, for example, can mean anything from a polite but superficial greeting to the most intense arousal. What makes a given touch more or less intense? Researchers have suggested a number of factors:

> what part of the body does the touching
>
> what part of the body is touched
>
> how long the touch lasts
>
> how much pressure is used
>
> whether there is movement after contact is made
>
> whether anyone else is present
>
> the situation in which the touch occurs
>
> the relationship between the persons involved

From this list you can see that there is, indeed, a complex language of touch. Because nonverbal

W e can turn now to the safer and more tender intimacies of the dance-floor. At parties, discotheques, dance-halls, and ballrooms, adults who are strangers to one another can come together and move around the room in an intimate frontal embrace. Individuals who are already friendly can also use the situation to escalate a non-touching relationship into a touching one. This special role that social dancing plays in our society is that it permits, in its special context, a sudden and dramatic increase in body intimacy in a way that would be impossible elsewhere. If the same full frontal embrace were performed between strangers, or partial strangers, outside the context of the dance-floor, the impact would be entirely different. Dancing, so to speak, devalues the significance of the embrace, lowering its threshold to a point where it can lightly be indulged in without fear of rebuff. Having permitted it to occur, it then gives a chance for it to work its powerful magic. If the magic fails to work, the formalities of the situation also permit retreat without ignominy.

Desmond Morris
Intimate Behavior

---

messages are inherently ambiguous, it's no surprise that this language can often be misunderstood. Is a hug playful or suggestive of stronger feelings? Is a touch on the shoulder a friendly gesture or an attempt at domination? Research suggests the interpretation can depend on a variety of factors, including the sex of the people involved, ethnic background, and marital status, among others. This sort of ambiguity shows the importance of checking to be sure your interpretations are accurate.

In spite of the need for making physical contact with others, North American society discourages much touching. Anyone who has traveled to other countries, particularly in Latin America, southern Europe, and parts of Africa, has noticed the differences in the amount of contact between citizens there and in the United States, Canada, and northern Europe.

In the United States, the amount of touching usually decreases with age (Knapp, 1978, pp. 244–246). Sixth-graders touch each other less than first-graders. Parents touch their older chil-

dren less often than their younger ones. Within our culture there are differences between the touching behavior of various groups. For instance, men touch each other much less than they touch women. Although this restraint might seem perfectly natural to someone brought up in a culture holding that touch between members of the same sex suggests homosexuality, a look at other cultures shows that prolonged hand contact, embracing, and even types of kissing go on between the most masculine of men and between the most feminine of women.

What touching does go on between adults in North American culture is highly prescribed by unwritten social rules. In the 1960s Sidney Jourard (1966) conducted a survey exploring touching behavior. He first divided the body into fourteen areas (such as top of head, face, hands, thighs, and so on), and asked 300 students in which areas they gave and received touches most often when interacting with parents, same-sex friends, and opposite-sex friends. Jourard found that body contact occurs most frequently between friends of the opposite sex, and is usually confined to upper portions of the body.

The data for Jourard's report were collected during 1963 and 1964. During the intervening years there has been much talk about the need for more touch. Has the actual amount of contact changed? Is any group more accessible to touch now than in 1964? Are different body parts more accessible? Do certain people have greater access to others? To answer these questions, Rosenfeld, Kartus, and Ray (1976) repeated Jourard's study twelve years later.

A large number of unmarried male and female undergraduate students between 18 and 22 years old completed a questionnaire asking how often and where on their bodies during the previous twelve months they were touched by their mother, father, closest same-sex friend, and closest opposite-sex friend. The body diagram presented to the subjects was divided into fourteen areas (see Figure 5–1). Touching remained about the same between parents and their children and also between same-sex friends. However, touch between opposite-sex friends increased.

Such data point a clear, if depressing, view of

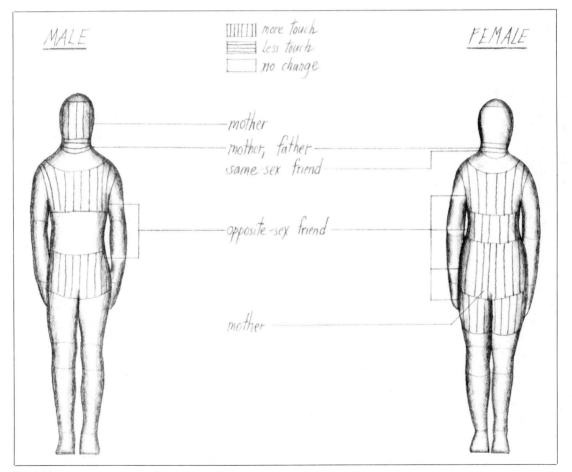

FIGURE 5–1

> he unconscious parental feelings communicated through touch or lack of touch can lead to feelings of confusion and conflict in a child. Sometimes a "modern" parent will say all the right things but not want to touch his child very much. The child's confusion comes from the inconsistency of levels: if they really approve of me so much like they say they do, why won't they touch me?
>
> William Schutz

touching in our society. As young children, most North Americans receive at least a modest amount of physical love and intimacy from their parents. The next time most can expect to receive this level of physical caring won't come until they have chosen a partner. Even then, the nurturing seemingly brought by physical contact will most often come only from that partner—a heavy demand for one person to carry.

Associated with (but not always the same as) the kind of love and intimacy we've been discussing is the sexual side of touching. It's obvious that sex can be one way of expressing caring for a partner. But especially in a touch-starved culture, sex can also serve another purpose not necessarily connected with intimate love or affection: It may simply be a socially acceptable way of touching and being touched by another human being. Although it's possible to argue that there's nothing wrong with making this kind of contact, it's sad to think that a sexual act is one of the very few ways to touch another person acceptably in a manner more personal than a handshake. We're only speculating, but see whether this idea makes sense to you: If we lived in a culture where physical contact was more acceptable, perhaps many people could achieve the touching they seem to need without resorting to sex out of desperation. Then sex would be valued and enjoyed when the time was right, not overused as the only way to bridge the gap between people.

Voice The voice itself is another channel of nonverbal communication. If you think about it for

a moment, you'll realize that a certain way of speaking can give the same word or words many meanings. For example, look at the possible meanings from a single sentence just by changing the word emphasis:

This is a fantastic communication book. (Not just any book, but *this* one in particular.)

This is a *fantastic* communication book. (This book is superior, exciting.)

This is a fantastic *communication* book. (The book is good as far as communication goes; it may not be so great as literature or drama.)

This is a fantastic communication *book*. (It's not a play or record; it's a book.)

It's possible to get an idea across without ever expressing it outright by accenting a certain word in a sentence. In *Nonverbal Communication in Human Interaction,* Mark Knapp (1978) quotes an example from *Newsweek.* It describes how Robert J. McCloskey, a State Department official in the Nixon administration, was able to express the government's position off the record:

McCloskey has three distinct ways of saying, "I would not speculate": spoken without accent, it means the department doesn't know for sure; emphasis on the "I" means "I wouldn't, but you may—and with some assurance"; accent on "speculate" indicates that the questioner's premise is probably wrong. (p. 322)

The voice communicates in many other ways—

through its tone, speed, pitch, number and length of pauses, volume, and nonfluencies (such as stammering or use of "uh," "um," and "er"). All these factors together are called *paralanguage,* and they can do a great deal to reinforce or contradict the message our words convey.

Sarcasm is one instance in which we use both emphasis and tone of voice to change a statement's meaning to the opposite of its verbal message. Experience this reversal yourself with the following three statements. First say them literally, and then say them sarcastically.

1. "Darling, what a beautiful little gown!"
2. "I really had a wonderful time on my blind date."
3. "There's nothing I like better than calves' brains on toast."

Albert Mehrabian (1972) and others have conducted experiments indicating that when the vocal factors (tone of voice, nonfluencies, emphasis, and so forth) contradict the verbal message (words), the vocal factors carry more meaning. They had subjects evaluate the degree of liking communicated by a message in which vocal clues conflicted with the words and found that the words had little effect on the interpretation of the message.

Communication through paralanguage isn't always intentional. Often our voices give us away when we're trying to create an impression different than our actual feelings. For example, you've probably had experiences of trying to sound calm and serene when you were really seething with inner nervousness. Maybe your deception went along perfectly for a while—just the right smile, no telltale fidgeting of the hands, posture appearing relaxed—and then, without being able to do a thing about it, right in the middle of your relaxed comments, your voice squeaked! The charade was over.

In addition to reinforcing or contradicting

messages, some vocal factors influence the way a speaker is perceived by others. For example, breathiness in a man causes him to be perceived as artistic, and in a woman causes her to be perceived as petite, pretty, and shallow. Both men and women suffer being viewed as the same stereotypes when they speak with a flat voice: They are perceived as sluggish, cold, and withdrawn. Both men and women also suffer stereotyping associated with an increase in speaking rate: They are perceived as more animated and extroverted. Nasality is probably the most socially offensive vocal cue, giving rise to a host of perceived undesirable characteristics.

The degree to which vocal factors communicate is extensive, as Lawrence Rosenfeld and Jean Civikly point out in *With Words Unspoken: The Nonverbal Experience* (1976). From vocal cues *alone* (people in these studies could not see the person speaking), we can determine age, differentiate "big" from "small" people, and judge personality characteristics, such as dominance, introversion, and sociability; we can detect certain emotions (although fear and nervousness, love and sadness, and pride and satisfaction are often confused). Interestingly, from vocal cues alone we can determine a person's status—even on the basis of *single word cues.* We don't need more than a few seconds' worth of a speech sample.

Proxemics and territoriality   Proxemics is the study of how people and animals use the space around them. Before we discuss this fascinating area of research, try the following experiment.

Choose a partner, go to opposite sides of the room, and face each other. Very slowly begin walking toward each other while carrying on a conversation. You might simply talk about how you feel as you experience the activity. As you move closer, be aware of any change in your

Once l heard a hospital nurse describing doctors. She said there were beside-the-bed doctors, who were interested in the patient, and foot-of-the-bed doctors, who were interested in the patient's condition. They unconsciously expressed their emotional involvement—or lack of it—by where they stood.

Edward Hall

feelings. Continue moving slowly toward each other until you are only an inch or so apart. Remember how you feel at this point. Now, while still facing each other, back up until you're at a comfortable distance for carrying on your conversation.

During this experiment your feelings will most likely change at least three times. During the first phase, when you were across the room from your partner, you probably felt unnaturally far away. Then, as you neared a point about three feet distant, you probably felt like stopping; this is the distance at which two people in our culture normally stand while conversing socially. If your partner wasn't someone you're emotionally close to, you probably began to feel quite uncomfortable as you moved through this normal range and came closer; it's possible that you had to force yourself not to move back. Some people find this phase so uncomfortable that they can't get closer than twenty inches or so to their partner.

The reason for your discomfort has to do with your spatial needs. Each of us carries around a sort of invisible bubble of *personal space* wherever we go. We think of the area inside this bubble as our own—almost as much a part of us as our own bodies. As you moved closer to your partner, the distance between your bubbles narrowed and at a certain point disappeared altogether: Your space had been invaded, and this is the point at which you probably felt uncomforta-

ble. As you moved away again, your partner retreated out of your bubble, and you felt more relaxed.

Of course, if you were to try this experiment with someone close to you—your husband, wife, girlfriend, or boyfriend—you might not have felt any discomfort at all, even while touching. On the other hand, if you'd been approaching someone who made you uncomfortable—a total stranger or someone you disliked—you probably would have stopped farther away from them. The reason is that our personal bubbles vary in size according to the person we're with and the situation we're in. It's precisely the varying size of our personal space—the distance that we put between ourselves and others—that gives a nonverbal clue to our feelings. For example, in a recent study by Edgar O'Neal and his associates (1980), the body-buffer zones of male undergraduates increased after they were insulted by experimenters.

In another study, Mark Snyder (1980) reported that the distance subjects unconsciously placed between themselves and others was a good indication of their prejudices. All the subjects were polled on their attitudes about homosexuality. Half the interviewers, who were confederates of the experimenter, wore "Gay and Proud" buttons and mentioned their membership in the Association of Gay Psychologists. The other interviewers wore no buttons and simply identified themselves as graduate students. Despite their expressions of tolerance, subjects seated themselves almost a foot further away from the apparently gay interviewers of the same sex.

Anthropologist Edward T. Hall (1969) has defined four distances we use in our everyday lives. He says that we choose a particular one depending upon how we feel toward others at a given time, and that by "reading" which distance people take, we can get some insight into their feelings.

Intimate distance   The first of Hall's zones begins with skin contact and ranges out to about eighteen inches. We usually use intimate distance with people who are emotionally close to us, and then mostly in private situations—making love, caressing, comforting, protecting. By allowing someone to move into our intimate distance, we let them enter our personal space. When we let them in voluntarily, it's usually a sign of trust: We've willingly lowered our defenses. On the other hand, when someone invades this most personal area without our consent, we usually feel threatened. You may have had this feeling during the last exercise when your partner intruded into your space without any real invitation from you. It also explains the discomfort we sometimes feel when forced into crowded places such as buses or elevators with strangers. At times like these

the standard behavior in our society is to draw away or tense our muscles and avoid eye contact. This is a nonverbal way of signaling, "I'm sorry for invading your territory, but the situation forced me."

In courtship situations a critical moment usually occurs when one member of a couple first moves into the other's intimate zone. If the partner being approached does not retreat, this usually signals that the relationship is moving into a new stage. On the other hand, if the reaction to the advance is withdrawal to a greater distance, the initiator should get the message that it isn't yet time to get more intimate. We remember from our dating experiences the significance of where on the car seat our companions chose to sit. If they moved close to us, it meant one thing; if they stayed jammed against the door, we got quite a different message.

From *The New Yorker,* November 14, 1983.

Personal distance   The second spatial zone ranges from eighteen inches at its closest point to four feet at its farthest. Its closer phase is the distance at which most couples stand in public. If someone of the opposite sex stands this near one partner at a party, the other partner is likely to feel uncomfortable. This "moving in" often is taken to mean that something more than casual conversation is taking place. The far range of personal distance runs from about two-and-a-half to four feet. It's the zone just beyond the other person's reach. As Hall puts it, at this distance we can keep someone "at arm's length." This choice of words suggests the type of communication that goes on at this range: The contacts are still reasonably close, but they're much less personal than the ones that occur a foot or so closer.

Test this zone for yourself. Start a conversation with someone at a distance of about three feet, and slowly move a foot or so closer. Do you notice a difference? Does this distance affect your conversation?

Social distance   The third zone ranges from four to about twelve feet out. Within it are the kinds of communication that usually occur in business situations. Its closer phase, from four to seven feet, is the distance at which conversations usually occur between salespeople and custom-ers and between people who work together. Most people feel uncomfortable when a salesclerk comes as close as three feet, whereas four or five feet nonverbally signals, "I'm here to help you, but I don't mean to be too personal or pushy."

We use the far range of social distance—seven to twelve feet—for more formal and impersonal situations. At this range we sit across the desk from our boss (or other authority figures). Sitting at this distance signals a far different and less relaxed type of conversation than if we were to pull a chair around to the boss's side of the desk and sit only three feet away.

Public distance   Public distance is Hall's term for the furthest zone, running outward from twelve feet. The closer range of public distance is the one that most teachers use in the classroom. In the further reaches of public space—twenty-five feet and beyond—two-way communication is almost impossible. In some cases it's necessary for speakers to use public distance to reach a large audience, but we can assume that anyone who chooses to use it when greater closeness is possible is not interested in a dialogue.

When our spatial bubble is invaded, we respond with what are called *barrier behaviors*, behaviors designed to create a barrier (or fix a broken one) between ourselves and other people. Invade someone's personal space and notice the reaction. At first the person is most likely simply to back away, probably without realizing what is happening. Next your partner might attempt to put an object between you, such as a desk, a chair, or some books clutched to the chest, all in an effort to get some separation. Then the other person will probably decrease eye contact (the "elevator syndrome," in which we can crowd in and even touch one another so long as we avoid eye contact). Furthermore, your reluctant partner might sneeze, cough, scratch, and exhibit any variety of behaviors to discourage your antisocial behavior. In the end, if none of these behaviors achieve the desired goal of getting some space between the two of you, the other person might "counterattack," gently at first ("Move back, will you?"), then more forcefully (probably with a shove).

Writers sometimes confuse personal space with a related concept: *territoriality*. Whereas personal space is the invisible bubble we carry around, the bubble that serves as an extension of our physical being, territory remains stationary.

Any geographical area, such as a room, house, neighborhood, or country, to which we assume some kind of "rights" is our territory. What's interesting about territoriality is that there is no real basis for the assumption of proprietary rights, of "owning" some area, but the feeling of "owning" exists nonetheless. My room in my house is *my room* whether I'm there or not (unlike my personal space which is carried around with me), and it's my room because I say it's my room. Although I could probably make a case for my room *really being* my room (as opposed to belonging to another family member or to the mortgage holder on the house), what about the desk I sit at in each class? I feel the same about the desk. It's *my desk*, even though it's certain that the desk is owned by the school and is in no way really mine.

How can you tell if you are territorial? Ask yourself: Is there some piece of land, some area, which you would defend against others? Are you uncomfortable when someone comes into your room uninvited, or when you're not there? Does the thought of your neighborhood showing an increase in crime make you want to fight back? Does defending your country sound like a good idea? Ethographers (people who study animal behavior and attempt to make parallels with human behavior) argue that we are territorial *in nature;* that is, like other animals, we human beings are biologically programmed to defend our territory (Ardrey, 1966).

Territoriality in animals serves a number of functions, such as providing a defended area for food and mating, and a place to hide from enemies. A territory also aids in the regulation of population density; only those controlling certain parts of the territory (usually the best pieces of land) tend to mate, thereby keeping the population in balance.

It is difficult to determine the advantages territoriality has for humans as a species. How-ever, certain advantages do exist for individuals, especially for those with high status. Generally, we grant people with higher status more personal territory and greater privacy. We knock before entering our supervisor's office, whereas the supervisor can usually walk into our work area without hesitating. In traditional schools professors have offices, dining rooms, and even toilets that are private, whereas the students, who are presumably less important, have no such sanctuaries. In the military greater space and privacy usually come with rank: Privates sleep forty to a barracks, sergeants have their own private rooms, and generals have government-provided houses.

Physical attractiveness   The importance of beauty has been emphasized in the arts for centuries. More recently, social scientists have begun to measure the degree to which physical attractiveness affects interaction between people. Recent findings, summarized by Knapp (1984: 141–144), Berscheid and Walster (1978), and Rosenfeld (1979), indicate that women who are perceived as attractive have more dates, receive higher grades in college, persuade males with greater ease, and receive lighter court sentences. Both men and women whom others view as attractive are rated as being more sensitive, kind, strong, sociable, and interesting than their less fortunate brothers and sisters. Who is most likely to succeed in business? Place your bet with the attractive job applicant. For example, shorter men have more difficulty finding jobs in the first place, and men over 6'2" receive starting salaries that average 12.4 percent higher than comparable applicants under six feet.

The influence of attractiveness begins early in life. Preschoolers, for example, were shown photographs of children their own age and asked to choose potential friends and enemies. The researchers found that children as young as three

If one wears a shoe known to be a runner's shoe, those knowledgeable in these matters can recognize another of their kind. Shoes are ranked in terms of status in the runner's culture, but for the purposes of achieving recognition as a member, it is sufficient merely to be sporting a running shoe; an Interval 305 New Balance or Brooks 270 will do the job.

Although any running shoe suffices to communicate "I am a runner," the kind of shoe worn does articulate the message further. For example, a person sporting a pair of Eugen Brutting Marathons, a shoe with a distinctive diamond embossed with the letters EB, communicates that his or her commitment to running is serious. These shoes cost approximately $12 more than other popular running shoes. They are known for their ultralight yet substantive construction. A person wearing them communicates that he or she knows a great deal about shoes, that he or she trains long and hard and for fast times.

Jeffrey E. Nash
Decoding the Runner's Wardrobe

---

agreed as to who was attractive ("cute") and unattractive ("homely"). Furthermore, they valued their attractive counterparts—both of the same and opposite sex—more highly. Also, preschool children rated by their peers as pretty were most liked, and those identified as least pretty were least liked. Children who were interviewed rated good-looking children as having positive social characteristics ("He's friendly to other children."), and unattractive children negatively ("He hits other children without reason.").

Teachers, unfortunately, share this prejudice. Teachers rated identical school reports, some with an attractive child's photo attached and others with an unattractive child's, differently: Unattractive children were given lower grades, presumed to have lower IQs, and thought to get along less well with their peers.

Fortunately, attractiveness is something we can control without having to call the plastic surgeon. We view others as beautiful or ugly, not just on the basis of the "original equipment" they come with, but also on *how they use that equipment*. Posture, gestures, facial expressions, and other behaviors can increase the attractiveness of an otherwise unremarkable person. Exercise can improve the way each of us looks. Finally, the way we dress can make a significant difference in the way others perceive us, as you'll now see.

Clothing   The way we dress tells others something about us. The armed forces, for instance, have developed uniforms partly as a way of showing who has what particular job and who's in charge. Thus, uniforms are a sort of nonverbal badge that describes the wearer's place in the military social system. Although many have a tendency to criticize the military as a rigid system that puts people into strictly defined classes, in many ways we also use clothing to categorize people.

Think about the people you know. Can you tell anything about their political or social philosophies by the way they dress? A good place to begin your survey is with the faculty at your school. Is there any relationship between the way instructors dress and their teaching style? Take a look at your friends. Do you find that the people who spend time together share the same ideas about clothing? Is there a "uniform" for political radicals and one for conservatives? Is there a high-fashion "uniform" that tells the public who's in style and who's out of it?

One setting in which dress is significant is in the employment interview. The importance of this situation has led to many books and articles describing how to behave to get a job offer. In a chapter titled "Forget Your Leisure Suit, but Not Your Bra," W. Pierson Newall (1979) concludes that dressing too differently from the interviewer can cast doubt on an applicant's qualifications. In H. Anthony Medley's *The Neglected Art of Being Interviewed* (1978), the author argues that 80 percent of the interviewer's opinion is formed before the first word is spoken. John P. Molloy (1976) refers to a survey of seventeen major industries that suggests that any clothing other than the most conservative can result in a negative rating from interviewers.

In a study conducted by Janelle Johnson (1981), 38 personnel representatives involved in recruiting and interviewing in the southwest were asked several questions regarding their attitudes toward applicants' appearance. One question was "What is the most predominant factor influencing your initial impression of interviewees?" Choices

Drawing by Richter; © 1968 The New Yorker Magazine, Inc.

"A general! Goodness gracious, you don't <u>look</u> like a general!"

were: physical attractiveness, résumé, appearance (dress), and manners. The majority of respondents (45 percent) indicated appearance as the most influential factor (followed by résumé with 33 percent and the other two items with 11 percent each).

Another question asked was how the first impression created by the applicant affected the rest of the interview. Choices were: not at all, not significantly, somewhat significantly, significantly, and it is the most important factor affecting the rest of the interview. The majority of respondents indicated that their first impression affected the rest of the interview either somewhat (42 percent) or significantly (37 percent).

At this point you might be thinking of the old saying, "You can't judge a book by its cover." How valid is such a statement? In an attempt to answer this question, psychologist Lewis Aiken (1963) conducted a study focusing on "wearer characteristics." His goal was to see whether there is any relationship between the type of clothing a person chooses to wear and personality. Aiken focused his study on female subjects and found that clothes do offer some clues about the characteristics of the wearer. For instance, Aiken found that women who had a high concern for decoration and style in dress also scored above average on traits such as conformity and sociability. Women who dressed for comfort scored high in the areas of self-control and extroversion. A great interest in dress correlated positively with compliance, stereotypic thinking, social conscientiousness, and insecurity. Those who dressed in high conformity to style also rated above average on social conformity, restraint, and submissiveness. Finally, women who stressed economy in their dress rated high on responsibility, alertness, efficiency, and precision.

To see whether Aiken's results held for men as well as women and to bring his research up to date, Lawrence Rosenfeld and Timothy Plax

(1977) conducted a follow-up investigation. They gave a battery of psychological examinations to a large number of male and female college students, and also administered a test that measured the subjects' attitudes toward clothes on four dimensions: clothing consciousness, exhibitionism, practicality, and the desire to design clothes.

Upon analyzing the results, some definite relationships between personality type and approach to clothing did emerge. For instance, both men and women who were not especially conscious of clothing style proved to be more independent than their more stylish counterparts. Highly exhibitionistic males were less sympathetic than other groups, and exhibitionistic women were more detached in their relationships. Men who dressed in a highly practical manner rated low on leadership orientation and were less motivated to form friendships, whereas those less concerned with practicality were more success-oriented and forceful.

Results such as these are fascinating, for they show that to some degree we *can* get an idea about human "books" from their covers. At the same time it's important to remember that research results are generalizations, and that not every clothes-conscious or exhibitionistic dresser fits into the pattern just described. Again, the best course is to treat your nonverbal interpretations as hunches that need to be checked out and not as absolute facts.

Environment   To conclude our look at nonverbal communication we want to emphasize the ways in which physical settings, architecture, and interior design affect our communication. Begin your thinking by recalling for a moment the different homes you've visited lately. Were some of these homes more comfortable to be in than others? Certainly a lot of these kinds of feelings are shaped by the people you were with, but

C ampuses are full of conscious and unconscious architectural symbolism. While the colleges at Santa Cruz evoke images of Italian hill towns as they might have been if the peasants had concrete, the administration building is another story. It appears to anticipate the confrontations between students and administration that marked the sixties. At Santa Cruz, administrative offices are located in a two-story building whose rough sloped concrete base with narrow slit windows gives it the look of a feudal shogun's palace. The effect is heightened by the bridge and landscaped moat that one crosses to enter the building. "Four administrators in there could hold off the entire campus," joked one student.

Sym Van Der Ryn (Chief Architect, State of California)

there are some houses where it seems impossible to relax, no matter how friendly the hosts. We've spent what seemed like endless evenings in what Mark Knapp (1978) calls "unliving rooms," where the spotless ashtrays, furniture coverings, and plastic lamp covers seemed to send nonverbal messages telling us not to touch anything, not to put our feet up, and not to be comfortable. People who live in houses like this probably wonder why nobody ever seems to relax and enjoy themselves at their parties. One thing is quite certain: They don't understand that the environment they have created can communicate discomfort to their guests.

There's a large amount of research that shows how the design of an environment can shape the kind of communication that takes place in it. In one experiment at Brandeis University, Maslow and Mintz (1956) found that the attractiveness of a room influenced the happiness and energy of people working in it. The experimenters set up three rooms: an "ugly" one, which resembled a janitor's closet in the basement of a campus building; an "average" room, which was a professor's office; and a "beautiful" room, which was furnished with carpeting, drapes, and comfortable furniture. The subjects in the experiment were asked to rate a series of pictures as a way of measuring their energy and

feelings of well-being while at work. Results of the experiment showed that while in the ugly room, the subjects became tired and bored more quickly and took longer to complete their task. Subjects who were in the beautiful room, however, rated the faces they were judging more positively, showed a greater desire to work, and expressed feelings of importance, comfort, and enjoyment. The results teach a lesson that isn't surprising: Workers generally feel better and do a better job when they're in an attractive environment.

Many business people show an understanding of how environment can influence communication. Robert Sommer, a leading environmental psychologist, described several such cases. In *Personal Space: The Behavioral Basis of Design* (1969), he points out that dim lighting, subdued noise levels, and comfortable seats encourage people to spend more time in a restaurant or bar. Knowing this fact, the management can control the amount of customer turnover. If the goal is to run a high-volume business that tries to move people in and out quickly, it's necessary to keep the lights shining brightly and not worry too much about soundproofing. On the other hand, if the goal is to keep customers in a bar or restaurant for a long time, the proper technique is to lower the lighting and use absorbent building materials that will keep down the noise level.

refuses to buy a chair or couch without sitting in it for at least half an hour to test the comfort.)

Sommer also describes how airports are designed to discourage people from spending too much time in waiting areas. The uncomfortable chairs, bolted shoulder to shoulder in rows facing outward, make conversation and relaxation next to impossible. Faced with this situation, travelers are forced to move to restaurants and bars in the terminal, where they're not only more comfortable but also more likely to spend money.

Casino owners in places such as Las Vegas also know how to use the environment to control behavior. To keep gamblers from noticing how long they've been shooting craps, playing roulette and blackjack, and feeding slot machines, they build their casinos without windows or clocks. Unless wearing a wristwatch, customers have no way of knowing how long they have been gambling or, for that matter, whether it's day or night.

In a more therapeutic and less commercial way physicians have also shaped environments to improve communications. One study showed that simply removing a doctor's desk made patients feel almost five times more at ease during office visits. Sommer found that redesigning a con-valescent ward of a hospital greatly increased the interaction between patients. In the old design seats were placed shoulder to shoulder around the edges of the ward. By grouping the chairs around small tables so that patients faced each other at a comfortable distance, the amount of conversations doubled.

Even the design of an entire building can shape communication among its users. Architects have learned that the way housing projects are designed controls to a great extent the contact neighbors have with each other. People who live in apartments near stairways and mailboxes have many more neighbor contacts than do those living in less heavily traveled parts of the building, and

Furniture design also affects the amount of time a person spends in an environment. From this knowledge came the Larsen chair, which was designed for Copenhagen restaurant owners who felt their customers were occupying their seats too long without spending enough money. The chair is constructed to put an uncomfortable pressure on the sitter's back if occupied for more than a few minutes. (We suspect that many people who are careless in buying furniture for their homes get much the same result without trying. One environmental psychologist we know tenants generally have more contacts with immediate neighbors than with people even a few doors away. Architects now use this information to design buildings that either encourage communication or increase privacy, and house hunters can use the same knowledge to choose a home that gives them the neighborhood relationships they want.

So far we've talked about how designing an environment can shape communication, but there's another side to consider. Watching how people use an already existing environment can be a way of telling what kind of relationships they want. For example, Sommer watched students in a college library and found that there's a definite pattern for people who want to study alone. While the library was uncrowded, students almost always chose corner seats at one of the empty rectangular tables. After each table was occupied by one reader, new readers would choose a seat on the opposite side and at the far end, thus keeping the maximum distance between themselves and the other readers. One of Sommer's associates tried violating these "rules" by sitting next to and across from other female readers when more-distant seats were available. She found that the approached women reacted defensively, signaling their discomfort through shifts in posture, gesturing, or eventually moving away.

Research on classroom environments is extensive. Probably the most detailed study was conducted by Raymond Adams and Bruce Biddle (1970). Observing a variety of classes from grades one, six, and eleven, they found that the main determinant of whether a student was actively and directly engaged in the process of classroom communication was that student's seating position. This finding held even when students were assigned seats, indicating that location, and not personal preferences, determined interaction.

Other studies by Robert Sommer and his colleagues (1978) found that students who sit opposite the teacher talk more, and those next to the teacher avoid talking at all. Also, the middle of the first row contains the students who interact most, and as we move back and to the sides of the classroom, interaction decreases markedly.

With an overwhelming lack of imagination we perpetuate a seating arrangement reminiscent of a military cemetery. This type of environment communicates to students that the teacher, who can move about freely while they can't, is the one who is important in the room, is the only one to whom anyone should speak, and is the person who has all the information. The most advanced curriculum has little chance of surviving without a physical environment that supports it.

As we draw this discussion of nonverbal communication to a close, realize that we haven't tried to teach you *how* to communicate nonverbally in this chapter—you've always known how. What we do hope you've gained here is a greater *awareness* of the messages you and others send. You can use this new awareness to understand your relationships, improve them, and make them more interpersonal in the best sense of the word.

Readings

Adams, Raymond, and Bruce Biddle. *Realities of Teaching: Explorations with Video Tape.* New York: Holt, Rinehart and Winston, 1970.

Aiken, Lewis R. "The Relationship of Dress to Selected Measures of Personality in Undergraduate Women." *Journal of Social Psychology* 80 (1963): 119–128.

Ardrey, Robert. *The Territorial Imperative.* New York: Dell, 1966.

Baker, Ellen, and Marvin E. Shaw. "Reactions to Interpersonal Distance and Topic Intimacy: A Comparison of Strangers and Friends." *Journal of Nonverbal Behavior* 5 (1980): 80–91.

Bakker, Cornelius B., and Marianne Bakker-Rabadau. *No Trespassing! Explorations in Human Territory*. San Francisco: Chandler and Sharp, 1973.

Bakwin, H. "Emotional Deprivation in Infants." *Journal of Pediatrics* 35 (1949): 512–521.

*Berscheid, Ellen, and Elaine Hatfield Walster. *Interpersonal Attraction*, 2d ed. Reading, Mass.: Addison-Wesley, 1978.

Birdwhistell, Ray L. *Kinesics and Context*. Philadelphia: University of Pennsylvania Press, 1970.

Blonston, Gary. "The Translator: Edward T. Hall." *Science 85* (July–August 1985): 78–85.

Burgoon, Judee, and Thomas Saine. *The Unspoken Dialogue*. Boston: Houghton Mifflin, 1978.

Byers, P., and H. Byers. "Nonverbal Communication and the Education of Children." In *Functions of Language in the Classroom*, C. B. Cazden, V. P. John, and D. Hymes, eds. New York: Teachers College Press, 1972.

Deasy, C. M. "When Architects Consult People." *Psychology Today* 3 (March 1970): 10.

DePaulo, B. M., M. Zuckerman, and R. Rosenthal. "Detecting Deception: Modality Effects." In L. Wheeler, ed., *Review of Personality and Social Psychology*, Vol. 1. Beverly Hills, Calif.: Sage, 1980.

Druckmann, D., R. M. Rozelle, and J. C. Baxter. *Nonverbal Communication: Survey, Theory, and Research*. Beverly Hills, Calif.: Sage, 1982.

Duncan, S. D., Jr. "On the Structure of Speaker-Auditor Interaction During Speaking Turns." *Language in Society* 2 (1974): 161–180.

Duncan, S. D., Jr. "Some Signals and Rules for Taking Speaking Turns in Conversation." *Journal of Personality and Social Psychology* 23 (1972): 283–292.

Duncan, S. D., Jr., and D. W. Fiske. "Dynamic Patterning in Conversation." *American Scientist* 67 (1979): 90–98.

Ekman, P., and W. V. Friesen. *Unmasking the Face: A Guide to Recognizing Emotions from Facial Clues*. Englewood Cliffs, N.J.: Prentice-Hall, 1975.

Ekman, P., and W. V. Friesen. "Detecting Deception from the Body or Face." *Journal of Personality and Social Psychology* 29 (1974): 288–298.

Ekman, P., and W. V. Friesen. "Constants Across Cultures in the Face and Emotion." *Journal of Personality and Social Psychology* 17 (1971): 124–129.

Ekman, P., and W. V. Friesen. "Nonverbal Leakage and Clues to Deception." *Psychiatry* 32 (1969): 88–106.

Ekman, P., W. V. Friesen, and J. Baer. "The International Language of Gestures." *Psychology Today* 18 (May 1984): 64–69.

Ellsworth, P. C., and L. D. Ross. "Intimacy in Response to Direct Gaze." *Journal of Experimental Social Psychology* 11 (1976): 592–613.

Ellyson, Steve L., John F. Dovidio, and Randi L. Corson. "Visual Behavior Differences in Females as a Function of Self-Perceived Expertise." *Journal of Nonverbal Behavior* 5 (1981): 164–171.

Exline, Ralph V., Steve L. Ellyson, and B. Long. "Visual Behavior as an Aspect of Power Role Relationships." In *Advances in the Study of Communication and Affect*, vol 2., P. Pilner, L. Krames, and T. Alloway, eds. New York: Plenum Press, 1975.

Feldman, Saul D. "The Presentation of Shortness in Everyday Life. Height and Heightism in American Society: Toward a Sociology of Stature." In *Lifestyles: Diversity in American Society*, 2d ed., S. D. Feldman and G. W. Thielbar, eds. Boston: Little, Brown and Company, 1975.

Garratt, G. A., J. C. Baxter, and R. M. Rozelle. "Training University Police in Black-American Nonverbal Behaviors: An Application to Police-Community Relations." *Journal of Social Psychology* 113 (1981): 217–229.

Greene, John O., H. Dan O'Hair, Michael Cody,

and Catherine Yen. "Planning and Control of Behavior During Deception." *Human Communication Research* 11 (1985): 335–364.

Gunther, Bernard. *Sense Relaxation: Below Your Mind*. New York: Macmillan, 1968.

*Hall, Edward T. *The Hidden Dimension*. Garden City, N.Y.: Anchor Books, 1969.

Halliday, J. L. *Psychosocial Medicine: A Study of the Sick Society*. New York: Norton, 1948.

Hegstrom, Timothy G. "Message Impact: What Percentage Is Nonverbal?" *Western Journal of Speech Communication* 43 (1979): 134–142.

Heslin, R., and T. Alper. "Touch: The Bonding Gesture." In *Nonverbal Interaction*, J. M. Wiemann and R. P. Harrison, eds. Beverly Hills, Calif.: Sage, 1983, pp. 47–75.

Hess, E. H., and J. M. Polt. "Pupil Size as Related to Interest Value of Visual Stimuli." *Science* 132 (1960): 349–350.

Johnson, Janelle M. "The Significance of Dress in an Interview." Unpublished paper, University of New Mexico, 1981.

Jones, Stanley E., and Elaine Yarbrough. "A Naturalistic Study of the Meanings of Touch." *Communication Monographs* 52 (1985): 19–56.

Jourard, Sidney M. "An Exploratory Study of Body Accessibility." *British Journal of Social and Clinical Psychology* 5 (1966): 221–231.

Katz, A. M., and V. T. Katz. *Foundations of Nonverbal Communication*. Carbondale, Ill.: Southern Illinois University Press, 1983.

Keyes, Ralph. "The Height Report." *Esquire* (November 1979): 31–43.

Kleinke, Chris R. "Compliance to Requests Made by Gazing and Touching Experimenters in Field Settings." *Journal of Experimental Social Psychology* 13 (1977): 218–223.

Kleinke, C. L., M. R. Lenga, T. B. Tully, F. B. Meeker, and R. A. Staneski. "Effect of Talking Rate on First Impressions of Opposite-Sex and Same-Sex Interactions." Presented at the meeting of the Western Psychological Association, Los Angeles, 1976.

Knapp, Mark L. *Interpersonal Communication and Human Relationships*. Boston: Allyn and Bacon, 1984.

Knapp, Mark L. *Nonverbal Communication in Human Interaction*, 2d ed. New York: Holt, Rinehart and Winston, 1978.

*La France, Marianne, and Clara Mayo. "A Review of Nonverbal Behaviors of Women and Men." *Western Journal of Speech Communication* 43 (1979): 96–107.

Leathers, Dale G. *Nonverbal Communication Systems*. Boston: Allyn and Bacon, 1978.

Maslow, A., and N. Mintz. "Effects of Aesthetic Surroundings: Initial Effects of Those Aesthetic Surroundings upon Perceiving 'Energy' and 'Well-Being' in Faces." *Journal of Psychology* 41 (1956): 247–254.

Mayo, C., and M. LaFrance. "Gaze Direction in Interracial Dyadic Communication." Presented at the meeting of the Eastern Psychological Association, Washington, D.C., 1973.

Medley, H. Anthony. *The Neglected Art of Being Interviewed*. Belmont, Calif.: Wadsworth, 1978.

Mehrabian, A. "Nonverbal Betrayal of Feeling." *Journal of Experimental Research in Personality* 5 (1971): 64–73.

Mehrabian, Albert. *Nonverbal Communication*. Chicago: Aldine-Atherton, 1972.

Mehrabian, A., and M. Williams. "Nonverbal Concomitants of Perceived and Intended Persuasiveness." *Journal of Personality and Social Psychology* 13 (1969): 37–58.

Molloy, John T. *Dress for Success*. New York: Wyden, 1975.

Molloy, John T. *The Men's and Women's Dress for Success Book*. Englewood Cliffs, N.J.: Prentice-Hall, 1976.

Montagu, Ashley. *Touching: The Human Significance of the Skin*. New York: Harper & Row, 1971.

Morsbach, H. "Aspects of Nonverbal Communication in Japan." *Journal of Nervous and*

Mental Disease 157 (1973): 262–277.

Newall, W. Pierson. *One on One*. New York: Focus Press, 1979.

Newsweek, "Updating the Hot Line to Moscow." April 30, 1984: 19.

Noller, Patricia. "Gaze in Married Couples." *Journal of Nonverbal Behavior* 5 (1980): 115–129.

O'Hair, Henry D., Michael J. Cody, and Margaret L. McLaughlin. "Prepared Lies, Spontaneous Lies, Machiavellianism, and Nonverbal Communication." *Human Communication Research* 7 (1981): 325–339.

O'Neal, Edgar C., Mark A. Brunault, Michael S. Carifio, Robert Troutwine, and Jaine Epstein. "Effect of Insult upon Personal Space Preferences." *Journal of Nonverbal Behavior* 5 (1980): 56–62.

Rosenfeld, Lawrence B. "Beauty and Business: Looking Good Pays Off." *New Mexico Business Journal* (April 1979) : 22–26.

*Rosenfeld, Lawrence B., and Jean M. Civikly. *With Words Unspoken: The Nonverbal Experience*. New York: Holt, Rinehart and Winston, 1976.

Rosenfeld, Lawrence B., Sallie Kartus, and Chett Ray. "Body Accessibility Revisited." *Journal of Communication* 26 (1976): 27–30.

Rosenfeld, Lawrence B., and Timothy G. Plax. "Clothing as Communication." *Journal of Communication* 27 (1977): 24–31.

*Rosenthal, Robert, and Bella M. DePaulo. "Expectancies, Discrepancies, and Courtesies in Nonverbal Communication." *Western Journal of Speech Communication* 43 (1979): 76–95.

Scheflen, Albert E. *How Behavior Means*. Garden City, N.Y.: Anchor Books, 1974.

Smith, David E., Frank N. Willis, and Joseph A. Gier. "Success and Interpersonal Touch in a Competitive Setting." *Journal of Nonverbal Behavior* 5 (1980): 26–34.

Snow, P. A. "Verbal Content and Affective Response in an Interview as a Function of Experimenter Gaze Direction." Master's thesis, Lakehead University, Thunder Bay, Ontario, Canada, 1972.

Snyder, M. "The Many Me's of the Self-Monitor." *Psychology Today* 14 (March 1980): 33–40, 92.

*Sommer, Robert. *Personal Space: The Behavioral Basis of Design*. Englewood Cliffs, N.J.: Prentice-Hall, 1969.

Sommer, Robert. *Tight Spaces*. Englewood Cliffs, N.J.: Prentice-Hall, 1978.

Streeter, L. A., R. M. Krauss, V. Geller, C. Olson, and W. Apple. "Pitch Changes During Attempted Deception." *Journal of Personality and Social Psychology* 35 (1977): 345–350.

Taylor, Anne P., and George Vlastos. *School Zone: Learning Environments for Children*. New York: Van Nostrand Reinhold, 1975.

Taylor, H. M. "American and Japanese Nonverbal Behavior." In *Papers in Japanese Linguistics* 3, J. V. Neustupny, ed. Melbourne: Monash University, 1974.

Thompson, James J. *Beyond Words: Nonverbal Communication in the Classroom*. New York: Citation Press, 1973.

Wachtel, P. "An Approach to the Study of Body Language in Psychotherapy." *Psychotherapy* 4 (1967): 97–100.

Watson, O. M. *Proxemic Behavior: A Cross-Cultural Study*. The Hague: Mouton, 1970.

Willis, Frank N., and Helen K. Hamm. "The Use of Interpersonal Touch in Securing Compliance." *Journal of Nonverbal Behavior* 5 (1980): 49–55.

Wilson, Glenn, and David Nias. "Beauty Can't Be Beat." *Psychology Today* 10 (September 1976): 96–98, 103.

Yarrow, L. J. "Research in Dimensions of Early Maternal Care." *Merrill-Palmer Quarterly* 9 (1963): 101–122.

Listening

After studying the material in this chapter

You should understand:

1. The frequency and importance of listening in interpersonal relationships.
2. Three common myths about listening.
3. The components of the listening process.
4. The four functions listening can serve.
5. The reasons people listen ineffectively.
6. Twelve guidelines for effective listening.
7. Six styles of listening that can be used to help others with their problems.

You should be able to:

1. Identify specific instances when you listen for information reception, empathy, criticism and discrimination, and other-affirmation.
2. Identify the circumstances (with whom and in what situations) when you listen ineffectively.
3. Identify the poor listening habits you exhibit in each ineffective listening situation.
4. Use the guidelines listed in the section of this chapter titled "Listening More Effectively" to develop a plan for improving your own listening behavior.
5. Identify the response style(s) you commonly use when responding to others' problems, and describe the combination of listening styles you could use to respond more effectively to these problems.

Author and psychiatrist Thomas Banville (1978) tells the following story. There was a ready-to-retire psychiatrist whose office shared the same floor with that of a young psychiatrist who had only recently entered practice. At the end of each day they would meet at the elevator, the older man fresh and full of energy, the younger one tired and worn. The younger doctor was amazed and finally asked, "How can you do it? All day long we both listen to patients describe their problems—and yet you leave work so fresh and relaxed, while I'm bushed." With a wry smile, the senior psychiatrist replied, "Who listens?"

The importance of listening

There's more than a grain of truth in this story. Listening *is* hard work, and most people *don't* give it their best effort. This shortcoming is especially discouraging because listening is a critically important communication skill. In a recent survey of adult learners' perceptions of the most important on-the-job communication skills (Wolvin, 1984), listening was ranked first. When subjects were asked what communication skills were most important in family and social settings, listening again ranked first (with expressing feelings second, building relationships third, informal conversations fourth, resolving conflicts fifth, and self-disclosure sixth).

Besides being one of the most important communication skills, listening is also the one used most often. About sixty years ago, Paul Rankin (1929) found that adults spent about 70 percent of their waking time communicating. Writing occupied 9 percent of the day, reading 16 percent, speaking 30 percent, and listening 45 percent. More recent studies confirm the importance of listening. Keefe (1971) found that executives spend about 63 percent of their communication time listening. The most recent

survey, pictured in Figure 6–1 (Barker et al., 1981), provides the following percentages for each type of communication: writing, 14; speaking, 16; reading, 17; and listening, 53. Listening was broken down further into listening to mass communication messages, such as radio and television, and listening to face-to-face messages. The former category accounted for 32 percent of the subjects' communication time, whereas the latter accounted for 21 percent—still more than any type of nonlistening communication.

Despite the importance of listening, the educational system provides surprisingly little training in this communication skill. Ralph Nichols and L. A. Stevens (1957) point out that the allotment of time for communication skills is upside-down in most school systems: The greatest amount of time is spent teaching the skills used least often. Writing is taught most often and used least; reading receives the second greatest amount of attention and is the third most used skill; speaking receives the third greatest amount of time and is the second most used skill; and listening—the most frequently used skill—is hardly taught at all (Steil, 1978). School, of course, isn't the only place where we learn how to communicate. Children manage to learn how to speak, for

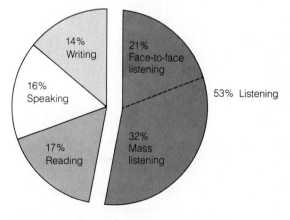

FIGURE 6–1 Types of communication activities

example, before setting foot in a classroom. Yet observing others outside the classroom is hardly an ideal way to learn good listening habits. Distracted parents and inattentive playmates are not always ideal models for a young child to emulate.

As you'll soon read, some poor listening is inevitable; but in other cases we can be better receivers by learning a few basic listening skills. The purpose of this chapter is to help you become a better listener by teaching you some important information about the subject. We'll talk about some common misconceptions concerning listening and show you what really happens when listening takes place. We'll discuss some poor listening habits and explain why they occur. Finally, we'll introduce you to some more effective alternatives, to increase both your own understanding and your ability to help others.

Myths about listening

In spite of its importance, listening is misunderstood by most people. Because these misunderstandings so greatly affect our communication, let's take a look at three common misconceptions.

Listening is not hearing   *Hearing* is the process wherein sound waves strike the eardrum and cause vibrations that are transmitted to the brain. *Listening* occurs when the brain reconstructs these electrochemical impulses into a representation of the original sound, and then gives them meaning. Barring illness, injury, or cotton plugs, hearing cannot be stopped. Your ears will pick up sound waves and transmit them to your brain whether you want them to or not.

Listening, however, is not so automatic. Many times we hear but do not listen. Sometimes we deliberately do not listen. Instead of paying

attention to words or other sounds, we avoid them. Often we block irritating sounds, such as a neighbor's power lawnmower or the roar of nearby traffic. We also stop listening when we find a subject unimportant or uninteresting. Boring stories, TV commercials, and nagging complaints are common examples of messages we avoid.

There are also cases when we honestly believe we're listening although we're merely hearing. For example, recall times when you think you've "heard it all before." It's likely that in these situations you might claim you were listening when in fact you had closed your mental doors to new information.

People who confuse listening with hearing often fool themselves into thinking that they're really understanding others, when in fact they're simply receiving sounds. As you'll see by reading this chapter, true listening involves much more than the passive act of hearing.

Skillfull listening is not natural   Another common myth is that listening is like breathing: a natural activity that people do well. "After all," this common belief goes, "I've been listening since I was a child. Why should I have to study the subject in school?"

This attitude is understandable, considering the lack of attention most schools devote to listening in comparison with other communication skills. From kindergarten to college most students receive almost constant training in reading and writing. Every year the exposure to literature continues, from Dick and Jane through Dostoyevsky. Likewise, the emphasis on writing continues without break. You could probably retire if you had a dollar for every composition, essay, research paper, and bluebook you have written since the first grade. Even spoken communication gets some attention in the curriculum. It's likely that you had a chance to take a public speaking class in high school and another one in college.

Compare all this training in reading, writing, and speaking with the almost total lack of instruction in listening. Even in college, there are few courses devoted exclusively to the subject. This state of affairs is especially ironic when you consider the fact that over 50 percent of our communication involves listening.

The truth is that listening is a skill much like speaking: Virtually everyone listens, but few people do it well. Your own experience should prove that communication often suffers due to poor listening. How many times have others misunderstood your clearest directions or expla-nations? How often have you failed to understand others because you weren't receiving their thoughts accurately? The answers to these ques-tions demonstrate the need for effective training in listening.

All listeners do not receive the same mes-sage   When two or more people are listening to a speaker, we tend to assume that they are each hearing and understanding the same message. In fact, such uniform comprehension isn't the case. Communication is *proactive:* Each person involved in a transaction of ideas or feelings responds uniquely. Recall our discussion of per-ception in Chapter 3, where we pointed out the many factors that cause each of us to perceive an event in a different manner. Physiological factors, social roles, cultural background, personal inter-ests, and needs all shape and distort the raw data we hear into uniquely different messages.

Components of listening

In his book *Listening Behavior,* Larry Barker (1971) describes the process of listening as having four components: hearing, attending, understanding, and remembering.

Hearing   As we already discussed, *hearing* is the physiological aspect of listening. It is the nonselective process of sound waves impinging on the ear. Insofar as these waves range between approximately 125 and 8000 cycles per second (frequency) and 55 to 85 decibels (loudness), the ear can respond. Hearing is also influenced by background noise. If a background noise is the same frequency as the speech sound, then the speech sound is said to be masked; however, if the background noise is of a different frequency than speech, it is called "white noise," and may or may not detract greatly from our ability to hear. Hearing is also affected by auditory fatigue, a temporary loss of hearing caused by continuous exposure to the same tone or loudness. People who spend an evening in a discotheque may experience auditory fatigue and, if they are exposed often enough, permanent hearing loss.

Attending   After the sounds are converted into electrochemical impulses and transmitted to the brain, a decision—often unconscious—is made whether to focus on them. The listening process started as a physiological one, but it quickly becomes a psychological one. An individual's needs, wants, desires, and interests determine what is *attended to.* If you're hungry, you are more likely to attend to the message about restaurants in the neighborhood from the person next to you than the competing message on the importance of communication from the speaker in front of the room.

Understanding   The next component, under-standing, is composed of several elements. First, understanding a message involves some recognition of the grammatical rules used to create that message. We find the children's books by Dr. Seuss amusing because he breaks the rules of grammar and spelling in interesting ways, and we are familiar enough with the rules to recognize this. Second, understanding depends upon our knowledge about the source of the message— whether the person is sincere, prone to lie, friendly, an adversary, and so on. Third, there is the social context. The time and place, for example, help us decide whether to take a friend's insults seriously or as a joke.

Understanding depends, generally, upon sharing common assumptions about the world. Consider the following sentences (Jerrold Katz and Jerry Foder, 1971):

I bought alligator shoes.
I bought horse shoes.

Because both sentences have the same grammatical structure and may be uttered by the same person (the first two components of understanding), they can be interpreted the same way. Both could indicate that a person bought two pairs of shoes, one made from alligator, the other from horse, or that two pairs of shoes were purchased, one for an alligator, the other for a horse. However, because of the common assumptions we share about the world, we understand that the first sentence refers to shoes made *from* alligator hides, and that the second refers either to shoes *for* horses or for playing a game.

Finally, understanding often depends on the ability to organize the information we hear into recognizable form. As early as 1948, Ralph Nichols related successful understanding to a large number of factors, most prominent among which were verbal ability, intelligence, and motivation.

A more recent investigation completed in 1979 by Timothy Plax and Lawrence Rosenfeld examined the relationship of a large number of ability,

personality, and motivational variables to the comprehension of organized and disorganized messages. They found that people who were successful at comprehending organized spoken messages, in comparison to those who were successful at comprehending disorganized messages, were generally more secure, more sensitive to others, and more willing to try to understand them. Those successful at comprehending disorganized spoken messages proved to be more insightful and versatile in their thinking.

Remembering   The ability to recall information once we've understood it is a function of several factors: the number of times the information is heard or repeated, how much information there is to store in the brain, and whether the information may be "rehearsed" or not.

Research conducted during the 1950s (Barker, 1971) revealed that people remember only about half of what they hear *immediately* after hearing it. They forget half even if they work hard at listening. This situation would probably not be too bad if the half remembered right after were retained, but it isn't. Within two months, half of the half is forgotten, bringing what we remember down to about 25 percent of the original message. This loss, however, doesn't take two months: People start forgetting immediately (within eight hours the 50 percent remembered drops to about 35 percent). Given the amount of information we process every day—from teachers, friends, the radio, TV, and other sources— the *residual message* (what we remember) is a small fraction of what we hear.

So far we have used the term "remembering" in connection with the long-term retention of information. Some, but not all, types of listening involve this long-term recall. There are actually two types of memory: short-term, limited in capacity and lasting from 20 seconds to one minute; and long-term, virtually unlimited in capacity (Wolvin and Coakley, 1985). It is possible to move information from short-term to long-term memory by rehearsing, or repeating it, as you probably do when you mentally repeat the name of an important person to whom you have just been introduced.

The results of short-term and long-term memory differ. A series of studies by Robert Bostrom (Bostrom and Bryant, 1980; Bostrom and Wald-hart, 1980) demonstrated that whereas long-term "lecture" listening is an excellent predictor of performance on a written examination (with little gain contributed by short-term listening), the opposite proved true for oral performance. In other words, short-term listening ability is closely related to measures of oral performance, whereas long-term comprehension is closely related to general measures of mental ability. These studies show that different types of listening skills are applicable in different contexts. "Listening," when used in the context of classroom performance, refers to long-term retention of information; but in the context of a conversation it most likely refers to short-term use of data. This difference helps explain why our feelings about a speaker often change when we need to listen for more than half

a minute: We are forced to put what we hear into long-term memory. It might also explain why some students who participate actively in class discussions do not achieve outstanding test scores. Their short-term listening skills are fine, but their long-term recall skills are poorly developed. .

Functions of listening

"All right," you might respond. "So I don't listen to everything I hear, I don't understand everything I listen to, and I don't remember everything I understand. I still seem to get along well enough. Why should I worry about becoming a better listener?" Author Rob Anderson (1979) suggests four benefits that can come from improving your listening skills.

Information reception   People who can understand and retain more information have a greater chance of becoming successful, however you define that term (Floyd, 1985). In school the advantages of listening effectively are obvious. Along with the skills of effective writing and reading, the ability to receive and understand the spoken word is a major key to academic success. The same holds true in the business and professional worlds. Understanding the instructions and advice of superiors and colleagues, learning about the needs and reactions of subordinates, and discovering the concerns of clients and other members of the public are important in virtually every job.

Even in personal life, the ability to receive and understand information is a key to success. Being a good listener can help you learn everything from car repair to first aid for houseplants to the existence of cheap restaurants. Socially, everyone knows the benefits of being able to hear and remember information about others whom we'd like to know better.

Empathy   A listener who was *only* able to receive and recall large amounts of information efficiently would be hardly more likable or valuable as a friend than a computer would be. Although the ability to receive data is admirable, personally helpful listeners are also able to empathize: to understand and "feel with" the emotions and thoughts of a speaker. An impressive body of research supports the idea that the ability to empathize is an important element in effective communication for many social roles: business supervisors, teachers, therapists and counselors, and of course, friends.

It's obvious that listening empathically can be a valuable way to help someone else with a problem; but developing the ability to empathize can also have personal payoffs for you as a listener. The most obvious one is the reward of having helped solve another person's problems. In addition, as an empathic listener, you can broaden your own understanding and often learn how to deal with issues in your own life. Just as it's helpful to hear the pleasures and problems of traveling to a new place before going there yourself, listening to another person's personal experiences can teach you what to think and do when you encounter similar circumstances.

Criticism and discrimination   In their interesting book *Teaching as a Subversive Activity*, Neil Postman and Charles Weingartner (1969) discuss this function of listening in their chapter on "Crap Detecting." They define a crap detector as someone who not only functions in a society, but *observes* it, noting its obsessions, fears, strengths, and weaknesses. Critical listeners are able to hear a speaker's words and understand the ideas without accepting them totally. The ability to listen analytically and critically differs radically from the kind of empathic reception just discussed, but it is equally important. Critical

listeners can help individuals and societies understand themselves and evaluate their ideas.

Other-affirmation   As Chapters 1 and 10
explain, a basic human need is to be recognized
and acknowledged by others. Listening is one of
the most fundamental means of giving this kind of
acknowledgment. The act of listening, of *choosing* to listen, is itself an affirmation of the speaker.
Whenever you listen, you are sending a nonverbal
message suggesting that the person speaking is
important. Of course, there are varying degrees
of importance, and there are also various degrees
of listening intensity reflecting this range of
valuing. A brief affirmation can come from pausing
to exchange a few minutes of chit-chat with an
acquaintance, whereas a much stronger message
of acknowledgment is reflected in your willingness
to spend hours hearing a friend talk over a
personal problem.

Barriers to listening

Given the importance of receiving information,
building empathy, critically discriminating, and
affirming others, it's obvious that listening well
can be valuable for both the receiver and the
speaker. In spite of this fact, we often do not
listen with much energy or concern. Why? Sad as
it may be, it's impossible to listen *all* the time, for
several reasons.

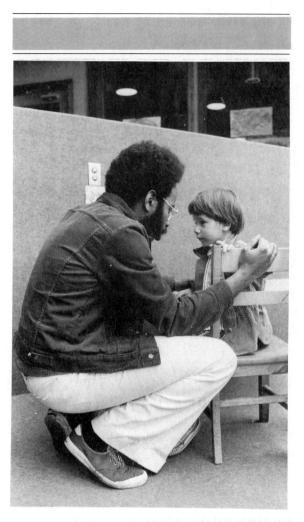

Hearing problems   If a person suffers from a
physical impairment that prevents either hearing
sounds at an adequate volume or receiving
certain auditory frequencies, then listening will
obviously suffer. Once a hearing problem has
been diagnosed, it's often possible to treat it. The
real tragedy occurs when a hearing loss goes
undiagnosed. In such cases both the person with
the defect and those surrounding can become
frustrated and annoyed at the ineffective communication that takes place. If you suspect that
you or someone you know might have a hearing
loss, it's wise to have a physician or audiologist
perform an examination.

Amount of input   The sheer amount of speech
most of us encounter every day makes it impossible to listen carefully to everything we hear. Many
of us spend almost half the time we're awake
listening to verbal messages from teachers, co-
workers, friends, family, salespeople, and total

T o be able to really listen, one should abandon or put aside all prejudices, preformulations, and daily activities. When you are in a receptive state of mind, things can be easily understood; you are listening when your real attention is given to something. But unfortunately most of us listen through a screen of resistance. We are screened with prejudices, whether religious or spiritual, psychological or scientific; or with our daily worries, desires, and fears. And with these for a screen, we listen. Therefore, we listen really to our own noise, to our own sound, not to what is being said.

J. Krishnamurti
The First and Last Personal Freedom

---

strangers (Barker et al., 1981). We often spend five or more hours a day listening to people talk. If you add these hours to those when we listen to radio and TV, you can see that it's virtually impossible for us to keep our attention totally focused for this length of time. Therefore, we periodically let our attention wander.

Personal concerns   A third reason we don't always listen carefully is that we're often wrapped up in personal concerns of more immediate importance to us than the message others are sending. It's hard to pay attention to someone else when you're anticipating an upcoming test or thinking about the wonderful time you had last night with good friends. When we still feel we have to "listen" politely to others, listening becomes a charade.

Rapid thought   Listening carefully is also difficult for a physiological reason. Although we're capable of understanding speech at rates up to 600 words per minute (Goldhaber, 1970), the average person speaks between 100 and 140 words per minute. Therefore we have a lot of "spare time" to spend with our minds while someone is talking. The temptation is to use this time in ways that don't relate to the speaker's ideas, such as thinking about personal interests,

daydreaming, planning a rebuttal, and so on. The trick is to use this spare time to understand the speaker's ideas better, rather than letting your attention wander.

"Noise"   Finally, the physical and mental worlds in which we live often present distractions that make it hard to pay attention to others. The sounds of other conversations, traffic, and music, as well as the kind of psychological noise discussed in Chapter 1, all interfere with our ability to hear well. Also, fatigue or other forms of discomfort can distract us from paying attention to a speaker's remarks. Consider, for example, how the efficiency of your listening decreases when you are seated in a crowded, hot, stuffy room full of moving people and other noises. In such circumstances even the best intentions aren't enough to ensure cogent understanding.

Before going any further we want to make it clear that we aren't suggesting that it's always desirable to listen intently, even when the circumstances permit. Given the number of messages to which we're exposed, it's impractical to expect yourself to listen well 100 percent of the time. Many of the messages sent at us aren't even worthwhile: boring stories, deceitful commercials, and remarks we've heard many times before. Given this deluge of relatively worthless information, it's important to realize that nonlistening behaviors are often reasonable. Our only concern is that you have the ability to be an accurate receiver when it really does matter.

Poor listening habits

Although it may not be necessary or desirable to listen effectively all the time, it's sad to realize that most people possess one or more bad habits that keep them from understanding truly important messages. As you read about the following poor listening behaviors, see which ones describe you.

Pseudolistening   Pseudolistening is an imitation of the real thing. "Good" pseudolisteners give the appearance of being attentive: They look you in the eye, nod and smile at the right times, and even answer you occasionally. Behind that appearance of interest, however, something entirely different is going on, for pseudolisteners use a polite facade to mask thoughts that have nothing to do with what the speaker is saying. Often pseudolisteners ignore you because of something on their mind that's more important to them than your remarks. Other times they may simply be bored, or think that they've heard what you have to say before, and so tune out your remarks. Whatever the reasons, the significant fact is that pseudolistening is really counterfeit communication.

Stage hogging   Stage hogs are only interested in expressing their ideas and don't care about what anyone else has to say. These people allow you to speak from time to time, but only so they can catch their breath, use your remarks as a basis for their own babbling, or to keep you from running away. Stage hogs really aren't conversing when they dominate others with their talk— they're making a speech and at the same time probably making an enemy.

Selective listening   Selective listeners respond only to the parts of a speaker's remarks that interest them, rejecting everything else. All of us are selective listeners from time to time; for instance, we screen out media commercials and music as we keep an ear cocked for a weather report or an announcement of time. In other cases selective listening occurs in conversations with people who expect a thorough hearing, but only get their partner's attention when the subject turns to their favorite topic—money, sex, a hobby, or some particular person. Unless and until you bring up one of these pet subjects, you might as well talk to a tree.

Filling in gaps   People who fill in the gaps like to think that what they remember makes a whole story. We remember half or less of what we hear, but these people manufacture information so that when they retell what they listened to, they can

"I'm sorry, what were you saying? I must
have dozed off for a second."

From *The New Yorker*, July 4, 1983.

At a lecture—only 12 percent listen

Bright-eyed college students in lecture halls aren't necessarily listening to the professor, the American Psychological Association was told yesterday.

If you shot off a gun at sporadic intervals and asked the students to encode their thoughts and moods at that moment, you would discover that:

- About 20 percent of the students, men and women, are pursuing erotic thoughts.
- Another 20 percent are reminiscing about something.
- Only 20 percent are actually paying attention to the lecture; 12 percent are actively listening.
- The others are worrying, daydreaming, thinking about lunch or—surprise— religion (8 percent).

This confirmation of the lecturer's worse fears was reported by Paul Cameron, 28, an assistant professor at Wayne State University in Detroit. The annual convention, which ends Tuesday, includes about 2000 such reports to 10,000 psychologists in a variety of meetings.

Cameron's results were based on a nine-week course in introductory psychology for 85 college sophomores. A gun was fired 21 times at random intervals, usually when Cameron was in the middle of a sentence.

San Francisco Sunday Examiner and Chronicle

---

give the impression they "got it all." Of course, filling in the gaps is as dangerous as selective listening: The message that's left is a distorted (not merely incomplete) version of the real message.

Assimilation to prior messages   We all have a tendency to interpret current messages in terms of similar messages remembered from the past. This phenomenon is called *assimilation to prior input.* A problem arises for those who go overboard with this tendency. They push, pull, chop, squeeze, and in other ways mutilate messages they receive to *make sure* they are consistent with what they heard in the past. This unfortunate situation occurs when the current message in some way conflicts with past beliefs.

Insulated listening   Insulated listeners are almost the opposite of their selective listening cousins. Instead of looking for something, these people avoid it. Whenever a topic arises they'd rather not deal with, insulated listeners simply fail to hear or acknowledge it. You remind them about a problem—an unfinished job, poor grades, or the like—and they'll nod or answer you and then promptly forget what you've just said.

Defensive listening   Defensive listeners take innocent comments as personal attacks. Teen-agers who perceive parental questions about friends and activities as distrustful snooping are defensive listeners, as are insecure breadwinners who explode any time their mates mention money, or touchy parents who view any questioning by their children as a threat to their authority and parental wisdom. It's fair to assume that many defensive listeners are suffering from shaky presenting images, and avoid admitting it by projecting their own insecurities onto others.

Ambushing Ambushers listen carefully to you, but only because they're collecting information that they'll use to attack what you have to say. The cross-examining prosecuting attorney is a good example of an ambusher. Needless to say, using this kind of strategy will justifiably initiate defensiveness on the other's side.

Insensitive listening Insensitive listeners offer the final example of people who don't receive another person's messages clearly. As we've said before, people often don't express their thoughts or feelings openly but instead communicate them through subtle and unconscious choice of words and/or nonverbal clues. Insensitive listeners aren't able to look beyond the words and behavior to understand hidden meanings. Instead, they take a speaker's remarks at face value.

It's important not to go overboard in labeling listeners as insensitive. Often a seemingly mechanical comment is perfectly appropriate.

When we speak we do not listen, my son and I.
I complain of slights, hurts inflicted on me.
He sings a counterpoint, but not in harmony.
Asking a question, he doesn't wait to hear.
Trying to answer, I interrupt his refrain.
This comic opera excels in disharmony only.

Lenni Shender Goldstein

Most often it is proper in situations involving *phatic* communication, in which a remark derives its meaning totally from context. For instance, the question, "How are you?" doesn't call for an answer when you pass an acquaintance on the street. In this context the statement means no more than, "I acknowledge your existence and I want to let you know that I feel friendly toward you." It is not an inquiry about the state of your health. Although insensitive listening is depressing, you would be equally discouraged to hear a litany of aches and pains every time you asked, "How's it going?"

Listening more effectively

After reading this far you probably recognize the need for better listening in many contexts. What

MOMMA by Mell Lazarus. Courtesy of Mell Lazarus and Field Newspaper Syndicate.

steps can you yourself take to become a better receiver?

Stop talking   Zeno of Citium put it most succinctly: "We have been given two ears and but a single mouth, in order that we may hear more and talk less." It is difficult to listen and talk at the same time. Talking includes the silent debating, rehearsing, and retorting that often goes on in our minds. The first step to better listening, then, is to keep quiet when another person speaks.

Put the speaker at ease   Help the speaker feel free to talk to you by working to create a supportive communication climate. Besides telling the speaker that you care about what is being said, look and act interested. Nonverbal cues associated with caring appear to be more important than a listener's verbal response. Good eye contact, a forward lean of the torso, and a warm tone of voice are three nonverbal expressions of empathy; together they seem to be twice as important as the words that accompany these behaviors (Haase and Tepper, 1972; Burgoon et al., 1984). Of course, the only way that such behaviors will be convincing over the length of a conversation is if you are sincerely interested in the speaker.

React appropriately   In order to help the speaker realize that you might be having problems understanding, offer positive and negative feedback. These behaviors can include nonverbal facial expressions: nodding, shaking your head, and so on, as well as verbal statements.

Concentrate   Focus your attention on the words, ideas, and the feelings of the speaker. Use the "extra" time you have listening to put the speaker's ideas into your own words, relate them to your experience, and think about any questions you might have.

Get rid of distractions   Avoid fidgeting with your pen, playing with a paper clip you've found, doodling, or writing the letter home that's been on your mind. Whenever possible, pick a listening environment that minimizes distractions such as passersby, telephone calls, loud noises, and so on. When you are stuck in a distracting setting, do your best to tune it out.

Don't give up too soon   Avoid interrupting until the other person expresses a complete thought: Clarity may be on the way! Statements that first seem obscure often make sense if you let the speaker talk for a while.

Avoid making assumptions   If you disagree with what you hear, don't assume that the speaker is "uninformed," "lying," or otherwise behaving dishonorably.

Don't argue mentally   Give the speaker a fair hearing; control your anger. If you argue mentally, you lose the opportunity to concentrate on what the speaker is saying. Also, when we mentally argue, we tend to place the other person in a fixed category, and thus cease responding to a unique person.

Listen for main points and supporting evidence   Critical listening will show that a speaker almost always advances one or more main points and backs them up with examples, stories, analogies, and other types of supporting material. One key to successful listening is to search for these main points, and then see if the speaker's support bears them out. A far less productive method is to dwell on an interesting story or comment while forgetting the speaker's main idea.

Share responsibility for the communication   Remember that communication is a transaction. We are simultaneously senders and

And, contrary to popular belief, it is usually the good talker who makes the best listener. A good talker (by which I do not mean the egomaniacal bore who always talks about himself) is sensitive to expression, to tone and color and inflection in human speech. Because he himself is articulate, he can help others to articulate their half-formulated feelings. His mind fills in the gaps, and he becomes, in Socrates' words, a kind of midwife for ideas that are struggling to be born.

This is why a competent psychiatrist is worth his weight in gold—and generally gets it. His listening is keyed for the half-tones and the dissonances that escape the untrained ear. For it is the mark of the truly good listener that he knows what you are saying often better than you do; and his playback is a revelation, not a recording.

Sydney J. Harris

---

receivers. Just as a good marriage requires both partners to give 100 percent of their effort, so a successful conversation demands the energy and skill of both parties.

Ask questions   Thus far we have been discussing listening methods basically passive in nature; that is, those that can be carried out silently. It's also possible to verify or increase your understanding in a more active way by asking questions to be sure you are receiving the speaker's thoughts and feelings accurately.

Although the suggestion to ask questions may seem so obvious as to be trivial, honestly ask yourself whether you take full advantage of this simple but effective method. It's often tempting to remain silent instead of being a questioner for two reasons. Sometimes you may be reluctant to show your ignorance by asking for further explanation of what seems as if it should be an obvious point. This reluctance is especially strong when the speaker's respect or liking is important to you. At such times it's a good idea to remember a quote attributed to Confucius: "He who asks a question is a fool for five minutes. He who does not ask is a fool for life."

A second reason people are often disinclined to ask questions is that they think they already understand a speaker; but do we in fact understand others as often or as well as we think? You can best answer by thinking about how often people misunderstand *you* while feeling certain that they know what you've meant. If you are aware that others should ask questions of you more often, then it's logical to assume that the same principle holds true in reverse.

Use active listening   Questioning is often a valuable tool for increasing understanding. Sometimes, however, it won't help you receive a speaker's ideas any more clearly, and it can even lead to further communication breakdown. To see how, consider the common example of asking directions to a friend's home. Suppose the instructions you've received are: "Drive about a mile and then turn left at the traffic signal." Now imagine that a few common problems exist in this simple message. First, suppose that your friend's idea of a mile differs from yours: Your mental picture of the distance is actually closer to two miles, whereas your friend's is closer to 300 yards. Next, consider that "traffic signal" really means "stop sign"; after all, it's common for us to think one thing and say another. Keeping these problems in mind, suppose you tried to verify your understanding of the directions by asking, "After I turn at the light, how far should I go?" to which your friend replied that the house is the third from the corner. Clearly, if you parted after this exchange, you would encounter a lot of frustration before finding the elusive residence.

What was the problem here? It's easy to see that questioning might not have helped you, for your original idea of how far to drive and where to turn were mistaken. Contained in such mistakes is the biggest problem with questioning, for such inquiries don't tell you whether you have accurately received the information that has *already* been sent.

Now consider another kind of feedback—one that would tell you whether you understand what had already been said before you asked additional questions. This sort of feedback involves restating in your own words the message you thought the speaker just sent, without adding anything new: "So you're telling me to drive down to the traffic light by the high school and turn toward the mountains, is that it?" Immediately sensing the problem, your friend could then reply, "Oh no, that's way too far. I meant that you should drive to the four-way stop by the park and turn there. Did I say stop light? I always do that when I mean stop sign!"

This simple step of restating what you thought the speaker said before going on is commonly termed *active listening,* and it is an important tool for effective listening. Remember that what is significant in active listening is to *paraphrase* the sender's words, not to parrot them. In other words, restate what you think the speaker has said in your own terms as a way of cross-checking the information. If you simply repeat the speaker's comments *verbatim,* you'll sound foolish or hard of hearing, and just as important, you still might be misunderstanding what's been said.

Because it's an unfamiliar way of responding, active listening may feel awkward when you first begin to use it; but by paraphrasing occasionally at first and then gradually increasing the frequency of such responses, you can begin to learn the benefits of this method.

Listening to help

So far we've talked about how becoming a better listener can help you to understand other people more often and more clearly. If you use the skills presented so far, you should be rewarded by communicating far more accurately with others every day. There's yet another way in which listening can improve your relationships. Strange as it may sound, you can often help other people solve their own problems simply by learning to listen—actively and with concern.

Before we introduce various methods of listening as a method of helping, read the following situations and think about how you would respond in each of them.

- You're speaking with a friend who has just been rejected from getting a badly wanted job. "I don't know what to do," your friend tells you. "I studied and worked two years to get that job, and it's all been for nothing."
- Another friend confesses, "My marriage seems to be on the rocks. We hardly talk anymore. Everything triggers a fight. We're in a rut, and it seems to be getting worse."
- At work or school, an acquaintance approaches you and says, "I can't decide whether to stay here or move up north. I have plenty of friends here and things are pretty good. On the other hand, I'd hate to give up a good job opportunity and find out it was a mistake. What do you think I should do?"

There are several ways in which you could have responded to these problems, none inherently good or bad. There's a proper time and place for each kind of response. Problems usually occur, though, when we use these ways in the wrong situations or depend upon one or two styles of response for all situations.

As you read the following descriptions of ways of responding, see which ones you most fre-quently used in the previous exercise, and notice the results that probably would have occurred.

Advising   When approached with another's problem, most people tend to advise: to help by offering a solution. Although such a response is sometimes valuable, often it isn't as helpful as you might think.

Often your suggestion may not offer the best course to follow, in which case it can even be harmful. There's often a temptation to tell others how we would behave in their place, but it's important to realize that what's right for one person may not be right for another. A related consequence of advising is that it often allows others to avoid responsibility for their decisions. A partner who follows a suggestion of yours that doesn't work out can always pin the blame on you. Finally, often people simply don't want advice: They may not be ready to accept it, instead needing simply to talk out their thoughts and feelings.

Before offering advice, then, you need to be sure that three conditions are present. First, you should be confident that your advice is correct. It's essential to resist the temptation to act like an authority on matters about which you know little. It's equally important to remember that just because a course of action worked for you doesn't guarantee that it will be correct for everybody. Second, you need to be sure that the person seeking your advice is truly ready to accept it. In this way you can avoid the frustration of making good suggestions, only to find that the person with the problem had another solution in mind all the time. Finally, when offering advice, you should be certain that the receiver won't blame you if the advice doesn't work out. You may be offering the suggestions, but the choice and responsibility of following them is up to the other person.

Judging   A judging response evaluates the sender's thoughts or behaviors in some way. The judgment may be favorable ("That's a good idea" or "You're on the right track now") or unfavorable ("An attitude like that won't get you anywhere"). In either case it implies that the person doing the judging is in some way qualified to pass judgment on the speaker's thoughts or actions.

Sometimes negative judgments are purely critical. How many times have you heard such responses as "Well, you asked for it!" or "I *told* you so!" or "You're just feeling sorry for yourself"? Although comments like these can sometimes serve as a verbal slap that brings problem-holders to their senses, they usually make matters worse by arousing defensiveness in the other person. After all, suggesting that someone is foolish or mistaken is an attack on the presenting image that most people would have a hard time ignoring or accepting.

There are other cases where negative judgments are less critical. These involve what we usually call constructive criticism, which is intended to help the problem-holder improve in the future. Friends give this sort of response about everything from the choice of clothing to jobs to friends. Another common setting for constructive criticism occurs in school, where instructors evaluate students' work in order to help them master concepts and skills. Even constructive criticism runs the risk of arousing defensiveness because it may threaten the self-concept of the person at whom it is directed.

Judgments have the best chance of being received when two conditions exist. First, the person with the problem should have requested an evaluation from you. In addition, your judgments should be genuinely constructive and not designed to be "putdowns." If you can remember to follow these two guidelines, your judgments will probably be less frequent and better received.

Analyzing   In analyzing a situation, the listener offers an interpretation to a speaker's message ("I think what's really bothering you is . . . "; "She's doing it because . . . "; or "Maybe the problem started when he . . . "). Interpretations are often effective ways to help people with problems to consider alternative meanings to a situation—ways they would have never thought of without your help. Sometimes a clear analysis will make a confusing problem suddenly clear, either suggesting a solution or at least providing an understanding of what is going on.

In other cases, an analysis can create more problems than it solves. There are two problems with analyzing. First, your interpretation may not be correct, in which case the sender may become even more confused by accepting it. Second, even if your analysis is accurate, sharing it with the sender might not be useful. There's a chance that it'll arouse defensiveness (analysis implies superiority and evaluativeness). Besides, the receiver may not be able to understand your view of the problem without working it out personally.

How can you know when it's helpful to offer an analysis? There are several guidelines to follow. First, it's important to offer your interpretation in a tentative way rather than as absolute fact. There's a big difference between saying, "Maybe the reason is . . . " and insisting, "This is the truth." Second, your analysis ought to have a reasonable chance of being correct. We've already said that a wild, unlikely interpretation can leave a person more confused than before. Third, you ought to be sure that the other person will be receptive to your analysis. Even if you're completely accurate, your thoughts won't help if the problem-holder isn't ready to consider what you say. Finally, you should be sure that your motive for offering an analysis is truly to help the other person. It's sometimes tempting to offer an analysis to show how brilliant you are or even to make the other person feel bad for not having thought of the right answer in the first place. Needless to say, an analysis offered under these conditions isn't helpful.

Questioning   A few pages ago we talked about questioning as one way for you to understand others better. A questioning response can also be a way of helping others think about their problem and understand it more clearly. For example, questioning can help a problem-holder define vague ideas more precisely. You might respond to a friend with a line of questioning: "You said Greg has been acting 'differently' toward you lately. What has he been doing?" "You told your roommates that you wanted them to be more helpful in keeping the place clean. What would you like them to do?"

Questions can also encourage a problem-holder to examine a situation in more detail by talking either about what happened or about personal feelings. For example: "How did you feel when they turned you down? What did you do then?" This type of questioning is particularly helpful when you are dealing with someone who is quiet or is unwilling under the circumstances to talk about the problem very much.

Although asking questions can definitely be helpful, there are two dangers that can come from using this style too much or at the wrong times. The first is that your questions may lead the help-seeker on a wild goose chase away from a solution to the problem. For instance, asking someone, "When did the problem begin?" might provide some clue about how to solve it—but it could also lead to a long digression that would only confuse matters. As with advice, it's important to be sure you're on the right track before asking questions.

A second danger is that questioning can also be a way of disguising advice or criticism. We've all been questioned by parents, teachers, or other figures who seemed to be trying to trap us or indirectly to guide us. In this way, questioning becomes a strategy and often implies that the person doing the asking already has some idea of what direction the discussion should take.

Supporting   Support can take several forms. Sometimes it involves reassuring: "You've got nothing to worry about—I know you'll do a good job." In other cases, support comes through comforting: "Don't worry. We all love you." We can also support people in need by distracting them with humor, kidding, and joking.

Sometimes a person needs encouragement, and in these cases a supporting response can be the best thing. In many other instances this kind of comment isn't helpful at all; in fact, it can even make things worse. Telling a person who is obviously upset that everything is all right or joking about what seems like a serious problem can communicate the idea that you don't think the problem is really worth all the fuss. People might see your comments as a putdown, leaving them feeling worse than before. As with the other styles we've discussed, supporting *can* be helpful, but only in certain circumstances.

Active listening   In active listening the receiver makes a paraphrasing statement that reflects both the *feelings* and the *thoughts* of the speaker. Imagine that a friend complained about a recent assignment: "I killed myself working on that paper. I deserved more than a lousy B-minus." An active listening response to such a comment would paraphrase both the speaker's ideas and the underlying emotions: "Sounds like you're really disappointed because the professor didn't appreciate the work you did."

Reflecting back a speaker's ideas and feelings in this way can be surprisingly helpful. First, it helps clarify the other person's concerns. If your paraphrasing is accurate, the speaker has a clear picture of the problem; and if you guess wrong, the speaker will correct you, and in doing so clarify the situation. In addition, your mention of the speaker's emotions can open up an important, unexplored area of concern. The emotional responses we have to problems are often more important than the problems themselves. For example, the grade on the paper mentioned above might only be a small part of your companion's problem, and focusing the discussion on that assignment might cause you both to ignore the other related areas of concern. On the other hand, encouraging the speaker to talk about frustration, anger, or disappointment lets the actual subject of the problem surface.

Besides the act of paraphrasing, a key element of active listening is empathy, or as an unknown writer put it, "To see with the eyes of another, to hear with the ears of another, to feel with the heart of another." The purpose of expressing empathy is, according to Byrnes and Yamamoto (1981), "to create an atmosphere of reassurance and understanding so that the feelings of the client [or any other person with whom you are interacting] may be expressed without mistrust or fear" (p. 343).

George Gazda and his associates (1977, p. 64) describe four types of response that they use to train teachers to respond empathically to students. The four levels are:

1. An irrelevant or hurtful response that does not appropriately attend to the surface feelings of the other person.
2. A response that only partially communicates an awareness of the surface feelings of the other person.
3. A response conveying understanding at the other person's level of expression. Surface feelings, in other words, are accurately reflected.

4. A response conveying understanding beyond the other person's level of immediate awareness. Underlying feelings are identified and reflected.

You can practice identifying each level of response by picturing the following situation, presented by Gazda: One of your married friends, a student in several classes with you, tells you the following: "It's getting tough to stay in school with what's happening at home. My family is losing out. With all the school work piled on, I have no time just to be with them and relax." Rate each of the following responses on a 1 (not empathic) to 4 (highly empathic) scale.

_____ 1. "Rearrange your schedule so you can be home more."

_____ 2. "You feel like an inadequate father and husband—as if you aren't really a part of the family because you don't have enough time to spend with them. That must feel terrible."

_____ 3. "You feel like you're spreading yourself too thin, taking on too much and missing out on your family life."

_____ 4. "You feel down because you're not with your family as much as you'd like because of school."

The first response is rated 1 on the empathy scale. It ignores surface feelings, is criticizing, and is probably irrelevant since the schedule is already set. The third response rates a 2: It suggests only a partial awareness of the other's feelings and ignores much of the other's statement. The fourth response rates a 3 on the empathy scale. It communicates an awareness of the surface feeling ("down"), and neither adds nor subtracts from what was said. This response says "I heard what you said and am attempting to understand how you feel." The second response earns a rating of 4. It goes beyond the speaker's present awareness and conveys an understanding of the underlying problem—feeling like an inadequate family member—as well as reflecting the content of what was said.

There are several reasons why active listening works so well. First, it takes the burden off you as a friend. Simply being there to understand what's on someone's mind often makes it possible to clarify the problems. You don't have to know all the answers to help. Also, helping by active listening means you don't need to guess at reasons or solutions that might not be correct. Thus, both you and your friend are saved from going on a wild goose chase after incorrect solutions.

A second advantage of active listening is that it's an efficient way to get through layers of hidden meanings. Often people express their ideas, problems, or feelings in strangely coded ways. Active listening can sometimes help cut through to the real meaning. Not too long ago a student came to an instructor and asked, "How many people get Ds and Fs in this class?" The instructor could have taken the question at face value and answered it, but instead he tried active listening. He replied, "Sounds like you've got some fears of doing poorly in here." After a few minutes of listening the instructor learned that the student was afraid that getting a low grade in a communication class would be equal to failing as a person.

The third advantage of active listening is that it's usually the best way to encourage people to share more of themselves with you. Knowing that you're interested will make them feel less threatened, and many will be willing to let down some of their defenses. In this sense active listening is simply a good way to learn more about someone, and a good foundation on which to build a relationship.

Regardless of the advantages, active listening isn't appropriate in all situations when someone wants help. Sometimes people are simply looking

for information and not trying to work out their feelings. At such times active listening would be out of place. If someone asks you for the time of day, you'd do better simply to give the information than to respond by saying, "You want to know what time it is." If you're fixing dinner and someone wants to know when it will be ready, it would be exasperating to reply, "You're interested in knowing when we'll be eating."

However, people do often hide an important feeling behind an innocent-sounding statement or question, and in such cases active listening on your part can usually bring their real concern into the open. But don't go overboard with the technique. Usually, if there's a feeling hidden behind a question you'll recognize some accompanying nonverbal clue—a change in your friend's facial expression, tone of voice, posture, and so on. It takes attention, concentration, and caring on your part.

You should realize that success in using active listening will depend on the attitude you bring to a situation. Too often people will think of active listening as a kind of gimmick they can use when some unpleasant situation arises. If you think about the technique this way, it is almost sure to fail. In fact, unless you truly mean what you say, you'll come across as being manipulative, phony, and uncaring. As you practice this listening skill, try to keep these points in mind:

1. *Don't actively listen unless you truly want to help the person.* There's nothing wrong with being too busy or preoccupied to help. You'll be doing both yourself and the other person a disservice if you pretend to care when you really don't.
2. *Don't try to listen actively if you're not willing to take the necessary time.* Listening with feedback isn't easy. If you're willing to make the effort, you'll probably be rewarded, but you'll only lose the speaker's trust if you commit yourself and then don't follow through.
3. *Don't try to impose your ideas on the other person.* Active listening means accepting other people's feelings and trusting that they can find their own solutions. Your efforts to moralize, to suggest, or to change the speaker might be helpful, but if you decide to use these approaches, do so honestly—don't mask them in the guise of active listening.
4. *Keep your attention focused on the sender.* Sometimes, as you listen to others share feelings, it's easy to become defensive, to relate their thoughts to your own life, or to seek further

information just to satisfy your own curiosity. Remember that active listening is a form of helping someone else. Keep your energy focused on this goal.

Readings

Anderson, Rob. *Students as Real People: Interpersonal Communication and Education.* Rochelle Park, N.J.: Hayden, 1979.

Arnett, R. C., and G. Nakagawa. "The Assumptive Roots of Empathetic Listening: A Critique." *Communication Education* 32 (October 1983): 368–378.

Axline, Virginia M. *Dibs: In Search of Self.* New York: Ballantine Books, 1967.

*Baddeley, Alan D. *The Psychology of Memory.* New York: Basic Books, 1976.

Banville, T. G. *How to Listen—How to Be Heard.* Chicago: Nelson-Hall, 1978.

Barker, L., R. Edwards, C. Gaines, K. Gladney, and F. Holley. "An Investigation of Proportional Time Spent in Various Communication Activities by College Students." *Journal of Applied Communication Research* 8 (1981): 101–109.

*Barker, Larry L. *Listening Behavior.* Englewood Cliffs, N.J.: Prentice-Hall, 1971.

Beier, Ernst G., and Evans G. Valens. *People-Reading: How We Control Others, How They Control Us.* New York: Stein and Day, 1975.

Bostrom, Robert N., and Carol L. Bryant. "Factors in the Retention of Information Presented Orally: The Role of Short-Term Listening." *Western Journal of Speech Communication* 44 (1980): 137–145.

*Bostrom, Robert N., and Enid S. Waldhart. "Components in Listening Behavior: The Role of Short-Term Memory." *Human Communication Research* 6 (1980): 221–227.

Burgoon, Judee K., David B. Buller, Jerold L. Hale, and Mark A. de Turck. "Relational Messages Associated with Nonverbal Behaviors."

Human Communication Research 10 (1984): 351–378.

Byrnes, D. A., and K. Yamamoto. "Some Reflections of Empathy." *School Counselor* 28 (1981): 343–345.

Cleveland, B. "Active Listening Yields Better Discussion." *Social Studies* 7 (1980): 218–221.

Dittmann, Allen T. "Developmental Factors in Conversational Behavior." *Journal of Communication* 22 (1972): 404–423.

*Floyd, James J. *Listening: A Practical Approach.* Glenview, Ill.: Scott, Foresman, 1985.

Foulke, Emerson, and Thomas Stricht. "Review of Research in Time-Compressed Speech." In *Time-Compressed Speech,* Sam Duker, ed. Metuchen, N.J.: Scarecrow Press, 1974.

*Gazda, George M., Frank R. Asbury, Fred J. Balzer, William C. Childers, and Richard P. Walters. *Human Relations Development: A Manual for Educators,* 2d ed. Boston: Allyn and Bacon, 1977.

Goldhaber, Gerald M. "Listener Comprehension of Compressed Speech as a Function of the Academic Grade Level of Subjects." *Journal of Communication* 20 (1970): 167–173.

Goss, B. *Processing Communication: Information Processing in Interpersonal Communication.* Belmont, Calif.: Wadsworth, 1982.

Haase, R. F., and D. T. Tepper. "Non-Verbal Components of Empathic Communication." *Journal of Counseling Psychology* 19 (1972): 417–424.

Haney, William V. *Communication and Interpersonal Relations: Text and Cases,* 4th ed. Homewood, Ill.: Richard D. Irwin, Inc., 1979.

Katz, Jerrold J., and Jerry A. Foder. "The Structure of a Semantic Theory." In *Readings in the Philosophy of Language,* Jay F. Rosenberg and Charles Travis, eds. Englewood Cliffs, N.J.: Prentice-Hall, 1971.

Keefe, W. F. *Listen Management.* New York: McGraw-Hill, 1971.

Kelley, Charles M. "Empathic Listening." In *Small Group Communication: A Reader,* 4th ed., Robert Cathcart and Larry Samovar, eds. Dubuque, Iowa: Wm. C. Brown, 1984.

Nichols, Ralph G. "Factors in Listening Comprehension." *Speech Monographs* 15 (1948): 154–163.

*Nichols, Ralph G., and L. A. Stevens. *Are You Listening?* New York: McGraw-Hill, 1957.

Palamatier, Robert A., and George McNinch. "Source of Gains in Listening Skill: Experimental or Pre-Test Experience?" *Journal of Communication* 22 (1972): 70–76.

Plax, Timothy G., and Lawrence B. Rosenfeld. "Receiver Differences and the Comprehension of Spoken Messages." *Journal of Experimental Education* 48 (1979): 23–28.

Postman, Neil, and Charles Weingartner. *Teaching as a Subversive Activity.* New York: Delacorte Press, 1969.

Rankin, Paul. "Listening Ability." In *Proceedings of the Ohio State Educational Conference's Ninth Annual Session,* 1929.

Rogers, Carl R. *On Becoming a Person.* Boston: Houghton-Mifflin, 1961.

Rossiter, Charles M. "Sex of the Speaker, Sex of the Listener, and Listening Comprehension." *Journal of Communication* 22 (1972): 64–69.

Steil, Lyman K. "Listen My Students . . . and You Shall Learn." *Towards Better Teaching* 11 (Fall 1978).

Steil, Lyman K., Larry L. Barker, and Kittie W. Watson. *Effective Listening: Key to Your Success.* Reading, Mass.: Addison-Wesley, 1983.

Stewart, J. "Interpretive Listening: An Alternative to Empathy." *Communication Education* 32 (October 1983): 379–391.

Weaver, Carl. *Human Listening: Processes and Behavior.* Indianapolis: Bobbs-Merrill, 1972.

*Wolff, F., N. C. Marsnik, W. S. Tacey, and R. G. Nichols. *Perceptive Listening.* New York: Holt, Rinehart and Winston, 1983.

Wolvin, Andrew D. "Meeting the Communication
Needs of the Adult Learner." *Communication
Education* 33 (1984): 267–271.

*Wolvin, Andrew, and Carolyn Coakley. *Listening,*
2d ed. Dubuque, Iowa: Wm. C. Brown, 1985.

Relationships

Seven

After studying the material in this chapter

You should understand:

1. The four dimensions of interpersonal relationships.

2. The ways content and relational messages are communicated in interpersonal relationships.

3. Eight reasons why people form relationships.

4. Knapp's stages of relationship formation and dissolution.

5. The communication-related characteristics that distinguish high-quality relationships.

6. The pressures that operate against friendships.

7. Sex-related variables influencing friendships.

8. Guidelines for making friendships work.

You should be able to:

1. Identify your relationships according to context, time, intimacy, and control/affinity dimensions.

2. Describe whether an important relationship of yours is complementary, symmetrical, or parallel.

3. Describe the progression of relational stages in one of your important relationships.

4. Identify the type of interpersonal attraction that explains an important relationship in which you are involved.

5. Describe how you can apply the guidelines on pages 175–176 to maintain or improve an important relationship.

Relationship is one of those words that people use a great deal, yet have a hard time defining. Take a moment to see if you can explain the term. It isn't as easy as it might seem.

The dictionary defines a relationship as "the mode in which two or more things stand to one another." This definition is true as far as it goes. You are tall in relation to some people and short in relation to others, and we are more or less wealthy only by comparison to others; but physical and economic relationships don't tell us much that is useful about interpersonal communication.

Interpersonal relationships involve the way people deal with one another *socially*. What is it about their social interaction that defines a relationship? What makes some relationships "good" and others "bad"? We can answer this question by recalling the three kinds of social needs introduced in Chapter 1: inclusion, control, and affection. When we judge the quality of a personal relationship, we are usually describing how well it meets those social needs. We can define the term *interpersonal relationship* as an association in which the parties meet each other's social needs to some degree.

Dimensions of interpersonal relationships

What qualities define a relationship? Is it the amount of time we spend together? The things we say and do? The way we feel about each other? By examining several ways of categorizing relationships we can take a fresh look at what makes some communication truly interpersonal.

Context   The most obvious way to classify relationships is by the contexts in which they occur. For example, the family provides a rich set of relationships for most of us. We also form relationships on the job, with fellow workers and in

some cases with members of the public. School, neighborhood, religious faith, sports, and hobbies—all these contexts form bases for relationships.

Despite the visibility of the communication setting, context doesn't play much role in shaping *interpersonal* relationships. Recall from Chapter 1 that we defined interpersonal communication as possessing three unique qualities: a minimum of stereotyping, development of unique rules, and increased self-disclosure. Once we consider these factors, it's apparent that no context guarantees them. Sadly, even husbands and wives or parents and children can have impersonal, superficial relationships. The parties go through the motions, rarely revealing themselves or working to create a unique arrangement that reflects their personalities. Clearly, then, context isn't useful as a basis for categorizing interpersonal relationships.

Time   The length of time a relationship lasts is one measure of its importance. We have all heard the line "our relationship goes back a long way," and we usually consider such statements as indicating how strong and valuable the relationship is. The same principle holds true for enemies. The length of time a dispute lasts is one measure of its importance. Not *all* long-standing relationships are important, however. Some can last for years and remain relatively superficial, like the neighbors who politely exchange clichés about the weather from time to time.

A better indicator of importance is the amount of time we *choose* to spend with others. You might work—or even party—with certain people out of obligation, but avoid them whenever possible. Time voluntarily spent is a partial indicator of a relationship's importance, but *how* the parties communicate when together is even more important, as we will now see.

Intimacy   Three kinds of intimacy help determine the importance of a relationship: intellectual, emotional, and physical. It is possible to be intimate with someone in one of these ways and not in others. You may, for example, share a relationship in which you're not physically close, but highly intimate on an emotional level.

One of the most prominent theories about how intimacy develops in relationships has been described by Irwin Altman and Dalmas Taylor in their book *Social Penetration: The Development of Interpersonal Relationships* (1973). These authors suggest that relationships develop in increments, moving from superficial to more personal levels. As two people learn more about each other, primarily through the process of self-disclosure, the relationship gains importance. Depending on the *breadth* of the information shared (for example, the number of topics you discuss) and the *depth* of that information, a rela-

tionship can be defined as casual or intimate. In the case of a casual relationship, the breadth may be high, but not the depth. A more intimate relationship is likely to have high breadth and high depth. Altman and Taylor visualize these two factors as an image of concentric circles (see Figure 7–1). Depth increases as you disclose information that is central to the relationship, information not available unless you provide it; for example, your personal goals, fears, and self-images. Altman and Taylor see relationship development as a progression from the periphery to the center of the circle, a process that typically takes time.

Based on this theory of *social penetration*, you can visualize a diagram in which a husband's relationship with his wife has high breadth and high depth, his relationship with his friend has low breadth and high depth, and his relationship with his boss is one of low breadth–low depth. Imagine what your own relationship with various people would look like. Figure 7–2 provides a typical example.

The Altman-Taylor model can be used to predict a variety of relationships. According to the theory, relationships proceeding rapidly to the central areas can be fragile. For example, an experience such as a "one-night stand" of sexual intimacy often lacks the accompanying transactions that build trust and understanding. When interpersonal conflict erupts, the relationship crumbles.

Control and affinity   An intimate relationship isn't always friendly or equal. Robert Carson (1969) argues that relationships can be described along two dimensions. One of these dimensions measures a range of behaviors from dominance or control on the one hand to unassertive, following behaviors on the other. This bipolar dimension is called "dominance/submission." The other dimension ranges from accepting, friendly, loving behavior at one extreme to hostile, punishing

"Actually, I'm seeking a meaningless relationship."
Drawing by Richter; © 1970 The New Yorker Magazine, Inc.

actions at the other. Carson terms this spectrum "love/hate," although "like/dislike" is probably a better label.

The most thorough treatment of this approach was carried out by Timothy Leary (1955, 1957). He described how this two-dimensional structure can characterize a variety of relationships (see Figure 7–3). For example, a cold and unfeeling person can be described as dominant/hostile; a person who is distrustful is hostile/submissive; a trusting person is submissive/loving; and someone who actively tries to help others can be characterized as loving/dominant.

Communication scholars frequently use the scheme first developed by Watzlawick, Beavin, and Jackson (1967) and later modified by Phillips and Wood (1983) and Wilmot (1979) to describe the distribution of control in a relationship. This scheme identifies three distinct relational structures: *complementary, symmetrical,* and *parallel.* A *complementary* relational structure is based on differences between the partners that complete each other. By their different behaviors, each

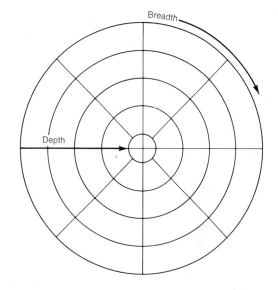

FIGURE 7–1   The Altman-Taylor model of social penetration

fulfills the other's needs. For example, a traditional marriage with a dominant husband and submissive wife is a complementary relationship. The male is expected to earn the money on which to live, whereas the female is expected to stay home

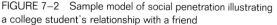

FIGURE 7–2   Sample model of social penetration illustrating a college student's relationship with a friend

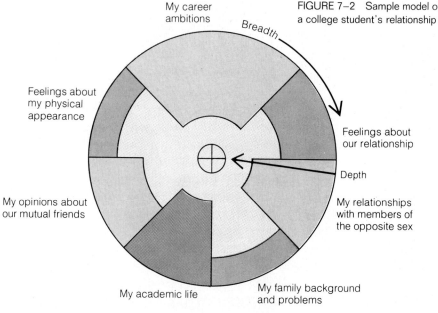

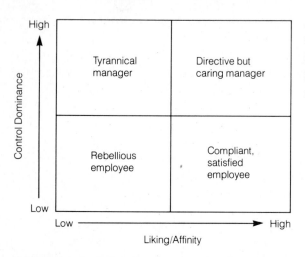

FIGURE 7–3 Interaction between control and affinity dimensions in working relationships

and take care of the house and children. The relationship is stable; they work as a team, and both perceive they can do more together than either could do individually. According to Phillips and Wood (1983, p. 151), two individuals in a complementary relationship "go together so that each works better in combination than alone."

Several attributes define a complementary relationship (Phillips and Wood, 1983; Wilmot, 1979): the relationship is based on differences between the partners; one partner occupies the superior or "one-up" position and the other occupies the submissive or "one-down" position; both individuals need each other to confirm their identities (for example, the submissive spouse is submissive only in the presence of the dominant spouse); each partner has distinct roles, rights, and obligations; the relationship reduces the partners' ability to function independently; and if the relationship is terminated, both partners are debilitated. Stability characterizes the relationship and is its avowed virtue.

Unlike the complementary structure, the *symmetrical* structure implies equality. A symmetrical structure is a balanced one: each of the individu-

als contributes equally to all facets of the relationship with the goal of balance or reciprocity. Balance and reciprocity are often a result of similarity between the partners; in fact, this similarity may be a source of its attraction (Hinde, 1979).

These attributes define a symmetrical relationship (Phillips and Wood, 1983; Wilmot, 1979): power is distributed equally among the partners; partners behave as if they are of equal status; each partner may initiate action; partners are highly independent (for example, each claims the right to make personal decisions, keep a private domain both inside and outside the relationship, and pursue a career); and both partners attempt to be either "one-up" or "one-down," that is, dominant or submissive. Partners in a symmetrical relationship believe that the structure of their relationship helps preserve their individuality.

A hybrid relational structure, *parallel,* combines the features of both the complementary and symmetrical structures. In this structure, participants are willing to employ both complementary and symmetrical communication patterns in their relationship (Phillips and Wood, 1983).

Here are the attributes of a parallel structure (Phillips and Wood, 1983; Wilmot, 1979): partners are committed to a common direction; partners realize that contributions to the relationship will vary from time to time and situation to situation; partners believe a certain amount of independence is necessary in some areas of the relationship; and both partners pursue common activities while retaining some separate interests. Flexibility is the hallmark of this relationship structure, with partners using either complementary or symmetrical interchanges depending upon the apparent needs of the relationship at a given moment.

In a recent investigation of perceptions of partners in each of the three types of relational structures (Harrington, 1984), it was found that the parallel relationship structure was favored by the vast majority of subjects. Apparently the open

m ost conversations seem to be carried out on two levels, the verbal level and the emotional level. The verbal level contains those things which are socially acceptable to say, but it is used as a means of satisfying emotional needs. Yesterday a friend related something that someone had done to her. I told her why I thought the person had acted the way he had and she became very upset and started arguing with me. Now, the reason is clear. I had been listening to her words and had paid no attention to her feelings. Her words had described how terribly this other person had treated her, but her emotions had been saying, "Please understand how I felt. Please accept my feeling the way I did." The last thing she wanted to hear from me was an explanation of the other person's behavior.

Hugh Prather

---

nature of the relationship allowed each of the subjects to maintain the relationship without compromising individual identity. The parallel structure also reflects the current popular view of a progressive relationship. The flexibility of the structure allows for greater social adaptability, an important and attractive asset in a rapidly changing social and professional world. The most rejected relationship was the complementary one with the female dominant and the male submissive, results that confirm Kaplan and Sedney's (1980) conclusion that in the United States people currently perceive such a family structure as pathological and a negative influence on children.

Communication in interpersonal relationships

By now it is clear that interpersonal relationships can be described in terms of their context, length, intimacy, locus of control, and affinity. How are these dimensions communicated?

Content and relational messages As you learned in Chapter 1, every message has a content and a relational dimension. The most obvious component of most messages is their content—the subject being discussed. The content of

statements like "It's your turn to do the dishes" or "I'm busy Saturday night" is obvious.

Content messages aren't the only information being exchanged when two people communicate. In addition, every message—both verbal and nonverbal—also has a second, *relational* dimension, which makes statements about how the parties feel toward one another (Watzlawick, Beavin, and Jackson, 1967, pp. 80–83). These relational messages deal with one or more of the social needs we have been discussing. Consider the two examples we just mentioned:

- Imagine two ways of saying, "It's your turn to do the dishes," one that is demanding and another that is matter-of-fact. Notice how the different nonverbal messages make statements about how the sender views control in this part of the relationship. The demanding tone says, in effect, "I have a right to tell you what to do around the house," whereas the matter-of-fact one suggests, "I'm just reminding you of something you might have overlooked."
- You can easily imagine two ways to deliver the statement "I'm busy Saturday night," one with little affection and the other with much liking.

Like these messages, every statement we make goes beyond discussing the subject at hand

and says something about the way the speaker feels about the recipient. You can prove this fact by listening for the relational messages implicit in your own statements to others and theirs to you.

Most of the time we are unaware of the relational messages that bombard us every day. Sometimes these messages don't capture our awareness because they match our belief about the amount of control, liking, or intimacy that is appropriate in a relationship. For example, you probably won't be offended if your boss tells you to drop everything and tackle a certain job, because you agree that supervisors have the right to direct employees. However, if your boss delivered the order in a condescending, sarcastic, or abusive tone of voice, you would probably be offended. Your complaint wouldn't be with the order itself, but with the way it was delivered. "I may work for this company," you might think, "but I'm not a slave or an idiot. I deserve to be treated like a human being."

Expression of relational messages   Exactly how are relational messages communicated? As the boss–employee example suggests, they are usually expressed nonverbally. To test this fact for yourself, imagine how you could act while saying, "Can you help me for a minute?" in a way that communicates each of the following relationships:

> superiority
> helplessness
> friendliness
> aloofness
> sexual desire
> irritation

Although nonverbal behaviors are a good source of relational messages, remember that they are ambiguous. The sharp tone you take as a personal insult might be due to fatigue, and the interruption you take as an attempt to ignore your

ideas might be a sign of pressure that has nothing to do with you. Before you jump to conclusions about relational clues, it is a good idea to verify the accuracy of your interpretation with the other person: "When you cut me off, I got the idea you're angry at me. Is that right?"

Not all relational messages are nonverbal. Social scientists use the term *metacommunication* to describe messages that refer to other messages. In other words, metacommunication is communication about communication. Whenever we discuss a relationship with others, we are metacommunicating: "I wish we could stop arguing so much," or "I appreciate how honest you've been with me." Verbal metacommunication is an essential ingredient in successful relationships. Sooner or later there are times when it becomes necessary to talk about what is going on between you and the other person. The ability to focus on the kinds of issues described in this chapter can be the tool for keeping the relationship on track.

Why we form relationships

Why do we form relationships with some people and not with others? Sometimes we have no choice: Children can't select their parents, and most workers aren't able to choose their colleagues. In many other cases, however, we seek out some people and actively avoid others. Social scientists have collected an impressive body of research on interpersonal attraction (see Berscheid and Walster, 1978; Hamachek, 1982).

Appearance   Most people claim that we should judge others on the basis of how they act, not how they look. The reality, however, is quite the opposite, especially in the early stages of a relationship. In one study, a group of over 700 men and women were matched as blind dates, allegedly for a "computer dance." After the party

was over, they were asked whether or not they would like to date their partners again. The result? The more physically attractive the person (as judged in advance by independent raters), the more likely he or she was to be seen as desirable. Other factors—social skills and intelligence, for example—didn't seem to affect the decision (Walster et al., 1966).

The influence of physical attractiveness begins early in life. From age five on, overweight boys are viewed by peers as socially offensive; tall, thin ones are judged as introverted and nervous; and muscular and athletic youngsters are seen as outgoing, active, and popular (Staffieri, 1967; Lemer and Gillert, 1969). The same principle continues into adult life. Handsome men and beautiful women are seen as more sensitive, kind, interesting, strong, poised, modest, sociable, outgoing, and exciting than their less attractive counterparts (Dion, Berscheid, and Walster, 1972). Attractiveness continues to be important well into middle age. Gerald Adams and Ted Huston (1975) found that adults in this group viewed attractive peers as more socially outgoing, more pleasant, and of higher social status than their less attractive counterparts.

Before you look in the mirror and conclude that your social prospects are hopeless, consider these encouraging facts. First, average-looking people with pleasing personalities are likely to be judged as being attractive (Berscheid and

Walster, 1978). Second, physical factors become less important as a relationship progresses. As Hamachek (1982, p. 59) puts it, "Attractive features may open doors, but apparently, it takes more than physical beauty to keep them open."

Similarity It's comforting to know someone who likes the things we like, who has similar values, and who may even be of the same race, economic class, or educational standing. This basis for the relationship, commonly and most appropriately known as the *similarity thesis,* is the most well substantiated of the several bases of relationship formation. The most common similarities between partners include age, education, race, religious and ethnic background, and socioeconomic status (Buss, 1985).

There are at least two possible hypotheses to study in the dynamics of similarity and interpersonal attraction: (1) people with similar attitudes are attracted to each other; and (2) people who are attracted to each other perceive themselves as similar, whether or not that's actually the case. Experiments support both of these ideas.

We like people who like what we like, and who dislike what we dislike. Several logical reasons exist for feeling this way. First of all, the other person serves as an external indication—a social validation—that we are not alone in our thinking, that we're not too "weird." Someone else *did* like the same controversial book as you. Therefore this other person offers good support for you, reinforcing your own sense of what is right.

Second, when someone is similar to you, you can make fairly accurate predictions—whether the person will want to eat at the Mexican restaurant or hear the concert you're so excited about. This ability to make confident predictions reduces uncertainty and anxiety.

There's a third explanation for the similarity thesis. It may be that when we learn that other people are similar to us, we assume they'll probably like us, so we in turn like them. The self-fulfilling prophecy creeps into the picture again.

Donn Byrne and his associates (Byrne, 1969; Byrne and Blaylock, 1963) verified that people are attracted to others they think similar. These researchers told subjects they would be participating in a group discussion, and that some of the other participants (strangers) would have similar opinions to theirs, whereas others would not. As expected, students expressed more liking for people who supposedly had views similar to their own, and judged these strangers to be more intelligent, better informed, more moral, and better adjusted than those assumed to have dissimilar attitudes. Recent evidence indicates, however, that rejection of an attitudinally dissimilar other decreases after conversation (Sunnafrank, 1985).

Research studies also support the second attraction-similarity relationship: When we like a person, we perceive that similarities exist with that individual. Studies by Byrne and Blaylock (1963) as well as by Levinger and Breedlove (1966) have found that the actual amount of similarity between husbands and wives is significantly less than the amount the partners *assume* to exist. In discussion of these findings, Ellen Berscheid and Elaine Walster (1978) speculate that couples deemphasize their disagreements in the interest of maintaining a harmonious relationship.

For either direction observed in this attraction-

similarity relationship, the research indicates that specific aspects of similarity must be considered. For example, does it matter that the person is similar to you in attitudes, but not in personality (or the converse)? The answer is yes. *Attitude similarity* carries more weight than *personality similarity*. Does it matter that you and the other person are similar on a small number of issues of greater importance to you both, than on a large number of other issues of lesser significance? Again, yes. Finally, are there any limitations to the degree of similarity and attraction between two people? Yes: A relationship can become *too* predictable, *too* patterned. This situation is the "I'm bored!" test of the relationship. It has also been found that people who are less anxious about whether or not others like them will associate with people having different appearances, experiences, and attitudes.

Similarity turns from attraction to dislike when we encounter people who are like us in many ways but who behave in a strange or socially offensive manner (Taylor and Mette, 1971; Cooper and Jones, 1969). For instance, you have probably disliked people others have said were "just like you" but who talked too much, were complainers, or had some other unappealing characteristic. In fact, there is a tendency to have stronger dislike for similar but offensive people than for those who are offensive but different. One likely reason is that such people threaten our self-esteem, causing us to fear that we may be as unappealing as they are. In such circumstances, the reaction is often to put as much distance as possible between ourselves and this threat to our ideal self-image.

Complementarity   The old saying "Opposites attract" seems to contradict the principle of similarity we just described. In truth, though, both are valid. Differences strengthen a relationship when they are *complementary*—when each partner's characteristics satisfy the other's needs. Couples, for instance, are more likely to be attracted to each other when one partner is dominant and the other passive (Winch, 1958). Relationships also work well when the partners agree that one will exercise control in certain areas ("You make the final decisions about money") and the other will take the lead in different ones ("I'll decide how we ought to decorate the place"). Strains occur when control issues are disputed.

In Chapter 1 we talked about how communication can satisfy human needs. We discussed Maslow's hierarchy of needs: physiological, safety, social, self-esteem, and self-actualization. We also looked at Schutz's theory that humans seek inclusion, control, and affection. These theories reflect the need-fulfillment thesis: the idea that people seek out each other and establish certain types of relationships because of the needs they want fulfilled at that time in their lives.

Studies that have examined successful and unsuccessful couples over a twenty-year period show the interaction between similarities and differences (Kelley, 1977, pp. 625–626). The research demonstrates that partners in successful marriages were similar enough to satisfy each other physically and mentally, but were different enough to meet each other's needs and keep the relationship interesting. The successful couples found ways to keep a balance between their similarities and differences, adjusting to the changes that occurred over the years.

Reciprocity   Being liked by others is a strong source of attraction, especially in the early stages of a relationship (Backman and Secord, 1959). At that time we are attracted to people who we believe are attracted to us. Conversely, we will probably not feel good about people who either attack or seem indifferent to us. After we get to know others, their liking becomes less of a factor. By then we form our preferences more from the

other reasons listed in this section.

It's no mystery why reciprocal liking builds attractiveness. People who approve of us bolster our feelings of self-esteem. This approval is rewarding in its own right, and it can also confirm a self-concept that says, "I'm a likable person."

You can probably think of cases where you haven't liked people who seemed to like you. These experiences usually fall into two categories. Sometimes we think the other person's supposed liking is counterfeit—an insincere device to get something from us. The acquaintance who becomes friendly when asking to borrow your car or the employee whose flattery of the boss seems to be a device to get a raise are examples. This sort of behavior really isn't "liking" at all.

The second category of unappealing liking occurs when the other person's approval doesn't fit with our own self-concept. We cling to an existing self-concept even when it is unrealistically unfavorable. When someone says you're good-looking, intelligent, and kind, but you believe you are ugly, stupid, and mean, you may choose to disregard the flattering information and remain in your familiar state of unhappiness. Groucho Marx summarized this attitude when he said he would never join any club that would have him as a member.

Exchange   Some relationships are based on an economic model called *exchange theory* (Thibaut and Kelley, 1959; Homans, 1961). This theory suggests that we often seek out people who can give us rewards—either physical or emotional—that are greater than or equal to the costs we encounter in dealing with them. When we operate on the basis of exchange, we decide (often unconsciously) whether dealing with another person is "a good deal" or "not worth the effort."

How do we determine what makes a relationship "a good deal"? Exchange theorist Harold Kelley suggests we base our decision on a comparison level of this relationship with ones we have had in the past (CL) or could have in the future (CL$_{alt}$). These comparisons allow for four predictions about relationships:

1. *Stable-satisfactory relationship:* The reward in the current relationship is higher than the general comparison level and the comparison level for alternatives. For example, you perceive that the person you are dating is "better" than your previous dates (the CL) and is better than other possible dates you could have (the CL$_{alt}$).

2. *Unstable-satisfactory relationship:* The reward in the current relationship is higher than the general comparison level, but lower than the comparison level for alternatives. For example, you perceive that the person you are dating is better than your previous dates (the CL), but is not better than other possible dates (the CL$_{alt}$).

3. *Stable-unsatisfactory relationship:* The reward in the current relationship is lower than the general comparison level, and higher than the comparison level for alternatives. For example,

you perceive that the person you are dating is not better than your previous dates (the CL), but is better than your other possible choices (the CL$_{alt}$).

4. *Unstable-unsatisfactory relationship:* The reward in the current relationship is lower than the general comparison level and lower than the comparison level for alternatives. For example, you perceive that the person you are dating is not better than other previous dates (the CL) and is not better than other possible choices (the CL$_{alt}$).

Now, to give this theory some intrigue, keep in mind that the comparison levels change over *time* (with age and experience, for example), and can change as a *situation* changes and as the *people* available for comparison change. For many people, unstable-satisfying relationships only last until a better, more desirable partner comes along. The same principle also holds true in the business world, where both employers and employees will only maintain a relationship as long as it's rewarding for both of them.

At its most blatant level, an exchange approach seems cold and calculating, but in some situations it can be reasonable. A healthy business relationship is based on how well the parties help one another out, and some friendships are based on an informal kind of barter: "I don't mind listening to the ups and downs of your love life because you rescue me when the house needs repairs." Even close relationships have an element of exchange. Husbands and wives tolerate each other's quirks because the comfort and enjoyment they get make the unhappy times worth accepting. Most deeply satisfying relationships, however, are built on more than just the benefits that make them a good deal.

Competency   We like to be around talented people, probably because we hope their skills and abilities will rub off on us. On the other hand, we are uncomfortable around those who are *too* competent—probably because we look bad by comparison (Bales, 1958).

Elliot Aronson and his associates (1966) demonstrated how competence and imperfection combine to affect attraction by having subjects evaluate tape recordings of candidates for a quiz program. One was a "perfect" candidate who answered almost all the questions correctly, and modestly admitted that he was an honor student, athlete, and college yearbook editor. The "average" candidate answered fewer questions correctly, had average grades, was a less successful athlete, and was a low-level member of the yearbook staff. Toward the end of half the tapes, the candidates committed a blunder, spilling coffee all over themselves. The remaining half of the tapes contained no such blunder.

These, then, were the four experimental conditions: (1) a person with superior ability who blundered; (2) a superior person who did not blunder; (3) an average person who blundered; and (4) an average person who did not.

The students who rated the attractiveness of these four types of people revealed an interesting and important principle of interpersonal attraction. The most attractive person was the superior candidate who blundered. Next was the superior person who did not blunder. Third was the average person who did not blunder. The least attractive person was the average person who committed the blunder.

Aronson's conclusion was that we like people who are somewhat flawed because they remind us of ourselves. There are some qualifications to this principle, however. People with especially positive or negative self-esteem find "perfect" people more attractive than those who are competent but flawed (Helmreich, Aronson, and Lefan, 1970). Furthermore, women tend to be more impressed by uniformly superior people, whereas men find desirable but "human" subjects

A proposal of marriage in our society tends to be a way in which a man sums up his social attributes and suggests to a woman that hers are not so much better as to preclude a merger or partnership in these matters.

Erving Goffman

especially attractive (Deaux, 1972). On the whole, though, the principle stands: The best way to gain the liking of others is to be good at what you do, but to admit your mistakes.

Disclosure   Telling others important information about yourself can help build liking. Sometimes the basis of this attraction comes from learning about ways we are similar, either in experiences ("I broke off an engagement myself") or in attitudes ("I feel nervous with strangers too"). Another reason why self-disclosure increases liking is because it is a sign of regard. When people share private information with you, it suggests they respect and trust you—a kind of liking that we've already seen increases attractiveness.

Not all disclosure leads to liking. Research shows that the key to satisfying self-disclosure is *reciprocity:* getting back an amount and kind of information equivalent to that which you reveal (Derlega, Wilson, and Chaikin, 1976; Altman, 1973). A second important ingredient in successful self-disclosure is *timing.* It's probably unwise to talk about your sexual insecurities with a new acquaintance or express your pet peeves to a friend at your birthday party. The information you reveal ought to be appropriate for the setting and stage of the relationship (Wortman et al., 1976; Archer and Berg, 1978). Chapter 8 contains a great deal of information on the subject of self-disclosure.

Copyright ©1965 by Saul Steinberg

Proximity As common sense suggests, we are likely to develop relationships with people we interact with frequently. In many cases, proximity leads to liking. We're more likely to develop

friendships with close neighbors than with distant ones, for instance; and several studies show that the chances are good that we'll choose a mate with whom we cross paths often. Facts like these are understandable when we consider that proximity allows us to get more information about other people and benefit from a relationship with them.

Familiarity, on the other hand, can also breed contempt. Evidence to support this fact comes from police blotters as well as university laboratories. Thieves frequently prey on nearby victims, even though the risk of being recognized is greater. Most aggravated assaults occur within the family or among close neighbors. Within the law, the same principle holds: You are likely to develop strong personal feelings of either like or dislike regarding others you encounter frequently.

It is interesting to note why people do *not* form relationships. Besides reasons related to avoidance of self-disclosure (see Chapter 8), Maxine Schnall (1981) describes a "social disease" she labels *commitmentphobia*. She describes commitmentphobia as the fear of entering into or sustaining an "exclusive, permanent relationship with a member of the opposite sex." Male commitmentphobes, Schnall suggests, often view commitment and entrapment as synonymous. Commitment to a woman means giving up traditional defenses, including control of others and emotional aloofness. One symptom of the commitmentphobic man is promiscuity. Another is the choice to remain alone, while a third is the apparent but insincere search for the "perfect wife."

The female commitmentphobe often views commitment as a dependency trap in which she will be forced to be subservient to her husband. Independence, bought with money and status, is one way to cope with commitmentphobia. Schnall argues that the problems of the commitmentphobic woman are greater than those of her male counterpart. For example, a single man fits into a stereotypic, acceptable role, whereas a single woman—even in the relatively enlightened 1980s—often is considered unusual.

Commitmentphobia is not limited to single people. Schnall concludes her article by discussing married commitmentphobes, people who complain incessantly about their marriages but never leave. She closes with the following advice:

> We need to reduce the fear of commitment by dispelling the notion that commitment is synonymous with the loss of identity. We must reassure ourselves and each other that it is possible to be both autonomous and deeply committed to one another. . . . A deep commitment to one person and the

experiences of a life lived together, far from being antithetical to personal fulfillment, are often pre-requisites for it.

The stages of a relationship

Whatever the attraction, relationships all wax and wane according to a similar pattern. Mark Knapp (1984) has broken the rise and fall of relationships into ten steps (see Table 7–1).

Initiating   The goals in the first stage are to show that you are interested in making contact and to show that you are the kind of person worth talking to. Communication during this stage is

TABLE 7–1 An overview of relational stages

PROCESS	STAGE	REPRESENTATIVE DIALOGUE
COMING TOGETHER	Initiating	"Hi, how ya doin'?" "Fine. You?"
	Experimenting	"Oh, so you like to ski . . . so do I." "You do?! Great. Where do you go?"
	Intensifying	"I . . . I think I love you." "I love you too."
	Integrating	"I feel so much a part of you." "Yeah, we are like one person. What happens to you happens to me."
	Bonding	"I want to be with you always." "Let's get married."
COMING APART	Differentiating	"I just don't like big social gatherings." "Sometimes I don't understand you. This is one area where I'm certainly not like you at all."
	Circumscribing	"Did you have a good time on your trip?" "What time will dinner be ready?"
	Stagnating	"What's there to talk about?" "Right. I know what you're going to say and you know what I'm going to say."
	Avoiding	"I'm so busy, I just don't know when I'll be able to see you." "If I'm not around when you try, you'll understand."
	Terminating	"I'm leaving you . . . and don't bother trying to contact me." "Don't worry."

Reprinted with permission from Mark L. Knapp, *Interpersonal Communication and Human Relationships* (Boston: Allyn and Bacon, 1984).

usually brief, and it generally follows conventional formulas: handshakes, remarks about innocuous subjects like the weather, and friendly expressions. These kinds of behavior may seem superficial and meaningless, but they are a way of signaling that you're interested in building some kind of relationship with the other person. They allow us to say without saying "I'm a friendly person, and I'd like to get to know you."

Experimenting   After making contact with a new person, we generally begin the search for common ground. This search usually begins with the basics: "Where are you from? What's your major?" From there we look for other similarities: "You're a runner too? How many miles do you do a week?"

The hallmark of experimenting is small talk. As Knapp (p. 36) says, this small talk is like Listerine: We hate it, but we take large quantities every day. We tolerate the ordeal of small talk because it serves several functions. First, it is a useful way to find out what interests we share with the other person. It also provides a way to "audition" the other person—to help us decide whether a relationship is worth pursuing. In addition, small talk is a safe way to ease into a relationship. You haven't risked much as you decide whether to proceed further. Finally, small talk *does* provide some kind of link to others. It's often better than being alone.

Intensifying   At the next stage the kind of truly interpersonal relationship defined in Chapter 1 begins. The amount of personal disclosure increases as the partners move away from stereotyped ways of behaving. The degree of risk here is matched by the potential for gain.

Several changes occur during intensifying. Forms of address become more informal: "Come over here, honey," "Hey Gordo, pass me a beer." The parties begin to refer to themselves as "we": "We'll see you at the picnic." Increased familiarity leads to verbal shortcuts. Instead of saying "You look tired. Did you have a hard day at work?," it's only necessary to ask "The boss again?" It is also during the intensifying stage that we begin to express directly feelings of commitment to one another: "I'm sure glad we met," "You're the best thing that's happened to me in a long time."

Integrating   As the relationship strengthens, the parties begin to take on an identity as a social unit. Invitations begin to come addressed to the couple. Social circles merge. The partners begin to take on each other's commitments: "Sure we'll spend Thanksgiving with your family." Common property may begin to be designated—our apartment, our car, our song. In this sense, the integration stage is a time when, in a sense, we give up some characteristics of our old selves and become a different person.

Bonding   During the bonding stage the parties make symbolic public gestures to show the world that their relationship exists. These gestures can take the form of a contract to be business partners or a license to be married. Bonding generates social support for the relationship. Custom and law both impose certain obligations on partners who have officially bonded.

Differentiating   Now that the two people have formed this commonality, they need to reestablish individual identities. How are we different? How am I unique? Former identifications as "we" now emphasize "I." Differentiation often first occurs when a relationship begins to experience the first, inevitable stress. Whereas a happy employee might refer to "our company," the description might change to "their company" when a raise or some other request isn't forthcoming. We see this kind of differentiation when parents argue

over the misbehavior of a child: "Did you see what *your* son just did?"

Differentiation can be positive, too, for people need to be individuals as well as parts of a relationship. The key to successful differentiation is the need to maintain commitment to a relationship while creating the space for members to be individuals as well.

Circumscribing   So far we have been looking at the growth of relationships. Although some reach a plateau of development, going on successfully for as long as a lifetime, others pass through several stages of decline and dissolution. In the circumscribing stage communication between members decreases in quantity and quality. Restrictions and restraints characterize

Leavetaking is the universal experience. From birth to death we face a continuum of partings. . . . Leavetaking is essential to growth. As we move into maturity—and beyond—we part from people, places, things, states of life. We must do this or we do not grow.

But the process is often painful. We cling to relationships longer than we should. We are shocked when we are taken leave of. Our resistance to the change that leavetaking brings compels us to maintain associations that we should have outgrown and makes us terribly vulnerable to the pain of rejection when an association is broken off. Sometimes we swing to the other extreme and sever relationships that we should have kept. Sometimes we take leave when we should but do it in ways that hurt ourselves and others.

M. R. Feinberg, G. Feinberg, and J. J. Tarrant
Leavetaking

---

this stage, and dynamic communication becomes static. Rather than discuss a disagreement (which requires some degree of energy on both parts), members opt for withdrawal: either mental (silence or daydreaming and fantasizing) or physical (where people spend less time together). Circumscribing doesn't involve total avoidance, which comes later. Rather, it entails a certain shrinking of interest and commitment.

Stagnation   If circumscribing continues, the relationship begins to stagnate. Members behave toward each other in old, familiar ways without much feeling. No growth occurs. The relationship is a hollow shell of its former self. We see stagnation in many workers who have lost enthusiasm for their job, yet continue to go through the motions for years. The same sad event occurs for some couples who unenthusiastically have the same conversations, see the same people, and follow the same routines without any sense of joy or novelty.

Avoiding   When stagnation becomes too unpleasant, parties in a relationship begin to create distance between each other. Sometimes they do it under the guise of excuses ("I've been

sick lately and can't see you") and sometimes directly ("Please don't call me; I don't want to see you now"). In either case, by this point the handwriting is on the wall about the relationship's future.

Terminating   Characteristics of this final stage include summary dialogues of where the relationship has gone and the desire to dissociate. The relationship may end with a cordial dinner, a note left on the kitchen table, a phone call, or a legal document stating the dissolution. Depending on each person's feelings, this stage can be quite short, or it may be drawn out over time, with bitter jabs at each other. In either case, termination doesn't have to be totally negative. Understanding each other's investments in the relationship and needs for personal growth may dilute the hard feelings.

Communication theorists used to believe that the ending of a relationship was little more than a reversal of the stages of coming together. Recent studies show that the matter isn't so simple. When both parties agree to end their relationship, the amount and kind of sharing does resemble a mirror image of that during the growth stages (Bordagaray-Sciolino, 1984). When one partner wants out and the other wants to keep the relationship together, however, the communication changes significantly.

The way a relationship ends depends on several factors, which Leslie Baxter (1984) identified after examining the breakups of 97 heterosexual romantic relationships. In addition to whether both or only one partner wants to end the relationship, these factors matter: whether the onset of relational problems is sudden or gradual, whether the partners use direct or indirect actions to dissolve the relationship, whether negotiations about the disengagement are brief or lengthy, whether there are attempts to save the relationship, and whether the final outcome is termination of the relationship or its continuation in some other form.

Besides these factors, Baxter (1982) and Cody (1982) found that the strategy partners use to disengage depends on the degree of intimacy their relationship had reached. In the least intimate relationships one partner simply withdraws (physically or emotionally) from the other. In slightly more intimate relationships one partner is likely to request they see less of each other. When intimacy has been greater, the disengaging partner makes an effort to explain the reason for leaving in a way that takes the other's feelings into account. In the most intimate relationships, the initiator expresses grief over the disengagement. In fact, Cody (1982) found that the more intimate the relationship, the greater the feeling of obligation to justify terminating it.

What happens to the degree of self-disclosure when a relationship ends? Danielle Bordagaray-Sciolino (1984) found that the *breadth* (number of topics chosen for disclosure) remains the same, but the *depth* of disclosure varies from one partner to the other. The person who wants to maintain the relationship decreases the level of intimacy (probably to avoid "rocking the boat," scaring the other away), whereas the partner who

wants to end it decreases the amount of information disclosed, while keeping the depth of disclosure about the same. Why would someone looking for a way out of a relationship keep disclosing personal information? One explanation is that this strategy allows for a graceful, relatively painless withdrawal that is less traumatic for the person left behind.

After outlining the ten steps of relational growth and decay, Knapp discusses several assumptions about his model. First, movement through the stages is generally sequential and systematic. We proceed at a steady pace and don't usually skip steps in the development. Second, movement can be forward or backward, and there is movement within stages. A relationship, for example, may experience a setback—a lessening of intimacy, a redefining of the relationship. Two people may repeat certain stages, and although the stages are the same, each cycle is a new experience. It may also be the case that certain relationships will stabilize at a particular stage. Many relationships stabilize at the experimenting stage (friend and work relationships), some stabilize at the intensifying stage, and a few stabilize at the bonding stage. With these assumptions in mind we can use Knapp's model as a set of developmental guidelines for movement within and between the stages of initiation and termination.

Friendship: a special relationship

Romantic and career relationships may come and go, but friendships are the interpersonal bond that can exist throughout a lifetime. Because friendship is so important, it deserves a special look in this chapter.

What makes a friend?   You probably have a variety of friends. If you are lucky, you have a few people whom you can count as special friends. Exactly what is it about these relationships that distinguish them from less personal ones? Michael Argyle and Monika Henderson (1984) found six rules that distinguish high-quality friendships from lower-quality ones. They seem to be the rules that must be kept if a friendship is to thrive.

1. Standing up for the other person when you are apart.
2. Sharing news of success with the other person.
3. Showing emotional support.
4. Trusting and confiding in each other.
5. Volunteering to help in time of need.
6. Striving to make the other happy when you are together.

These rules are similar to the eight characteristics that Muriel James and Louis Savary (1976) defined as important to friendships. Notice that the following traits take on different levels of importance as a friendship matures.

Availability and *shared activities* are particularly important in the initial stages of a relationship. You expect to spend time with the other person, getting together to work on the term project, having lunch or dinner, or maybe, talking during TV commercials. If these expectations are not met, the relationship may never develop beyond an acquaintanceship. In most cases, being available presumes face-to-face interactions, but there are also times when we maintain availability through written letters or telephone calls. When you're feeling down and depressed, you may surprise yourself by what you do. Sometimes you call someone you haven't spoken to in months, someone who may not even be a "close" friend, and at other times you write to someone who presumes you died or ran off for a tour of the world. No matter, the person is still available, and that's what is important.

Expectations common to the intermediate phases of relationships include *caring, honesty,* *confidentiality,* and *loyalty.* You expect them from the other person, and you expect to provide them yourself if the relationship is to be reciprocal. Sometimes we forget that others expect the same treatment from us!

Although the degree of caring will vary with the type of relationship, James and Savary offer the following definition:

> Caring is not the same as using the other person to satisfy one's own needs. Neither is it to be confused with such things as well-wishing, or simply having an interest in what happens to another. Caring is a process of helping others grow and actualize themselves. It is a transforming experience.

In like manner, honesty, confidentiality, and loyalty are expected in all types of relationships. Honesty in a relationship does not mean that you need to tell everything to the other person, but that you are honest about matters relevant to that relationship, while maintaining a respect for the other person's sense of privacy. Confidentiality and loyalty are two agreements made in relationships, at times in unstated and assumed ways, and sometimes in a formal (written) legal manner.

Understanding and *empathy* are the "bonuses" of a relationship. Many relationships can maintain themselves based on the other characteristics, but those that are particularly strong have a mutually high degree of understanding and empathy. Sue and Mary each understand how the other works and thinks, and they can empathize with each other's feelings. It's not that they are so predictable as to be boring, but they do know each other's ways of thinking and feeling almost as well as they know their own. Usually, these features of a relationship take time to develop, and they require clear communication between the two people involved. Each must be willing to express needs, feelings, and wishes as accurately as possible, and each must practice the skills of active listening for the other person.

Pressures on friendships   Many times strong friendships wither away. Sad as this change may be, it's not surprising, for there are both external and internal pressures on such friendships. The *external* pressures include physical circumstances, such as moving away from friends or changing jobs, and the existence of other competing people and relationships. Two people who have been friends throughout their school years, for example, may experience new tensions when one marries, or when other friends compete for time and attention. Friends usually come in pairs, and there's a good reason why that's so. In three-person interactions it is almost impossible for one participant to extend attention to both of the other two simultaneously. Unless each person is quite secure in the relationship and apart from it, most triadic arrangements cannot survive the tensions.

Internal factors can also pressure a friendship. One common internal pressure occurs when partners grow at different rates. For instance, a relationship that was born out of one person's dependency on the other loses its main reason for existing if the weaker partner becomes more self-reliant. Similarly, a friendship once based on agreement to avoid discussing any conflicts will be threatened if one person suddenly becomes willing to tackle disputes directly. When such changes occur, the maintenance of the friendship depends on the ability of both persons to adapt to the new conditions. Therefore, friendships lasting for long periods are often quite different now than they were at earlier times. The partners were wise enough to adapt to their personal changes rather than clinging to the old ways of relating which may have been comfortable and enjoyable, but are now gone.

Not all friendships can survive these pressures. It's important to realize that the end of a friendship does not always mean that the people have failed. Rather, it may simply reflect the fact that one or both partners has changed and now seeks a different (not necessarily better) type of interaction. Of course, this kind of ending is easier to accept if both people have other relationships that can support their needs.

One way to avoid the brutal self-attacks that can follow a separation is to see the friendship not as a *fraction* of you, but as what James and Savary call an additional "third self." There's you, me, and *us*. If the friendship changes or dissolves, the separate entities of you and me still exist intact and completely, and a new friendship will bring with it another third self.

Liking and loving   The word "friend" is rather vague. Although we clearly see a relationship with a friend as more intimate than one with a "coworker" or "pal" and less intimate than one with a "spouse," "lover," or "steady" (Knapp, Ellis, and Williams, 1980), it is hard to define exactly how intimate a friendship relationship really is. This difficulty may stem from our inability to draw the line between "liking" and "loving."

The unabridged edition of the *Random House Dictionary of the English Language* (1969) defines "like" as "to take pleasure in; find agreeable or congenial to one's taste . . . to regard with favor . . . find attractive. . . . " The definition of

"love" takes up twice the space of "like" and, unfortunately, does not provide twice the clarity. "Love" is defined as "the profoundly tender or passionate affection for a person of the opposite sex . . . a feeling of warm personal attachment or deep affection . . . beloved person; sweetheart . . . " and so on for twenty different definitions and uses, including number 19: "like."

Some of the confusion about love comes from its equivocal nature. In truth, people use the word "love" in a variety of ways, even to describe their romantic relationships. After surveying Canadian and English subjects, John Alan Lee (1973) identified several very different uses of the term. To make these distinctions more clear, he gave each type its own label.

Eros   The erotic lover regards love as life's most important activity. Attraction to the partner is strong, and the relationship is intense, both emotionally and physically. The erotic lover prefers feelings be mutual but does not demand it: there is little possessiveness or fear of rivals.

Ludus   The ludic lover considers love a game, a pleasant pastime, which requires neither much feeling nor commitment. The game is played for mutual enjoyment; it requires self-control and detachment, with just the right level of intensity. Lies and insincerity are often part of the rules of this game, although there is no desire to hurt the other person.

Storge   Storgic love is love without intensity or excitement: it is an extension of friendship and affection. Storgic lovers have a relaxed relationship that is part of their ongoing lives. Characteristic of this type of love is the tendency to share interests and activities, but not feelings about the relationship itself.

Mania   Often called "romantic love," manic love is intense, obsessive, and painful. Manic lovers are out of control, continuously creating problems to intensify how they feel. Life without the partner's love is not worth living, so manic lovers abuse themselves to win the other's love, to force the other into greater and greater expressions of love. A rather dramatic relationship, manic love rarely ends happily.

Pragma   The pragmatic lover looks for contentment, a mate with whom a long-term compatible relationship can be formed. Emotional extremes are avoided because they can get in the way of reciprocated affection and mutual problem-solving.

Agape   Agapic love is completely altruistic and deeply compassionate, given without ulterior motives or expectations of something in return. The agapic lover cares for the other, whether the other wants it or not, whether the love is deserved or not.

Metaphors for love   One way to recognize which type of love people are seeking or describing is through the metaphors they use. Philosopher Robert Solomon (1981) suggests that the metaphor we use when thinking about love both shapes and reflects the way we behave with a partner. Solomon outlines a number of metaphors for love and describes the consequences of using each.

Love as a game   We often hear people talking about love as if it were a contest in which one person emerges as the winner. The term itself is a common one: the "game" of love. People "play the field," often trying to "score." Strategies—including lying and flattery—that lead to domination are common: after all, "All's fair. . . . " "Playing hard to get" is another common tactic. For most game players, relationships are short-lived.

Love as a fair exchange   This view of love is based on the economic model of receiving fair

value for one's goods and services. People who adopt this metaphor talk about their relationship being "a good arrangement," and say they are getting "a good (or lousy) deal" from their partners. When things go wrong the complaint is "It isn't worth it anymore." As these metaphors suggest, the overriding question for these love-traders is "What am *I* getting out of this?" The value of the relationship is measured by whether the return on one's investment (of time, energy, money, good will, and so on) is worth the effort. Social exchange theory, introduced earlier in this chapter, explores this economic metaphor.

Love as communication   Some people (including a few students in communication courses, we fear) measure love in terms of how well the lovers send and receive messages. For them, Solomon suggests, the essential moment is the "heavy conversation." "We really get through to each other," they say proudly. Their "feedback" is good, and "openness" is the ultimate goal—regardless of whether the messages are supportive or hostile. In other words, in the communication model, *expression* of feelings is more important than the content of those emotions. The result of this attitude is interaction that is all form and little substance: *making* love as opposed to *loving.*

Communication is important in a loving relationship, of course, but as a *means,* and not an end in itself. When expression of feelings becomes more important than the content of those feelings, something is wrong.

Love as work   Some people view love as an important job, and their language reflects this attitude. They "work on," "work out," or "work at" the relationship. They see nothing wrong with having fun, but their primary objective is to build a successful relationship in the face of life's inevitable obstacles. Solomon points out that some devotees of the work model pick the most inept or inappropriate partners "rather like buying a run-down shack—for the challenge" (p. 87). They feel somehow superior to couples who are merely happy together, and admire those who have survived years of fights and other pain for "making it work."

Love as a flame   Solomon states that "red-hot" lovers act as if they were Mr. Coffee machines, "bubbling over, occasionally overflowing, getting too hot to handle, and occasionally bursting from too much pressure" (p. 94). Partners who expect this sort of emotional fire can become disappointed when things "cool down," and may look for ways to "spice up their relationship." Unfortunately, the likelihood of those flames of love burning brightly for a long period is slim; and rather than settling for mere warmth, these romantic pyromaniacs frequently find themselves looking for a new flame.

Love as banal   Banal lovers stand in almost direct opposition to their red-hot counterparts. Although few lovers intentionally seek a relationship based on blandness, this approach is a common one. Bland, unexcited lovers use bland, unexciting metaphors. The word "thing" is overused. It can describe a sex organ, profession or hobby ("doing one's thing"), or a problem. The bland, high-level abstraction that banal lovers often use is "relationship": clinically accurate, but hardly suggestive of any emotion.

Solomon presents other metaphors, including the dramatic model, in which lovers strive for catharsis (often playing before onlookers); the contract model, which emphasizes "commitment" and "obligation"; and the biological metaphor, which stresses that people are "made for each other."

People rarely select a metaphor consciously. In the case of love, the linguistic model we use is likely to come from the models to which we're exposed, both in the media and in our personal experience. Once a metaphorical view of love exists, we tend to behave in ways that support it. We can speculate that one source of difficulty for many couples is the partners' fundamentally different views of how their relationship "ought" to be. What metaphor do you use? Is it appropriate?

Gender and friendship   Several studies have looked at friends selected by men and by women. Do men and women differ in their perceptions of friendship and choices of friends? In a survey of college students, Myron Brenton (1974) found that men place more value on friends who provide intellectual stimulation than do women. Traits such as honesty, trust, and acceptance were important to both men and women, but were more important to women. He observed that men and women use different techniques for meeting with friends of the same sex. Traditionally, men get together with their male friends to go fishing, play ball or poker, and to have a few drinks. Women get together with their female friends at volunteer organizations, book clubs, craftwork sessions, and bridge games. For women, there has been a distinct absence of sports-based social activities. Caldwell and Peplau (1977) found that women see friendship as a means for sharing feelings, whereas men determine friends according to similar interests in physical activities.

In 1976, Gerald Phillips and Nancy Metzger published the results of an extensive investigation of friendship. College students completed a lengthy questionnaire called "The Friendship Protocol," which included questions about the subject's closest friend of the same sex, opinions about male-female relationships, and comments about friendship in general. Responses to the questionnaire provided the following differences.

Men tended to agree with these statements:

1. It is easy to make friends.

2. It is possible to size up a friend to see what the friend might provide.
3. Commitment to a friend should be made only when mutuality is proved.
4. If someone hurts you, it is all right to hurt back.
5. Commitment to friends should not interfere with commitment to yourself.

Women tended to agree with these statements:

1. Friendship should be spontaneous.
2. People should talk about the nature of their friendship.
3. Friend-making is a skill that can be learned.
4. I want to understand people.
5. It is possible to be friends with employees or students.

Based on responses to the inventory, Phillips and Metzger concluded that men are more approving of a planned and calculating relationship, whereas women are more concerned with the emotional aspects of the relationship and its spontaneity. Such differences may be the product of the socialization process for men and women.

Making friendships work   In a study called "Happily Ever After and Other Relationship Styles: Advice on Interpersonal Relations in Popular Magazines, 1951–1973," Virginia Kidd (1975) described two media views of relationships. First, there is a static vision: "Relationships don't change, and people live happily ever after." Second, there is a more realistic vision that emphasizes the dynamic nature of communication. Individuals are constantly changing, and so too are the relationships they share. This second vision implies that we can improve our relationship effectiveness if we understand the transactional nature of the communication process and practice such communication skills as active listening, conflict management, and self-disclosure.

Caring is a process of helping others grow and actualize themselves. It is a transforming experience.

Muriel James and Louis M. Savary
The Heart of Friendship

In accordance with Kidd's categories of relationships, William Wilmot (1979) discusses four important principles about relationships:

Relationships do change   Change is inevitable, and relationships are no exception to the rule. Unfortunately, sometimes we do get stuck in our relationships. We stifle ourselves and others with expectations that each of us remain the same. We impose restrictions and often fight to keep relationships from being redefined. An extreme case can be observed in a parent who continues to treat a forty-six-year-old son as the baby, not as an adult and friend. Consider your own relationships. Do you accept the fact that your relationships will change?

Relationships require attention   As Wilmot notes, "Participants have to *keep working on their relationships until the day they die.*" He makes another comment: "If we all worked on our relationships as much as we did our jobs, we would have a richer emotional life." Work takes at least forty hours a week of your time. How much time do you devote to developing your close relationships?

Good relationships meet the expectations of the participants   Your satisfaction with a relationship is a function of how well that relationship meets *your* goals. For example, people get married for a variety of reasons: companionship, status, love, a good sex life, a name, money. So long as the two people sharing that relationship fulfill their expectations, the relationship is satisfying for them.

Conflicts arise when the expectations differ and cannot be met with that relationship. What expectations do you have? What do you want from your relationships?

Relationships can be improved by dealing directly with relational issues The nature of the relationship and its functions are defined by the people, not by some mystical outside force. Knowing how a relationship forms and how it can change should increase the quality of that relationship. Rather than hoping problems won't occur and avoiding them when they do arise, do you use your best communication skills to prevent and confront your interpersonal problems?

Readings

Adams, G. R., and T. L. Huston. "Social Perception of Middle-Aged Persons Varying in Physical Attractiveness." *Developmental Psychology* 11 (1975): 657–658.

Altman, I. "Reciprocity of Interpersonal Exchange." *Journal for the Theory of Social Behavior* 3 (1973): 249–261.

*Altman, Irwin, and Dalmas Taylor. *Social Penetration: The Development of Interpersonal Relationships.* New York: Holt, Rinehart and Winston, 1973.

Archer, R., and J. Berg. "To Encourage Intimacy, Don't Force It." *Psychology Today* (November 1978): 39–40.

Argyle, M., and M. Henderson. "The Rules of Friendship." *Journal of Social and Personal Relationships* 1 (1984): 211–237.

Aronson, E., B. Willerman, and J. Floyd. "The Effect of a Pratfall on Increasing Interpersonal Attractiveness." *Psychonomic Science* 4 (1966): 227–228.

Backman, C. W., and P. F. Secord. "The Effect of Perceived Liking on Interpersonal Attraction." *Human Relations* 12 (1959): 379–384.

Bales, R. "Task Roles and Social Roles in Problem Solving Groups." In E. E. Maccoby, T. M. Newcomb, and E. L. Hartley, eds., *Readings in Social Psychology,* 3d ed. New York: Holt, Rinehart and Winston, 1958, pp. 437–447.

Baxter, L. A. "Strategies for Ending Relationships: Two Studies." *Western Journal of Speech Communication* 46 (1982): 223–241.

Baxter, L. A. "Trajectories of Relationship Disengagement." *Journal of Social and Personal Relationships* 1 (1984): 29–48.

Bell, Jeff, and Aza Hadas. "On Friendship." Paper presented to the WYOTANA Conference, University of Montana, June 1977.

*Berscheid, E., and E. H. Walster. *Interpersonal Attraction,* 2d ed. Reading, Mass.: Addison-Wesley, 1978.

Bordagaray–Sciolino, D. *The Role of Self-Disclosure as a Communication Strategy During Relationship Termination.* Thesis, University of North Carolina at Chapel Hill, 1984.

Brenton, Myron. *Friendship.* New York: Stein and Day, 1974.

Buley, Jerry L. *Relationships and Communication.* Dubuque: Kendall/Hunt, 1977.

Buss, D. M. "Human Mate Selection." *American Scientist* 73 (January–February 1985): 47–51.

Byrne, Donn. "Attitudes and Attraction." In *Advances in Experimental Social Psychology* 4, L. Berkowitz, ed. New York: Academic Press, 1969.

Byrne, Donn, and Barbara Blaylock. "Similarity and Assumed Similarity of Attitudes Between Husbands and Wives." *Journal of Abnormal and Social Psychology* 67 (1963): 636–640.

Caldwell, Mayta Ann, and Letitia A. Peplau. "Sex Differences in Friendship." Paper presented to the Western Psychological Association Convention, Seattle, Washington, April 1977.

Carson, Robert C. *Interaction Concepts of Personality.* Chicago: Aldine, 1969.

Cody, M. J. "A Typology of Disengagement Strategies and Examination of the Role of Intimacy, Reactions to Inequity, and Relational

Problems in Strategy Selection." *Communication Monographs* 49 (1982): 148–170.

Cooper, J., and E. E. Jones. "Opinion Divergence as a Strategy to Avoid Being Miscast." *Journal of Personality and Social Psychology* 13 (1969): 23–30.

Deaux, K. "To Err Is Humanizing: But Sex Makes a Difference." *Representative Research in Social Psychology* 3 (1972): 20–28.

Derlega, V. J., M. Wilson, and A. L. Chaikin. "Friendship and Disclosure Reciprocity." *Journal of Personality and Social Psychology* 34 (1976): 578–582.

Dion, K., E. Berscheid, and E. Walster. "What Is Beautiful Is Good." *Journal of Personality and Social Psychology* 24 (1972): 285–290.

Duck, S. W. "A Topography of Relationship Disengagement and Dissolution." In *Personal Relationships 4: Dissolving Personal Relationships,* S. W. Duck, ed. London: Academic Press, 1982. pp. 1–30.

Feinberg, M. R., G. Feinberg, and J. J. Tarrant. *Leavetaking.* New York: Simon and Schuster, 1978.

Hamachek, D. E. *Encounters with Others: Interpersonal Relationships and You.* New York: Holt, Rinehart and Winston, 1982.

Harrington, Mark Randall. *The Relationship Between Psychological Sex-Type and Perceptions of Individuals in Complementary, Symmetrical, and Parallel Relationships.* Thesis, University of North Carolina at Chapel Hill, 1984.

Helmreich, R., E. Aronson, and J. Lefan. "To Err Is Humanizing—Sometimes: Effects of Self-Esteem, Competence, and a Pratfall on Interpersonal Attraction." *Journal of Personality and Social Psychology* 16 (1970): 259–264.

*Hendrick, C., and S. Hendrick. *Liking, Loving, and Relating.* Monterey, Calif.: Brooks/Cole, 1983.

Hinde, R. A. *Towards Understanding Relationships.* London: Academic Press, 1979.

Homans, George C. *Social Behavior: Its Elementary Form.* New York: Harcourt, Brace, 1961.

James, Muriel, and Louis M. Savary, *The Heart of Friendship.* New York: Harper & Row, 1976.

Kaplan, A. G., and M. A. Sedney. *Psychology and Sex Roles: An Androgynous Perspective.* Boston: Little, Brown, 1980.

Kelley, E. L., cited in J. V. McConnell. *Understanding Human Behavior,* 2d ed. New York: Holt, Rinehart and Winston, 1977.

Kelley, Harold H. *Personal Relationships: Their Structure and Processes.* Hillsdale, N.J.: Lawrence Erlbaum Associates, 1979.

Kidd, Virginia. "Happily Ever After and Other Relationship Styles: Advice on Interpersonal Relations in Popular Magazines, 1951–1973." *Quarterly Journal of Speech* 61 (1975): 31–39.

*Knapp, M. L. *Interpersonal Communication and Human Relationships.* Boston: Allyn and Bacon, 1984.

Knapp, M. L., D. G. Ellis, and B. A. Williams. "Perceptions of Communication Behavior Associated with Relationship Terms." *Communication Monographs* 47 (1980): 262–278.

Leary, Timothy. "The Theory and Measurement Methodology of Interpersonal Communication." *Psychiatry* 18 (1955): 147–161.

Leary, Timothy. *Interpersonal Diagnosis of Personality.* New York: Ronald, 1957.

Lee, J. A. *The Colors of Love: An Exploration of the Ways of Loving.* Don Mills, Ontario: New Press, 1973.

Lemer, R. M., and E. Gillert. "Body Build Identification, Preference, and Aversion in Children." *Developmental Psychology* 1 (1969): 456–463.

Levinger, George, and James Breedlove. "Interpersonal Attraction and Agreement." *Journal of Personality and Social Psychology* 3 (1966): 367–372.

Parlee, Mary Brown, and the editors of *Psychology Today.* "The Friendship Bond: PT's Survey Report on Friendship in America." *Psychology*

Today 13 (October, 1979): 43–45, 49–50, 53–54, 113.

*Phillips, Gerald M., and Nancy J. Metzger. *Intimate Communication.* Boston: Allyn and Bacon, 1976.

Phillips, Gerald M., and Julia T. Wood. *Communication and Human Relationships: The Study of Interpersonal Relationships.* New York: Macmillan, 1983.

Ragan, S., and R. Hopper. "End-Frame Talk: How to Exit Intimate Relationships." Paper presented to the Speech Communication Association, 1977.

Rogers, Carl. "The Characteristics of a Helping Relationship." In C. Rogers, *On Becoming a Person.* Boston: Houghton Mifflin, 1961.

Rogers, L. E., and R. V. Farace. "Analysis of Relational Communication in Dyads: New Measurement Procedures." *Human Communication Research* 3 (1975): 222–239.

*Rubin, Zick. *Liking and Loving.* New York: Holt, Rinehart and Winston, 1973.

Schnall, Maxine. "Commitmentphobia." *Savvy* 2 (1981): 37–41.

Selman, Robert L., and Anne P. Selman. "Children's Ideas About Friendship: A New Theory." *Psychology Today* 13 (October 1979): 71–72, 74, 79–80, 114.

Solomon, Robert C. "The Love Lost in Clichés." *Psychology Today* (October 1981): 83–94.

Staffieri, J. "A Study of Social Stereotype of Body Image in Children." *Journal of Personality and Social Psychology* 7 (1967): 101–104.

Sunnafrank, Michael. "Attitude Similarity and Interpersonal Attraction During Early Communicative Stages: A Research Note on the Gen-
eralizability of Findings to Opposite-Sex Relationships." *Western Journal of Speech Communication* 49 (1985): 73–80.

Swenson, Clifford H. *Introduction to Interpersonal Relations.* Glenview, Ill.: Scott, Foresman, 1973.

Taylor, S., and D. Mette. "When Similarity Breeds Contempt." *Journal of Personality and Social Psychology* 20 (1971): 75–81.

Thibaut, John W., and Harold H. Kelley. *The Social Psychology of Groups.* New York: Wiley, 1959.

Villard, Kenneth L., and Leland J. Whipple. *Beginnings in Relational Communication.* New York: Wiley, 1976.

Walster, E., E. Aronson, D. Abrahams, and L. Rottman. "Importance of Physical Attractiveness in Dating Behavior." *Journal of Personality and Social Psychology* 4 (1966): 508–516.

*Walster, E., and M. Walster. *A New Look at Love.* Reading, Mass.: Addison-Wesley, 1978.

Watzlawick, P., J. Beavin, and D. D. Jackson. *Pragmatics of Human Communication.* New York: W. W. Norton, 1967.

Wilmot, William W. *Dyadic Communication,* 2d ed. Reading, Mass.: Addison-Wesley, 1979.

Winch, R. *Mate-Selection: A Study of Complementary Needs.* New York: Harper & Row, 1958.

Wortman, C. B., P. Adosman, E. Herman, and R. Greenberg. "Self-Disclosure: An Attributional Perspective." *Journal of Personality and Social Psychology* 33 (1976): 184–191.

Wright, Paul H. "Toward a Theory of Friendship Based on a Conception of Self." *Human Communication Research* 4 (1978): 196–207.

Self-Disclosure

After studying the material in this chapter

You should understand:

1. How self-disclosure is defined.
2. How the Johari Window represents the degrees of self-disclosure in a dyadic relationship.
3. How receivers judge whether another's message is self-disclosing.
4. Eight reasons people self-disclose, and which are most common in various contexts.
5. The types, functions, and extent of white lies.
6. How gender affects self-disclosure.
7. The risks and benefits of self-disclosure.
8. The relationship among self-disclosure, relational stage, and interpersonal attraction.

You should be able to:

1. Identify the degree to which you engage in self-disclosure with individuals in your life and the circumstances in which you do so.
2. Use the Johari Window model to represent the level of self-disclosure in one of your relationships.
3. Express the reasons you self-disclose in a selected relationship.
4. Identify the types, extent, functions, and consequences of white lies you tell.
5. Name the potential risks and benefits of disclosing in a selected situation.
6. Use the guidelines in this chapter to decide whether or not to disclose important information in one of your relationships.

The dream is a common one. You suddenly find yourself without clothes—on the street, at work, at school, or maybe in a crowd of strangers. Everyone else is fully dressed, while you stand alone, naked and vulnerable. Maybe others see you and respond with curiosity or hostility or laughter. Possibly you seem to be invisible, searching for shelter before you are recognized. Whatever the details, dreams of this sort are usually disturbing.

You needn't be a psychoanalyst to figure out that the nakedness here is symbolic, representing the fear of disclosing oneself in other ways, dropping the masks and facades that we often show to the world. Laughter hides pain; a relaxed pose covers tension; a veneer of certainty masks confusion, and we fear being found out.

Why are we often afraid of opening up to others? Why not let others know who we really are? In his thoughtful book, *What Are You Afraid Of?: A Guide to Dealing with Your Fears*, John T. Wood (1976) suggests an answer:

> I am afraid to be who I am with you . . . I am afraid to be judged by you, I am afraid you will reject me. I am afraid you will say bad things about me. I am afraid you will hurt me. I am afraid, if I really am myself, you won't love me—and I need your love so badly that I will play the roles you expect me to play and be the person that pleases you, even though I lose myself in the process.

There probably isn't a person over the age of six who wouldn't understand these words. At one time or another all of us are afraid to disclose personal information to others. As Wood suggests, the biggest reason for hiding this information is usually fear of rejection. As we'll soon see, there are other reasons as well.

Because the issue of self-disclosure is such a crucial one in interpersonal communication, we want to spend this chapter looking at it in detail. We'll talk about what self-disclosure is and how it differs from other types of communication. We'll see how one's sex influences disclosure. We will look at the benefits and apparent drawbacks of disclosing. Finally, we'll offer some suggestions for when self-disclosure is appropriate. Let's begin by defining our terms.

What is self-disclosure?

What do we mean when we use the term "self-disclosure"? How does the process operate in interpersonal relationships? We need to begin our discussion by answering these questions.

A definition of self-disclosure You might argue that aside from secrets, it's impossible *not* to make yourself known to others. After all, every time you open your mouth to speak, you're revealing your tastes, interests, desires, opinions, beliefs, or some other bit of information about yourself. Even when the subject isn't a personal one, your choice of what to speak about tells the listener something about who you are. If you recall Chapter 5, each of us communicates nonverbally even when we're not speaking. For instance, a yawn might mean that you're tired or bored, a shrug of your shoulders might indicate uncertainty or indifference, and how close or how far you choose to stand from your listener may be taken as a measure of your friendliness or comfort.

If every verbal and nonverbal behavior in which you engage is self-revealing, how can self-disclosure be distinguished from any other act of communication? Psychologist Paul Cozby (1973) begins to answer this question. He suggests that in order for a communication act to be considered self-disclosing it must meet the following criteria: (1) it must contain personal information about the sender; (2) the sender must communicate this information verbally; and (3) another person must

Which of us has known his brother?
Which of us has looked into his father's heart:
Which of us has not remained forever prison-
   bent?
Which of us is not forever a stranger and alone?

Thomas Wolfe

be the target. Put differently, the content of self-disclosing communication is the *self,* and information about the self is *purposefully communicated to another person.*

Although this definition is a start, it ignores the fact that some messages intentionally directed toward others are not especially revealing. For example, telling others that you dislike eating clams is quite different from announcing that you dislike some aspect of their personality. Let's take a look at several factors that further distinguish self-disclosure from other types of communication.

Honesty   It almost goes without saying that true self-disclosure has to be honest. It's not revealing to say, "I've never felt this way about anyone before" to every Saturday night date, or to preface every lie with the statement, "Let me be honest. . . . "

What about cases where individuals do not know themselves well enough to present accurate information? Are these unintentionally false statements self-disclosing? For our purposes, the answer is yes. As long as you are honest and accurate to the best of your knowledge, the communication can qualify as an act of self-disclosure. On the other hand, both painting an incomplete picture of yourself (telling only part of what's true), or avoiding saying anything at all about yourself, are not self-disclosive acts.

Depth   A self-disclosing statement is generally regarded as being personal—containing relatively

"deep" rather than "surface" information. Of course, what is personal and intimate for one person may not be for another. You might feel comfortable admitting your spotty academic record, short temper, or fear of spiders to anyone who asks, whereas others would be embarrassed to do so. Even basic information such as "How old are you?" can be extremely revealing for some people.

Availability of information   Several researchers in the area of self-disclosure argue that self-disclosing messages must contain information the other person is not likely to know at the time or be able to obtain from another source without a great deal of effort, if at all.

For example, describing your conviction for a drunk-driving accident might feel like an act of serious disclosure, for the information concerns you, is offered intentionally, is honest and accurate, and considered personal. However, if the other person could obtain that information elsewhere without much trouble—from a glance at the morning newspaper or from various gossips, for example—your communication would not be an act of self-disclosure.

Context of sharing   Sometimes the self-disclosing nature of a statement comes from the setting in which it is uttered. For instance, relatively innocuous information about family life seems more personal when a teacher shares it with the class. This sort of sharing creates a more personal atmosphere because it changes the relationship from a purely "business" level to a more intimate one.

We can summarize our definitional tour by saying that an act of self-disclosure: (1) *has the self as content;* (2) *is intentional;* (3) *is directed at another person;* (4) *is honest;* (5) *is revealing;* (6) *contains information generally unavailable from other sources;* and (7) *gains much of its intimate nature from the context in which it is expressed.*

Although many acts of communication may be self-revealing, this definition makes it clear that few of our statements may be classified as self-disclosure. Pearce and Sharp (1973) estimate that as little as 2 percent of our communication qualifies as self-disclosure. Other writers agree with the point, if not the exact percentage (Berne, 1964; Powell, 1968; Steele, 1975). Consider your own communication. How often do you disclose?

A model of self-disclosure   One way to illustrate how self-disclosure operates in communication is to look at a device called the *Johari Window,* developed by Joseph Luft and Harry Ingham (Luft, 1969).

Imagine a frame that contains everything there is to know about you: your likes and dislikes, your goals, your secrets, your needs—everything (Figure 8–1).

FIGURE 8–1

Of course, you aren't aware of everything about yourself. Like most people you're probably discovering new things about yourself all the time. To represent this, we can divide the frame containing everything about you into two parts: the part you know about, and the part of which you are not aware (Figure 8–2).

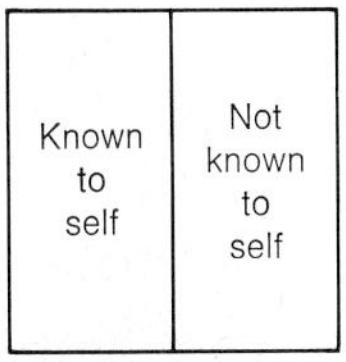

FIGURE 8–2

We can also divide the frame containing everything about you in another way. In this division one part represents the things about you that others know, and the second part contains the things about you that you keep to yourself. Figure 8–3 represents this view.

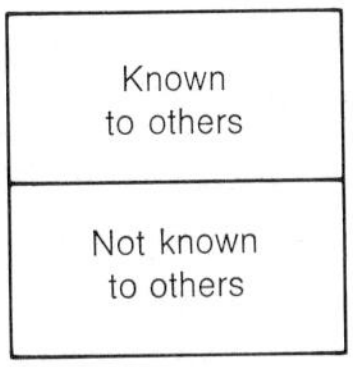

```
┌─────────────┐
│  Known      │
│  to others  │
├─────────────┤
│  Not known  │
│  to others  │
└─────────────┘
```

FIGURE 8–3

When we place these two divided frames one atop the other, we have a Johari Window. By looking at Figure 8–4 you can see that it divides everything about you into four parts.

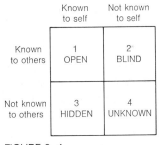

FIGURE 8–4

Part 1 represents the information of which both you and the other person are aware. This part is your *open area.* Part 2 represents the *blind area:* information of which you are unaware, but the other person knows. You learn about information in the blind area primarily through feedback. Part 3 of the Johari Window represents your *hidden area:* information that you know but aren't willing to reveal to others. Items in this hidden area become public primarily through self-disclosure, which is the focus of this chapter. Part 4 of the Johari Window represents information that is *unknown* to both you and others. At first the unknown area seems impossible to verify. After all, if neither you nor others know what it contains, how can you be sure it exists at all? We can deduce its existence because we are constantly discovering new things about ourselves. It is not unusual to discover, for example, that you have an unrecognized talent, strength, or weakness. Items move from the unknown area either directly into the open area when you share your insight, or through one of the other areas first.

The relative size of each area in our personal Johari Windows changes from time to time, according to our moods, the subject we are discussing, and our relationship with the other person. Despite these changes, most people's overall style of disclosure could be represented by a single Johari Window. Figure 8–5 pictures windows representing four extreme interaction styles.

Style 1 depicts a person who is neither recep-

tive to feedback nor willing to self-disclose. This person takes few risks, and may appear aloof and uncommunicative. The largest quadrant is the unknown area: such people have a lot to learn about themselves, as do others.

Style 2 depicts a person who is open to feedback from others but does not voluntarily self-disclose. This person may fear exposure, possibly because of a lack of trusting others. People who fit this pattern may appear highly supportive at first. After all, they want to hear *your* story, and appear willing to deny themselves by remaining quiet. Then this first impression fades, and eventually you see them as distrustful and detached. A Johari Window describing such people has a large hidden area.

Style 3 in Figure 8–5 describes people who discourage feedback from others, but disclose freely. Like the people pictured in diagram 2 they may distrust others' opinions. They certainly seem self-centered. Their largest quadrant is the blind area: They do not encourage feedback, and so fail to learn much about how others view them.

Style 4 depicts people who are both willing to disclose information about themselves and open to others' ideas. They are trusting enough to seek the opinions of others and share their own. In extreme, this communication style can be intimidating and overwhelming because it violates the usual expectations of how nonintimates ought to behave. In moderation, however, this open style provides the best chance for developing highly interpersonal relationships.

Interpersonal communication of any significance is virtually impossible if the individuals involved have little open area. Going a step further, you can see that a relationship is limited by the individual who is less open, that is, who possesses the smaller open area. Figure 8–6 illustrates this situation with Johari Windows. A's window is set up in reverse so that A's and B's open areas are adjacent. Notice that the amount of communication (represented by the arrows connecting the

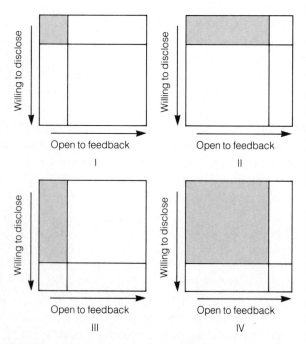

FIGURE 8–5   Four styles of disclosure

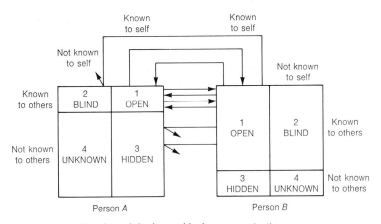

FIGURE 8–6 How limited disclosure blocks communication

two open areas) is dictated by the size of the smaller open area of A. The arrows originating from B's open area and being turned aside by A's hidden and blind areas represent unsuccessful attempts to communicate.

You have probably found yourself in situations that resemble Figure 8–6. Perhaps you have experienced the frustration of not being able to get to know someone who was too reserved. Perhaps you have blocked another person's attempts to build a relationship with you in the same way. Whether you picture yourself more like Person A or Person B, the fact is that self-disclosure on both sides is necessary for the development of any interpersonal relationship. This chapter will describe just how much self-disclosure is optimal and of what type.

The receiver's perception So far we have been looking at self-disclosure from the sender's (discloser's) viewpoint. After all, a receiver can't always be certain whether a given act of communication is truly intentional, honest, and revealing and contains information unavailable elsewhere. Suppose, for example, that at a party you met someone who remarked, "I've never felt comfortable in places like this." Is your companion disclosing? The content of the communication concerns the self and is directed at another per-

son (you); but is the statement intentional, honest, revealing, and unavailable elsewhere? You might guess at the answers to these questions, but you could not know for sure.

Although the sender may be best suited to judge whether a message is self-disclosive, the receiver of the message also makes judgments about the communication. What characteristics of a message or sender impress receivers as being most disclosive? Recent investigations have begun to answer this question.

In a series of studies conducted by Gordon Chelune (1981; Chelune, Skiffington, and Williams, 1981), subjects were asked to rate the degree to which they believed a speaker was self-disclosing from 0 (indicating the speaker totally withheld personal information) to 100 (indicating total disclosure). These ratings were then compared to a number of objective behaviors exhibited by the speakers:

Self-references: statements descriptive of the speaker

Self-reference percent: number of self-references divided by the total number of statements made

Positive self-reference percent: percentage of statements describing favorable attributes of the speaker

Negative self-reference percent: percentage of statements describing unfavorable attributes of the speaker

Intimacy: depth of verbal content, measured on a five-point scale

Affective manner of presentation: degree of congruence between the intimacy level and the manner in which it was presented

Rate of disclosure: number of self-references per minute

Results indicate that all of these factors shape a receiver's evaluation of how much self-disclosure a sender is exhibiting. The single best predictor of subjects' ratings was intimacy, with rate of disclosure and congruent affective manner the next most influential factors. Chelune also found, interestingly, that men were consistently seen as being more disclosing than women (for both male and female raters), possibly reflecting the stereotyped notion that men do not self-disclose very much; hence, any disclosure is "a lot."

Other elements of a communication situation also affect the receiver's perception of another's self-disclosure. Chris Kleinke (1979) discusses variables such as social context (location, subject, people), the appropriateness of the information disclosed (highly intimate disclosure early in a relationship is usually viewed as inappropriate), attributions made about the discloser's motives ("Why is she telling me this?"), and individual characteristics of both the sender and receiver (self-image, dogmatism, neuroticism, anxiety, and need for approval). All of these factors need to be considered when determining how much and what kind of self-disclosure is appropriate.

Reasons for self-disclosure

Although the amount of self-disclosure varies from one person to another, all of us share important information about ourselves at one time or another. For what reasons? Derlega and Grzelak (1979) present a variety of reasons a person might have for disclosing in any particular situation. We can build upon their work and divide these reasons into several categories.

Catharsis   Sometimes you might disclose information in an effort to "get it off your chest." In a moment of candor you might, for instance, share your regrets about having behaved badly in the past.

Self-clarification   Sometimes you can clarify your beliefs, opinions, thoughts, attitudes, and feelings by talking about them with another person. This sort of "talking the problem out" occurs in many psychotherapies, but it also goes on in other contexts, all the way from good friends to bartenders or hairdressers.

Self-validation   If you disclose information ("I think I did the right thing . . . ") with the hope of seeking the listener's agreement, you are seeking validation of your behavior—confirmation of a belief you hold about yourself. On a deeper level, this sort of self-validating disclosure seeks confirmation of important parts of your self-concept.

Reciprocity   A well-documented conclusion from research is that one act of self-disclosure begets another (Derlega and Chaikin, 1975). Thus, in some situations you may choose to disclose information about yourself to encourage another person to begin sharing.

Impression formation   In some situations you may choose to self-disclose to create a particular impression of yourself. Dating behavior, particularly on the first few dates, is often aimed at creating a favorable impression. To look good, we sometimes share selected bits of information about ourselves—for example, our accomplishments or goals.

Relationship maintenance and enhancement   Relationships need disclosure to stay healthy and develop. If you don't reveal how you're feeling about your partner—not to mention other parts of your life—then the subjects of your interaction become limited and shallow.

Social control   Revealing personal information may increase your control over the other person, and sometimes over the situation in which you and the other person find yourselves. For example, an employee who tells the boss that another firm has made overtures probably will have an increased chance of getting raises and improvements in working conditions.

Manipulation   Although most of the preceding reasons might strike you as being manipulative, they often aren't premeditated strategies. There

are cases, however, when an act of self-disclosure is calculated in advance to achieve a desired result. Of course, if a disclosure's hidden motive ever becomes clear to the receiver, the results will most likely be quite unlike the intended ones.

To determine which of these reasons for self-disclosing are most important, Lawrence Rosenfeld and Leslie Kendrick (1984) asked college students to describe which ones would be their reasons for disclosing in a variety of situations. These situations varied in three respects:

the target of the self-disclosure (friend or stranger)

the setting (alone or in a group)

intimacy (intimate or nonintimate)

For example, the *friend alone/intimate* situation was: "It's evening and you are alone with your

"Bob, as a token of my appreciation for this wonderful lunch I would like to disclose to you my income-tax returns for the past four years."
From *The New Yorker*, October 22, 1984, p. 34.

boy or girl friend in his or her home." The *friend alone/nonintimate* situation was: "You are in the library with a friend." The *group of strangers/ nonintimate* situation was: "You are introduced to a group of strangers."

The study showed that whether the target was a stranger or a friend had the strongest influence on the reason for disclosing. When the target was a friend, the top three reasons for disclosing were (from most to least important) relationship maintenance and enhancement, self-clarification, and reciprocity. The primary objective of disclosing to friends appears to be to help the relationship grow and solidify, with reciprocity functioning as the process that allows this growth to happen. The importance of self-clarification shows that friendships also have a personal (as opposed to relational) function. It appears that friendships provide the kind of security that allows us to share our private thoughts in an attempt to sort things out.

When the target was a stranger, the top reason for disclosing was reciprocity. People offer information to elicit information from others. This information provides a basis for deciding whether to continue the relationship, and how personal it is likely to be. The second reason for disclosing to strangers was impression formation. In other words, we often reveal information to strangers that will make us look good. This information, of course, is usually positive—at least in the early stages of a friendship.

"White lies": an alternative to self-disclosure?

Whether the motive is catharsis, impression formation, self-clarification, or any of the others you just read about, the basis for all self-disclosure is truthfulness. In contrast, lying is a deliberate attempt to hide or misrepresent the truth.

Although most people would agree that lying to gain advantage over an unknowing subject is wrong, another kind of mistruth—the "white lie"—is both a popular and often acceptable type of communication. White lies are defined (at least by those who tell them) as being unmalicious, or even helpful.

Whether or not they are benign, white lies are certainly common. In one study (Turner, Edgely, and Olmstead, 1975), 130 subjects were asked to keep track of the truthfulness of their everyday conversational statements. Only 38.5 percent of these statements—slightly more than a third— proved to be totally honest. What reasons do people give for being deceitful so often?

Motives for lying   When subjects in the study by Turner and his associates were asked to give a lie-by-lie account of their motives for concealing or distorting the truth, five major reasons emerged. The most frequent motive (occurring in 55.2 percent of the lies) was *to save face*. Lying of this sort is often given the approving label of "tact," and is used "when it would be unkind to be honest but dishonest to be kind" (Bavelas, 1983, p. 132). Sometimes a face-saving lie prevents embarrassment for the recipient, as when you pretend to remember someone at a party whom you really don't recall ever having seen before. In other cases a lie protects the teller from embarrassment. You might, for example, cover up your mistakes by blaming them on outside forces: "You didn't receive the check? It must have been delayed in the mail."

The second most frequent motivation for lying was *to avoid tension or conflict* (22.2 percent). Sometimes it seems worthwhile to tell a little lie to prevent a large conflict. You might, for example, compliment a friend's bad work, not so much for your friend's sake but to prevent the hassle that would result if you told the truth. Likewise, you might hide feelings of irritation to avoid a

The personality of man is not an apple that has to be polished, but a banana that has to be peeled. And the reason we remain so far from one another, the reason we neither communicate nor interact in any real way, is that most of us spend our lives in polishing rather than peeling.

Man's lifelong task is simply one, but it is not simple: to remove the discrepancy between his outer self and his inner self, to get rid of the "persona" that divides his authentic self from the world.

This persona is like the peeling on a banana: It is something built up to protect from bruises and injury. It is not the real person, but sometimes (if the fear of injury remains too great) it becomes a lifelong substitute for the person.

The "authentic personality" knows that he is like a banana, and knows that only as he peels himself down to his individuated self can he reach out and make contact with his fellows by what Father Goldbrunner calls "the sheer maturity of his humanity." Only when he himself is detached from his defensive armorings can he then awaken a true response in his dialogue with others.

Most of us, however, think in terms of the apple, not the banana. We spend our lives in shining the surface, in making it rosy and gleaming, in perfecting the "image." But the image is not the apple, which may be wormy and rotten to the taste.

Almost everything in modern life is devoted to the polishing process, and little to the peeling process. It is the surface personality that we work on—the appearance, the clothes, the manners, the geniality. In short, the salesmanship: We are selling the package, not the product.

Sydney J. Harris

---

fight: "I'm not mad at you; it's just been a tough day." The motive for this sort of lying can be charitably described as promoting relational stability (Camden, Motley, and Wilson, 1984).

A third motive for lying (given 9.9 percent of the time) is *to guide social interaction.* You might, for instance, pretend to be glad to see someone you actually dislike or fake interest in a dinner companion's boring stories to make a social event pass quickly. Children who aren't skilled or interested in these social lies are often a source of embarrassment for their parents.

Affecting interpersonal relationships was a

fourth motive for lying, offered as a reason by the experimental subjects 9.6 percent of the time. Some lies in this category are attempts to *expand* the relationship: "I'm headed that way. Can I give you a ride?" "I like science fiction too. What have you read lately?" Lies to make yourself look good also fall into this category, such as calling yourself a "management trainee" when you really are a clerk who might someday be promoted. Other relational lies are attempts to reduce interaction. Sometimes we lie to escape an unpleasant situation: "I really have to go. I should be studying for a test tomorrow." In other cases people lie to end an entire relationship: "You're too good for me. I don't deserve a wonderful person like you."

The fifth and last motive revealed by 3.2 percent of the subjects was *to achieve personal power.* Turning down a last-minute request for a date by claiming you're busy can be one way to put yourself in a one-up position, saying in effect "Don't expect me to sit around waiting for you to call." Lying to get confidential information—even for a good cause—also falls into the category of achieving power.

This five-part scheme isn't the only way to categorize lies. Camden, Motley, and Wilson (1984) created the taxonomy outlined in Table 8–1. Their framework is more complicated than the five-part one above, and covers some types of lies that don't fit into the simpler scheme. Exaggerations,

for example, are lies told to boost the effect of a story. In exaggerated tales the fish grow larger, hikes grow longer and more strenuous, and so on. The stories may be less truthful, but they become more interesting—at least to the teller.

Beneficiaries of lying Most people think "white lies" are told for the benefit of the recipient. In fact, the majority of subjects in the Turner, Edgely, and Olmstead study claimed such lying was "the right thing to do." Other research paints a less flattering picture of who benefits most from social lying. Hample (1980) found that two out of every three lies are told for "selfish reasons." A look at Table 8–1 seems to make this figure too conservative. Of the 322 lies recorded, 244 (75.8 percent) were for the benefit of the liar. Only 70 (21.1 percent) were for the benefit the person

TABLE 8–1 Types of white lies and their frequency

	BENEFIT SELF	BENEFIT OTHER	BENEFIT THIRD PARTY
Basic Needs	68	1	1
A. Acquire resources	29	0	0
B. Protect resources	39	1	1
Affiliation	128	1	6
A. Positive	65	0	0
1. Initiate interaction	8	0	0
2. Continue interaction	6	0	0
3. Avoid conflict	48	0	0
4. Obligatory acceptance	3	0	0
B. Negative	43	1	3
1. Avoid interaction	34	1	3
2. Leave-taking	9	0	0
C. Conversational control	20	0	3
1. Redirect conversation	3	0	0
2. Avoid self-disclosure	17	0	3
Self-Esteem	35	63	1
A. Competence	8	26	0
B. Taste	0	18	1
C. Social desirability	27	19	0
Other	13	5	0
A. Dissonance reduction	3	5	0
B. Practical joke	2	0	0
C. Exaggeration	8	0	0

From Camden, Motley, and Wilson (1984), p. 315.

hearing the lie, while a mere 8 (2.5 percent) were intended to aid a third party.

Before we become totally cynical, however, the researchers urge a charitable interpretation. After all, most intentional communication behavior—truthful or not—is designed to help the speaker achieve a goal. Therefore, it's unfair to judge white lies more harshly than other types of messages. If we define selfishness as the extent to which some desired resource or interaction is denied to the person hearing the lie or to a third party, then only 111 lies (34.7 percent) can be considered truly selfish. This figure may be no worse than the degree of selfishness in honest messages.

Lying may be so common because it provides an easy way to manage difficult situations. In this regard, successful liars may be viewed as possessing a certain kind of communicative competence or skill. On the other hand, if lying is merely the easiest response to a difficult situation, liars may be viewed as lacking the competence to present the truth in ways that achieve the same goals without dishonesty.

Are white lies an ethical alternative to self-disclosure? Although we hesitate to answer the question with an unqualified "yes," the research cited in this section makes it clear that few people can claim that their communication is totally honest. Perhaps the right questions to ask are whether a small lie is truly in the interests of the receiver, and whether such a lie is the only effective way to behave.

Sex differences in self-disclosure

Are men and women equally willing to communicate in a disclosing way? Sidney Jourard (1971) was one of the first researchers to explore this question. Using his Self-Disclosure Questionnaire he found that females disclose more than males.

He explained his results by discussing what he called the "lethal male role"—that is, males are socialized not to disclose and so build up more tension in their daily lives, which results in early death—and the notion that females are socialized to be open and self-disclosing.

More-recent research isn't so certain: Some studies support Jourard's early findings, some indicate that there is no difference between the amount males and females disclose, and a few studies indicate that males disclose more (although these studies are fewest in number). It appears that the relationship between gender and self-disclosure is not a simple, clear-cut one. For example, males disclose more about their family relationships, interests, and tastes. Also, males appear to disclose less negative and more neutral information about themselves than females. Finally, Cash and Soloway (1975) found that males who perceive themselves as attractive self-disclose more than other males, whereas females who perceive themselves as attractive disclose less than other females.

In clarifying the relationship between sex and self-disclosure, Lawrence Rosenfeld, Jean Civikly, and Jane Herron (1979) found that the relationship is indeed a complex one, calling for the consideration of a number of variables before any conclusions can be drawn. In general, they found that males disclose more to strangers than females do, and are more willing to disclose superficial things about themselves, such as their work, attitudes, and opinions. Males are also less intimate and less personal than females. One clear finding is that both men and women generally prefer self-disclosure with members of the opposite sex (Rosenfeld, 1982).

When the target of disclosure is a friend and not a stranger, it's difficult to predict how either males or females will self-disclosure. Is the revealer alone or in a group? Is the topic an intimate one, or rather impersonal? At least these two questions must be answered before any predictions can be made.

Self-disclosure in families differs according to sex. A study by Victor Daluiso (1972) reported that daughters received the lion's share of disclosure from the parents and, probably as a consequence, had a more accurate perception of their parents. Sons received less disclosure than they gave, and they gave less than their sisters. This information suggests that the pattern for later life may be established in the family: Males have a tendency to disclose less intimate information about themselves than females.

Adrienne Abelman (1976) uncovered some fascinating connections between self-disclosure and family relationships. Among her many conclusions were the following: (1) mutual self-disclosure exists, but primarily between the parents and their children of the same sex; (2) a daughter's satisfaction with her family is related to her father's degree of self-disclosing to his wife; (3) men seem to rely on self-disclosing with their wives to obtain family satisfaction, whereas women seem to rely on self-disclosing with their children in order to obtain the same thing (which may account for why a father's disclosure to his wife is a determinant of their daughter's satisfaction); (4) information family members have about each other is related to the degree to which each family member self-discloses.

Men and women differ in their self-disclosing behaviors, but do they *avoid* opening up for the same or different reasons? Rosenfeld (1979) investigated this question in a study in which men and women in beginning speech courses were asked to respond to reasons why people might avoid self-disclosure. (See Table 8–2.) Before reading the results of the survey, you might want to complete the questionnaire for yourself.

Use the following scale to indicate the extent to which you use each reason to avoid self-disclosing.

1 Almost always
2 Often

TABLE 8–2 Reasons for nondisclosure

_____ 1. I can't find the opportunity to self-disclose with this person.

_____ 2. If I disclosed, I might hurt the other person.

_____ 3. If I disclosed, I might be evaluating or judging the other person.

_____ 4. I cannot think of topics that I would disclose.

_____ 5. Self-disclosure would give the other person information to use against me at some time.

_____ 6. If I disclosed, it might cause me to make personal changes.

_____ 7. Self-disclosure might threaten relationships I have with people other than the close acquaintance to whom I disclose.

_____ 8. Disclosure is a sign of weakness.

_____ 9. If I disclosed, I might lose control over the other person.

_____ 10. If I disclosed, I might discover I am less than I wish to be.

_____ 11. If I disclosed, I might project an image I do not want to project.

_____ 12. If I disclosed, the other person might not understand what I was saying.

_____ 13. If I disclosed, the other person might evaluate me negatively.

_____ 14. Self-disclosure is a sign of some emotional disturbance.

_____ 15. Self-disclosure might hurt our relationship.

_____ 16. I am afraid that self-disclosure might lead to an intimate relationship with the other person.

_____ 17. Self-disclosure might threaten my physical safety.

_____ 18. If I disclosed, I might give information that makes me appear inconsistent.

_____ 19. Any other reason: _____

_____.

3   Sometimes
4   Rarely
5   Almost never

An analysis of responses to the questionnaire indicated that there is a great deal of similarity between why males and females avoid self-disclosure. The reason most commonly identified by both men and women was, "If I disclosed, I might project an image I do not want to project."

Important differences exist, too. For males, subsequent reasons (in order of importance) included: "If I disclosed, I might give information that makes me appear inconsistent"; "If I disclosed, I might lose control over the other

person"; and "Self-disclosure might threaten relationships I have with people other than the close acquaintance to whom I disclose." Taken as a group, these reasons provide insight into the predominant reason why men avoid self-disclosure: "If I disclose to you I might project an image I do not want to, which could make me look bad and cause me to lose control over you. This trouble might go so far as to affect relationships I have with people other than you." *The object is to maintain control*, which may be hampered by self-disclosure.

For females, reasons in addition to "If I disclosed, I might project an image I do not want to project" included (in order of importance): "Self-disclosure would give the other person information to use against me at some time"; "Self-disclosure is a sign of some emotional disturbance"; and "Self-disclosure might hurt our relationship." Taken as a group, these reasons add up to the following: "If I disclose to you I might project an image I do not want to, such as my being emotionally ill, which you might use against me and which might hurt our relationship." *The object is to avoid personal hurt and problems with the relationship,* both of which may result from self-disclosure.

Other analyses have supplemented these results. Males are expected not to disclose (Lewis, 1978). Men are socialized to compete, and sharing private information can seem incompatible with winning. Also, some men may be reluctant to share positive feelings toward others of the same sex because of a fear known as "homophobia," the fear of homosexuals or of appearing to be a homosexual. Expressions of vulnerability are perceived as feminine, as are expressions of affection.

Women, on the other hand, are expected to be more disclosing than men (Hacker, 1981). This expectation is based on women having been taught to value relationships and develop intimacy. Also, females are more likely to have had positive experiences when self-disclosing as children, and they expect that future disclosure will lead to continued positive results.

Risks and benefits of self-disclosure

Is self-disclosure "good" or "bad"? There are two answers to this question: "both" and "it depends." On the one hand, disclosure is both a means and an end of interpersonal relationships. Revealing important information about ourselves is a way to grow closer and build trust. The information we learn about others through disclosure is often what transforms our relationships from superficial, stereotyped role-playing arrangements into unique, deeply fulfilling ones. On the other hand, too much disclosure or disclosure that is poorly timed can lead to consequences ranging from mild annoyance and disappointment to downright rage and grief. We need to look, then, at both the benefits and risks of disclosing to gain a clearer idea of when it is—and isn't—an effective type of communication.

Risks of self-disclosure   The reasons for avoiding self-disclosure are summed up best by John Powell, who answers the question posed in the title of his book, *Why Am I Afraid to Tell You Who I Am?* (1968):

> I am afraid to tell you who I am, because, if I tell you who I am, you may not like who I am, and that's all I have.

Revealing private information can be risky, both for the person who does the disclosing and those who hear it. These risks fall into several categories:

1. *Self-disclosure might lead to rejection.* Powell cited this risk in the quote above.

A: I don't want to keep any secrets from you. At the reunion last year I met my old sweetheart, and we made love.

B: You have fifteen minutes to pack your bags and get out of here!

2. *Self-disclosure might lead to the projection of a negative image.* Even if disclosure of unappealing information doesn't lead to total rejection, it can create a negative impression that diminishes both the other person's respect and your self-esteem.

A: I earned a C average last semester.

B: Really? You must be a real dummy!

3. *Self-disclosure might lead to a decrease in the satisfaction obtained from a relationship.* Relationships can be weakened when the wants and needs of the parties are different.

A: Let's get together with Wes and Joanne Saturday night.

B: To tell you the truth, I'm tired of seeing Wes and Joanne. I don't have much fun with them.

A: But they're my best friends . . .

4. *Self-disclosure might lead to a loss of control in the relationship.* Once you confess a secret weakness, your control over how the other person views you has diminished.

A: I'm sorry I was sarcastic. That's my way of hiding how inferior I feel sometimes.

B: Is that it? I'll never let you put me down again!

5. *Self-disclosure might hurt the other person.* Revealing hidden information may leave you feeling temporarily better, but it leaves others, especially insecure people, with lowered self-esteem.

"Hah! This is the Old King Cole nobody ever sees."

From The New Yorker, November 14, 1983.

i think of my poems and songs
as hands
and if i don't hold them out to you
i find i won't be touched

if i keep them
in my pocket
i would never get to see you
seeing me
seeing you

and though i know from experience
many of you
for a myriad of reasons
will laugh
and spit
and walk away unmoved
still
to meet those of you
who do reach out
is well worth the risk
                        the pain

so
here are my hands
do what you will

Ric Masten

A: Well, since you asked, I have been bored lately when we've been together.

B: I know. It's my fault. I don't see how you can stand me at all!

6. *Lying often appears to have greater benefit for the listener.* Honesty doesn't always seem to be the best policy.

A: I worked three months on this painting, and I want you to have it. What do you think of it?

B: The thought is really sweet, but I don't like the painting.

The above risks make it clear that self-disclosure doesn't always lead to happily-ever-after outcomes. In addition to these situational hazards, there are cultural dangers associated with disclosing. Like it or not, many people view revealing personal information—even in close relationships—as a kind of weakness, exhibitionism, or mental illness. Although these beliefs seem to be growing less pervasive, it is still important to consider whether the other person will welcome the information you share.

Paradoxical as it sounds, a final risk of self-disclosure is that it often leads to increased awareness. As you reveal yourself to others, you often learn more about yourself. This awareness can expose a need for you to change, which might be difficult or painful. If ignorance is bliss, self-awareness can sometimes be quite the opposite—at least temporarily.

Benefits of self-disclosure   Although revealing personal information has its risks, the potential benefits are at least as great. Self-disclosure —of the right type, communicated at the right time, in the right way—has three benefits.

Better relationships   The effect of self-disclosure on personal relationships works in two directions: We like people with whom we reciprocally disclose, and we disclose with people whom we like. Cozby (1973) describes a study in which subjects who had just spent a short time getting acquainted chose to disclose the greatest amount of information to partners whom they liked the most, and the smallest amount of information to those they liked the least. After a period of interaction, the subjects were asked again to rate their liking for their partners. An analysis showed that the partners who had disclosed the greatest amount of information were liked the best.

Self-disclosure plays a very important role in our close relationships. According to Derlega (1984, p. 4), "It enables the relationship partners to coordinate necessary actions and to reduce ambiguity about one another's intentions and the

Something there is that doesn't love a wall,
That sends the frozen-ground-swell under it,
And spills the upper boulders in the sun;
And makes gaps even two can pass abreast.
 . . . The gaps I mean,
No one has seen them made or heard them
 made,
But at spring mending-time we find them there.
I let my neighbor know beyond the hill;
And on a day we meet to walk the line
And set the wall between us once again.
We keep the wall between us as we go.
To each the boulders that have fallen to each. . . .
We wear our fingers rough with handling them.
Oh, just another kind of outdoor game,
One on a side. It comes to little more:
There where it is we do not need the wall:
He is all pine and I am apple orchard.
My apple trees will never get across
And eat the cones under his pines, I tell him.
He only says, "Good fences make good
 neighbors."
Spring is the mischief in me, and I wonder
If I could put a notion in his head:
"*Why* do they make good neighbors? Isn't it
Where there are cows? But here there are no
 cows.
Before I built a wall I'd ask to know
What I was walling in or walling out,
And to whom I was like to give offense.
Something there is that doesn't love a wall,
That wants it down." . . .
 . . . I see him there
Bringing a stone grasped firmly by the top
In each hand, like an old-stone savage armed.
He moves in darkness as it seems to me,
Not of woods only and the shade of trees.
He will not go behind his father's saying,
And he likes having thought of it so well
He says again, "Good fences make good
 neighbors."

Robert Frost, *"Mending Wall"*

meaning of their behavior." Perhaps because of this, the importance of self-disclosure in marriage is well documented. Self-disclosure has been found to be positively related to marital satisfaction (Miller and Lefcourt, 1982; Waring and Chelune, 1983). One recent study revealed that distressed couples who sought counseling disclosed less information to one another and communicated more ambiguously than nondistressed couples (Chelune, Rosenfeld, and Waring, in press). Couples recognize the value of disclosure: Disclosing couples give their present relationships higher evaluations and have more positive expectations than do partners who disclose less (Troost, 1977).

Whether lack of self-disclosure is a cause or a symptom of troubled marriages isn't clear. However, couples who learn to change their communication styles are likely to find their relationships grow stronger. A number of studies have demonstrated that increased self-disclosure can improve troubled marriages (Jacobson, 1984; Waring, 1981). With the guidance of a skilled counselor or therapist, partners can learn constructive ways to open up. Many of the guidelines for constructive disclosure are contained in this chapter. Often, however, a couple with a backlog of hidden hurts and resentments needs the help

of a third party to unload their emotional baggage without causing more damage.

Whether or not the relationship is an intimate one, it's a mistake to believe that if some self-disclosure is good, then more disclosure is better. In fact, as Figure 8–7 shows, there is a curvilinear relationship between liking and self-disclosure (Cozby, 1972; Lange and Grove, 1981). People who disclose too little are not well liked for an obvious reason: It's impossible to get to know them. On the other hand, those who disclose too much aren't popular either. They are viewed as lacking judgment and trustworthiness. One key to better relationships, then, is to engage in a moderate amount of self-disclosure.

The amount of disclosing that goes on in satisfying relationships seems to vary according to the relational stage (Won-Doornick, 1979). As the relationship progresses from early stages of initiating and experimenting, partners spend less time exchanging nonintimate information. The clichés and trivial facts that are a necessary part of getting acquainted are less satisfying when a relationship intensifies. Interestingly, however, the growth of intimacy doesn't appear to continue indefinitely: When the relationship reaches a peak of bonding, the level of self-disclosure begins to diminish. Your personal experience probably matches this research. An intense period of self-disclosure is exciting and rewarding, but it's difficult to maintain. Mature relationships are a mixture of everyday, relatively superficial information and occasional deeper revelations.

Mental health Besides being necessary for the success of interpersonal relationships, appropriate self-disclosure promotes mental health. Cozby summarizes the research on this area:

> Persons with positive mental health (given that they can be identified) are characterized by high disclosure to a few significant others and medium disclosure to others in the social environment.

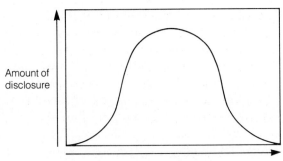

FIGURE 8–7 Relationship between self-disclosure and interpersonal attraction

Individuals who are poorly adjusted (again assuming a suitable identification can be made) are characterized by either high or low disclosure to virtually everyone in the social environment (Cozby, 1973, p. 78).

The relationship between self-disclosure and mental health is obvious, if somewhat circular. Most experts consider the ability to form and maintain satisfying interpersonal relationships as one element of mental health. Because it is impossible to carry on these relationships without a degree of self-disclosure, it follows that self-disclosure and mental health go hand in hand.

There is an additional way in which self-disclosure and personal adjustment are related. It takes a great deal of energy to keep feelings hidden from significant others. Withholding important information can create stress that leads to less effective behavior and even physical discomfort (Jourard, 1971; Mowrer, 1968). The feelings we experience when we have finally opened up—freedom, relief, "as if a weight was taken off your shoulders"—come from freeing up the energy used to keep the information private. Mentally healthy people are not burdened by an excessive load of unexpressed feelings and ideas.

Self-understanding Sharing your thoughts and feelings appropriately can lead to learning more about yourself. Disclosure leads to self-understanding in two steps. First, the act of sharing information often leads to new insights. Simply talking about a subject aloud often reduces the confusion that comes from turning a feeling over and over in your mind. Second, your disclosure boosts the odds that the other person will also reveal information—about you, the subject you are discussing, and the relationship you share. Research shows that disclosure is reciprocal: the more information you reveal, the more you are likely to receive (Chelune, 1979). In this way,

> **Sometimes a neighbor whom we have disliked for a lifetime for his arrogance and conceit lets fall a single commonplace remark that shows us another side, another man, really; a man uncertain, puzzled, and in the dark like ourselves.**
>
> Willa Cather

feedback from others can lead to increased self-awareness.

When to self-disclose

Self-disclosure is a special kind of sharing, not appropriate for every situation. Let's take a look at some guidelines that can help you recognize how to express yourself in a way that's rewarding for you and the others involved.

1. Is the other person important to you? There are several ways in which someone might be important. Perhaps you have an ongoing relationship deep enough so that sharing significant parts of yourself justifies keeping your present level of togetherness intact. Perhaps the person to whom you're considering disclosing is someone with whom you've previously related on a less personal level. Now you see a chance to grow closer, and disclosure may be the path toward developing that personal relationship.

There's still another category of "important person" to whom self-disclosure is sometimes appropriate: strangers who are players in what has been called the "bus rider phenomenon." Sometimes when we meet a total stranger whom we'll probably never see again (on a bus, plane, or elsewhere), we reveal the most intimate parts of our lives. It's sometimes possible to call such strangers "important people" because they provide a safe outlet for expressing important feelings which otherwise would go unshared.

2. Is the risk of disclosing reasonable? Take a realistic look at the potential risks of self-disclosure. Even if the probable benefits are great, opening yourself up to almost certain rejection may be asking for trouble. For instance, it might be foolhardy to share your important feelings with someone you know is likely to betray your confidences or ridicule them. On the other hand, knowing that your partner is trustworthy and supportive makes the prospect of speaking out more reasonable. In anticipating risks, be sure that you are realistic. It's sometimes easy to imagine all sorts of disastrous consequences of your opening up, when in fact such horrors are quite unlikely to occur.

3. Is the amount and type of disclosure appropriate? A third point to realize is that there are degrees of self-disclosure, so that telling others about yourself isn't an all-or-nothing decision you must make. It's possible to share some facts, opinions, or feelings with one person while reserving riskier ones for others. In the same vein, before sharing important information with someone who does matter to you, you might consider testing her or his reactions by disclosing less-personal data. Remember, too, that even the closest long-term relationships aren't characterized by a constant exchange of disclosure. Rather, they are a mixture of much everyday, non-intimate information and less frequent but more personal messages. Finally, realize that even intimate partners need to be sensitive to the timing of a message. If the other person is tired, preoccupied, or grumpy, it may be best to postpone an important conversation.

4. Is the disclosure relevant to the situation at

"I'm a very sensual person. How about you, Mr. Gellerman?"

Drawing by Stan Hunt © The New Yorker Magazine, Inc.

hand? Self-disclosure doesn't require long confessions about your past life or current thoughts unrelated to the present. On the contrary, it ought to be directly pertinent to your present conversation. It's ludicrous to picture the self-disclosing person as someone who blurts out intimate details of every past experience. Instead, our model is someone who, when the time is appropriate, trusts us enough to share the hidden truths that affect our relationship.

Usually, then, the subject of appropriate self-disclosure involves the present, the "here and now" as opposed to "there and then." "How am I feeling now?" "How are we doing now?" These are appropriate topics for sharing personal thoughts and feelings. There are certainly times when it's relevant to bring up the past, but only as it relates to what's going on in the present.

5. *Is the disclosure reciprocated*? There's nothing quite as disconcerting as talking your heart out to someone, only to discover that the other person has yet to say anything to you that is half as revealing. You think to yourself, "What am I doing?" Unequal self-disclosure creates an unbalanced relationship, one doomed to fall apart.

There are few times when one-way disclosure

is acceptable. Most of them involve formal, therapeutic relationships in which a client approaches a trained professional with the goal of resolving a problem. For instance, you wouldn't necessarily expect your physician to begin sharing his or her personal ailments with you during an office visit. Nonetheless, it's interesting that one frequently noted characteristic of effective psychotherapists, counselors, and teachers is a willingness to share their feelings about a relationship with their clients.

6. *Will the effect be constructive?* Self-disclosure can be a vicious tool if it's not used carefully. Every person has a psychological "beltline," and below that beltline are areas about which the person is extremely sensitive. Jabbing at a "below the belt" area is a sure-fire way to disable another person, though usually at great cost to the relationship. It's important to consider the effects of your candor before opening up to others. Comments such as, "I've always thought you were pretty unintelligent" or, "Last year I made love to your best friend" *may* sometimes resolve old business and thus be constructive, but they also can be devastating—to the listener, to the relationship, and to your self-esteem.

7. *Is the self-disclosure clear and understandable?* When expressing yourself to others, it's important that you share yourself in a way that's intelligible. This means describing the *sources* of your message clearly. For instance, it's far better to describe another's behavior by saying, "When you don't answer my phone calls or drop by to visit anymore . . . " than to complain vaguely, "When you avoid me . . . "

It's also vital to express your *thoughts* and *feelings* explicitly. "I feel worried because I'm afraid you don't care about me" is more understandable than "I don't like it . . . "

Readings

Abelman, Adrienne K. "The Relationship Between Family Self-Disclosure, Adolescent Adjustment, Family Satisfaction, and Family Congruence." *Dissertation Abstracts International* 36 (1976): 4248A.

Bavelas, I. "Situations That Lead to Disqualifications." *Human Communication Research* 9 (1983): 130–145.

Berne, Eric. *Games People Play.* New York: Grove Press, 1964.

Burke, Ronald J., Tamara Weir, and Denise Harrison. "Disclosure of Problems and Tensions Experienced by Marital Partners." *Psychological Reports* 38 (1976): 531–542.

Camden, C., M. T. Motley, and A. Wilson. "White Lies in Interpersonal Communication: A Taxonomy and Preliminary Investigation of Social Motivations." *Western Journal of Speech Communication* 48 (1984): 309–325.

Cash, T. F., and D. Soloway. "Self-Disclosure Correlates of Physical Attractiveness: An Exploratory Study." *Psychological Reports* 36 (1975): 579–586.

Chelune, G. J., L. B. Rosenfeld, and E. M. Waring. "Spouse Disclosure Patterns in Distressed and Nondistressed Couples." *American Journal of Family Therapy* (in press).

*Chelune, Gordon J., ed. *Self-Disclosure.* San Francisco: Jossey-Bass, 1979.

Chelune, Gordon J. "Toward an Empirical Definition of Self-Disclosure: Validation in a Single Case Design." *Western Journal of Speech Communication* 45 (1981): 269–276.

Chelune, Gordon J., Stephen T. Skiffington, and Connie Williams. "A Multidimensional Analysis of Observers' Perceptions of Self-Disclosing Behavior." *Journal of Personality and Social Psychology* 41 (1981): 599–606.

Cozby, P. "Self-Disclosure, Reciprocity, and Liking." *Sociometry* 35 (1972): 151–160.

*Cozby, Paul C. "Self-Disclosure: A Literature Review." *Psychological Bulletin* 79 (1973): 73–91.

Daluiso, Victor E. "Self-Disclosure and Perception of that Self-Disclosure Between Parents and Their Teen-Age Children." *Dissertation Abstracts International* 33 (1972): 420B.

Derlega, Valerian J. "Self-Disclosure and Intimate Relationships." In *Communication, Intimacy, and Close Relationships*, V. J. Derlega, ed. Orlando: Academic Press, 1984.

Derlega, Valerian J., and Alan L. Chaikin. "Privacy and Self-Disclosure in Social Relationships." *Journal of Social Issues* 33 (1978): 102–115.

*Derlega, Valerian J., and Alan L. Chaikin. *Sharing Intimacy: What We Reveal to Others and Why*. Englewood Cliffs, N.J.: Prentice-Hall, 1975.

Derlega, Valerian J., Bonnie Durham, Barbara Gockel, and David Sholis. "Sex Differences in Self-Disclosure: Effects of Topic Content, Friendships, and Partner's Sex." *Sex Roles* 7 (1981): 433–448.

Derlega, Valerian J., and Janusz Grzelak. "Appropriateness of Self-Disclosure." In *Self-Disclosure*, Gordon J. Chelune, ed. San Francisco: Jossey-Bass, 1979.

Derlega, Valerian J., Midge Wilson, and Alan L. Chaikin. "Friendship and Disclosure Reciprocity." *Journal of Personality and Social Psychology* 34 (1976): 578–582.

Egan, Gerard. *Encounter: Group Processes for Interpersonal Growth*. Belmont, Calif.: Brooks/Cole, 1970.

Gergen, Kenneth J. *The Concept of Self*. New York: Holt, Rinehart and Winston, 1971.

Giffin, Kim, and Bobby R. Patton. *Personal Communication in Human Relations*. Columbus, Ohio: Charles E. Merrill, 1974.

Gilbert, Shirley J. "Self-Disclosure, Intimacy and Communication in Families." *Family Coordinator* 25 (1976): 221–231.

Gilbert, Shirley J., and Gale G. Whiteneck. "Toward a Multidimensional Approach to the Study of Self-Disclosure." *Human Communication Research* 2 (1976): 347–355.

Goodstein, Leonard D., and Virginia M. Reinecker. Factors Affecting Self-Disclosure: A Review of the Literature." In *Progress in Experimental Personality Research* VII, Brendan A. Maher, ed. New York: Academic Press, 1974.

Hacker, Helen Mayer. "Blabbermouths and Clams: Sex Differences in Self-Disclosure in Same-Sex and Cross-Sex Friendship Dyads." *Psychology of Women Quarterly* (Spring 1981): 385–401.

Hample, D. "Purposes and Effects of Lying." *Southern Speech Communication Journal* 46 (1980): 33–47.

Hendrick, Susan S. "Self-Disclosure and Marital Satisfaction." *Journal of Personality and Social Psychology* 40 (1981): 1150–1159.

Jacobson, N. S. "A Component Analysis of Behavioral Marital Therapy: The Relative Effectiveness of Behavior Exchange and Communication/Problem-Solving Training." *Journal of Consulting and Clinical Psychology* 52 (1984): 295–305.

Jourard, Sidney M. *Disclosing Man to Himself*. Princeton, N.J.: Van Nostrand, 1968.

Jourard, Sidney M. "Healthy Personality and Self-Disclosure." *Mental Hygiene* 43 (1959): 499–507.

*Jourard, Sidney M. *The Transparent Self*, 2d ed. Princeton, N.J.: Van Nostrand, 1971.

Kleinke, Chris L. "Effects of Personal Evaluations." In *Self-Disclosure*, Gordon J. Chelune, ed. San Francisco: Jossey-Bass, 1979.

Lange, Jonathan I., and Theodore G. Grove. "Sociometric and Autonomic Responses to Three Levels of Self-Disclosure in Dyads." *Western Journal of Speech Communication* 45 (1981): 355–362.

Lederer, W. J. *Marital Choices*. New York: W. W. Norton, 1981.

Lewis, Robert A. "Emotional Intimacy Among Men." *Journal of Social Issues* 34 (1978): 108–121.

Luft, Joseph. *Of Human Interaction*. Palo Alto, Calif.: National Press Books, 1969.

Lyons, Arthur. "Personality of High and Low Self-Disclosers." *Journal of Humanistic Psychology* 18 (1978): 83–86.

Miller, R. S., and H. M. Lefcourt. "The Assessment of Social Intimacy." *Journal of Person-*

ality *Assessment* 46 (1982): 514–518.

Moriwaki, Sharon Y. "Self-Disclosure, Significant Others and Psychological Well-Being in Old Age." *Journal of Health and Social Behavior* 14 (1973): 226–232.

Mowrer, Orval Hobart. "Loss and Recovery of Community: A Guide to the Theory and Practice of Integrity Therapy." In *Innovations to Group Psychotherapy*, George M. Gazda, ed. Springfield, Ill.: Charles C. Thomas, 1968.

Pearce, W. Barnett, and Stewart M. Sharp. "Self-Disclosing Communication." *Journal of Communication* 23 (1973): 409–425.

Powell, John. *Why Am I Afraid to Tell You Who I Am?* Niles, Ill.: Argus Communications, 1968.

*Rosenfeld, Lawrence B. "Self-Disclosure Avoidance: Why Am I Afraid to Tell You Who I Am?" *Communication Monographs* 46 (1979): 63–74.

Rosenfeld, Lawrence B. "Self-Disclosure and Target Characteristics." Unpublished manuscript, University of New Mexico, 1981.

Rosenfeld, Lawrence B., Jean M. Civikly, and Jane R. Herron. "Anatomical Sex, Psychological Sex, and Self-Disclosure." In *Self-Disclosure,* Gordon J. Chelune, ed. San Francisco: Jossey-Bass, 1979.

Rosenfeld, Lawrence B., and W. Leslie Kendrick. "Choosing to Be Open: Subjective Reasons for Self-Disclosing." *Western Journal of Speech Communication* 48 (1984): 326–343.

Rubin, Zick. "Lovers and Other Strangers: The Development of Intimacy in Encounters and Relationships." *American Scientist* 62 (1974): 182–190.

Steele, Fritz. *The Open Organization: The Impact of Secrecy and Disclosure on People and Organizations.* Reading, Mass.: Addison-Wesley, 1975.

Troost, K. M. "Communication in Marriage." *Dissertation Abstracts* 37 (1977): 8003A.

Turner, R. E., C. Edgely, and G. Olmstead. "Information Control in Conversation: Honesty Is Not Always the Best Policy." *Kansas Journal of Sociology* 11 (1975): 69–89.

Walker, Lilly S., and Paul H. Eright. "Self-Disclosure in Friendship." *Perceptual and Motor Skills* 42 (1976): 735–742.

Waring, E. M. "Facilitating Marital Intimacy through Self-Disclosure." *American Journal of Family Therapy* 9 (1981): 33–42.

Waring, E. M., and Gordon J. Chelune. "Marital Intimacy and Self-Disclosure." *Journal of Clinical Psychology* 39 (1983): 183–190.

Wheeless, Lawrence R., and Janis Grotz. "The Measurement of Trust and Its Relationship to Self-Disclosure." *Human Communication Research* 3 (1977): 250–257.

Williams, Margery. *The Velveteen Rabbit.* New York: Avon, 1975.

Won-Doornick, M. J. "On Getting to Know You: The Association Between the Stage of Relationship and Reciprocity of Self-Disclosure." *Journal of Experimental Social Psychology* 15 (1979): 229–241.

Wood, John T. *What Are You Afraid Of?: A Guide to Dealing with Your Fears.* New York: Spectrum Books, 1976.

Emotions

After studying the material in this chapter

You should understand:

1. The four components of emotion.
2. The factors that influence the expression of emotion in contemporary society.
3. The benefits of expressing emotions appropriately.
4. The characteristics of facilitative and debilitative emotions.
5. The relationship between activating events, thoughts, and emotions.
6. Seven fallacies that result in unnecessary, debilitative emotions.
7. The steps in the rational-emotive approach to coping with debilitative feelings.

You should be able to:

1. Observe the physical and cognitive manifestations of some emotions you experience.
2. Label your own emotions accurately.
3. Identify the degree to which you express your emotions and the consequences of this level of expression.
4. Realize which of your emotions are facilitative and which are debilitative.
5. Identify the fallacious beliefs that have led you to experience some debilitative emotions.
6. In a specific situation, apply the rational-emotive approach to managing your debilitative emotions.
7. Determine the appropriate circumstances and methods for expressing some emotion you have not disclosed.

At one time or another you've probably imagined how different life would be if you became disabled in some way. The thought of becoming blind, deaf, or immobile is certainly frightening, and though a bit morbid, it can remind you to appreciate the faculties you do have. Now, have you ever considered how life would be if you somehow lost your ability to experience emotions?

Although life without feelings certainly wouldn't be as dramatic or crippling as other disabilities, consider its effect. Never again would you experience the excitement of Christmas or the first sunny day of spring. You would never enjoy a movie, book, or piece of art—or even find it interesting. Happiness, confidence, and love would be nothing but words to you. Of course, an emotionless life would also be free of boredom, frustration, fear, and loneliness—but most of us would agree that giving up pleasure is too steep a price to pay for freedom from pain.

This fantasy demonstrates the important role that emotions play in our relationships as well as in other parts of life. Because feelings play such a fundamental role in interpersonal communication, we will take a close look at them in this chapter. We'll explore exactly what feelings are, discuss the ways in which they are handled in contemporary society, and see how recognizing and expressing them can improve relationships. We'll explore a method for coping with troublesome,

"What the hell was *that*? Something just swept over me—like contentment or something."

Drawing by Weber; © 1981 The New Yorker Magazine, Inc.

debilitating feelings that can inhibit rather than help your communication. And finally, we'll look at some guidelines which should give you a clearer idea of when and how to express your emotions effectively.

What are emotions?

Suppose that a visitor from Spock's planet Vulcan asked you to explain emotions. What would you say? You might start by saying that emotions are things that we feel. This definition doesn't say much, because you would probably describe feelings as being synonymous with emotions. Social scientists who study the role of feelings generally agree that there are four components to our emotions.

Physiological changes   When a person experiences strong emotions, many bodily changes occur. For example, the physical aspects of fear include an increased heartbeat, a rise in blood pressure, an increase in adrenalin secretions, an increase in blood sugar, a slowing of digestion, and a dilation of the pupils. Some of these changes offer a significant clue to our emotions once we become aware of them. For instance, one woman we know began focusing on her internal messages and learned that every time she returned to the city from a vacation she felt an empty feeling in the pit of her stomach. From what she'd already learned about herself, she knew that this sensation always accompanied things she dreaded. Then she realized she was much happier in the country.

Another friend of ours had always appeared easygoing and agreeable, even in the most frustrating circumstances. After focusing on internal messages, he discovered his mild behavior contrasted strongly with the tense muscles and headaches that he got during trying times. This new awareness led him to realize that he did indeed experience frustration and anger—and that he somehow needed to deal with these feelings if he was going to feel truly comfortable.

Nonverbal manifestations   A quick comparison between the emotionless Spock of *Star Trek* and full-blooded humans tells us that feelings show up in many nonverbal behaviors. Postures, gestures, facial expression, body positioning, and distance all provide clues suggesting our emotional state.

One of the first social scientists to explore the relationship between emotion and behavior was Charles Darwin. In 1872 Darwin published *The Expression of Emotion in Man and Animals,* which asserted that humans and certain other creatures seemed to behave in similar ways when enraged. Later researchers confirmed the premise that among humans, at least, the most basic emotional expressions are universal. A. G. Gitter and his colleagues (1972) found that people from a variety of cultures all agreed on the facial expressions that indicate emotions such as fear, sadness, happiness, and pain. Chapter 5 discussed the value of observing nonverbal messages as clues to emotion.

Cognitive interpretations   The physiological aspects of fear, such as a racing heart, perspiration, tense muscles, and a boost in blood pressure, are surprisingly similar to the physical changes that accompany excitement, joy, and other emotions. In other words, from measuring the physical condition of someone experiencing a strong emotion, it would be difficult to determine whether the person was trembling with fear or quivering with excitement. The recognition that the bodily components of most emotions are similar led some psychologists (see Schachter and Singer, 1962; Valins, 1966) to conclude that the experience of fright, joy, or anger comes primarily from the *label* that we give to the same physical symptoms. If the cause of the physiological changes is unexplained, the person experiencing them uses situational cues—presumed relevant to the physiological arousal—to make a decision about the cause. An emotional state, therefore, is the product of an unexplained physiological arousal plus relevant situational cues. This cognitive explanation of emotion has been labeled *attribution theory*. Psychologist Philip Zimbardo (1977) offers a good example of attribution in action:

> I notice I'm perspiring while lecturing. From that I infer I am feeling nervous. If it occurs often, I might even label myself a "nervous person." Once I have the label, the next question I must answer is "Why am I nervous?" Then I start to search for an appropriate explanation. I might notice some students leaving the room, or being inattentive. I am nervous because I'm not giving a good lecture. That makes me nervous. How do I know it's not good? Because I'm boring my audience. I am nervous because I am a boring lecturer and I want to be a good lecturer. I feel inadequate. Maybe I should open a delicatessen instead. Just then a student says, "It's hot in here. I'm perspiring and it makes it tough to concentrate on your lecture." Instantly, I'm no longer "nervous" or "boring."

In his book *Shyness*, Zimbardo (1977) discusses the consequences of making inaccurate or exaggerated attributions. In a survey of more than 5000 subjects, over 80 percent described themselves as having been shy at some time in their lives, while more than 40 percent considered themselves presently shy. Most significantly, the "not shy" people behaved in virtually the *same way* as their shy counterparts. They would blush, perspire, and feel their hearts pounding in certain social situations. The biggest difference between the two groups seemed to be the label with which they described themselves. This difference is significant. Someone who notices the symptoms we've described and thinks, "I'm such a shy person!" will most likely feel more uncomfortable and communicate less effectively than a person with

Half our mistakes in life arise from feeling where we ought to think, and thinking where we ought to feel.

John Churton Collins

the same symptoms who thinks, "Well, I'm a bit shaky here, but that's to be expected."

Verbal expression   The fourth component of emotion is verbal expression. As Gerard Egan (1977) points out, there are several ways to express a feeling verbally. The first is through single words like those in Table 9–1: I'm angry, excited, depressed, curious, and so on. Many people are limited to these single word expressions, and suffer from impoverished emotional vocabularies. They have a hard time describing more than a few basic feelings, such as "good" or "bad," "terrible" or "great."

Another way of expressing feelings verbally is to use descriptive words or phrases: "I feel all jumbled up," "I'm on top of the world," and so on. As long as such terms aren't too obscure—for example, "I feel somnolent"—they can effectively express your emotional state.

It's also possible to express emotions by describing what you'd like to do: "I feel like singing"; "I'd like to cry"; "I feel like running away." Often these expressions capture the emotion clearly, but in other cases they can be confusing. For instance, if somebody told you, "Every time I see you I want to laugh," you wouldn't know whether you were an object of enjoyment or ridicule.

The ability to express emotions verbally is crucial to effective communication. For example, notice the difference between the comments in each pair:

> "When you kiss me and nibble on my ear, I think you want to make love."

TABLE 9–1 Some emotions			
affectionate	envious	joyful	seductive
afraid	evasive	judgmental	self-pitying
alarmed	evil	lively	self-reliant
alienated	excited	lonely	sexy
alone	exhilarated	lovable	shallow
angry	fatalistic	loved	shy
anxious	fearful	loving	silly
apathetic	feminine	masculine	sincere
appreciated	flirtatious	masked	sinful
attractive	friendly	masochistic	sluggish
awkward	frigid	melancholy	soft
beaten	frustrated	misunderstood	sorry
beautiful	generous	needy	stubborn
bewildered	genuine	old	stupid
brave	gentle	optimistic	suicidal
calm	giddy	out of control	superior
caring	glad	overcontrolled	supported
closed	grateful	oversexed	supportive
comfortable	grudging	paranoid	suspicious
committed	guilty	passionate	sympathetic
compassionate	gutless	peaceful	tender
competent	happy	persecuted	terrified
concerned	hateful	pessimistic	threatened
confident	homicidal	phony	tolerant
confused	hopeful	pitiful	torn
contented	hopeless	playful	touchy
cowardly	hostile	pleased	triumphant
creative	humorous	possessive	two-faced
cruel	hurt	preoccupied	ugly
curious	hyperactive	prejudiced	unsure
cut off	ignored	pressured	understanding
defeated	immobilized	protective	unresponsive
defensive	impatient	proud	uptight
dejected	inadequate	quiet	useless
dependent	incompetent	rejected	vindictive
depressed	indecisive	remorseful	violent
deprived	inferior	repelled	weary
desperate	inhibited	repulsive	weepy
disappointed	insecure	restrained	wishy-washy
domineering	insincere	reverent	youthful
eager	involved	sad	zany
easygoing	isolated	sadistic	zealous
embarrassed	jealous	secure	zesty

"When you kiss me and nibble on my ear, I think you want to make love and I feel excited (or disgusted)."

"Ever since we had our fight, I've been avoiding you."

"Ever since we had our fight, I've been avoiding you because I've been so embarrassed (or so angry)."

Many people think they're clearly expressing their feelings, when in fact their statements are emotionally counterfeit. For instance, it may sound emotionally revealing to say, "I feel like going to a show," or "I feel we've been seeing too much of each other." Neither of these statements actually exhibits emotional content. In the first sentence, the word "feel" really represents an intention: "I *want* to go to a show." In the second sentence, the "feeling" is really a thought: "I *think* we've been seeing too much of each other." The absence of emotion in each case becomes recognizable when you add a word with genuine feeling to the sentence. For instance, "I'm *bored* and I want to go to a show," or "I think we've been seeing too much of each other and I feel *confined.*"

Emotions in contemporary society

Once you can detect these kinds of counterfeit emotional statements, you notice that most people do little sharing of their feelings. Count the number of genuine emotional expressions you

hear over a two- or three-day period. You'll probably discover that emotional expressions are rare. People are generally comfortable making statements of fact and often delight in expressing their opinion, but they rarely disclose how they feel.

Why do people fail to express their feelings? There are several reasons. First, *our society discourages the expression of most feelings.* From the time children are old enough to understand language, they learn that the range of acceptable emotions is limited. We are told: "Don't get angry at your brother"; "That isn't funny"; "There's no reason to feel bad"; "Don't get so excited!"; and "For God's sake, don't cry." Each of these messages denies its recipient the right to experience a certain feeling. Anger isn't legitimate, and neither is fear. There's something wrong with finding certain situations humorous. Feeling bad is considered silly. Excitement isn't desirable, so keep your emotions under control. Finally, don't make a scene by crying.

Often such parental admonitions are nothing

The Thinker

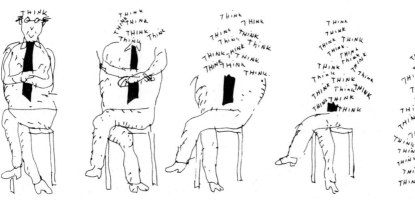

What other dungeon is so dark as one's own heart! What jailer so inexorable as one's self!

Nathaniel Hawthorne

---

more than a coded request for some peace and quiet. Repeated often enough, the underlying instruction comes through loud and clear—only a narrow range of emotions is acceptable to share or experience.

In addition, the actions of most adults create a model suggesting that grownups shouldn't express too many feelings. Expressions of affection are fine within limits: A hug and kiss for Mom is all right, but a young man should shake hands with Dad. Affection toward friends becomes less and less frequent as we grow older, so that even a simple statement such as "I like you" is seldom heard between adults.

Second, *expression of emotions is further limited by the requirements of many social roles.* Salespeople are taught always to smile at customers, no matter how obnoxious. Teachers are portrayed as paragons of rationality, supposedly representing their field of expertise and instructing their students with total impartiality. Students are rewarded for asking "acceptable" questions and otherwise being submissive creatures.

Furthermore, stereotyped sex roles discourage people from freely expressing certain emotions. The stereotype states that men don't cry and are rational creatures. They must be strong, emotionally and physically. Aggressiveness is a virtue ("the Marine Corps builds men"). Women, on the other hand, are often socialized in a manner that allows them to express their emotions by crying. The stereotype states that women should be irrational and intuitive. A certain amount of female determination and assertiveness is appealing, but when faced with a man's resistance they ought to defer (Pearson, 1985).

The third reason people fail to express their emotions is the result of all these restrictions: *many of us lose the ability to recognize emotions and to feel deeply.* As a muscle withers away when it is unused, so our capacity to recognize and act on certain emotions reduces. It's hard to cry after spending a lifetime fulfilling the role society expects of a man, even when the tears are inside. After years of denying your anger, the ability to recognize that feeling takes real effort. For someone who has never acknowledged love for friends, accepting the emotion can be difficult indeed.

The fourth and final reason concerns the fear of self-disclosure we explored in Chapter 8. In a society that discourages the expression of feelings, *emotional self-disclosure can be risky.* For a parent, boss, or teacher whose life has been built on the presumption of confidence and certainty, it may be frightening to say, "I'm sorry, I was wrong." A person who has made a life's work out of not relying on others has a hard time saying, "I'm lonesome. I want your friendship."

Moreover, a person who musters up the courage to share such feelings still risks suffering unpleasant consequences. Others might misunderstand: An expression of affection might be construed as a romantic come-on, and a confession of uncertainty might appear to be a sign of weakness. Another risk is that emotional honesty might make others feel uncomfortable. Finally, there's always a chance that emotional candor could be used against you, either out of cruelty or thoughtlessness.

Benefits of expressing emotions appropriately

Given all the social conditioning and personal risks that discourage us from expressing feelings, it's understandable why so many people are emotionally uncommunicative. This situation is

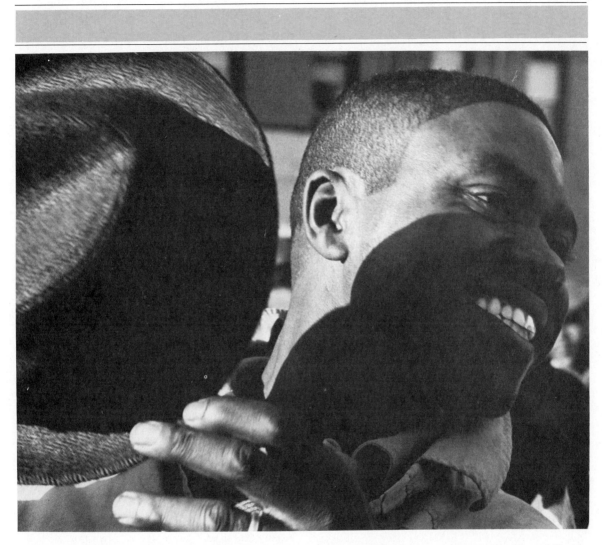

especially unfortunate when we look at the benefits that can flow from sharing feelings appropriately.

Physical health   Sharing emotions is healthy. In fact, keeping your feelings pent up can lead to psychosomatic illnesses. We're not referring to hypochondria, in which people believe they are ill but aren't, or malingering, in which they pretend to be sick. A psychosomatic disease is real: It

does not differ from an organically induced illness. What distinguishes a psychosomatic illness is its psychological basis. The pain comes from a physical condition, but the problem has its origins in some aspect of the person's psychological functioning. Psychosomatic problems can grow out of the chronic stress that results when unexpressive people don't share their feelings. The physiological changes that accompany strong emotions (digestion slows, heartbeat increases, adrenalin is secreted, and respiration grows quicker) are short-lived for people who can express their feelings, whereas those who fail to act on these impulses develop a continual state of physiological tension. This tension damages the digestive tract, lungs, circulatory system, muscles, joints, and the body's ability to resist infections. It even hastens the process of aging (McQuade and Aikman, 1974).

Hypertension (high blood pressure) and heart trouble can also have their roots in chronic stress. Over a five-year period Flanders Dunbar (1947) studied a random sample of 1600 cardiovascular patients at Columbia Presbyterian Medical Center in New York City. She found that four out of five patients shared common emotional characteristics, many of which were representative of either nonassertive or aggressive communicators. In fact, most of the patients were argumentative, had trouble expressing their feelings, and kept people at a distance. McQuade and Aikman describe other characteristics of cardiovascular sufferers: they are easily upset but unable to handle upsetting situations, anxious to please but longing to rebel, and alternately passive and irritable.

Evidence also suggests that nonassertive people are prone to yet another physical problem. The immunological system, which protects the body against infection, apparently functions less effectively when a person is under stress. The body doesn't always respond quickly enough to infection; and sometimes the body even responds incorrectly, as in the case of allergic reactions. Stress has even been diagnosed as one cause of the common cold. Stress or anxiety alone is not sufficient to cause these disorders; a source of infection must also be present. However, as research by Swiss physiologist Hans Selye (1956) suggests, persons subjected to stress have an increased chance of contracting infectious disease. Selye states, "If a microbe is in or around us all the time and yet causes no disease until we are exposed to stress, what is the cause of our illness, the microbe or the stress?"

Men have a higher incidence of stress-related ailments such as ulcers, and there may be a link between these ailments and stereotypical male nonexpressiveness. "Why Men Don't Cry" (1984), a report on the work of biochemist William Frey, points out tears from crying (not the kind associated with peeling onions) contain certain chemicals that build up in the body during stress. Crying rids the body of these chemicals and reduces the level of stress. Men, who cry about one-fifth as much as women (about once a month), may be adversely affecting their health.

All this talk about psychosomatic illness is not intended to suggest that nonassertion or nonexpressiveness automatically leads to ulcers and heart trouble, or perhaps worse. Obviously, many shy or aggressive people never suffer from such ailments and many assertive people do. There are also many other sources of stress in our society: financial pressures, the problems of people we care for, pollution, crime, and the nagging threat of war, to name a few. Nonetheless, an increasing amount of evidence suggests that the person who is not fully expressive increases the risk of developing physical disabilities. Just as nonsmokers are less likely to contract lung cancer than their pack-a-day counterparts, skillful communicators have a better chance of living a healthy life.

Increased intimacy   Beyond the physiological benefits, another advantage of expressing emotions is the chance of reaching greater intimacy with others. A friend of ours, reflecting on his marriage, affirmed this point.

For the longest time I held back a lot of feelings from my wife which I thought would hurt her. I did spare her feelings, but by holding back I also felt more and more like a stranger to her. It finally got to the point where I was hiding so much of how I truly felt that instead of an honest, growing marriage, I felt like I was carrying on a charade. Finally I couldn't stand the experience of being isolated from the woman I was committed to spending my life with, and so I began to share the things that were going on inside me—the uncomfortable feelings as well as the pleasant ones. As we really began to talk about who we were again, we uncovered a lot of feelings which we had both been out of touch with. I won't say that this kind of sharing has made our life together easier—it's often hard for one of us to face how the other feels—but I can definitely say that we feel closer now than we have in a long time.

A note of caution: Sharing every emotion you experience at the time is not always wise. When deciding whether to express a feeling that is difficult for you or another person to handle, read the guidelines for self-disclosure in Chapter 8.

Conflict resolution   Although expressing feeling can sometimes lead to trouble, the consequences of not sharing them can be just as bad. When people don't communicate, boring marriages don't change, friendships continue in hurtful patterns, and job conditions stay unpleasant. How long can such destructive patterns go on? Surely there comes a time when it's necessary either to share emotions or to give up on the relationship. Moreover, research on conflict resolution conducted by David Johnson (1971) and others suggests that the skillful expression of emotions actually increases the quality of problem solving. After all, unresolved feelings can create obstacles that keep individuals and groups from dealing most effectively with their problems. On the other hand, once the participants in a conflict have expressed their feelings, they're in a position to resolve the problems that led to them. Chapter 11 introduces several methods for handling interpersonal conflicts constructively.

Coping with debilitative feelings: A cognitive approach

At this point you may think that experiencing and expressing emotions is always beneficial. Actually, this position is extreme: Some feelings do little good for anyone. For instance, feeling dejected can sometimes provide a foundation upon which to grow ("I'm so miserable now that I must do something to change"). Often, however, depression prevents people from acting effectively. The same point can be made about rage, terror, and jealousy: Most of the time these emotions do little to promote personal well-being or to improve relationships.

Debilitative vs. facilitative emotions   We need to make a distinction, then, between *facilitative* emotions, which contribute to effective functioning, and *debilitative* emotions, which hinder or prevent effective performance. The difference between facilitative and debilitative emotions isn't one of quality so much as degree. For instance, a certain amount of anger or irritation can be constructive, since it often stimulates a person to improve the unsatisfying conditions. Rage, on the other hand, usually makes matters worse. The same is true for fear. A little bit of nervousness before an important athletic contest or job interview might boost you just enough to improve your performance (mellow athletes or actors usually don't do well). Total terror is something else. One big difference, then, between facilitative and debilitative emotions is their *intensity*.

As Gerald Kranzler (1974) points out, intense feelings of fear or rage cause trouble in two ways. First, the strong emotions keep you from thinking clearly. We've seen students in public speaking classes whose fear is so great that they can't even remember their name, let alone the subject of their speech. Second, intense feelings lead to

an urge to act, to do *something, anything* to make the problem go away. Because a person who feels so strongly doesn't think clearly, the resulting action might cause more trouble. At one time or another we've all lashed out in anger, saying words we later regretted. A look at almost any newspaper provides a grim illustration of the injury and death that follow from the physical assaults of intensely angry people.

A second characteristic of debilitative feelings is their extended *duration.* Feeling depressed for a while after the breakup of a relationship or the loss of a job is natural. Spending the rest of one's life grieving over the loss accomplishes nothing. In the same way, staying angry at someone for a wrong inflicted long ago can be just as punishing to the grudge-holder as to the wrongdoer.

Of all the debilitative emotions, two are common and harmful enough in interpersonal relationships to deserve special mention here. They are anger and jealousy.

Anger   Although anger may be facilitative, its intensity and duration often make it debilitative. We are taught early in life to hide our feelings of anger. The feelings do not go away, however, and they frequently manifest themselves in harmful ways. In some cases the anger builds up until it explodes in a surprising, destructive manner. In other instances the anger smolders inside, almost literally "eating away at our guts" in the form of psychosomatic illnesses. For instance, S. W. Wolf (1965) found that the mucous lining protecting the inside of the stomach responds minute by minute to both conscious and unconscious emotions. When a person becomes angry, the lining becomes inflamed, producing excessive amounts of acids and gastric juices. In fact, ulcers have been produced experimentally in animals by subjecting them to stress (Sawrey, 1956). People who develop ulcers have stomachs that are almost constantly in a state of agitation, a condition often caused by a failure to express their feelings appropriately. "Appropriately" does not necessarily mean "immediately" or "loudly." In fact, recent evidence (Tavris, 1982, 1983) indicates that expressing anger makes you angrier, perpetuates an angry attitude, and may establish an anger habit.

Millard Bienvenu (1976), in his study of unmarried couples, found that withdrawal was a usual response to feelings of anger. He discovered that effective communicators were distinguished from ineffective ones by the way they handled their anger. We will have more to say about appropriate ways for dealing with anger, both later in this chapter and in Chapter 11.

John Jones and Anthony Banet (1976) discuss a common and destructive "anger cycle." They view anger as a response to the perception of an event as threatening one's physical or psychological well-being. The perception of such a threat begins the anger cycle. The second step occurs when the individual analyzes (correctly or incorrectly) the possible danger the threat poses. The third part of the cycle includes an assessment of the individual's power to deal with the threat. The cycle completes itself in one of two ways: If the threat is not very great or the individual feels powerful enough to handle it, a calm or purposeful response follows. If, however, the threat seems great and the individual seems powerless to handle it, anger can emerge as a response. Notice that anger can be a cover-up for other feelings, such as fear or frustration.

Jealousy   Jealousy is actually a combination of many feelings. It includes measures of inadequacy, inferiority, powerlessness, hurt, suspicion, bitterness, and anger. Colleen Kelley (1980) defines jealousy as "the fear of losing to a third party something to which one feels one has a right and which one finds desirable. Thus jealousy involves (1) a valued thing, (2) a perceived threat

of loss of this thing to (3) a usurper" (p. 138). Much like anger, jealousy contains a threat against which we feel powerless. The reaction is impulsive: We want to strike out.

Gordon Clanton and Lynn Smith (1976) delineate three possible kinds of loss that determine the strength of one's jealousy. The first is loss of face, or humiliation. Compare, for example, the difference between the slight embarrassment you might feel if a friend beat you in a tennis match and the humiliation you might be likely to feel if your spouse ran off with your best friend. In addition to humiliation, a second type of loss involves the inability to control events. Using our previous example, you would see the person who "belongs" to you slip away, with nothing you could do about it. The third type of loss is partnership. The loss of a significant other and all that person represents is extremely serious.

Larry Constantine, in his book *Treating Relationships* (1976), claims that jealousy and jealous behavior are neither intrinsically healthy and good nor unhealthy and bad. Jealousy only becomes a problem when it interferes with successful functioning in a chosen lifestyle or relationship. If it consumes an excessive amount of energy, alienates the other person in the relationship, or is a response to only imaginary threats, it is dysfunctional; however, where the danger is real, jealousy may indeed be a functional response. Barbara Brown (1979) details some of the functional aspects of jealousy. First, it can help limit the complexity of the interpersonal situations in which the couple operates to a level that they can tolerate. Also, it can serve as an early warning signal that some aspects of the relationship need to be clarified and worked out more thoroughly: Jealousy may serve to draw attention to differences in the partners' assumptions and expectations.

In general, women and men experience and express their jealousy differently (Corzine, 1981; Mace, 1981): Men are more apt to deny feelings of jealousy, whereas women are more apt to acknowledge them; men are more likely than women to express their jealousy through rage and violence and follow such outbursts with feelings of despondency; a jealous man is likely to focus on the sexual activity of the partner outside the relationship, whereas a jealous woman is likely to focus on the emotional involvement between her partner and some third person; and men are more likely to externalize the cause of the jealousy, blaming the partner, the third person, or "circumstances," whereas women are more likely to blame themselves.

In another study, Ray and Tucker (1980) also found that males and females differed in their expression of jealousy. Men reported greater concern with loss of face, while women were more concerned with losing a partner. This finding makes sense, because many men do not want to view themselves as weak or inferior, positions that are associated with loss of face.

Thinking and feeling   Our goal, then, is to find a method for getting rid of debilitative feelings while remaining sensitive to the more facilitative emotions. Fortunately, such a method was developed by cognitive psychologists such as Aaron Beck (1976) and Albert Ellis (1977). This method is based on the idea that the key to changing feelings is to change unproductive thinking. Let's see how it works.

For most people, emotions seem to have a life of their own. People wish they could feel calm when approaching strangers, yet their voices quiver. They try to appear confident when asking for a raise, but their eyes twitch nervously. Many people would say that the strangers or the boss *make* them feel nervous, just as they would say that a bee sting causes them to feel pain. They connect physical and emotional discomfort in the following way:

ACTIVATING EVENT	CONSEQUENCES
bee sting	physical pain
meeting strangers	nervous feelings

When looking at emotions in this way, people may believe they have little control over how they feel. The causal relationship between physical pain and emotional discomfort (or pleasure) isn't, however, as great as it seems. Cognitive psychologists and therapists argue that it is not *events*, such as meeting strangers or being jilted by a lover, that cause people to feel poorly, but rather the *beliefs they hold* about these events.

Ellis tells a story that clarifies this point. Imagine yourself walking by a friend's house and seeing your friend come to a window and call you a string of vile names. (You supply the friend and the names.) Under these circumstances, it's likely that you would feel hurt and upset. Now imagine that instead of walking by the house, you were passing a mental institution when the same friend, who was obviously a patient there, shouted the same offensive names at you. In this case, your reaction would probably be quite different; most likely, you'd feel sadness and pity.

In this story the activating event—being called names—was the same in both cases, yet the emotional consequences were very different. The reason for the different feelings has to do with the pattern of thinking in each case. In the first instance you would most likely think that your friend was angry with you, and imagine you must have done something terrible to deserve such a response. In the second case you would probably assume that your friend had experienced some psychological difficulty, so you would probably feel sympathetic.

This example illustrates that it is people's *interpretations* of events that determine their feelings. Therefore, a more accurate model for emotions would look this way:

ACTIVATING EVENT	THOUGHT OR BELIEF	CONSEQUENCES
being called names	"I've done something wrong."	hurt, upset
being called names	"My friend must be sick."	pity, sympathy

The key, then, to understanding and changing feelings lies in the pattern of thought. Consider the part of you that, like a little voice, whispers in your ear. Take a moment now and listen to what the voice is saying.

Did you hear the voice? It was quite possibly saying, "What little voice? I don't hear any voices!" This little voice talks to you almost constantly:

"Better pick up a loaf of bread on the way home."

"I wonder when he's going to stop talking."

"It's sure cold today!"

"Are there two or four cups in a quart?"

At work or at play, while reading the paper or brushing teeth, we all tend to think. This thinking voice rarely stops. It may fall silent for a while when you're running, riding a bike, or meditating, but most of the time it rattles on.

Irrational beliefs This process of self-talk is essential to understanding debilitative feelings. Ellis suggests that many debilitative feelings come from accepting a number of irrational beliefs—we'll call them fallacies here—that lead to illogical conclusions, and, in turn, to debilitating feelings.

The fallacy of perfection People who accept this myth believe that a worthwhile communicator should be able to handle any situation with complete confidence and skill. Whereas such a standard of perfection might serve as a goal and a source of inspiration (rather like making a hole in one for a golfer), it's totally unrealistic to expect that you can reach or maintain this level of behavior. The truth is, people simply aren't perfect. Perhaps the myth of the perfect commu-

nicator comes from believing too strongly in novels, TV, or films. In these media perfect characters are often depicted, such as the perfect mate or child, the totally controlled and gregarious host, and the incredibly competent professional. Although these images are certainly appealing, people will inevitably come up short when compared to these fabrications.

People who accept the belief that it's desirable and possible to be a perfect communicator come to think that people won't appreciate them if they are imperfect. Admitting mistakes, saying "I don't know," or sharing feelings of uncertainty or discomfort thus seem to be social defects. Given the desire to be valued and appreciated, these people are tempted at least to try to *appear* perfect. They assemble a variety of social masks, hoping that if they can fool others into thinking that they are perfect, perhaps they'll find acceptance. The costs of such deception are high. If others ever detect that this veneer of confidence is a false one, then the person is considered a phony. Even if the facade goes undetected, the performance consumes a great deal of psychological energy, and diminishes the rewards of approval.

David Burns, in "The Perfectionist's Script for Self-Defeat" (1980), delineates the costs and benefits of perfectionism. The list of benefits, especially lasting ones, is nonexistent because early successes rarely are maintained; the list of costs is a long one. For example, impaired health, troubled relationships, painful mood swings, anxiety, and decreased productivity (which is ironic since the perfectionist's goal is often higher productivity). The fear of failure, of being less than perfect, often causes the perfectionist to avoid risks, take the safe routes, and engage in the safe

I never was what you would call a fancy skater—and while I seldom actually fell, it might have been more impressive if I had. A good resounding fall is no disgrace. It is the fantastic writhing to avoid a fall which destroys any illusion of being a gentleman. How like life that is, after all!

Robert Benchley

---

relationships. The perfectionist sets high goals (out of fear of being second-rate), fears rejection if less than perfect, becomes upset over making a mistake, and keeps pushing harder to do better in the future.

The irony for these people is that their efforts are unnecessary. Research by Eliot Aronson (1972) and others suggests that the people we regard most favorably are those who are competent but not perfect. Why? First, many people see the acts of would-be perfectionists as the desperate struggle that they are. It's obviously easier to like someone who is not trying to deceive you than someone who is. Second, most people become uncomfortable around a person regarded as perfect. Knowing they don't measure up to certain standards, most people are tempted to admire this superhuman only from a distance.

Not only can subscribing to the myth of perfection keep others from liking you, it also acts as a force to diminish self-esteem. How can you like yourself when you don't measure up to your own standards? You become more liberated each time you comfortably accept the idea that you are not perfect. For example: Like everyone else, you sometimes have a hard time expressing yourself. Like everyone else, you make mistakes from time to time, and there is no reason to hide it. You are honestly doing the best you can to realize your potential, to become the best person you can be.

The fallacy of approval Another mistaken belief is based on the idea that it is vital—not just desirable—to obtain everyone's approval. Communicators who subscribe to this belief go to incredible lengths to seek acceptance from people who are significant to them, even to the extent of sacrificing their own principles and happiness. Adherence to this irrational myth can lead to some ludicrous situations, such as feeling nervous because people you really don't like seem to disapprove of you, or feeling apologetic when you are not at fault, or feeling embarrassed after behaving unnaturally to gain another's approval.

The myth of acceptance is irrational. It implies that some people are more respectable and more likable because they go out of their way to please others. Often this implication simply isn't true. How respectable are people who have compromised important values simply to gain acceptance? Are people highly thought of who repeatedly deny their own needs as a means of buying approval? Genuine affection and respect are hardly due such characters. In addition, striving for universal acceptance is irrational because it is simply not possible. Sooner or later a conflict of expectations is bound to occur. One person approves of a certain kind of behavior, whereas another approves only the opposite course of action.

Don't misunderstand: Abandoning the fallacy of approval does not mean living a life of selfishness. It's still important to consider the needs of others. It's also pleasant—one might even say necessary—to strive for the respect of certain people. The point is that the price is too high when people must abandon their needs and principles in order to gain this acceptance.

The fallacy of shoulds One huge source of unhappiness is the inability to distinguish between what *is* and what *should be*. For instance, imagine a person who is full of complaints about the world:

"There should be no rain on weekends."
"People ought to live forever."
"Money should grow on trees."
"We should all be able to fly."

Beliefs such as these are obviously foolish. However pleasant such wishing may be, insisting that the unchangeable should be altered won't affect reality one bit. Yet many people torture themselves by engaging in this sort of irrational thinking: They confuse "is" with "ought." They say and think:

"That guy should drive better."
"She shouldn't be so inconsiderate."
"They ought to be more friendly."
"You should work harder."

In each of these cases the person *prefers* that people behave differently. Wishing that things were better is perfectly legitimate, and trying to change them is, of course, a good idea; but it is unreasonable for people to *insist* that the world operate just as they want it to. Parents wish their children were always considerate and neat. Teachers wish that their students were totally fascinated with their subjects and willing to study diligently. Consumers wish that inflation wasn't such a problem. As the old saying goes, those wishes and a dime (now fifty cents) will get you a cup of coffee.

Becoming obsessed with shoulds yields three bad consequences. First, this obsession *leads to unnecessary unhappiness.* People who are constantly dreaming about the ideal are seldom satisfied with what they have. For instance, partners in a marriage who focus on the ways in which their mate could be more considerate, sexy, or intelligent have a hard time appreciating the strengths that drew them together in the first place.

Second, it *keeps you from changing unsatisfying conditions.* One instructor, for example, constantly complains about the problems at the university: The quality of teaching should be improved, pay ought to be higher, the facilities should be upgraded, and so on. This person could be using the same energy to improve these conditions. Of course, not all problems have solutions; but when they do, complaining is rarely the most productive method of improvement. As one college administrator puts it: "Rather than complain about the cards you are dealt, play the hand well."

Finally, this obsession *tends to build a defensive climate in others.* Imagine living around someone who insisted that people be more punctual, work harder, or refrain from using certain language. This kind of carping is obviously irritating. It's much easier to be around people who comment without preaching.

© 1963 United Feature Syndicate Inc.

The fallacy of overgeneralization One type of overgeneralization occurs when a person bases a belief on a limited amount of evidence. Consider the following statements:

> "I'm so stupid! I can't understand how to do my income tax."

> "Some friend I am! I forgot my best friend's birthday."

In these cases people have focused on a limited shortcoming as if it represented everything. Sometimes people forget that despite their difficulties, they have solved tough problems, and that although they can be forgetful, they're often caring and thoughtful.

A second, related category of overgeneralization occurs when we exaggerate shortcomings:

> "You *never* listen to me."
> "You're *always* late."
> "I can't think of *anything*."

Upon closer examination, such absolute statements are almost always false and usually lead to discouragement or anger. It's better to replace overgeneralizations with more accurate messages:

> "You often don't listen to me."
> "You've been late three times this week."
> "I haven't had any ideas I like today."

The fallacy of causation People who live their lives in accordance with this myth believe they should do nothing that can hurt or in any way inconvenience others because it will *cause* them to feel a particular way. For example, you might visit friends or family out of a sense of obligation rather than a genuine desire to see them because, you believe, not to visit them will cause them to feel hurt. Did you ever avoid objecting to behavior that you found troublesome because you didn't want to cause the person to feel angry? You may, on occasion, have pretended to be attentive—even though you were running late for an appointment and in a rush—because you didn't want to cause the speaker to feel embarrassed for "holding you up." Then there were the times when you substituted praise for more honest negative responses in order to avoid *causing* the other person to feel hurt.

A reluctance to speak out in such situations often results from assuming that one person can cause another's emotions—that you hurt, confuse, or anger others. Actually, this assumption is seldom correct. A person doesn't *cause* feelings in others; rather, others *respond* to your behavior with feelings of their own. Your behavior is, at most, an *invitation* to the other person. Like other kinds of invitations, the other person can respond in a variety of ways, including not at all. Consider how strange it sounds to suggest that people *make* others fall in love with them. Such a statement simply doesn't make sense. It would be more correct to say that people first act in one way or another; then others may or may not fall in love as a result of these actions. In the same way, it's incorrect to say that people *make* others angry, upset, even happy. Behavior that upsets or pleases one person might not bring any reaction from another. More accurately, people's responses are determined as much by their own psychological makeup as by others' behavior.

Restricting communication because of the myth of causation can produce three damaging consequences. First, *people often will fail to meet your needs.* There's little likelihood that people will change their behavior unless they know that it affects you in a negative way.

Second, *you are likely to resent the person about whose behavior you fail to complain.* Although this reaction is illogical, as these feelings have never been known, logic doesn't change the fact that burying the problem usually builds up hostility.

Third, *once your deceptiveness is discovered, others may find it difficult to determine when you are genuinely upset.* Even your most fervent assurances become suspect, as others can never be sure when you are concealing resentments. In many respects, assuming responsibility for others' feelings is not only irrational, but counterproductive.

The fallacy of helplessness The next fallacy suggests that satisfaction in life is determined by

A man said to the universe:
"Sir, I exist!"
"However," replied the universe,
"The fact has not created in me
A sense of obligation."

Stephen Crane

forces beyond control. People with this outlook continuously see themselves as victims:

"There's no way a woman can get ahead in this society. It's a man's world, and the best thing I can do is to accept it."

"I was born with a shy personality. I'd like to be more outgoing, but there's nothing I can do about that."

"I can't tell my boss that she is putting too many demands on me. If I did, I might lose my job."

The error in such statements becomes apparent once a person realizes that few paths are completely closed. Most "can't" statements can, in fact, more correctly be rephrased in one of two ways.

The first is to say that you *won't* act in a certain way, that you *choose* not to do so. For instance, you may choose not to stand up for your rights or to follow unwanted requests, but it is usually inaccurate to claim that some outside force keeps you from doing so. The other way to rephrase a "can't" is to say that you *don't know how* to do something. Examples of this sort of situation include not knowing how to complain in a way that reduces defensiveness, or not being aware of how to conduct a conversation. Many difficulties that a person claims can't be solved do have solutions: The task is to discover those solutions and to work diligently at applying them.

When viewed in this light, many "can'ts" are really rationalizations to justify not wanting to change. Once people persuade themselves that

**There is nothing good or bad but thinking
makes it so.**

Shakespeare, *Hamlet*

_____

there's no hope, it's easy for them to give up trying. On the other hand, acknowledging that there
is a way to change—even though it may be difficult—puts the responsibility for the predicament
on your shoulders. Knowing that you can move
closer to your goals makes it difficult to complain
about the present situation. You *can* become a
better communicator.

The fallacy of catastrophic expectations   Some
fearful people operate on the assumption that if
something bad can happen, it probably will—a
position similar to Murphy's Law. These statements are typical of such an attitude:

"If I invite them to the party, they probably
won't want to come."

"If I speak up in order to try and resolve a conflict, things will probably get worse."

"If I apply for the job I want, I probably won't be
hired."

"If I tell them how I really feel, they'll probably
laugh at me."

It's undoubtedly naive to blithely assume that all
of your interactions with others will meet with
success, but it's equally wrong to assume you will
fail. One consequence of this attitude is that you'll
be less likely to be expressive at important times.
To carry the concept to its logical extreme, imagine people who fear *everything:* How could they
live their lives? They wouldn't step outside in the
morning to see what kind of day it was for fear
they'd be struck by lightning or a falling airplane.
They wouldn't drive a car for fear of a collision.
They wouldn't engage in any exercise for fear the

strain might cause a heart attack. Do these examples seem ridiculous? Consider if you have ever
withdrawn from communicating because you were
afraid of unlikely consequences. A certain amount
of prudence is wise, but carrying caution too far
can lead to a life of lost opportunities.

Even when one acts in spite of catastrophic
fantasies, problems occur. One way to escape
from the myth of catastrophic failure is to reas-
sess the consequences that would follow if you
failed in your efforts to communicate. Failing in a
given situation usually isn't as bad as it seems.
What if people do laugh? Suppose you don't get
the job? What if others do get angry at certain
remarks? Are these matters really *that* serious?

A rational-emotive approach   How can a
person overcome irrational thinking? Ellis and
Harper (1977) developed a simple yet effective
approach that helps people cut down on self-
defeating thinking that leads to debilitative emotions.

Monitor your emotional reactions   The first step
is to recognize debilitative emotions. (Of course,
it's also nice to be aware of pleasant feelings
when they occur.) As suggested earlier, one way
to notice feelings is through physiological
responses, such as butterflies in the stomach,
racing heart, hot flashes, and so on. Some such
reactions may call for a trip to the emergency
room of the local hospital, but more often these
feelings reflect strong emotion. You can also recognize certain ways of behaving that suggest a
strong emotion, such as stomping instead of normal walking, being unusually quiet, or speaking in
a sarcastic tone of voice.

Does it seem strange to suggest that you look
for emotions that should be immediately apparent? The fact is, people often suffer from debilitating feelings for some time without noticing them.

For example, at the end of a trying day you've probably caught yourself frowning, only to realize that you've been wearing that mask for some time.

Notice the activating event   Once you're aware of how you're feeling, the next step is to figure out what event activated the response. Sometimes this activating event is obvious. For instance, a common source of anger is being accused unfairly (or fairly) of behaving foolishly, or being rejected by somebody personally important.

Other times there isn't a single activating event, but a series of small incidents that build toward a critical mass, later triggering a debilitative feeling. This series of incidents may happen when you're trying to work or sleep and are continually interrupted, or when you suffer a string of small disappointments.

The best way to recognize activating events is to notice the circumstances that accompany debilitative feelings. Perhaps they occur when you're around *specific people*. In other cases you might be bothered by certain *types of individuals*, of a given age, role, background, and so forth. Certain *settings* may also stimulate unpleasant emotions: parties, work, or school. In other cases, the *topic* of conversation is the factor that sets you off, whether it be politics, religion, sex, or some other subject.

Record your self-talk   Now analyze the thoughts that link the activating event to the feeling. Let's look at a pair of examples to see how the steps work in practice.

Scott noticed that he became nervous (emotional reaction) whenever he tried to talk with an attractive woman he'd like to date (activating event). After some observation, he discovered that his self-talk included:

> **. . . our perceptions about the causes of anger can be affected just by talking about them and deciding on an interpretation.**
>
> Carol Tavris

1. *"I'm behaving like a fool."*
2. *"I don't know what to say to her."*
3. *"She'd never want to go out with me."*
4. *"I'm no good with women."*

Brenda became infuriated at a friend whom she described as a "leech." This friend would call Brenda frequently, sometimes three or four times a day. She also dropped in for visits at awkward times without being invited. Brenda found that her self-talk focused on the statements:

1. *"After all the hints I've dropped, she should get the idea and leave me alone."*
2. *"She's driving me crazy."*
3. *"I'm a coward for not speaking up and telling her to quit bothering me."*
4. *"If I do tell her, she'll be crushed."*
5. *"There's no solution to this mess. I'm damned if I tell her to leave me alone and damned if I don't."*

Monitoring your self-talk might be difficult at first, but if you persevere, you'll soon be able to identify the thoughts that lead to your debilitative feelings. Once you habitually recognize the internal monologue, you'll identify your thoughts quickly and easily.

Dispute your irrational beliefs   The next step is the key to success in the rational-emotive approach. Use the discussion of irrational beliefs on pages 219–224 to discover which of your internal statements are based on mistaken thinking.

You can see how this process works by looking at how Scott disputed his self-talk instead of accepting his earlier beliefs. He examined each of his statements one at a time to discover which were reasonable.

A man is hurt not so much by what happens as by his opinion of what happens.

Montaigne

---

1. "This is an exaggeration. I'm certainly not perfect, but I'm not a fool either. A fool would behave much worse than I do. It's more accurate to say that I'm behaving like a nervous guy around a pretty woman, which is exactly the case. There's nothing unusual about that."
2. "This is an accurate statement. I'm not sure what to say, so I'm searching for a good topic."
3. "This is an irrational, catastrophic belief. She may not want to go out, but on the other hand, she might want to. The only way I'll know is to ask her. In the meantime, it's foolish to expect the worst."
4. "This is an exaggeration. Based on my past experience I'd say that I have my strengths and weaknesses when it comes to dealing with women. My drawbacks are that I get nervous and tend to get a crush on lots of nice, beautiful women with whom I probably wouldn't get along. On the other hand, I'm honest and kind, and I've had some good times with some fine women."

Brenda examined her self-talk in the same way.

1. "If she was perfect, then she would be more sensitive. Because she's an insensitive person, she's behaving just as I'd expect her to do. I'd sure like her to be more considerate, but there's no rule that says she should be."
2. "This is a bit melodramatic. I definitely don't like her interruptions, but there's a big difference between being irritated and going crazy. Besides, even if I was losing my mind, it wouldn't be accurate to say that she was driving me crazy, but rather that I'm letting her get to me. (It is fun to feel sorry for myself, though.)"
3. "This is an exaggeration. I am afraid to tell her, but that doesn't make me a coward. It makes me a less than totally self-assured person. This confirms my suspicion that I'm not perfect."

4. "There's a chance that she'll be disappointed if she knows that I've found her irritating. But I have to be careful not to catastrophize here. She would probably survive my comments and even appreciate my honesty once she gets over the shock. Besides, I'm not sure that I want to take the responsibility of keeping her happy if it leaves me feeling irritated. She's a big person, and if she has a problem she can learn to deal with it."
5. "I'm playing helpless here. There must be a way I can tell her honestly while still being supportive."

After reading about this method of dealing with unpleasant emotions, some readers have the following objections:

The rational-emotive approach sounds like nothing more than trying to talk yourself out of feeling bad. This accusation is totally correct: Cognitive therapists believe that it is possible to convince yourself to feel differently. After all, we talk ourselves *into* debilitative emotions, so what's wrong with talking ourselves *out* of them?

This kind of disputing sounds unnatural. "I don't talk to myself in sentences and paragraphs," many people say. There's no need to dispute your irrational beliefs in any particular literary style. You can be as colloquial as you want. The importance here is to understand clearly what thoughts led you into your debilitative feeling, so you can clearly dispute them. When the technique is new for you, write or talk out your thoughts in order to make them clear. After you've had some practice, you will be able to do these steps in a quicker, less formal way.

Rational-emotive thinking seems to turn people into calculating, emotionless machines. This objection is simply not true. There's nothing wrong with having facilitative emotions: They are the stuff that makes life worth living. The goal of this approach is to get rid of the debilitative, harmful emotions that keep us from functioning well. Just as you remove weeds from a garden to let vegetables and flowers grow, so you can use rational thinking to weed out unproductive, harmful feelings to leave room for the productive, positive ones.

This technique appears to promise too much. It seems unrealistic to think that you could rid yourself of *all* unpleasant feelings. Rational-emotive thinking probably won't solve emotional problems totally, but it *can* reduce the amount, intensity, and duration of debilitative feelings. This method is not the answer to all your problems, but it can make a significant difference, which is not a bad accomplishment.

Sharing feelings: when and how?

Now that we've talked about how to deal with debilitative emotions, the question remains: What is the best way to share facilitative feelings with others? It's obvious that indiscriminately sharing every feeling of boredom, fear, affection, irritation, and so on, would often cause trouble. On the other hand, we can clearly strike a better balance between denying or downplaying feelings on the one hand and totally cutting loose with them on the other. The suggestions that follow are some guidelines on when and how to express emotions. They will give you the best chances for improving your relationships.

Recognize your feelings   It's an obvious but important fact that you can share your feelings best when you're aware of what they are. As we've already said, there are a number of ways in which feelings can become evident. Physiological changes can clearly indicate emotions. Monitoring your nonverbal behaviors (facial expression, voice tone, posture, and so on) is another excellent way to keep in touch with your feelings (see Chapter 5). You can also recognize your feelings by monitoring your self-talk as well as the verbal messages you send to others. It's not far from

the verbal statement "I hate this!" to the realization "I'm angry (or bored, or nervous, or embarrassed)." Any way you recognize your feelings, the same point applies: It's important to know how you feel in order to tell others about those feelings.

Share multiple emotions   Many times the feeling we express isn't the only one we're experiencing. Consider the case of Heidi and Mike at a party. The subject of self-defense has come up, and Heidi recounts the time Mike drunkenly picked a fight in a bar, only to receive a sound beating from a rather short, elderly, pudgy customer. Later Mike confronts Heidi angrily, "How could you? That was a rotten thing to say. I'm furious at you." Mike's anger may be justified, but he failed to share with Heidi the emotion that preceded and in fact was responsible for his anger, namely the embarrassment when a secret he hoped to keep private was exposed to others. If he had shared this primary feeling, Heidi could have understood his rage and responded in a more constructive way. Anger often isn't the primary emotion, although it's the one we may express. In addition to embarrassment, it's often preceded by confusion, disappointment, frustration, or sadness. In each of these cases it's important to share the primary feeling as well as the anger that follows it.

According to Carol Tavris (1982), most emotions aren't "pure," but combinations that reflect the complex structure of most of our problems and our lives. It's common to feel mingled hurt and jealousy, rage and fear. Parents feel combined anger and worry when a teenager returns home from a date three hours late. Joy and guilt are a common combination among those working to establish independence from their families. Ventilating only one component of the mix as Mike did, expressing his anger without so much as a nod to his embarrassment, emphasizes that emotion to the exclusion of the others. In this circumstance, according to Tavris, "You aren't ventilating the anger; you're practicing it" (p. 32). Indeed, Mike may just convince himself that anger is *all* he feels.

Robert Plutchik (1980) developed the "emotion wheel" pictured in Figure 9–1 to illustrate the distinction between eight primary emotions (placed inside the perimeter of the wheel) and eight mixed emotions, based on combinations of the primary emotions (placed outside the wheel). Whether or not you agree with the emotions Plutchik identifies as primary, the emotion wheel suggests that many feelings should be described in more than a single term. To say that you feel "glad" a friend called to make peace after an argument probably doesn't tell the whole story. Other emotions you're probably experiencing (and might want to share) could include relief, embarrassment (that you didn't call first), gratitude, and nervousness.

This kind of complexity explains why so many scholars have compared emotions to colors: some primary and some secondary—and appearing in an almost infinite range of shades.

Another way emotions are like colors is in their intensity. The half-globe in Figure 9–2 illustrates this point clearly. Each vertical slice represents the range of a primary emotion from its mildest to its most intense state. This model shows the importance not only of choosing the right emotional family when expressing yourself, but also of describing the strength of the feeling. Some people fail to communicate clearly because they understate their emotions, failing to let others know how strongly they feel. To say you're "annoyed" when a friend breaks an important promise, for example, would probably be an understatement. In other cases, people chronically overstate the strength of their feelings. To them, everything is "wonderful" or "terrible." The

FIGURE 9–1   The emotion wheel: primary and mixed emotions

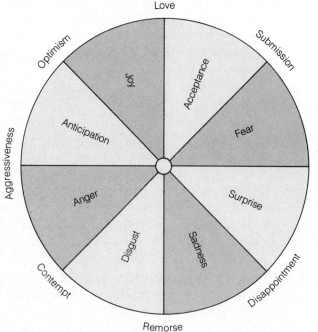

FIGURE 9–2 Intensity of emotions

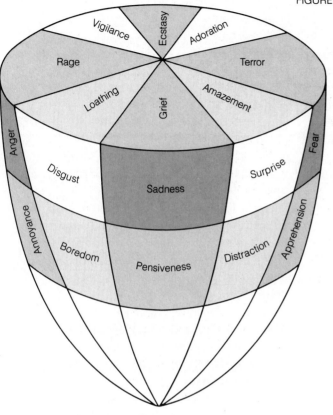

problem with this sort of exaggeration is that when a truly intense emotion comes along, they have no words left to describe it adequately. If chocolate chip cookies from the local bakery are "fantastic," how does it feel to fall in love?

Distinguish feeling from acting When children are infants, they often go through long spells of late-night crying. Most parents experience moments in the wee hours of the morning when they are so tired that they feel like leaving home with all its noise and confusion. Needless to say, they rarely follow through on this impulse.

Of course, most of us would like to be the kind of people who are totally patient, accepting, and rational, but we're not. Although we don't always want to act on our immediate feelings, we also don't want to ignore them so that they'll build up inside and eventually consume us. For this reason we feel best when we can express what's happening, and then decide whether or not we'll act on it.

For instance, it may be appropriate to acknowledge nervousness in some new situations, even though you might not choose to show it. Likewise, you can acknowledge attraction to certain men or women even though you might not choose to act on these feelings. It's possible to get in touch with the boredom you sometimes experience in meetings and classes, even though you'll most likely resist falling asleep or walking out. In other words, just because you feel a certain way doesn't mean you must always act it out.

This distinction is extremely important, for it can liberate you from the fear that acknowledging and sharing a feeling will commit you to some disastrous course of action. If, for instance, you say to a friend, "I feel so angry that I could punch you in the nose," it becomes possible to explore exactly why you feel so furious and then to resolve the problem that led to the anger. Pretending that nothing is the matter, on the other hand, will do nothing to diminish resentful feelings, which can go on to contaminate a relationship.

Accept responsibility for your feelings
Although you often experience a feeling in response to the behavior of others, it's important to understand that others don't *cause* your feelings. In other words, people don't make you sad, happy, and so on; *you* are responsible for the way you react. Look at it this way: It's obvious that people are more easily upset on some days than on others. Little things that usually don't bother you can suddenly bring on a burst of emotion. Therefore it isn't the things or people themselves that determine your reactions, but rather how you feel about them at a given time. If, for example, you're especially harassed due to the press of unfinished work, you may react angrily to a personal joke a friend has made. Was the friend responsible for this upset? No, it's more correct to say that the pressure of work—something within you—set off the anger. The same principle holds true for other emotions: Unrequited love doesn't break our hearts; we allow ourselves to feel hurt, or rather, we simply *are* hurt. A large dose of alcohol doesn't make us sad or happy; those emotions are already within us.

Wayne Dyer (1976), outlining his positive measures for dealing with debilitative emotions and irrational beliefs, includes accepting responsibility. He argues that we need to remind ourselves that

it is not what others do that bothers us, but our *reactions* to it.

> Decide that any and all unhappiness that you choose will never be the result of someone else, but rather that it will be the result of you and your own behavior. Remind yourself constantly that any externally caused unhappiness reinforces your own slavery, since it assumes that you have no control over yourself or them, but they have control over you. (p. 171)

It's important to make sure that language reflects the fact of self-responsibility for feelings. Instead of "You're making me angry," say "I'm getting angry." Instead of "You hurt my feelings," say "I feel hurt when you do that." People don't make us like or dislike them, and pretending that they do denies the responsibility each of us has for our own emotions.

Choose the best time and place   When you do choose to share your feelings with another person, it's important to pick a time and place that's appropriate. Often the first flush of a strong feeling is not the best time to speak out. If you're awakened by the racket caused by a noisy neighbor, by storming over to complain you might say things you'll regret later. In such a case it's probably wiser to wait until you have thought out carefully how you might express your feelings. If your goals include maintaining a relationship with the other person or gaining some kind of cooperation, expressing your feelings at the wrong time or in the wrong place *might* feel good for a moment, but the lasting effects may be costly.

Even after you've waited for the first flush of feeling to subside, it's still important to choose the time that's best suited to the message. Being rushed, tired, or disturbed by some other matter are all good reasons for postponing the sharing of a feeling. Often, dealing with emotions can take a great amount of time and effort, and fatigue or distraction will make it difficult to devote enough energy to follow through on the matter you've started. In the same manner you ought to be sure that the recipient of your message is ready to listen before sharing.

Speak clearly and unambiguously Either out of confusion or discomfort we sometimes express emotions in an unclear way. Sometimes this entails using many words where one will do better. For example, "Uh, I guess what I'm trying to say is that I was pretty upset when I waited for you on the corner where we agreed to meet at 1:30 and you didn't show up until 3:00" would be better stated as, "I was angry when you were an hour and a half late." One key to making emotions clear is to realize that you most often can summarize a feeling in a few words. In the same way, a little thought can probably provide brief reasons for feeling a certain way.

Another way the expression of a feeling may be confused is by discounting or qualifying it: "I'm *a little* unhappy"; "I'm *pretty* excited"; "I'm *sort of* confused." Of course, not all emotions are strong ones—we do experience degrees of sadness and joy—but some communicators have a tendency to discount almost every feeling.

Still another way the expression of an emotion becomes confused is when it is sent in a code. This coding most often happens when the sender is uncomfortable about sharing the feeling in question. Some codes are verbal ones, as when the sender hints at the message. For example, an indirect way to say "I'm lonesome" might be, "I guess there isn't much happening this weekend, so if you're not busy why don't you drop by?" This indirect code does have its advantages: It allows the sender to avoid the self-disclosure of expressing an unhappy feeling, and it also serves as a safeguard against the chance of being rejected outright. On the other hand, such a message is so indirect that the chances of the real feeling being recognized are reduced. For this

reason people who send coded messages stand less of a chance of having their emotions understood and their needs met.

Finally, you can express yourself clearly by making sure that you and your partner understand that your feeling is centered on a specific set of circumstances, rather than being indicative of the whole relationship. Instead of saying "I resent you," say "I resent you when you don't keep your promises." Rather than "I'm bored with you," say "I'm bored when you talk about money." Be aware that, in the course of knowing anyone, you're bound to feel positive at some times and negative at others. By limiting comments to the specific situation, you can express a feeling directly without jeopardizing the relationship.

Readings

Adler, Ronald B. *Confidence in Communication: A Guide to Assertive and Social Skills.* New York: Holt, Rinehart and Winston, 1977.

Aronson, Eliot. *The Social Animal.* New York: Viking Press, 1972.

Beck, Aaron T. *Cognitive Therapy and the Emotional Disorders.* New York: International Universities Press, 1976.

Bienvenu, Millard J., Sr. "Inventory of Anger Communication (IAC)." In *The 1976 Annual Handbook for Group Facilitators,* J. William Pfeiffer and John E. Jones, eds. La Jolla, Calif.: University Associates, Inc., 1976.

Brown, Barbara B. *New Mind, New Body: Bio-Feedback—New Directions for the Mind.* New York: Harper & Row, 1979.

Burns, David D. "The Perfectionist's Script for Self-Defeat." *Psychology Today* 14 (November 1980): 34–52.

*Buscaglia, Leo F. *Love.* Thorofare, N.J.: Charles B. Slack, Inc., 1972.

Buscaglia, Leo F. *Personhood.* Thorofare, N.J.: Charles B. Slack, Inc., 1978.

Caraskadon, T. G. "Help Seeking in the College Student: Strength and Weakness." In *Psychological Stress in the Campus Community*, L. Bloom, ed. New York: Behavioral Publications, 1975.

Clanton, Gordon, and Lynn G. Smith. *Jealousy.* Englewood Cliffs, N.J.: Prentice-Hall, 1976.

Constantine, Larry L. *Treating Relationships.* Lake Mills, Iowa: Graphic, 1976.

Coon, Dennis. *Introduction to Psychology: Exploration and Application.* St. Paul, Minn.: West, 1977.

Corzine, William L. *The Phenomenon of Jealousy: A Theoretical and Empirical Analysis.* New York: Macmillan, 1981.

Dunbar, Flanders. *Mind and Body: Psychosomatic Medicine.* New York: Random House, 1947.

Dyer, Wayne W. *Your Erroneous Zones.* New York: Avon Books, 1976.

Egan, Gerard. *You and Me: The Skills of Communicating and Relating to Others.* Monterey, Calif.: Brooks/Cole, 1977.

*Ellis, Albert, and Robert Harper. *A New Guide to Rational Living.* North Hollywood, Calif.: Wilshire Books, 1977.

Gitter, A. G., H. Block, and D. Mostofsky. "Race and Sex in the Perception of Emotion." *Journal of Social Issues* 170 (1972): 63–78.

Jakubowski, Patricia, and Arthur Lange. *The Assertive Option.* Champaign, Ill.: Research Press, 1978.

Johnson, David. "The Effects of Expressing Warmth and Anger upon the Actor and the Listener." *Journal of Counseling Psychology* 18 (1971): 571–578.

Jones, John E., and Anthony G. Banet, Jr. "Dealing with Anger." In *The 1976 Annual Handbook for Group Facilitators*, J. William

Pfeiffer and John E. Jones, eds. La Jolla, Calif.: University Associates, Inc., 1976.

Kelley, Colleen. "Jealousy: A Proactive Approach." In *The 1980 Annual Handbook for Group Facilitators*, J. William Pfeiffer and John E. Jones, eds. La Jolla, Calif.: University Associates, Inc., 1980.

Kranzler, Gerald. *You Can Change How You Feel: A Rational-Emotive Approach.* Eugene, Ore.: RETC Press, 1974.

Lazarus, Arnold, and Allen Fay. *I Can If I Want To.* New York: William Morrow, 1975.

Mace, David R. "Two Faces of Jealousy." *McCall's* (April 1981): 58–63.

McQuade, A., and A. Aikman. *Stress: What It Is and What It Does to You.* New York: E. P. Dutton, 1974.

Pearson, J. C. *Gender and Communication.* Dubuque, Iowa: Wm. C. Brown, 1985.

Phillips, Gerald M. *Help for Shy People.* Englewood Cliffs, N.J.: Prentice-Hall, 1981.

Plutchik, R. *Emotion: A Psychoevolutionary Synthesis.* New York: Harper & Row, 1980.

Powell, John. *The Secret of Staying in Love.* Niles, Ill.: Argus, 1974.

Ray, Lisa, and Raymond Tucker. "The Emotional Components of Jealousy: A Multivariate Investigation." Unpublished paper, Bowling Green State University, 1980.

Sawrey, W. "An Experimental Investigation of the Role of Psychological Factors in the Production of Gastric Ulcers in Rats." *Journal of Comparative Physiological Psychology* 49 (1956): 457–461.

Schachter, S., and J. Singer. "Cognitive, Social and Physiological Determinants of Emotional State." *Psychological Review* 69 (1962): 379–399.

Selye, Hans. *The Stress of Life.* New York: McGraw-Hill, 1956.

Spielman, Philip. "Envy and Jealousy: An Attempt

at Clarification." *Psycho-Analytic Quarterly* 40 (1971): 59–82.

Tavris, C. "Anger Defused." *Psychology Today* 16 (November 1982): 25–35.

Tavris, C. *Anger: The Misunderstood Emotion.* New York: Simon and Schuster, 1983.

Timmons, F. R. "Research on College Dropouts." In *Psychological Stress in the Campus Community,* L. Bloom, ed. New York: Behavioral Publications, 1975.

Valins, S. "Cognitive Effects of False Heart-Rate Feedback." *Journal of Personality and Social Psychology* 4 (1966): 400–408.

"Why Men Don't Cry." *Science Digest* 92 (June 1984): 24.

Wolf, S. W. *The Stomach.* Oxford: Oxford University Press, 1965.

Wood, John T. *How Do You Feel?* Englewood Cliffs, N.J.: Prentice-Hall, 1974.

*Zimbardo, Philip. *Shyness: What It Is, What to Do About It.* Reading, Mass.: Addison-Wesley, 1977.

Communication Climate

After studying the material in this chapter

You should understand:

1. The definition of communication climate.
2. The basic characteristics of confirming and disconfirming responses.
3. The nature of positive and negative communication spirals.
4. Types of disconfirming responses.
5. The relationship between the presenting self and defensive responses.
6. Types of defensive responses.
7. The types of messages that are likely to build confirming communication climates.
8. The ways of responding nondefensively to critical messages.

You should be able to:

1. Identify some confirming and disconfirming messages in your own relationships.
2. Identify your defensive responses in a relationship, the parts of your presenting self you are defending, and the consequences.
3. Given a set of disconfirming messages, supply more confirming alternatives.
4. Supply appropriate nondefensive responses to real or hypothetical criticism.

How would you describe your most important relationships? Fair and warm? Stormy? Hot? Cold? Just as physical locations have characteristic weather patterns, interpersonal relationships have unique climates, too. You can't measure the interpersonal climate by looking at a thermometer or glancing at the sky, but it's there nonetheless. Every relationship has a feeling, a pervasive mood that colors the goings-on of the participants.

What is communication climate?

The term *communication climate* refers to the social/psychological tone of a relationship. A climate doesn't involve specific activities as much as the way people feel about each other as they carry out those activities. Consider two interpersonal communication classes, for example. Both meet for the same length of time and follow the same syllabus. It's easy to imagine how one of these classes might be a friendly, comfortable place to learn, whereas the other could be cold and tense—even hostile. The same principle holds for families, co-workers, and other relationships: Communication climates are a function of the way people feel about one another, not so much the tasks they perform.

Like their meteorological counterparts, communication climates are shared by everyone involved. It's rare to find one person describing a relationship as open and positive, while the other characterizes it as cold and hostile. Also, just like the weather, communication climates can change over time. A relationship can be overcast at one time and sunny at another.

Confirming and disconfirming climates

What makes some climates positive and others negative? A short but accurate answer is that *communication climate is determined by the degree to which people see themselves as val-*ued. Communicators who perceive others in a relationship as being concerned about their welfare feel positive, whereas those who feel unimportant or abused bring negative attitudes to the relationship.

The kinds of messages that deny the value of others have been called *disconfirming responses.* A disconfirming response expresses a lack of regard for the other person, either by disputing or ignoring some important part of that person's message. This disregard, of course, is a severe blow to the receiver's self-esteem. It's disturbing enough to be told your idea is "wrong," but at least this sort of attack leaves some room for argument. More extreme types of disconfirming responses go beyond criticizing the content of a particular message to assault the worth of the person who is speaking—either overtly or simply by disregarding the person entirely.

A *confirming response,* on the other hand, is one in which the speaker acknowledges the other person as important. Unlike disconfirming responses, which invite us to feel unappreciated or ignored, confirming responses invite us to feel valued: Our existence is acknowledged and our importance is confirmed.

Studies by Sieburg (1969), Mix (1972), and others suggest that the most important single factor affecting outcomes in both family and organizational settings is communication that implies acceptance or rejection, confirmation or disconfirmation. For example, Clarke (1973) found that perceived confirmation was a better predictor of marital satisfaction and attraction than self-disclosure, and Cissna and Keating (1979), who also studied married couples, found that husbands and wives whose spouses communicated with them in a direct and empathic way were likely to feel confirmed by their partners.

Confirmation and disconfirmation also has been studied in educational settings. Sundell (1972) studied the behavior of teachers and students in

junior high schools and found that confirming teachers were confirmed by their students, and disconfirming teachers were disconfirmed by their students. Jacobs (1973) found that reactions to interviews between professors and students were determined to a large extent by the professors' confirming behavior. Students who were deliberately disconfirmed by their professors during the interview were more dissatisfied with the interview experience and their own performance than those who were deliberately confirmed. Lawrence Rosenfeld (1983) found that supportiveness is of major importance for distinguishing liked from disliked classes, with liked classes described as more supportive. (The level of defensiveness was about the same in both classes.) Teacher behavior in liked classes was described primarily as *empathic*, whereas teacher behavior in disliked classes was described primarily as *superior*. A recent investigation by Rosenfeld and Jarrard (1985) found that the climate of classes with male professors perceived as sexist was less supportive, more defensive, and less involving than those of professors perceived as nonsexist. Perceived sexism in female professors was found to be unrelated to descriptions of climate.

Finally, a study by Heineken (1980) focused on the therapeutic setting in an attempt to determine whether psychiatric patients disconfirm more than "normal" individuals. She found that the frequency of disconfirming responses was significantly higher for groups of psychiatric patients.

How communication climates develop As soon as two people start to communicate, a climate begins to develop. Verbal messages certainly contribute to the tone of a relationship, but many climate-shaping messages are nonverbal. The very act of approaching others is confirming, whereas avoiding them can be disconfirming. Smiles or frowns, the presence or absence of eye contact, tone of voice, use of personal space . . . all these cues and others send messages about how the parties feel about one another.

Once a climate is formed, it can take on a life of its own and grow in a self-perpetuating spiral. This sort of cycle is most obvious in regressive spirals, when a dispute gets out of hand (Wilmot, 1979, p. 123):

A: (*mildly irritated*) Where were you? I thought we agreed to meet here a half hour ago.

B: (*defensively*) I'm sorry. I got hung up at the library. I don't have as much free time as you do, you know.

A: I wasn't *blaming* you, so don't get so touchy. I do resent what you just said, though. I'm plenty busy. And I've got lots of better things to do than wait around for you!

B: Who's getting touchy? I just made a simple comment. You've sure been defensive lately. What's the matter with you?

Friendship is like a fishhook; the further it goes in, the harder it is to pull out.

Gerald Suttles

Fortunately, spirals can work in a progressive direction too (Wilmot, 1979, p. 122). One confirming behavior leads to a similar response from the other person, which in turn leads to further confirmation by the first party.

Spirals—whether positive or negative—rarely go on indefinitely. When a negative spiral gets out of hand, the parties might agree to back off from their disconfirming behavior. "Hold on," one might say, "this is getting us nowhere." At this point there may be a cooling-off period, or the parties might work together more constructively to solve their problem. If the partners pass the "point of no return," the relationship may end (Leary, 1955). As you read in Chapter 1, it's impossible to take back a message once it has been sent, and some exchanges are so lethal that the relationship can't survive them. Positive spirals also have their limit: Even the best relationships go through rocky periods, in which the climate suffers. The accumulated good will and communication skill of the partners, however, can make these times less frequent and intense. Therefore, most relationships pass through cycles of progression and regression, as pictured in Figure 10–1.

FIGURE 10–1 Progressive and regressive spiral phases of a marital dyad (William W. Wilmot, *Dyadic Communication*, 2d ed. Reading, Mass.: Addison-Wesley, 1979, p. 126)

Progressive stages — Critical limit

Regressive stages — Critical limit

Characteristics of disconfirming communication

Disconfirming communication is common enough and damaging enough that it deserves special attention.

Disconfirming messages Disconfirming messages communicate a lack of appreciation for the recipient. As we have already said, disagreeing can be one type of disconfirmation, but not the most damaging kind. Disagreement at least acknowledges the other's position. Far worse are responses that ignore other's ideas, or even their existence. Sieburg and Larson (1971) describe seven such types of disconfirming responses.

Impervious response An impervious response fails to acknowledge the other person's communicative attempt, either verbally or nonverbally. Failing to return a phone call is an impervious response, as is not responding to another's letter. Impervious responses also happen in face-to-face settings. They are especially common when adults and children communicate. Parents often become enraged when they are ignored by their children; likewise, children feel diminished when adults pay no attention to their questions, comments, or requests.

Interrupting response Another kind of behavior commonly occurs when one person begins to speak before the other is through making a point.

Customer: I'm looking for an outfit I can wear on a trip I'm . . .

Salesperson: I've got just the thing. It's part wool and part polyester, so it won't wrinkle at all.

C: Actually wrinkling isn't that important. I want something that will work as a business outfit and . . .

S: We have a terrific blazer that you can dress up or down, depending on the accessories you choose.

C: That's not what I was going to say. I want something that I can wear as a business outfit, but it ought to be on the informal side. I'm going to . . .

S: Say no more. I know just what you want.

C: Never mind. I think I'll look in some other stores.

Irrelevant response It is disconfirming to respond with comments totally unrelated to what the other person was just saying.

A: What a day! I thought it would never end. First the car overheated and I had to call a tow truck, and then the computer broke down at work.

B: Listen, we have to talk about a present for Ann's birthday. The party is on Saturday, and I only have tomorrow to shop for it.

A: I'm really beat. You won't believe what the boss did. Like I said, the computer was down, and in the middle of that mess he decided he absolutely had to have the sales figures for the last six months.

B: I just can't figure what would suit Ann. She's been so generous to us, and I can't think of anything she needs.

A: Why don't you listen to me? I beat my brains out all day and you don't give a damn.

B: And you don't care about me!

Tangential response Unlike the three behaviors just discussed, a tangential comment does acknowledge the other person's communication. However, the acknowledgment is used to steer the conversation in another direction. Tangents can come in two forms: (1) The tangential "shift," which is an abrupt change in conversation; and (2) the tangential "drift," which makes a token connection with what the other person is saying and slowly moves the conversation in another direction entirely.

Consider the following situation: A student rushes up to the teacher at the end of class to discuss the grade on a recent exam.

Student: Dr. Jones, I'd like to talk about my grade on the exam.

Dr. Jones: Fine. But you'd better hurry along so you're not late for your next class.

This response is a tangential shift, executed rather adroitly. Jones acknowledges the student's remark ("fine"), then abruptly changes direction ("hurry along . . ."). Following is an example of a tangential drift:

Dr. Jones: Fine. We'll have to discuss the test. I also used to be concerned with understanding things I got wrong on tests. Of course, I was also concerned with punctuality! You'd better hurry along now so you're not late for the next class.

In this case, Jones indicates readiness to discuss the examination, but goes on to talk about something unrelated. A tangential response, if done well, can keep the other person guessing about how the change in the conversation's direction was accomplished.

Impersonal response In an impersonal message the speaker conducts a monologue filled with impersonal, intellectualized, and generalized statements. The speaker never really interacts with the other on a personal level.

Employee: I've been having some personal problems lately and I'd like to take off early a couple of afternoons to clear them up.

Boss: Ah, yes. We all have personal problems. It seems to be a sign of the times.

Ambiguous response Ambiguous communication contains a message with more than one meaning. The words are highly abstract or have meanings private to the speaker alone.

A: I'd like to get together with you soon. How about Tuesday?

B: Uh, maybe so. Anyhow, see you later.

C: How can I be sure you mean it?

D: Who knows what anybody means?

Incongruous response An incongruous response contains two messages that seem to deny or contradict each other, one at the verbal level and the other at the nonverbal level.

He: Darling, I love you!

She: I love you too. (*giggles*)

Teacher: Did you enjoy the class?

Student: Yes. (*yawns*)

Defensive communication Probably no type of communication clouds an interpersonal climate more quickly or severely than a defensive spiral. One verbal attack leads to another, and soon the dispute gets out of control, leaving an aftermath of hurt and bitterness that is difficult—sometimes even impossible—to repair.

The word "defensiveness" suggests protecting yourself from attack, but what kind of attack? Few of the times you become defensive involve a physical threat. If you're not threatened by bodily injury, what *are* you guarding against? To answer this question we need to talk more about the presenting self, introduced in Chapter 2.

Recall that the presenting self consists of the physical traits, personality characteristics, attitudes, aptitudes, and all the other parts of the image you want to present to the world. Actually,

The worst sin towards our fellow creatures is not to hate them, but to be indifferent to them; that's the essence of inhumanity.

George Bernard Shaw

---

it is a mistake to talk about a single presenting self. In truth, we try to project different selves to different people. You might, for instance, try to impress a potential employer with your seriousness and friends with your playfulness. Of course, not all parts of your presenting self are equally significant. Letting others know that you are right-handed or a Gemini is probably less important to you than convincing them you are good-looking or loyal.

We defend this presenting self when we perceive it has been attacked. To understand this process, imagine what might happen if someone attacked an important part of your presenting self. Suppose that:

- An instructor labeled you as an idiot, when you regard yourself as reasonably bright.
- An acquaintance accused you of being snobbish, when you believe you are friendly.
- An employer called you lazy, when you see yourself as a hard worker.

You have four choices in such situations: accept, attack, distort, or avoid.

Accepting the critic's judgment   When faced with an attack on your presenting self, you can agree with the critic. In the situations above, you could agree that you are stupid, snobbish, or lazy. If you sincerely accepted these evaluations, you would not feel or act defensively. Instead, you would adjust your presenting self—at least to this critic—to include the new judgment.

Sometimes, however, you aren't willing to accept attacks on your presenting self. The accusations of your critic may be false. You

might, for instance, be working extremely hard on a job when you're accused of laziness. In a more extreme example, you might be telling the truth when someone accuses you of lying. Even in cases like these, when defensive *feelings* are justified, defensive *behavior* is usually counterproductive. Complaining, justifying, and other defensive reactions rarely change a critic's mind. In fact, they usually intensify the attack. Also, defensive responses reduce the chance of gaining your partner's cooperation or enhancing your relationship. The final section of this chapter will suggest more productive ways to communicate when you have been criticized unfairly.

You might also be unwilling to accept criticism even when it *is* valid, because it doesn't support the image you want to project. It's difficult to admit you were cheap, unfair, or foolish— especially since these traits don't seem to gain the companionship and approval you are seeking.

If you aren't willing to accept the judgments of others, you are faced with what Leon Festinger (1957) called *dissonance*. Dissonance is an uncomfortable condition, and communicators try to resolve it three ways.

Attacking the critic   Counterattacking follows the old maxim that the best defense is a good offense. Attacks can take several forms.

- *Verbal aggression*   Sometimes the recipient directly assaults the critic. "Where do you get off calling me sloppy?" you might storm to a roommate. "You're the one who leaves globs of toothpaste in the sink and dirty clothes all over the bedroom!" This sort of response shifts the blame onto the critic, without acknowledging that the original judgment might be true. Other attacks on the critic are completely off the subject: "You're in no position to complain about my sloppiness. At least I pay my share of the bills on time." Again, this response resolves

the dissonance without ever addressing the validity of the criticism.

- *Sarcasm* Disguising the attack in a barbed, humorous message is a less direct form of aggression. "You think I ought to study more? Thanks for taking a break from watching soap operas and eating junk food to run my life." Sarcastic responses might score high on wit and quick thinking, but their hostile, disconfirming nature usually leads to a counterattack and a mutually destructive defensive spiral.

Distorting the critical information A second way of defending a perceived self that is under attack is to somehow distort the information in a way that leaves the presenting self intact—at least in the eyes of the defender. There are a number of ways to distort dissonant information.

- *Compensation* Compensators emphasize a strength in one area to cover up a weakness in another. A guilty parent might keep up the facade of being conscientious by protesting: "I may not be around much, but I give those kids

They defend their errors as if they were defending their inheritance.

Edmund Burke

---

the best things money can buy!" Likewise, you might try to convince yourself and others that you are a good friend by compensating: "Sorry I forgot your birthday. Let me give you a hand with that job." There's nothing wrong with most acts of compensation in themselves. The harm comes when they are used insincerely to maintain a fictitious presenting image.

- *Rationalization*   A rationalizer invents logical but untrue explanations of undesirable behavior. "I would help you out, but I really have to study," you might say as a convenient way to avoid an unpleasant chore. "I'm not overeating," you might protest to another critic who you secretly admit is on target. "I have a busy day ahead, and I need to keep my strength up."

- *Regression*   Another way to avoid facing attack is to play helpless, claiming you *can't* do something when in truth you *don't want* to do it. "I'd like to have a relationship with you, but I just can't: I'm not ready." "I wish I could do the

job better, but I just can't: I just don't understand it." The test for regression is to substitute the word "won't" for "can't." In many cases it becomes clear that "It's not my fault" is a fiction.

Avoiding dissonant information   A third way to protect a threatened presenting image is to avoid information altogether. Avoidance can take several forms.

- *Physical avoidance*   Steering clear of people who attack a presenting self is an obvious way to avoid dissonance. Sometimes physical avoidance may be wise. There's little profit in being battered by hostile or abusive criticism. In other cases, however, the relationship may be important enough and the criticism valid enough that avoiding the situation only makes matters worse.

- *Repression*   Sometimes we mentally block out dissonant information. You might, for instance, know that you ought to discuss a problem with a friend, boss, or instructor, yet put the idea out of your mind whenever it arises. It's even possible to repress a problem in the face of a critic. Changing the subject, acting as if you don't

understand, and even pretending you don't hear the criticism all fall into this category.

- *Apathy*   Another avoidance response is to acknowledge unpleasant information but pretend you don't care about it. You might, for instance, sit calmly through a friend's criticism and act as if it didn't bother you. Similarly, you might respond to the loss of a job by acting indifferently: "Who cares? It was a dumb job anyhow."

It's important to recognize that, in their purest sense, all these defensive reactions involve two kinds of deception. The first involves convincing the critic (and possibly others) that your presenting image is valid. Just as central is the need to convince *yourself* that the presenting image is accurate.

Creating positive communication climates

Despite the fact that nobody wants them, poor communication climates do occur. They are rarely deliberate creations: More often they grow from either lack of communication skill or carelessness. The following information should help you prevent stormy climates from developing in your relationships, and offers suggestions on how to change unhealthy climates that now exist.

Initiating positive climates   The best time to create a positive climate is at the beginning of a relationship, when there's no negative history to overcome. It's at this time that you can most easily create messages that allow people to believe you value them.

Notice the word *believe* in the preceding sentence. It isn't enough to care about others: They have to *know* that you care. Sometimes communicating this concern can be difficult. You may have to overcome the other person's insecurities

It is a curious psychological fact that the man who seems to be "egotistic" is not suffering from too much ego, but from too little.

Sydney J. Harris

("Why would anyone care about me?"). You might need to overcome a suspicious attitude ("What's he after, being so nice?"). Finally, you might have to overcome a bad reputation ("I've heard about *her*"), whether or not it's deserved.

A variety of researchers have defined the elements of a positive climate (for example, Gibb, 1961; Barbour and Goldberg, 1974; Eadie, 1982). Many of their descriptions are too vague to be of much use: "be accepting," "be empathic," and so on. The following guidelines translate a body of abstract advice into behaviors you can use to create confirming climates in your own relationships.

Acknowledge the other person   Acknowledging isn't as obvious as it might seem. Pseudolistening (described in Chapter 6) is as disconfirming as it is common. A wandering glance, vacant expression, and unattentive posture all suggest you aren't really paying attention to a conversational partner. In addition, the disconfirming behaviors on pages 240–241 also show a lack of acknowledgment: Besides ignoring the person outright, you can interrupt, give irrelevant, tangential, ambiguous, or incongruous responses, and act impersonally—all behaviors that imply a disconfirming "I don't care about you" attitude.

By contrast, an acknowledging response shows that you understand the speaker. A complete acknowledgment has two elements. The first is to acknowledge the speaker's *ideas.* One way to show you understand the speaker's ideas is to ask intelligent questions. An even clearer way to show you understand is to paraphrase the message, using the skill outlined in Chapter 6:

> "So you think I'm making a big mistake by dropping the class, both because I'll be quitting and because I might need the information someday—is that it?"

> "It sounds like you think we're going overboard on holiday presents again this year, and that we have to find a way of cutting back."

Notice that messages like these don't agree or disagree with the sender. Rather, they show that you understand what the other person is saying. Conveying this sort of understanding might seem trivial until you realize how often others fail to acknowledge your ideas, and how frustrated this lack of acknowledgment leaves you.

A second, more thorough kind of acknowledgment conveys your understanding of the speaker's *feelings,* as well as thoughts. Again, the best way to show your understanding is by paraphrasing:

> "You really feel confident that changing the work schedule will work, huh? It sounds like you're excited about giving it a try."

> "I never realized it before, but it sounds like you resent the way I kid you about your accent. You think I'm putting you down, and that's what makes you angry. Is that right?"

This sort of paraphrasing response accomplishes two things. First, it guarantees that you have indeed understood the other person accurately. If your paraphrase is incorrect, your partner can correct you: "It's not so much that I get mad when you tease me about my accent. It's that I feel hurt." In addition, paraphrasing shows that you respect others enough to hear them out—a genuine confirmation of their value.

Realize that acknowledging a message isn't the same thing as *agreeing* with it. You can still respond with your own ideas; but taking time first to understand the other person can make the difference between a positive, constructive climate and a negative, defensive spiral.

Demonstrate an open-minded attitude

Communicators with closed minds state or imply "I don't care what you have to say—my mind is made up." Gibb (1961) terms this disconfirming attitude "certainty," and he points out how it is likely to generate a defensive reaction. The communication climate will be far more positive if you listen to others' ideas without immediately disputing them. Ask questions, by all means, but make sure they are sincere requests for information and not ambushes. Notice the difference between a genuine question ("Can you explain how that would work?") and a hostile one ("Are you crazy? How can you even imagine that would work?"). Sometimes the difference between a sincere question and a veiled attack lies in the way you ask it. Imagine confirming and disconfirming ways of saying "Why do you want to do that?"

Edward deBono (1973) suggests a method for thinking and communicating open-mindedly. Rather than taking sides on an issue, he suggests, you and the other party should cooperatively explore all the positive aspects of an issue, then consider all the negative aspects, and finally think about all the aspects that are neither positive nor negative, but still interesting. Working *with* the other party to develop these lists sends the confirming relational message "I care about what you have to say," whereas staking out an opposing position communicates the opposite.

Agree whenever possible Public speakers have always realized the importance of stressing "common ground" they share with an audience. The same principle is just as valuable in other settings: Emphasizing shared beliefs makes it easier to discuss disagreements. A moment's thought will show that you probably share many important beliefs with others—even those whose positions you dislike. Both pro- and anti-abortionists, for example, can agree that an unwanted pregnancy poses a terrible dilemma for many women. Most supporters and opponents of the Equal Rights Amendment both believe that women should be treated equally under the law. Recognizing shared beliefs like these won't resolve disagreements, but it can create a climate that makes discussion more productive.

Describe, don't evaluate   Statements that judge another person are likely to provoke a defensive reaction (Gibb, 1961). Evaluative language has often been described as "you" language, since most such statements contain an accusatory use of that word. For example:

> "You made a fool of yourself last night."
> "You smoke too much."
> "You're not doing your share of the work."

In contrast to this sort of evaluative language is what Gibb calls *descriptive* communication, or "I" language. Rather than judging another's behavior, a descriptive statement explains the personal effect of the other's action. For example, instead of saying "You talk too much," a descriptive communicator might say "When you don't give me a chance to say what's on my mind, I get frustrated." This sort of descriptive statement contains three elements: (1) an account of the other person's behavior, (2) an explanation of the consequences of that behavior, and (3) a description of the speaker's feelings. Notice how the three statements listed above become more confirming when rephrased as descriptions:

> "When you told those jokes last night, everyone seemed uncomfortable. I was really embarrassed."

> "When you smoke so much, I worry about your health. I wonder what might happen to you—and me—if you keep it up."

> "When you take a break every ten or fifteen minutes, I wind up doing most of the work. I don't mind that once in a while, but I'm getting fed up."

Show concern for the other person's interests   Defensiveness is likely when one person tries to impose an idea on others with little regard for their needs or interests. This sort of controlling behavior isn't only disconfirming—it's often unnecessary. A more productive attitude is what Gibb terms *problem-orientation:* asking "How can we solve this problem?" instead of "How can I overcome the other person?"

A problem-oriented approach works on large issues (How can we live together with such different personalities?) and small ones (How can we watch different TV shows at the same hour?). In every case, the key to success is to strive for an answer that satisfies everyone's needs. Chapter 11 offers detailed information on this sort of "win-win" problem solving. For now it's important to recognize that simply *striving* for this sort of outcome builds a positive communication climate.

Communicate honestly   One of the surest ways to cloud a communication climate is to get caught lying. Dishonesty and manipulation are disconfirming for two reasons. First, they imply that you don't have the other person's best interests in mind. Second, this approach suggests you thought you could deceive the other person, and almost no one likes to be regarded as a gullible fool.

Paradoxical as it seems, candor too can be a kind of manipulation. Some people use honesty in a calculating way, revealing just enough information to get what they want. When discovered, this

and in a way that is easy for the other person to understand. This means using the kinds of communication described earlier in this section, such as common ground and descriptive language. Saying "You look terrible in that outfit" isn't confirming. Notice how much better it is to say "I think it's great that you're trying to change your look, but I'd like you better in another color." For more advice about how to combine honesty and effectiveness, refer to the guidelines for self-disclosure in Chapter 8.

Transforming negative climates   The preceding pages have described how to build a positive communication climate at the beginning of a relationship and how to maintain a positive climate once it's started. What about cases in which negative feelings already exist? Changing the climate in these cases is like slowing down a runaway horse: You have to stop the animal before you can begin to move toward your destination.

One of the biggest barriers to overcoming poor climates is the torrent of negative criticism characterizing so many of them. Because the problem of handling criticism is so difficult and important, we'll devote the rest of this chapter to it. When you're finished reading, you should have acquired some workable skills to help you in these difficult cases.

In order to handle criticism constructively you need to have available honest, nonmanipulative ways of dealing with criticism without feeling the need to justify yourself or to counterattack. There are two such methods, each of which at first appears to be almost childishly simple, yet in practice has proved over and over to be among the most valuable assertive skills (see also Smith, 1975).

kind of candor can backfire, for it leaves the victim feeling like a sucker—hardly the kind of outcome that leads to a positive climate.

Honest messages are only confirming when they meet two conditions. First, they must grow out of a sincere concern for the other person's welfare. Honesty used as a weapon can destroy a relationship quicker than almost any other type of communication: "You want honesty? To tell the truth, I think you're stupid!" Second, the honest message needs to be delivered at the right time

When criticized, seek more information
Seeking more information makes good sense

when you realize that it's foolish to respond to a critical attack until you understand it. Even comments that upon first consideration appear to be totally unjustified or foolish often prove to contain at least a grain of truth, and sometimes much more.

Many readers object to the idea of asking for details when they are criticized. Their resistance grows from confusing the act of *listening open-mindedly* to a speaker's comments with *accepting* them. Once you realize that you can listen to, understand, and even acknowledge the most hostile comments without necessarily accepting them, it becomes much easier to hear another person out. If you disagree with a speaker's objections, you will be in a much better position to explain yourself once you understand them. On the other hand, after carefully listening to the other's remarks, you just might see that they are valid, in which case you have learned some valuable information about yourself. In either case you have everything to gain and nothing to lose by hearing the critic out.

Of course, after years of instinctively resisting criticism, this habit of hearing the other person out will take some practice. To make matters more clear, here are several ways in which you can seek additional information from your critics.

1. Ask for specifics. Often the vague attack of a critic is practically useless, even if you sincerely want to change. Abstract accusations such as, "You're being unfair" or "You never help out" can be difficult to understand. In such cases it is a good idea to request more specific information from the sender. "What do I *do* that's unfair?" is an important question to ask before you can judge whether the accusation is correct. "When haven't I helped out?" you might ask prior to agreeing with or disputing the accusation.

If you solicit specifics by using questions and are accused of reacting defensively, the problem may be in the *way* you ask. Your tone of voice and facial expression, posture, or other nonverbal clues can give the same words radically different connotations. For example, think of how you could use the words, "Exactly what are you talking about?" to communicate either a genuine desire to know or your belief that the speaker is crazy. It's important to request specific information only when you genuinely want to learn more from the speaker, for asking under any other circumstances will only make matters worse.

2. Guess about specifics. On some occasions even your sincere and well-phrased requests for specific details of another's criticism won't meet with success. Sometimes your critics won't be able to define precisely the behavior they find offensive. In these instances you'll hear such comments as, "I can't tell you exactly what's wrong with your sense of humor—all I can say is that I don't like it." In other cases your critics may know the exact behavior they don't like but seem to get a perverse satisfaction out of making you struggle to figure it out. Then you hear such comments as, "Well, if you don't know what you did to hurt my feelings, I'm certainly not going to tell you!"

Needless to say, failing to learn the details of another's criticism when you genuinely want to know them can be a frustrating experience. In instances like these you can often learn more clearly what is bothering your critic by *guessing* at the specifics of a complaint. In a sense you become both detective and suspect, with the goal being to figure out exactly what "crime" you have committed. Like the technique of asking for specifics, guessing must be done with good will if it's to produce satisfying results. You need to convey to the critic that for both of your sakes you're truly interested in finding out what is the matter. Once you have communicated this intention, the emotional climate generally becomes more comfortable, because in effect both you and the critic are seeking the same goal.

Here are some typical questions you might hear from someone guessing about the details of another's criticism:

"So you object to the language I used in writing the paper. Was my language too formal?"

"O.K. I understand that you think the outfit looks funny. What is it that's so bad? Is it the color? Does it have something to do with the fit? The fabric?"

"When you say that I'm not doing my share around the house, do you mean that I haven't been helping enough with the cleaning?"

3. Paraphrase the speaker's ideas. Another strategy for learning more about criticism is to draw out confused or reluctant speakers by paraphrasing their thoughts and feelings and using the active listening skills described in Chapter 6. Paraphrasing is especially good in helping others solve their problems. Given that people generally criticize you because your behavior creates some problem for them, the method is especially appropriate for such times.

One advantage of paraphrasing is that you don't have to come up with any guesses about the specifics of your behavior that might be offensive. By clarifying or amplifying what you understand critics to be saying, you'll learn more about their objections. A brief dialogue between a disgruntled customer and a store manager especially talented at paraphrasing might sound like this one:

Customer: The way you people run this store is disgusting! I just want to tell you that I'll never shop here again.

Manager: *(reflecting the customer's feeling)* It seems that you're quite upset. Can you tell me your problem?

C: It isn't *my* problem, it's the problem your salespeople have. They seem to think it's a great inconvenience to help a customer find anything around here.

M: So you didn't get enough help locating the items you were looking for, is that it?

C: Help? I spent twenty minutes looking around in here before I even talked to a clerk. All I can say is that it's a hell of a way to run a store.

M: So what you're saying is that the clerks seemed to be ignoring the customers?

C: No. They were all busy with other people. It just seems to me that you ought to have enough help around to handle the crowds that come in at this hour.

M: I understand now. What frustrated you the most was the fact that we didn't have enough staff to serve you promptly.

C: That's right. I have no complaint with the service I get once I'm waited on, and I've always thought you had a good selection here. It's just that I'm too busy to wait so long for help.

M: Well, I'm glad you brought this to my attention. We certainly don't want loyal customers going away mad. I'll try to see that it doesn't happen again.

This conversation illustrates two advantages of paraphrasing. First, often the intensity of the attack abates once the critic realizes that the complaint is being heard. Often criticism grows from the frustration of unmet needs—in this case, a lack of attention. As soon as the manager genuinely demonstrated interest in the customer's plight, the customer began to feel better, and was able to leave the store relatively calm. Of course this sort of active listening won't always mollify your critic, but even when it doesn't, there's still another benefit that makes the technique worthwhile. In the sample conversation, for instance, the manager learned some valuable information by taking time to understand the customer. The manager discovered that there were certain times when the number of employees was insufficient to help the crowd of shoppers, and that the delays at these times seriously annoyed at least some shoppers, threatening a loss in business. This knowledge is certainly important, and by reacting defensively to the customer's complaint, the manager would not have learned from it. As you read earlier, even apparently outlandish criticism often contains at least a grain of truth, so a person who is genuinely interested in improving would be wise to hear it out.

4. Ask about the consequences of your behavior. As a rule people complain about your actions only when some need of theirs is not being met. One way to respond to this kind of criticism is to find out exactly what troublesome consequences your behavior has for them. You'll often find that actions that seem perfectly legitimate to you cause some difficulty for your critic; once you have understood this consequence, comments that previously sounded foolish take on a new meaning.

A: You say that I ought to have my cat neutered. Why is that important to you?

B: Because at night he picks fights with my cat, and I'm tired of paying the vet's bills.

C: Why do you care whether I'm late to work?

D: Because when the boss asks where you are, I feel obligated to make up some story so you won't get in trouble, and I don't like to lie.

E: Why does it bother you when I lose money at poker? You know I never gamble more than I can afford.

F: It's not the cash itself. It's that when you lose you're in a grumpy mood for two or three days, and that's no fun for me.

5. Solicit additional complaints. Although the idea might at first sound outlandish, once you've understood one complaint, it's often beneficial to see if there is anything else about your behavior that bothers your critic. Soliciting additional complaints can be a good idea for the simple reason that if you can learn one valuable lesson from a

"What do you mean 'Your guess is as good as mine'? My guess is a hell of a lot <u>better</u> than your guess!"

single criticism, you ought to double your knowledge by hearing two.

Of course, it isn't always wise to seek additional gripes, at least not immediately. You should be sure that you understand the first complaint before tackling another one at the same time. Resolving the complaint sometimes means agreeing to the other's demands for change, but in other circumstances it can mean hearing out the other's request and promising to think about it. In still other instances the critic really doesn't expect you to change; in such cases resolution can simply mean that you've taken the time and spent the effort to understand the criticism.

You can see how solicitation of additional criticism works by returning to the conversation between the store manager and a disgruntled customer.

M: I can promise you that I'll see what I can do about having more employees on hand during busy periods. While you're here, I'd like to know if you can think of any other ways we could improve our operation.

C: What? You really want to know what else I think you're doing wrong?

M: Sure. If we're not aware of ways we could do better, we'll never change.

C: Well, the only other thing I can think of is the parking situation. A lot of times I'll come by and have to wait several minutes for a delivery truck to unload before I can get into the lot from the south side. I wish you could have the trucks park somewhere else or unload at a quieter hour.

M: That's a good point. We can't always control when the drivers from other companies will show up, but I can sure give their dispatchers a call and see what can be done. I want to say that I appreciate your thoughts. Even when we have our bad days around here, it's important to us that we do every-

thing we can to make this a good place to shop.

Sometimes soliciting and understanding more information from a critic isn't enough. What do you do, for instance, when you fully understand the other person's objections and still feel a defensive response on the tip of your tongue? You know that if you try to protect yourself, you'll wind up in an argument; on the other hand, you simply can't accept what the other person is saying about you. The solution to such a dilemma is outrageously simple, and is discussed in the following section.

When criticized, agree with the speaker   But, you protest, how can you honestly agree with comments that you don't believe are true? The following pages will answer this question by showing that there's virtually no situation in which you can't honestly accept the other person's point of view and still maintain your position. To see how, you need to realize that there are four different types of agreement, each of which you can express in different circumstances.

1. Agree with the truth. Agreeing with the truth is easy to understand, though not always to practice. You agree with the truth when another person's criticism is factually correct:

> "You're right, I am angry."
>
> "I suppose I *was* being defensive."
>
> "Now that you mention it, I did get pretty sarcastic."

Agreeing with the facts seems quite sensible when you realize that certain matters are indisputable. If you agree to be somewhere at 4:00 and don't show up until 5:00, you *are* late, no matter how good your explanation for tardiness is. If you've broken a borrowed object, run out of gas, or failed to finish a job you started, there's no point in denying the fact. In the same way, if you're honest you will have to agree with many interpretations of your behavior, even when they're not flattering. You do get angry, act foolishly, fail to listen, and behave inconsiderately. Once you rid yourself of the myth of perfection, it's much easier to acknowledge these truths.

If it's so obvious that the descriptions others give of your behaviors are often accurate, why is it so difficult to accept them without being defensive? The answer to this question lies in a confusion between agreeing with the *facts* and accepting the *judgment* that so often accompanies them. Most critics don't merely describe the action that offends them, they also evaluate it, and it's this evaluation that we resist:

"It's silly to be angry."
"You have no reason for being defensive."
"You were wrong to be so sarcastic."

It's judgments like these that we resent. By realizing that you can agree with—even learn from—the descriptive part of many criticisms and still not accept the accompanying evaluations, you'll often have a response that is both honest and nondefensive. A conversation between a teacher and a student illustrates this point.

Teacher: Look at this paper! It's only two pages long and it contains twelve misspelled words. I'm afraid you have a real problem with your writing.

Student: You're right. I know I don't spell well at all.

T: I don't know what's happening in the lower grades. They just don't seem to be turning out people who can write a simple, declarative sentence.

S: You're not the first person I've heard say that.

T: I should think you'd be upset by the fact that after so much time in English composition

Love your enemies, for they tell you your faults.

Benjamin Franklin

_____

classes you haven't mastered the basics of spelling.

S: You're right. It does bother me.

Notice that in agreeing with the teacher's comments the student did not in any way demean herself. Even though there might have been extenuating circumstances to account for her lack of skill, the student didn't find it necessary to justify her errors, because she wasn't saddled with the burden of pretending to be perfect. By simply agreeing with the facts she was able to maintain her dignity and avoid an unproductive argument.

Of course, in order to reduce defensiveness it's important that your agreements with the facts are honest ones admitted without malice. It's humiliating to accept descriptions that aren't accurate, and maliciously pretending to agree with these only leads to trouble. You can imagine how unproductive the above conversation would have been if the student had spoken the same words in a sarcastic tone. Only agree with the facts when you can do so sincerely. Although it won't always be possible, you'll be surprised at how often you can use this simple response.

Agreeing with criticism is fine, but by itself it isn't an adequate response to your critic. For instance, once you've admitted to another that you are defensive, habitually late, or sarcastic, you can expect the other to ask what you intend to do about this behavior. Such questions are fair ones. In most cases it would be a mistake simply to understand another's criticism, to agree with the accusations, and then to go on behaving as before. Such behavior makes it clear that you have no concern for the speaker. The message that comes through is, "Sure, now I understand what I've done to bother you. You're right, I have been doing it and I'll probably keep on doing it. If you don't like the way I've been behaving, that's tough!" Such a response might be appropriate for dealing with people you genuinely don't care about—manipulative solicitors, abusive strangers, and so on—but it is clearly not suitable for people who matter to you.

Before reading on, then, understand that responding nondefensively to criticism is only the *first step* in resolving the conflicts that usually prompt another's attack. In order to manage your conflicts fully, you'll need to learn the skills described in Chapter 11.

2. Agree with the odds. Sometimes a critic will point out possible unpleasant consequences of your behavior:

> "If you don't talk to more people, they'll think you're a snob."

> "If you don't exercise more, you'll wind up having a heart attack one of these days."

> "If you run around with that crowd, you'll probably be sorry."

Often such comments are genuinely helpful suggestions that others offer for your own good. In other cases, however, they are really devices for manipulating you into behaving the way your critic wants. For instance, "If we go to the football game, you might catch cold" could mean, "I don't want to go to the football game." "You'll probably be exhausted tomorrow if you stay up late" could be translated as, "I want you to go to bed early." Chapter 11 will have more to say about such methods of indirect aggression, but for now it is sufficient to state that such warnings often generate defensiveness. A mother-son argument shows this outcome:

Mother: I don't see why you want to ride that motorcycle. You could wind up in an accident so easily. (*states the odds for an accident*)

Son: Oh, don't be silly. I'm a careful driver, and besides you know that I never take my bike on the freeway. (*denies the odds*)

M: Yes, but every time I pick up the paper I read about someone being hurt or killed. There's always a danger that some crazy driver will miss seeing you and run you off the road. (*states the odds of an injury*)

S: Oh, you worry too much. I always look out for the other driver. And besides, you have a lot better maneuverability on a motorcycle than in a car. (*denies the odds for an injury*)

M: I know you're careful, but all it takes is one mistake and you could be killed. (*states the odds for being killed*)

S: Somebody is killed shaving or taking a shower every day, but you don't want me to stop doing those things, do you? You're just exaggerating the whole thing. (*denies the odds for being killed*)

From this example you can see that it's usually counterproductive to deny another's predictions. You don't convince the critic, and your mind stays unchanged as well. Notice the difference when you agree with the odds (though not the demands) of the critic.

M: I don't see why you want to drive that motorcycle. You could wind up in an accident so easily. (*states the odds for an accident*)

S: I suppose there is a chance of that. (*agrees with the odds*)

M: You're darned right. Every time I pick up the newspaper I read about someone being hurt or killed. There's always a danger that some crazy driver will miss seeing you and run you off the road. (*states the odds for an injury*)

S: You're right, that could happen (*agrees with the odds*), but I don't think the risk is great enough to keep me off the bike.

M: That's easy for you to say now. Some day you could be sorry you didn't listen to me. (*states the odds for regret*)

S: That's true. I really might regret driving the bike some day. (*agrees with the odds*)

Notice how the son simply considers his mother's predictions and realistically acknowledges the chance that they might come true. While such responses might at first seem indifferent and callous, they can help the son to avoid the pitfall of indirect manipulation. Suppose the conversation was a straightforward one in which the mother was simply pointing out the danger of motorcycle riding to her son. He acknowledged that he understood her concern and even agreed with the possibility that her prediction could come true. If, however, her prediction was really an indirect way of saying, "I don't want you to ride any more," then the son's response would force her into making her demand clear, allowing him to deal with it openly. At this point they might be able to figure out a solution that lets the son satisfy his need for transportation and excitement and at the same time allows the mother to alleviate her concern.

In addition to bringing hidden agendas into the open for resolution, agreeing with the odds has the added advantage of helping you become aware of some possible consequences of your actions that you might not have previously considered. Instead of blindly denying the chance that your behavior is inappropriate, agreeing with the odds will help you take an objective look at whether your course of action is in fact the best one. You might agree with your critic that the odds are such that you really should change your behavior.

3. Agree in principle. Often criticism comes in the form of abstract ideals against which you're unfavorably compared:

"I wish you wouldn't spend so much time on your work. Relaxation is important too, you know."

"You shouldn't expect so much from your kids. Nobody's perfect."

"What do you mean, you're not voting? The government is only going to get better when people like you take more of an interest in it."

"You mean you're still upset by that remark? You ought to learn how to take a joke better."

In such instances it's entirely possible for you to accept the principle upon which the criticism is based and still continue to behave as you have been doing. This apparent inconsistency is sensible for two reasons. First, no abstract statement applies to every instance of human behavior. For instance, although relaxation is important, there are occasions where it is appropriate to throw yourself totally into your work for a period of time. While it is unfair to put excessive demands on one's children, in some cases it becomes necessary for them to behave in an exceptional manner. As the Bible says, there is a time for every purpose, and what might usually be right isn't always so.

A second reason why you might agree in principle with a criticism but not change your behavior is precisely because people *are* inconsistent. Not being totally rational, we often do things that aren't in our best interests or those of another person. Again the myth of perfection needs debunking: You're not a saint, so it's unrealistic to expect that you'll always behave like one. As authors and teachers of assertive communication, we can relate to this principle. There are occasions when we find ourselves behaving in a very unassertive manner: failing to define our problems and goals behaviorally, expecting ourselves to improve in some way all at once instead of changing in gradual steps, and (ironically enough) becoming defensive in the face of criticism. In the face of such situations our inner dialogues often go something like this one:

Top dog: Boy, are you a hypocrite. Here you are, the expert on assertiveness, and you can't even take a little criticism yourself. Do as I say, not as I do, eh?

Underdog: *(whining)* Well, it's not just my fault, you know. I do the best I can, but sometimes other people are so obnoxious that . . . Wait a second. You're right *(agreeing with principle)*. I probably ought to be able to accept criticism better, but I guess I still haven't managed totally to master everything I teach. Maybe after a little longer I'll get better. I sure hope so for everybody's sake!

4. Agree with the critic's perception. What about times when there seems to be no basis whatsoever for agreeing with your critic? You've listened carefully and asked questions to make sure you understand the objections, but the more you listen, the more positive you are that they are totally out of line: There is no truth to the criticism, you can't agree with the odds, and you can't even accept the principle the critic puts forward. Even in these cases there's a way of agreeing—this time not with the critics' conclusions, but with their right to perceive things their way.

A: I don't believe you've been all the places you were just describing. You're probably just making all this up so we'll think you're hot stuff.

B: Well, I can see how you might think that. I've known people who lie to get approval.

C: I want to let you know right from the start that I was against hiring you for the job. I think the reason you got it was because you're a woman.

D: I can understand why you'd believe that with all the antidiscrimination laws on the books. I hope that after I've been here for a while you'll change your mind.

E: I don't think you're being totally honest about your reasons for wanting to stay home. You say that it's because you have a headache, but I think you're avoiding Mary and Walt.

F: I can see why that would make sense to you since Mary and I got into an argument the last time we were together. All I can say is that I do have a headache.

Responses such as these tell critics that you're acknowledging the reasonableness of their perception, even though you don't choose to accept it yourself or change your behavior. This coping style is a valuable one, for it lets you avoid the debates over who is right and who is wrong, which can turn an exchange of ideas into an argument. Notice the difference in the following scenes between Amy and Bob.

Disputing the perception:

Amy: I don't see how you can stand to be around Josh. The guy is so crude that he gives me the creeps.

Bob: What do you mean, crude? He's a really nice guy. I think you're just touchy.

A: Touchy! If it's touchy to be offended by disgusting behavior, then I'm guilty.

B: You're not guilty about anything. It's just that you're too sensitive when people kid around.

A: Too sensitive, huh? I don't know what's happened to you. You used to have such good judgment about people. . . .

Agreeing with the perception:

A: I don't see how you can stand to be around Josh. The guy is so crude that he gives me the creeps.

B: Well, I enjoy being around him, but I guess I can see how his jokes would be offensive to some people.

A: You're damn right. I don't see how you can put up with him.

B: Yeah. I guess if you didn't appreciate his humor, you wouldn't want to have much to do with him.

Notice how in the second exchange Bob was able to maintain his own position without attacking Amy's in the least. This acceptance is the key ingredient for successfully agreeing with your critics' perceptions: When it is present, you make it clear that in no way are you disputing their views of the matter. Because you have no intention of attacking your critics' views, they are less likely to be defensive.

All of these responses to criticism may appear to buy peace at the cost of denying your feelings. However, as you can see by now, counterattacking usually makes matters worse. The nondefensive responses you have just learned won't solve problems or settle disputes by themselves. They *will* make a constructive dialogue possible, setting the stage for a productive solution. How to achieve these productive solutions is the topic of Chapter 11.

Readings

Adler, Ronald B. *Confidence in Communication: A Guide to Assertive and Social Skills.* New York: Holt, Rinehart and Winston, 1977.

Barbour, Alton, and Alvin A. Goldberg. *Interpersonal Communication: Teaching Strategies and Resources.* Annandale, Va.: ERIC/RCS Speech Communication Module, 1974.

Blake, Robert R., and Jane S. Mouton. *The Managerial Grid.* Houston: Gulf Publishing Co., 1964.

Buber, Martin. "Distance and Relation." *Psychiatry* 20 (1957): 97–104.

*Cissna, Kenneth N. Leone, and Suzanne Keating. "Speech Communication Antecedents of Perceived Confirmation." *Western Journal of Speech Communication* 43 (1979): 48–60.

Clarke, F. Patrick. *Interpersonal Communication Variables as Predictors of Marital Satisfaction-Dissatisfaction.* Doctoral dissertation, University of Denver, 1973.

Coon, Dennis. *Introduction to Psychology: Exploration and Application,* 2d ed. St. Paul, Minn.: West, 1981.

Dance, Frank, and Carl Larson. *The Functions of Human Communication.* New York: Holt, Rinehart and Winston, 1976.

deBono, E. *Lateral Thinking: Creativity Step by Step.* New York: Harper & Row, 1973.

Deutsch, Morton A. "Trust and Suspicion." *Journal of Conflict Resolution* 2 (1958): 265–279.

Eadie, W. F. "Defensive Communication Revisited: A Critical Examination of Gibb's Theory." *Southern Speech Communication Journal* 47 (1982): 163–177.

Festinger, L. *A Theory of Cognitive Dissonance.* Stanford, Calif.: Stanford University Press, 1957.

*Gibb, Jack R. "Defensive Communication." *Journal of Communication* 11 (September 1961): 141–148.

Gordon, Thomas. *T.E.T.: Teacher Effectiveness Training.* New York: David McKay, 1977.

Hays, Ellis R. "Ego-Threatening Classroom Communication: A Factor Analysis of Student Perceptions." *Speech Teacher* 19 (1970): 43–48.

Heineken, J. R. *Disconfirming Responses in Psychiatric Patients.* Doctoral dissertation, University of Denver, 1980.

Horney, Karen. *Our Inner Conflicts: A Constructive Theory of Neurosis.* New York: Norton, 1945.

Jacobs, Merelyn R. *Levels of Confirmation and Disconfirmation in Interpersonal Communication.* Doctoral dissertation, University of Denver, 1973.

Kelman, Herbert C. "Compliance, Identification, and Internalization." *Journal of Conflict Resolution* 2 (1958): 51–60.

Laing, R. D. *Self and Others.* New York: Pantheon, 1961.

Leary, T. "The Theory and Measurement Methodology of Interpersonal Communication." *Psychiatry* 18 (1955): 147–161.

McGregor, Douglas. *Human Side of Enterprise.* New York: McGraw-Hill, 1960.

Mix, Clarence R. *Interpersonal Communication Patterns, Personal Values, and Predictive*

Accuracy: An Exploratory Study. Doctoral dissertation, University of Denver, 1972.

Powell, John. *Why Am I Afraid to Tell You Who I Am?* Chicago: Argus Communications, 1969.

Redding, W. Charles. *Communication Within the Organization.* New York: Industrial Communication Council, 1972.

Rokeach, Milton. *The Open and Closed Mind.* New York: Basic Books, 1960.

Rosenfeld, Lawrence B. *Analyzing Human Communication,* 2d ed. Dubuque, Iowa: Kendall/ Hunt, 1983.

Rosenfeld, Lawrence B. "Communication Climate and Coping Mechanisms in the College Classroom." *Communication Education* 32 (1983): 167–174.

Rosenfeld, Lawrence B., and Mary W. Jarrard. "The Effects of Perceived Sexism in Female and Male College Professors on Students' Descriptions of Classroom Climate." *Communication Education* 34 (1985): 205–213.

Shostrom, Everett L. *Man, the Manipulator.* New York: Basic Books, 1960.

Sieburg, Evelyn. "Confirming and Disconfirming Communication in an Organizational Setting." *Personnel Woman* 18 (1974): 4–11.

*Sieburg, Evelyn. "Confirming and Disconfirming Organizational Communication." In *Communication in Organizations,* J. Owen, P. Page, and G. Zimmerman, eds. New York: West, 1976.

Sieburg, Evelyn. *Dysfunctional Communication and Interpersonal Responsiveness in Small Groups.* Doctoral dissertation, University of Denver, 1969.

Sieburg, Evelyn, and Carl Larson. "Dimensions of Interpersonal Response." Paper presented to the International Communication Association, Phoenix, Arizona, 1971.

Smith, Manuel. *When I Say No, I Feel Guilty.* New York: Bantam Books, 1975.

Sundell, Wayne. *The Operation of Confirming and Disconfirming Verbal Behavior in Selected Teacher-Student Interactions.* Doctoral dissertation, University of Denver, 1972.

Watzlawick, Paul, Janet Beavin, and Don Jackson. *Pragmatics of Human Communication: A Study of Interactional Patterns, Pathologies, and Paradoxes.* New York: W. W. Norton, 1967.

*Wilmot, W. W. *Dyadic Communication.* Reading, Mass.: Addison-Wesley, 1979.

Eleven

Resolving Conflicts

After studying the material in this chapter

You should understand:

1. The four elements of conflict.
2. That conflict is natural and inevitable.
3. The characteristics of functional and dysfunctional conflicts.
4. The differences among nonassertiveness, indirect aggression, direct aggression, and assertiveness.
5. The characteristics of win-lose, lose-lose, and win-win problem-solving.

You should be able to:

1. Recognize and accept the inevitability of conflicts in your life.
2. Identify the behaviors that characterize your dysfunctional conflicts and suggest more functional alternatives.
3. Identify the conflict styles you use most commonly and evaluate their appropriateness.
4. Use the win-win problem-solving approach to resolve an interpersonal conflict.

Once upon a time there was a world with no conflicts. The leaders of each nation recognized the need for cooperation and met regularly to solve any potential problems before they could grow. They never disagreed on areas needing attention or on ways to handle these areas, and so there were never any international tensions, and of course there was no war.

Within each nation things ran just as smoothly. The citizens always agreed on who their leaders should be, so elections were always unanimous. There was no social friction between various groups. Age, race, and educational differences did exist, but each group respected the others and all got along harmoniously.

Personal relationships were always perfect. Strangers were always kind and friendly to each other. Neighbors were considerate of each other's needs. Friendships were always mutual, and no disagreements ever spoiled people's enjoyment of one other. Once people fell in love—and everyone did— they stayed happy. Partners liked everything about each other and were able to satisfy each other's needs fully. Children and parents agreed on every aspect of family life and never were critical or hostile toward each other. Each day was better than the one before.

Of course, everybody lived happily ever after.

This story is obviously a fairy tale. Regardless of what we may wish for or dream about, a conflict-free world just doesn't exist. Even the best communicators, the luckiest people, are bound to wind up in situations when their needs don't match the needs of others. Money, time, power, sex, humor, aesthetic taste, as well as a thousand other issues, arise and keep us from living in a state of perpetual agreement.

For many people the inevitability of conflict is a depressing fact. They think that the existence of ongoing conflict means that there's little chance for happy relationships with others. Effective communicators know differently. They realize that although it's impossible to *eliminate* conflict, there are ways to *manage* it effectively. Managing conflict skillfully can open the door to healthier, stronger, and more satisfying relationships.

What is conflict?

Stop reading and make a list of as many different conflicts as you can recall. Include both conflicts you've experienced personally and ones that only involved others.

This list will probably show you that conflict takes many forms. Sometimes there's angry shouting, as when parents yell at their children. In other cases, conflicts involve restrained discussion, as in labor-management negotiations or legal trials. Sometimes conflicts are carried on through hostile silence, as angry couples act when conducting an unspoken feud. Finally, conflicts may wind up in physical fighting between friends, enemies, or even total strangers.

Whatever forms they may take, all interpersonal conflicts share certain similarities. Joyce Frost and William Wilmot (1985) provide a thorough definition of conflict. They state that conflict is *an expressed struggle between at least two interdependent parties who perceive incompatible goals, scarce rewards, and interference from the other parties in achieving their goals.* Let's look at the various parts of this definition so as to develop a clearer idea of conflicts in people's lives.

Expressed struggle   Another way to describe an expressed struggle is to say that both parties in a conflict know that some disagreement exists. For instance, you may be upset for months because a neighbor's loud stereo keeps you from getting to sleep at night, but no conflict exists between the two of you until the neighbor learns about your problem. Of course, the expressed struggle doesn't have to be verbal. You can show your displeasure with somebody without saying a word. A dirty look, the silent treatment, or avoiding the other person are all ways of expressing yourself. One way or another, both parties must know that a problem exists before they're in conflict.

Perceived incompatible goals   All conflicts look as if one party's gain would be another's loss. For instance, consider the neighbor whose stereo keeps you awake at night. Doesn't somebody have to lose? If the neighbor turns down the noise, then he loses the enjoyment of hearing the music at full volume; but if the neighbor keeps the volume up, then you're still awake and unhappy.

The goals in this situation really aren't completely incompatible—solutions do exist that allow both parties to get what they want. For instance, you could achieve peace and quiet by closing your windows or getting the neighbor to close his. You might use a pair of earplugs, or perhaps the neighbor could get a set of earphones, allowing the music to play at full volume without bothering anyone. If any of these solutions prove workable, then the conflict disappears.

Unfortunately, people often fail to see mutually satisfying answers to their problems. As long as they *perceive* their goals to be mutually exclusive, then, although the conflict is unnecessary, it is still real.

Perceived scarce rewards   Conflicts also exist when people believe there isn't enough of something to go around. The most obvious example of a scarce resource is money—a cause of many conflicts. If a worker asks for a raise in pay and the boss would rather keep the money or use it to expand the business, then the two parties are in conflict.

Time is another scarce commodity. As authors and family men, all three of us are constantly in the middle of struggles about how to use the lim-

ited time we have at home. Should we work on this book? Visit with our wives? Play with our children? Enjoy the luxury of being alone? With only twenty-four hours in a day, we're bound to wind up in conflicts with our families, editors, students, and friends—all of whom want more of our time than we have available to give.

Interdependence   However antagonistic they might feel, the parties in a conflict are dependent upon each other. The welfare and satisfaction of one depends on the actions of another. If not, then even in the face of scarce resources and incompatible goals there would be no need for conflict. Interdependence exists between conflicting nations, social groups, organizations, friends, and lovers. In each case, if the two parties didn't need each other to solve the problem, they would go separate ways. In fact, many conflicts go unresolved because the parties fail to understand their interdependence. One of the first steps toward resolving a conflict is to take the attitude that "we're all in this together."

Conflict is natural and inevitable

Frost and Wilmot's definition goes on to assert that conflicts are bound to occur, even to the most happy, successful, lucky people. It's vitally important to recognize the inevitability of conflict, for failing to do so can lead to a lot of unnecessary grief. Expecting life to be free of conflict is like expecting the weather to be perfect every day. If you maintain this kind of hope, you're bound to be disappointed. On the other hand, having a more realistic attitude about the weather can help you get through (and even take advantage of) stormy days.

Even after we recognize the inevitability of conflict, most people tend to view it as an unpleasant though necessary activity, similar to figuring out income taxes or visiting the dentist. A quick look at our culture reveals several reasons for this bad image. The first relates to unrealistic teaching. From the time children can understand speech, most of them are raised on a diet of fairy tales that paint the ideal world as free of conflicts. The storybook ending of living "happily ever after" implies that if people are truly good, they live harmonious lives that are free of any friction. Many TV shows perpetuate this image. Although TV characters do have problems, they're inevitably simple enough to be cleared up before the final commercial, hardly a reflection of real life.

When TV and newspapers show conflicts in the real world, most of the struggles cannot be called constructive. Soldiers and innocent civilians die in wars, angry demonstrators riot, and social groups shout angrily at each other. This sort of hostility and violence is hardly a testimonial to the benefits of conflict.

In addition, many families present conflict as dangerous and undesirable. Some parents are verbally or physically abusive to each other and their children. Because people learn from models, their children may grow up to be the same kind of fighters as their parents. This modeling is why so many adults who are child-beaters were, as children, victims of abuse themselves. In other cases, the horror of viewing destructive aggression may lead children to avoid conflicts when they grow up.

At the other end of the spectrum, families in which conflicts are not acknowledged create the idea that confrontations are to be avoided. Many parents never acknowledge the conflicts that they feel with each other, even to themselves. When disagreements do come up, they're handled privately—"Not in front of the children." Many parents feel compelled to keep up a "couple front," making it look to the children as if adults agreed on everything. Parental advice and commands repeatedly suggest that conflict is bad:

"Now don't get angry. . . . "

"Don't talk back."

"There's nothing to fight about."

"If you can't say something nice, don't say anything."

Moreover, adults without noticeable conflicts are presented as models:

"She doesn't have an angry bone in her body."

"He's such a calm person."

"They're always so friendly."

Teachings such as these are confusing to children who *know* that they experience conflict. What's a youngster to do when a brother or sister won't share, when parents are critical, when friends are uncooperative or cruel? Surely turning the other cheek isn't *always* the answer.

While children hear so much preaching about being nice, they're also being presented with messages that praise aggressiveness. Sports heroes frequently wind up in fights, often to the noisy approval of fans. Sarcasm and humor are often used as effective putdowns by the same adults who talk so much about kindness. Grownups who preach about pleasantness threaten ominously, "If you don't stop fighting you'll be sorry!"

Why is it that overt disagreement seems to be such a taboo in our society? What forces so many people to express their conflicts indirectly in such destructive, crazy ways? The answer lies in what Herbert Simons (1972) has termed a "system view" of conflict. Communicators who hold this view believe (usually not consciously) that maintaining the status quo is an extremely important goal, and that people should avoid rocking the boat in any way—even when the present system is clearly unsatisfactory.

The tendency to keep an unsatisfying system

I'm lonesome; they are all dying; I have hardly a warm personal enemy left.

James McNeill Whistler

---

running smoothly occurs in many settings. Both managers and employees continue plugging away at old ways of doing business rather than face the challenge of developing better methods. Teachers and students often look with hostility at each other across a gap of mutual mistrust and fear. Many families suffer through what Thoreau called lives of "quiet desperation," rather than speaking up and trying to change their lives.

Many people support the status quo only because they don't acknowledge that conflicts can be positive, and because they don't possess the skills to manage their disagreements constructively. This chapter should help you develop an awareness of the skills involved in managing conflicts.

So far, we've discussed beliefs about conflict that apply equally to both sexes. In addition, most of us have been exposed to the idea that men and women "ought" to deal with disagreements in different ways (Pearson, 1985). Probably the biggest difference has to do with emotions. The cultural stereotype of female behavior holds that women have a great capacity for expressing emotions, whereas men are generally expected to be more "logical" and issue-oriented. Therefore, for many people of both sexes, it's more appropriate to hear a woman say she's disappointed or confused than it does to hear a man send the same messages. The same holds true for nonverbal expressions. Whereas most people wouldn't be surprised to see a woman cry, the same behavior coming from a man is usually more of a shock.

Just as many people are used to perceiving women as extremely emotional, so they also find it easier to accept assertiveness when it comes from a man. Even in these relatively liberated

times, many people find the widely circulated guide "How to Tell a Businessman from a Businesswoman" amusing:

> A businessman is aggressive; a businesswoman is pushy.
>
> He loses his temper because he's so involved in his job; she's bitchy.
>
> He follows through; she doesn't know when to quit.
>
> He's firm; she's stubborn.
>
> He isn't afraid to say what he thinks; she's opinionated.

In the last decade, there has been increasing recognition that such stereotypes have more to do with cultural conditioning than with biology. Yet even the most ardent liberationists will admit that many people—both men and women—still accept and live by these attitudes.

Functional and dysfunctional conflicts

Some bacteria are "good," aiding digestion and cleaning up waste, whereas others are "bad," causing infection. There are helpful forest fires, which clean out dangerous accumulations of underbrush, and harmful ones, which threaten lives and property. In the same way, some conflicts can be beneficial. They provide a way for relationships to grow by solving the problem at hand and often improving other areas of interaction as well. Other conflicts can be harmful, causing pain and leaving a relationship weaker. Communication scholars usually describe harmful conflicts as *dysfunctional* and beneficial ones as *functional*.

What makes some conflicts functional and others dysfunctional? Usually the difference doesn't rest in the subject of the conflict, for it's possible to have good or poor results on almost any issue.

Sometimes certain individual styles of communication are more productive than others. In other cases the success or failure of a conflict will depend on the method of resolution the parties choose. We'll talk more about types of conflict resolution later in this chapter. We want now to describe several symptoms that distinguish functional from dysfunctional conflicts.

Integration vs. polarization   In a dysfunctional conflict biases are rampant. Participants see themselves as "good" and the other person as "bad"; their actions as "protective" and the other's as "aggressive"; their behavior as "open and trustworthy" and the other's as "sneaky and deceitful." Researchers Robert Blake and Jane Mouton (1964) found that people engaged in this kind of polarization underestimate the commonalities shared with the other person, and so miss areas of agreement and good will.

By contrast, participants in a functional conflict realize that the other person's needs may be legitimate too. A person who is allergic to cigarette smoke recognizes that smokers aren't nec-

Well-washed and well-combed domestic pets grow dull; they miss the stimulus of fleas.

Francis Galton

---

essarily evil people who delight in inflicting torment, while the smoker sympathizes with the other's need for cleaner air. In such issues functional conflict is marked by mutual respect.

Cooperation vs. isolation   Participants in a dysfunctional conflict see each other as opponents and view the other's gain as their loss: "If you win, I lose" is the attitude. This belief keeps partners from looking for ways to agree or finding solutions that can satisfy them both. People rarely try to redefine the situation in more constructive ways, and seldom give in, even on noncritical issues.

A more functional approach recognizes that by cooperating it may be possible to find an answer that leaves everyone happy. Even nations basically hostile to each other often recognize the functional benefits of cooperating. For example, the United States and the Soviet Union have clear-cut differences in certain areas, yet work together in fields such as disease control, halting air piracy, and disarmament. This same kind of cooperation is possible in interpersonal conflicts. We will have a great deal to say about cooperative problem solving later in this chapter.

Agreement vs. coercion   In destructive conflicts the participants rely heavily on power to get what they want. "Do it my way, or else" is a threat commonly stated or implied in dysfunctional conflicts. Money, favors, friendliness, sex, and sometimes even physical coercion become tools for forcing the other person to give in. Needless to say, victories won with these kinds of power plays don't do much for a relationship.

More enlightened communicators realize that power plays are usually a bad idea, not only on ethical grounds but because they often have a way of backfiring. Because it's rare that a party in a relationship is totally powerless, it's possible to win a battle only to lose a war. One classic case of the dysfunctional consequences of using power to resolve conflicts occurs in families where authoritarian parents make their children's requests into "unreasonable demands." It's easy enough to send a five-year-old out of a room for some real or imagined misbehavior, but when that child grows into a teenager there are many ways of striking back.

Deescalation vs. escalation   In destructive conflicts the problems seem to grow larger instead of smaller. As you read in Chapter 10, defensiveness is reciprocal: The person you attack is likely to strike back even harder. We've all had the experience of seeing a small incident get out of hand and cause damage out of proportion to its importance.

One clear sign of functional conflict is that in the long run the behavior of the participants solves more problems than it creates. We say "long run" because facing up to an issue instead of avoiding it frequently makes life more difficult for a while. In this respect handling conflicts functionally is rather like going to the dentist: You may find it a little (or even a lot!) painful for a while, but you're only making matters worse by not facing the problem.

Focusing vs. drifting   In dysfunctional conflicts the partners often bring in issues having little or nothing to do with the original problem. Take for example a couple who originally are having trouble deciding whether to spend the holidays at his or her parents' home. As they begin to grow frustrated at their inability to solve the dilemma, one of them says:

A: *"Your mother is always trying to latch onto us!"*

B: *"If you want to talk about latching on, what about your folks? Ever since they loaned us that money they've been asking about every dime we spend."*

A: *"Well, if you could ever finish with school and hold down a decent job, we wouldn't have to worry about money so much. You're always talking about wanting to be an equal partner, but I'm the one paying all the bills around here."*

You can imagine how the conversation would go from here. Notice how the original issue became lost as the conflict expanded. It's obvious that this kind of open-ended hostility is unlikely to solve any of the problems it brings up, not to mention the potential for creating problems not even existing before.

One characteristic of communicators who handle conflict well is their ability to keep focused on one subject at a time. Unlike those dysfunctional battlers whom George Bach and Peter Wyden (1968) call "kitchen sink fighters," skillful communicators might say, "I'm willing to talk about how my parents have been acting since they made us that loan, but first let's settle the business of where to spend the holidays." In other words, for functional problem solving, the rule is "one problem at a time."

Foresight vs. shortsightedness   Short-sightedness can produce dysfunctional conflicts even when partners do not lose sight of the original issue. One common type of shortsightedness occurs when disputants try to win a "battle" and wind up losing the "war." Friends might argue about who started a fight; but if you succeed in proving that you were "right" at the cost of the friendship, then the victory is a hollow one. Another type of shortsightedness happens when partners are so interested in defending their own

A quarrel between friends, when made up, adds a new tie to friendship, as experience shows that the callosity formed round a broken bone makes it stronger than before.

St. Francis De Sales

---

solution to a problem that they overlook a different solution that would satisfy both their goals. A final type of shortsightedness occurs when one or both partners jump into a conflict without planning the necessary steps. We will have more to say about preventing these last two types of shortsightedness in a few pages.

Positive vs. negative results   So far we've looked at the differences between the *processes* of functional and dysfunctional conflicts. Now let's compare the *results* of these different styles.

Dysfunctional conflict typically has three consequences. First, no one is likely to get what was originally sought. In the short run it may look as if one person might win in a dispute while the other loses, but most often both parties suffer in some way. For instance, an instructor might win by forcing an unpopular grading system on students who clearly would lose out if they received grades lower than the ones they believed they deserved. However, in situations such as this, instructors also fail to get what they want, for instead of trying to truly understand and master the material, the students will most likely become preoccupied with beating the system by simply memorizing facts, trying to "psych out" the forthcoming exams, or even cheating. Obviously this behavior prevents good learning, which means that the instructor has failed. In the long run, everyone has lost.

A second consequence of dysfunctional conflicts is that they threaten the future of the relationship. Let's return to the feuding couple. It's easy to imagine how the resentments of both partners would affect their behavior. For example, it's unlikely that either would feel affectionate after such an exchange, and so we might expect their home life to deteriorate: As their disappointment grows, they would probably be less willing to help each other in their usual ways. If this couple can't solve their original problems, it's likely that dissatisfaction with each other will grow like a cancer until it has poisoned almost every part of their relationship. This effect of individual conflicts on an overall relationship explains why it's important to deal successfully with seemingly inconsequential matters such as arriving on time for appointments or who takes out the trash, for every time partners don't resolve a small conflict they weaken their entire relationship.

Failure to resolve interpersonal problems is also personally destructive to each participant. We discussed the range of emotions in Chapter 9. Take a moment now to think about the feelings you've experienced when you were engaged in an unresolved conflict. It's likely that you felt (and still may feel) inadequate, foolish, unworthy, unlikable, or unlovable. Poorly managed conflicts have a strong effect on our self-esteem that can linger for years, threatening both our peace of mind and our future relationships with others.

In contrast to these dismal outcomes, functional conflicts have positive results. One benefit to skillfully handling issues is that interpersonal involvement increases. When we engage in a conflict productively, we get excited, motivated to act. In contrast to an apathetic person, the functional communicator is determined to do something to make the relationship better.

Skillfully handled conflict also promotes growth in a relationship. Along with restoring harmony, dealing with a conflict teaches people things about each other they didn't know before. They learn more about each other's needs and how such needs can be satisfied. Feelings are clarified. Backgrounds are shared. Of course growth can

occur in nonconflict situations too; the point here is that dealing with problems can be an opportunity for getting to know each other better. Moreover, conflicts provide the opportunity for new kinds of sharing. We often fail to know where another person stands on an issue until that issue is confronted.

Constructive conflict also provides a safe outlet for the feelings of frustration and aggression that are bound to occur in any relationship. When people accept the inevitable fact that they'll occasionally disagree with each other, they can be willing to let their partners express that disagreement, and in so doing defuse a great deal of it. One characteristic of good interpersonal communicators is that they allow each other to blow off steam without taking offense.

Finally, functional conflicts allow each person involved to establish a personal identity within the relationship. To see how important this individual identity is, think back to the early stages of your relationships. (Try to recall a wide variety: romantic, friendship, business, academic.) In many cases the earliest stages of relationships are marked by such a desire to promote harmony that the members behave unnaturally: They're so polite, so concerned with each other's happiness that they ignore their own needs and wants. In this effort to keep everything smooth, the parties give up a bit of themselves. When conflicts finally do surface, each gives the other a chance to take a stand, to say, "I understand what you want, but let me tell you what's important to *me*." Conflicts handled skillfully allow the relationship to grow while at the same time letting each person remain an individual.

Personal conflict styles

People have their individual styles of handling conflict—characteristic approaches they take when their needs appear incompatible with what others want. Sometimes a style is helpful and sometimes not. In either case people should recognize their own styles so they can make the styles work for them.

What's your style of handling conflict? Find out by thinking about how two hypothetical characters—Sally and Ralph—manage a problem that you might find familiar.

Sally and Ralph have been friends for several years, ever since they moved into the same apartment building. They had always exchanged favors in a neighborly way, but lately Ralph has been depending more and more on Sally. He asks her to care for his cat and houseplants almost every other weekend while he travels, borrows food and cash without returning them, and drops in to talk about his unhappy love life at least once a week. Until lately, Sally hasn't minded much, but now she's getting tired of Ralph's behavior.

Read the four groups of responses below and rank them in the order you would be most likely to use them. Mark your most likely response number 1, your next most likely number 2, and so on.

—— Steer clear of Ralph as much as possible. Pretend not to be home when he drops by. Make excuses for why you can't help him with his problems. *or* Do the favors for Ralph, hoping he'll stop imposing soon. After all, nobody's perfect, and it isn't worth making an issue.

—— Do the favors for Ralph, but let him know you aren't happy. Hint about the inconvenience of helping him. Sigh when he asks another favor. Make an occasional sarcastic remark about how much you enjoy being Ralph's housekeeper and psychotherapist. When he asks if you're upset with him, deny anything is wrong. Men-

tion your unhappiness to some mutual friends, hoping they'll tell Ralph to back off.

—— Ralph can't take a hint, so you tell him directly that you're fed up with his demands. Say you don't mind helping once in a while, but let him know he's taken advantage of your friendship. Warn him that continued impositions will threaten your friendship.

—— Tell Ralph that you're beginning to feel uneasy about his requests. Let him know that you value his friendship, and want to keep feeling good about him. Explain that's why you're telling him this, and ask him to work with you to find a way to solve his problems that's less of a strain for you.

Make sure you have ranked your responses before going on. Each of the choices above represents a different style of behavior in conflicts. These four styles are explained below and summarized in Table 11–1. As you read on, see which ones best describe the way you manage your own conflicts.

Nonassertion   Nonassertive behavior is the inability or unwillingness to express thoughts or feelings when necessary. Sometimes nonassertion comes from a lack of confidence. In other cases, people lack awareness or skill in more direct, effective means of expression.

One variety of nonassertive behavior is avoidance. People who avoid conflicts usually believe it's easier to put up with the status quo than to face the problem head on and try to solve it. This sort of avoidance has its costs, however: ongoing frustration, a loss of self-respect, and the risk of damaging an entire relationship.

Every time Sally hides from Ralph or changes the subject so he won't ask her for a favor, she

TABLE 11–1 Styles of conflict				
	NONASSERTIVE	DIRECTLY AGGRESSIVE	INDIRECTLY AGGRESSIVE	ASSERTIVE
Approach to Others	I'm not O.K., You're O.K.	I'm O.K., You're not O.K.	I'm O.K., You're not O.K. (But I'll let you think you are.)	I'm O.K., You're O.K.
Decision Making	Lets others choose.	Chooses for others. They know it.	Chooses for others. They don't know it.	Chooses for self.
Self-Sufficiency	Low.	High or low.	Looks high but usually low.	Usually high.
Behavior in Problem Situations	Flees, gives in.	Outright attack.	Concealed attack.	Direct confrontation.
Response of Others	Direspect, guilt, anger, frustration.	Hurt, defensiveness, humiliation.	Confusion, frustration, feelings of manipulation.	Mutual respect.
Success Pattern	Succeeds by luck or charity of others.	Beats out others.	Wins by manipulation.	Attempts "no lose" solutions.

Adapted with permission from S. Phelps and N. Austin, *The Assertive Woman* (San Luis Obispo, Calif.: Impact, 1974), p. 11, and Gerald Piaget, *Training in Assertive Communication: A Practical Manual*, 3d ed. (Portola Valley, Calif.: IAHB, 1980).

becomes uncomfortable and probably leaves Ralph feeling the same way. After this avoidance goes on for a while, it's likely that whatever enjoyment Sally and Ralph had found together will be eclipsed by their new way of relating, and the friendship will degenerate into an awkward, polite shell.

This kind of avoidance is particularly sad because the immediate fears of dealing with an issue are usually way out of proportion to what is likely to happen. Avoiders are not to blame; they may not know any better way to act. We simply want to point out the typically unsatisfactory results of such a conflict style.

In a few cases, however, avoidance may be the best course. If a conflict is short-lived, it might not be worth resolving. For example, you might let a friend's annoying grumpiness pass, knowing that the friend has been sick lately but will soon feel better. If the issue is genuinely a minor one, you might decide not to confront a person with it. You may have a neighbor, for instance, whose lawn sprinklers occasionally hit your newly washed car.

In your opinion, this annoyance may not even be worth mentioning. You also might reasonably choose to keep quiet if the conflict occurs in an unimportant relationship, as with an acquaintance whose language you find offensive but whom you don't see often.

Accommodation is another type of nonassertive response. Accommodators deal with conflict by giving in, putting the other's needs ahead of their own. Certainly, accommodation is sometimes appropriate, such as when the other person's needs really are more important than yours. For instance, if a friend wants to have a serious talk and you feel playful, you'd most likely honor the friend's request, particularly if the person is facing some kind of crisis and wants your help. In most cases, however, accommodators fail to assert themselves either because they don't value themselves sufficiently, or because they don't know how to ask for what they want.

Indirect aggression Indirectly aggressive communicators express their dissatisfaction in a disguised manner. Psychologist George Bach (1968) describes indirect aggression as "crazymaking." He uses this term because of the effect such behavior usually has on its target. There are a number of crazymaking ways to deal with conflict indirectly. One is through guilt: "Never mind, I'll do all the work myself. Go ahead and have a good time. Don't worry about me." Hinting is another form of indirect aggression: "When do you think you can get around to finishing the job?" Sometimes nonverbal behavior is a way to express aggression indirectly: a loud sigh, pained expression, or a disdainful laugh can get a message across. If the target of these messages asks about them, the indirect aggressor can always deny the conflict exists. Even humor—especially sarcasm—can be used as a way to send aggressive messages.

There are a number of risks to indirect approaches like these. First, they may not work. The other person might miss your message and continue with the undesirable behavior. On the other hand, the target of your indirect message might understand your message clearly, but refuse to comply, possibly out of irritation at your underhanded style of communicating. Even when indirect aggression proves successful in the short run, it can have unpleasant consequences over a longer period of time. You might get immediate compliance ("All right, I'll help you with the damn thing"), but create a resentful climate that will harm the relationship in the future.

Direct aggression   Where the nonasserter underreacts, a directly aggressive communicator overreacts, lashing out to attack the source of displeasure. Common consequences of direct aggression are anger and defensiveness on one hand, and hurt and humiliation on the other. In either case, aggressive communicators build themselves up at the expense of others. A directly aggressive attack can often lead to an

The test of a man or woman's breeding is how they behave in a quarrel.

George Bernard Shaw

equally combative reaction, starting a destructive spiral that can expand beyond the original dispute and damage the entire relationship.

Assertion   An assertive statement expresses the speaker's thoughts and feelings directly and clearly, without judging or dictating to others. A complete assertive message usually contains five parts (Miller et al., 1975):

1. The *behavior* that prompted the message. As you learned in Chapter 4, a behavioral description should describe only what can be observed.
2. The communicator's *interpretation* of the behavior described in step 1. It's important to label this statement as subjective, and not a matter of fact. For instance, "I get the idea you're mad at me" is a better interpretive statement than "I know you're mad at me."
3. The *feelings* that grow from the communicator's interpretation. Notice the difference between the statement "I get the idea you're mad at me" and the more complete description "I get the idea you're mad at me *and I feel hurt* (or defensive, confused, or sorry)." Review Chapter 9 for suggestions on how to express emotions clearly.
4. The *consequences* of the sense data, interpretation, and feelings described so far. Consequences can focus on three areas: what happens to the *speaker* ("When you tease me, I avoid you"), what happens to the *target of the message* ("When you drink too much, you start to drive dangerously"), or on what happens to *others* ("When you play the stereo loudly, it wakes up the baby").
5. Some sort of *intention statement*. Some inten-

tion statements are *requests* ("I hope you'll come again"). Others describe *how you plan to act* ("Unless we can work out some sort of studying arrangement, I may have to find a new place to live").

Sally could have used this format to express herself assertively to Ralph: "Ralph, I've been bothered by some things lately and I'd like to talk them over with you. (She identifies the problem as hers, and not Ralph's.) When you ask me to take care of your apartment two or three times a month and borrow food and cash without returning them (behavior), I don't think you realize the inconveniences I face (interpretation). I didn't mind until recently—that's why I haven't said anything before—but I'm starting to feel resentful (feeling), and I don't want to spoil our friendship (intention). I'd like to figure some way I can help you when you really need it, but without it being quite so much of a burden on me (another intention)."

Expressing yourself assertively doesn't guarantee you'll get what you want, but it often increases the chances of success. An additional benefit of such an approach is that it maintains the self-respect of both parties. As a result, people who manage their conflicts assertively usually feel better about themselves and each other afterward—not often the case with other styles.

Which style to use?   A look at your own behavior and that of others will show you that few people use the same conflict style all the time. For instance, take the average worker (Rahim,

From *The New Yorker*, August 29, 1983, p. 67.   "Want to fight?"

1983) who smoothes things over with his boss by being obliging and compromises to get what he wants from others with whom he works. Although he often lets others have their own way on the job, his behavior is completely different with his friends away from work. With them he's a collaborator, interested in discovering their needs and working to satisfy them as well as his own.

His style fits still another pattern with his children. Rather than deal with problems involving them, he'll avoid the issue in any way possible: making jokes, pretending to "forget" about his promises to discuss a problem, or retreating into his work. Many of us are like this man, changing our behaviors to suit various circumstances.

The person in this example changes conflict styles depending on whom he's dealing with; but context isn't the only determinant of which style to use. Sometimes people switch styles depending on the issue involved. For instance, you might be inclined to compromise on an issue that isn't vitally important to you, whereas you'd be more likely to confront others when the problem is a critical one.

Another factor governing our choice of conflict style is the mood we happen to be in. On some days you're probably most inclined to be an accommodator, giving in to the demands or desires of others. At other times you might be feeling angry or grouchy and be inclined to compete, even on unimportant issues.

Many communicators use one or two styles exclusively, because these ways of relating are the only ones they know. We've already seen that patterns of thinking and acting are formed early in life, and during these first critical years (and often beyond) many people see only avoiding, smoothing over, and competition. Not knowing that there are other alternatives that might be more effective, they use these styles throughout their lives to handle their own conflicts. This lack of awareness about effective communication styles explains why so many educators see a need for training parents in communication skills, so that children will grow from the start learning ways of relating that will help them throughout adulthood.

Even when aware of different conflict styles, some communicators rely heavily on only one or two. These behaviors are usually ones that worked well in the past, so the tendency is to continue relying on them, even though their usefulness may be gone. Frost and Wilmot cite the example of the man who is "stuck" in the style of a 1960s protester, seeing every issue as a fight against the establishment. This man identifies reflexively with the underdog, without considering whether the underdog is correct. He sees those in power as always evil and wrong, and tries to use any power at his disposal to defeat those "enemies." This man finds enemies where none exist, and creates problems unnecessarily.

Another common example of relying on long-standing but obsolete behavior is the student who accommodates and withdraws from those in authority because standing up to such people in the past met with punishment. It may make sense to give in to a harsh parent or authoritarian teacher when you're small and powerless, but such behavior isn't necessary as an adult, especially when others are interested in dealing constructively with problems.

It should now be clear that there's no single "best" style of dealing with conflict. What's appropriate behavior for communicating with a police officer you believe has unfairly given you a speeding ticket might not be the best way to act with a neighbor whose dog is digging up your garden. The right way to talk to your neighbor might not work at all when discussing the way you've drifted apart with an old friend. The key to success, then, is to develop a *repertoire* of conflict styles, so that when issues come up you'll be able to choose the way of communicating that works best for the given situation. Before introducing a new style of communicating to add to that repertoire, we next want to offer some guidelines to tell whether the styles of communication you're presently using are helping or hindering your conflicts.

Methods of conflict resolution

So far we have been describing individual conflict styles. These styles combine to form one of three outcomes. In the following pages we will look at each of these three outcomes and suggest how to make the most desirable one occur.

Win-lose   Win-lose conflicts are ones in which one party gets satisfaction while the other comes up short. People resort to this method of resolving disputes when they perceive a situation as being an "either-or" one: Either I get my way, or you get your way. The most clear-cut examples of win-lose situations are certain games, such as baseball or poker, in which the rules require a winner and a loser. Some interpersonal issues seem to fit into this win-lose framework: two co-workers seeking a promotion to the same job, say, or a couple arguing over how to spend their limited money.

Power is the distinguishing characteristic in win-lose problem solving, for it's necessary to defeat an opponent to get what you want. The most obvious kind of power is physical. Some parents threaten their children with warnings such as "Stop misbehaving or I'll send you to your room." Adults who use physical power to deal with each other usually aren't so blunt, but the threat often exists nonetheless. For instance, behind the legal system is the implied threat, "Follow the rules or we'll lock you up."

Real or implied force isn't the only kind of power used in conflicts. People who rely on authority of many types engage in win-lose methods without ever threatening physical coercion. In most jobs supervisors have the potential to use authority in the assignment of working hours, job promotions, desirable or undesirable tasks, and of course in the power to fire an unsatisfactory employee. Teachers can use the power of grades to coerce students to act in desired ways.

Intellectual or mental power can also be a tool for conquering an opponent. Everyone is familiar with stories of how a seemingly weak hero defeats a stronger enemy through cleverness, showing that brains can triumph over brawn. In a less admirable way, crazymakers can defeat their partners in effective, if destructive, ways: by inducing guilt, avoiding issues, withholding desired behaviors, pseudoaccommodating, and so on.

Even the usually admired democratic principle of majority rule is a win-lose method of resolving conflicts. However fair it may be, this system results in one group getting its way and another being unsatisfied.

There are some circumstances in which the win-lose method may be necessary, as when there are truly scarce resources, and when only one party can achieve satisfaction. For instance, if two suitors want to marry the same person, only one can succeed. To return to an earlier example, it's often true that only one applicant can be hired for a job. Still, don't be too willing to assume that your conflicts are necessarily win-lose. Many situations seeming to require a loser can be resolved to everyone's satisfaction.

There is a second kind of situation wherein win-lose is the best method of conflict. Even when cooperation is possible, if the other person insists on defeating you, then the most logical response might be to defend yourself by fighting back. "It takes two to tango," the old cliché goes, and it also takes two to cooperate.

A final and much less frequent justification for trying to defeat another person occurs when the other party is clearly behaving in a wrongful man-

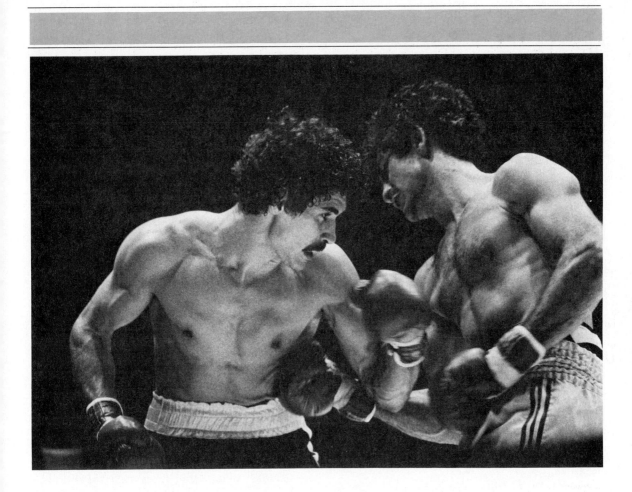

ner, and when defeating that person is the only way to stop the wrongful behavior. Few people would deny the importance of restraining a person who is deliberately harming others, even if the belligerent person's freedom is sacrificed in the process. It seems justifiable to coerce others into behaving as we think they should only in the most extreme circumstances.

Lose-lose   In lose-lose methods of problem solving neither side is satisfied with the outcome. Although the name of this approach is so dis-

couraging that it's hard to imagine how anyone could willingly use the method, in truth lose-lose is a fairly common approach to handling conflicts.

Compromise is the most respectable form of lose-lose conflict resolution. In compromising, all the parties are willing to settle for less than they want because they believe that partial satisfaction is the best result they can hope for. In *Interpersonal Conflict Resolution*, Alan Filley (1975) makes an interesting observation about our attitudes toward this method. Why is it, he asks, that if someone says, "I will compromise my values," we view the action unfavorably; yet we talk admiringly about parties in a conflict who compromise to reach a solution? Although compromises may be the best obtainable result in some conflicts, it's important to realize that both people in a dispute can often work together to find much better solutions. In such cases "compromise" is often a negative concept.

Most of us are surrounded by the results of bad compromises. Consider a common example, the conflict between one person's desire to smoke cigarettes and another's need for clean air. The win-lose outcomes on this issue are obvious: Either the smoker abstains or the non-smoker gets polluted lungs. Neither solution is mutually satisfying. A compromise whereby the smoker only gets to enjoy a rare cigarette or must retreat outdoors to smoke, and the nonsmoker still must inhale some fumes or feel like an ogre, is hardly better. Both sides still have lost considerable comfort and good will.

The costs involved in still other compromises are even greater. For example, if a divorced couple compromises on child care by haggling over custody and then finally grudgingly splits the time with its youngsters, it's hard to say that anybody has won.

Compromises aren't the only lose-lose solutions, or even the worst ones. There are many instances in which the parties both strive to be winners, but as a result of the struggle both wind up losers. On the international scene, many wars illustrate this sad point. A nation that gains military victory at the cost of thousands of lives, large amounts of resources, and a damaged national conscience hasn't truly won much. On the interpersonal level the same principle holds true. Most of us have seen battles of pride in which both parties strike out and both suffer. There should be a better alternative, and fortunately, there often is.

Win-win   As its name suggests, the outcome of a win-win problem-solving style is different than win-lose conflicts. Results that satisfy everyone are no accident: They are usually the result of an approach that is very different from the ones we've discussed so far (see Table 11–2).

In win-win problem solving the goal is to find a solution that satisfies the needs of everyone involved. Not only do the partners avoid trying to win at each other's expense, but there's a belief that by working together it's possible to find a solution in which everybody reaches her or his goals without needing to compromise.

One way to understand how no-lose problem solving works is to look at a few examples.

A boss and her employees get into a conflict over scheduling. The employees often want to shift the hours they're scheduled to work in order to accommodate personal needs, whereas the boss needs to be sure that the operation is fully staffed at all times. After some discussion they arrive at a solution that satisfies everyone: The boss works up a monthly master schedule indicating the hours during which each employee is responsible for being on the job. Employees are free to trade hours among them-

TABLE 11–2 Differences between win-lose and win-win problem solving

WIN-LOSE	WIN-WIN
Conflicting interests	Shared interests
Negotiations based on power	Negotiations based on trust
Low self-disclosure	High self-disclosure
Concern only for self	Concern for self and other

The first fight is a ritual, a test of the relationship. Very often it will be provoked deliberately, usually over a false issue (I know a couple who fell out forever, after a very promising start, over whether the Marx Brothers were greater than W. C. Fields), just to see what happens. Do they really care? How do they both feel? How deeply? Of course, all it really proves is that they can survive until the next fight.

Jane O'Reilly

---

selves, as long as the operation is fully staffed at all times.

A conflict about testing arises in a college class. Due to sickness or other reasons a certain number of students need to take exams on a makeup basis. The instructor doesn't want to give these students any advantage over their peers, and doesn't want to go through the task of making up a brand new test for just a few people. After working on the problem together, instructor and students arrive at a no-lose solution. The instructor will hand out a list of twenty possible exam questions in advance of the test day. At examination time five of these questions are randomly drawn for the class to answer. Students who take makeups will draw from the same pool of questions at the time of their test. In this way, makeup students are taking a fresh test without the instructor having to create a new exam.

A newly married husband and wife found themselves arguing frequently over their budget. The husband enjoyed buying impractical and enjoyable items for himself and the house, whereas the wife feared that such purchases would ruin their carefully constructed budget. Their solution was to set aside a small amount of money each month for purchases. The amount was small enough to be affordable, yet gave the husband a chance to escape from their Spartan lifestyle. Additionally, the wife was satisfied with the arrangement, because the luxury money was now a budget category by itself, which got rid of the "out of control" feeling that came when her husband made unexpected purchases. The plan worked so well that the couple continued to use it even after their income rose, by increasing the amount devoted to luxuries.

Although such solutions might seem obvious when you read them here, a moment's reflection will show you that such cooperative problem solving is all too rare. People faced with these types of conflicts often resort to such dysfunctional styles of communicating as withdrawing, avoiding, or competing, and wind up handling the issues in a manner resulting in either a win-lose or lose-lose outcome. As we said earlier, it's a shame to see one or both parties in a conflict come away unsatisfied when they could both get what they're seeking by communicating in a no-lose manner.

Win-win problem solving works best when it follows a seven-step approach, based on a plan developed by Deborah Weider-Hatfield (1981).

1. Define your needs   Begin by deciding what it is you want or need. Sometimes the answer is obvious, as in our earlier example of the neighbor whose loud stereo music kept others awake. In other instances, however, the apparent problem masks a more fundamental one. Consider an example: After dating for a few months, Beverly started to call Jim after they parted for the evening—a "goodnight call." Although this calling was fine with Jim at the beginning, he began to find it irritating after several weeks.

At first Jim thought his aggravation focused on the nuisance of talking late at night when he was ready for sleep. More self-examination showed that his irritation centered on the relational message he thought Beverly's calls implied: that she

I will not play at tug o' war.
I'd rather play at hug o' war.
Where everyone hugs
Instead of tugs,
Where everyone giggles
And rolls on the rug,
Where everyone kisses,
And everyone grins,
And everyone cuddles,
And everyone wins.

Shel Silverstein

---

was either snooping on Jim or was so insecure she needed constant assurances of his love. Once he recognized the true sources of his irritation, Jim's needs became clear: 1) to have Beverly's trust and 2) to be free of her insecurities.

Because your needs won't always be clear, it's often necessary to think about a problem alone, before approaching the other person involved. Sometimes talking to a third party can help you sort out your thoughts. In either case, you should explore both the apparent content of your dissatisfaction and the relational issues that may lurk behind it.

2. Share your needs with the other party Once you've defined your needs, it's time to share them with the other person. Two guidelines are important here. First, be sure to choose a time and place that is suitable. Unloading on a tired or busy partner lowers the odds your concerns will be well received. Likewise, be sure you are at your best: Don't bring an issue up when your anger might cause you to say things you'll later regret, when your discouragement blows the problem out of proportion, or when you're distracted by other business. Making a date to discuss the problem—after dinner, over a cup of coffee, or even a day in advance—can often

boost the odds of a successful outcome.

The second guideline for sharing a problem is to use the descriptive "I" language outlined in Chapter 10 and the assertive message format on pages 271–272. Rather than implying blame, messages worded in this way convey how your partner's behavior affects you. Notice how Jim's use of the assertive message format conveys a descriptive, nonjudgmental attitude as he shares his concern with Beverly: "When you call me after every date (sense data), I begin to wonder whether you're checking up on me (interpretation of Beverly's behavior). I've also started to think that you're feeling insecure about whether I care about you, and that you need lots of reassurance (more interpretation). I'm starting to feel closed in by the calls (feeling), and I feel myself pulling back from you (consequence). I don't like the way we're headed, and I don't think it's necessary. I'd like to know whether you are feeling insecure, and to find a way that we can feel sure about one another's feelings without needing so much reassurance (intentions)."

3. Listen to the other person's needs Once your own wants and needs are clear, it's time to find out what the other person wants and needs. (Now the listening skills described in Chapter 6 and the supportive behaviors described in Chapter 10 become most important.) When Jim began to talk to Beverly about her telephoning, he learned some interesting things. In his haste to hang up the phone the first few times she called, he had given her the impression that he didn't care about her once their date was over. Feeling insecure about his love, she called as a way of getting his attention and expressions of love.

Once Jim realized this fact, it became clear that he needed to find a solution that would leave Beverly feeling secure and at the same time allow him to feel unpressured.

Arriving at a shared definition of the problem

requires skills associated with creating a supportive and confirming climate. The ability to be non-judgmental, descriptive, and empathic are important support-producing behaviors. Both Jim and Beverly needed to engage in active listening to discover all the details of the conflict.

When they're really communicating effectively, partners can help each other clarify what it is that they're seeking. Truly believing that their happiness depends on the other's satisfaction, they actively try to analyze what obstacles need to be overcome.

4. Generate possible solutions   In the next step the partners try to think of as many ways to satisfy both of their needs as possible. They can best do so by "brainstorming"—inventing as many potential solutions as they can. The key to success in brainstorming is to seek quantity without worrying about quality. The rule is to prohibit criticism of all ideas, no matter how outlandish they may sound. An idea seeming farfetched can sometimes lead to a more workable one. Another rule of brainstorming is that ideas aren't personal property. If one person makes a suggestion, the other should feel free to suggest another solution that builds upon or modifies the original one. The original solution and its offshoots are all solutions that will be considered later. Once partners get over their possessiveness about ideas, the level of defensiveness drops and both people can work together to find the best solution without worrying about whose idea it is.

All of the supportive and confirming behaviors discussed in Chapter 10 are important during this step. Two, however, stand out as crucial: the ability to communicate provisionalism rather than certainty, and the ability to refrain from premature evaluations of any solution. The aim of this step is to generate *all* the possible solutions—whether immediately reasonable or not. By behaving provisionally and avoiding any evaluation until all the

solutions are generated, creative and spontaneous behavior is encouraged. The final result is a long list of solutions which most likely contains the best solution, one which might not have been expressed if the communication climate were defensive.

Jim and Beverly used brainstorming to generate solutions to their telephone problem. Their list consisted of: continuing the calling but limiting the time spent on the phone; limiting the calls to a "once in a while" basis; Beverly's keeping a journal that could serve as a substitute for calling; Jim's calling Beverly on a "once in a while" basis; cutting out all calling; moving in together to eliminate the necessity for calling; getting married; and breaking up. Although some of these solutions were clearly unacceptable to both of them, they listed all the ideas they could think of, preparing themselves for the next step in no-lose problem solving.

5. Evaluate the possible solutions and choose the best one   The time to evaluate the solutions is after they have all been generated, after the partners feel they have exhausted all the possibilities. In this step, the possible solutions generated during the previous step are evaluated for their ability to satisfy the mutually shared goal. How does each solution stand up against the individual and mutual goals? Which solution satisfies the most goals? Partners need to work cooperatively in examining each solution and in finally selecting the best one.

It is important during this step to react spontaneously rather than in a strategic fashion. Selecting a particular solution because the other person finds it satisfactory, while seemingly a "nice" thing to do, is as manipulative a strategy as getting the other person to accept a solution satisfactory only to you. Respond as you feel as solutions are evaluated, and encourage your partner to do the same. Any solution agreed upon as

**Our marriage used to suffer from argu-
ments that were too short. Now we argue
long enough to find out what the argument
is about.**

Hugh Prather
Notes to Myself

"best" has little chance of satisfying both partners' needs if it was strategically manipulated to
the top of the list.

The solution Beverly and Jim selected as satisfying her need to feel secure, his need to be
undisturbed before turning in, and their mutual
goal of maintaining their relationship at a highly
intimate level was to limit both the frequency and
length of the calls. Also, Jim agreed to share in
the calling.

6. Implement the solution   Now the time comes
to try out the idea selected to see if it does,
indeed, satisfy everyone's needs. The key questions to answer are *who* does *what* to *whom*,
and *when*?

Before Jim and Beverly tried out their solution,
they went over the agreement to make sure it
was clear. This step proved to be important, for a
potential misunderstanding existed. When will the
solution be implemented? Should Beverly wait a
few weeks before calling? Should Jim begin the
calling? They agreed that Jim would call after their
next date.

Another problem concerned their different definitions of length. How long is too long? They
decided that more than a few minutes would be
too long.

The solution was implemented after they discussed the solution and came to mutual agreement about its particulars. This process may
seem awkward and time consuming, but both
Beverly and Jim decided that without a clear

understanding of the solution, they were opening
the door to future conflicts.

Interestingly, the discussion concerning their
mutual needs and how the solution satisfied them
was an important part of their relationship
development. Jim learned that Beverly felt insecure about his love (sometimes); Beverly learned
that Jim needed time to himself, and that this
need did not reflect on his love for her. Soon after
implementing the solution they found that the
problem ceased to exist. Jim no longer felt the
calls were invading his privacy, and Beverly, after
talks with Jim, felt more secure about his love.

7. Follow up the solution   To stop after selecting
and implementing a particular solution assumes
any solution is forever, that time does not change
things, that people remain constant, and that
events never alter circumstances. Of course this
assumption is not the case: As people and circumstances change, a particular solution may
lose its effectiveness or, on the other hand,
increase its effectiveness. Regardless, it remains
for a follow-up evaluation to take place.

After you've tested your solution for a short
time, it's a good idea to *plan* a meeting to talk
about how things are going. You may find that you
need to make some changes or even rethink the
whole problem.

Reviewing the effects of your solution does not
mean that something is wrong and must be corrected. Indeed, everything may point to the conclusion that the solution is still working to satisfy
the individuals' needs and the mutually shared
goal, and that the mutually shared goal is still
important to you.

It is important at this stage in the no-lose problem-solving process to be honest with yourself as
well as the other person. It may be difficult for you
to say, "We need to talk about this again," yet it
could be essential if the problem is to remain
resolved. Planning a follow-up talk at the same

time the solution is first implemented is important.

Beverly and Jim decided to wait one month before discussing the effects of their solution. Their talk was short, because both felt the problem no longer existed. Also, their discussions helped their relationship grow: They learned more about each other, felt closer, and developed a way to handle their conflicts constructively.

The win-win approach seems too good to be true. Reassuringly enough, research shows that seeking mutual benefit is not only desirable—it works. In fact, it works far better than a win-lose approach.

Professor Robert Axelrod (1984) presented subjects with a bargaining situation called "prisoner's dilemma," in which they could choose either to cooperate or betray a confederate. There are three types of outcomes in prisoner's dilemma: One partner can win big by betraying a confederate, both can win by cooperating, or both can lose by betraying one another.

Although cynics might assume that the most effective strategy is to betray a partner (a win-lose approach), Axelrod demonstrates that cooperation is actually the best hard-nosed choice. He staged a tournament in which participants played against a computer that was programmed to represent several negotiating strategies. The winning strategy was one called "Tit-for-Tat." It starts out by cooperating and continues to cooperate until the other party betrays it. After that, the program always does what the other player did on the previous move. It never punishes an opponent more than once for a betrayal, and it will always cooperate if the other player does.

A win-win Tit-for-Tat strategy succeeds for several reasons (Kinsley, 1984). First, it isn't a sucker. It responds quickly to betrayal, discouraging others from taking unfair advantage. At the same time, it is quick to forgive. It doesn't hold a grudge: as soon as the other party cooperates, it does too. Finally, it isn't too sneaky. By making its

behavior obvious and predictable, Tit-for-Tat creates an atmosphere of trust.

There are certainly some conflicts that can't be resolved with win-win outcomes. Only one suitor can marry the prince or princess, and only one person can be hired for the advertised job. Most of the time, however, good intentions and creative thinking can lead to outcomes that satisfy everyone's needs.

Readings

Axelrod, R. *The Evolution of Cooperation.* New York: Basic Books, 1984.

*Bach, George R., and Peter Wyden. *The Intimate Enemy.* New York: Avon, 1968.

Blake, Robert R., and Jane S. Mouton. *The Managerial Grid.* Houston: Gulf Publishing Co., 1964.

Ellis, Donald G., and B. Aubrey Fisher. "Phases of Conflict in Small Group Development." *Human Communication Research* 1 (1975): 195–212.

Fahs, Michael L. "The Effects of Self-Disclosing Communication and Attitude Similarity on the Reduction of Interpersonal Conflict." *Western Journal of Speech Communication* 45 (1981): 38–50.

Filley, Alan C. *Interpersonal Conflict Resolution.* Glenview, Ill.: Scott, Foresman, 1975.

Filley, Alan C., Robert J. House, and Steven Kerr. *Managerial Process and Organizational Behavior,* 2d ed. Glenview, Ill.: Scott, Foresman, 1976.

*Fisher, R., and W. Ury. *Getting to Yes: Negotiating Agreement Without Giving In.* Boston: Houghton Mifflin, 1981.

*Frost, Joyce Hocker, and William W. Wilmot. *Interpersonal Conflict,* 2d ed. Dubuque, Iowa: Wm. C. Brown, 1985.

Gordon, Thomas. *Parent Effectiveness Training.* New York: Peter H. Wyden, 1970.

Jandt, Fred E. *Conflict Resolution Through Communication.* New York: Harper & Row, 1973.

Kinsley, M. "It Pays to Be Nice." *Science* 222 (1984): 162.

Miller, S., E. W. Nunnally, and D. B. Wackman. *Alive and Aware: How to Improve Your Relationships Through Better Communication.* Minneapolis: Interpersonal Communication Programs, 1975.

Pearson, J. C. *Gender and Communication.* Dubuque, Iowa: Wm. C. Brown, 1985.

*Rahim, M. A. "A Measure of Styles of Handling Interpersonal Conflict." *Academy of Management Journal* 26 (1983): 368–376.

Rosenfeld, Lawrence B. *Now That We're All Here . . . Relations in Small Groups.* Columbus, Ohio: Charles E. Merrill, 1976.

Simons, Herbert. "Persuasion in Social Conflicts: A Critique of Prevailing Conceptions and a Framework for Future Research." *Speech Monographs* 39 (1972): 227–247.

Tavris, C. *Anger: The Misunderstood Emotion.* New York: Simon and Schuster, 1982.

*Thomas, Kenneth. "Conflict and Conflict Management." In *Handbook of Industrial and Organizational Psychology*, Marvin D. Dunnette, ed. Chicago: Rand McNally, 1976.

*Weider-Hatfield, Deborah. "A Unit in Conflict Management Skills." *Communication Education* 30 (1981): 265–273.

Name Index

A

Abelman, A., 192, 202
Abrahams, D., 178
Adams, G., 159, 176
Adams, R., 123
Adler, R., 231, 257
Adosman, P., 178
Aiken, L., 120, 123
Aikman, A., 17, 214, 232
Alexander, H., 90
Alper, T., 109, 125
Alpern, M., 62
Alsbrook, L., 63
Altman, I., 154, 163, 176
Anderson, R., 134, 148
Apple, W., 126
Archer, R., 163, 176
Ardrey, R., 117, 123
Argyle, M., 170, 176
Armao, R., 50, 63
Armstrong, J., 78, 90
Arnett, R., 148
Aronson, E., 163, 176, 177, 178, 220, 231
Asbury, F., 149
Auden, W., 41
Austin, N., 270
Axelrod, R., 281
Axline, V., 148

B

Bach, G., 267, 271, 281
Backman, C., 161, 176
Baddeley, A., 148
Baer, J., 99, 100, 124
Baird, J., 63, 89, 90
Baker, E., 123
Bakker, C., 124
Bakker-Rabadau, M., 124
Bakwin, H., 108, 124
Bales, R., 163, 176
Balzer, F., 149
Banet, A., 217, 232
Banville, T., 129, 148
Barbour, A., 245, 257
Bardwick, J., 54, 63

Barker, L., 129, 131, 132, 135, 148, 149
Barnlund, D., 16
Baron, P., 58, 63
Bartoshuk, L., 48, 63
Bateson, G., 67, 90
Bavelas, I., 188, 202
Baxter, J., 124
Baxter, L., 169, 176
Beavin, J., 12, 17, 46, 64, 155, 157, 178, 258
Beck, A., 218, 231
Beier, E., 148
Bem, S., 54, 55, 63
Benchley, R., 220
Bennetts, L., 61, 63
Berg, J., 163, 176
Berger, C., 90
Berne, E., 183, 202
Berryman, C., 87, 88, 90
Berscheid, E., 42, 117, 124, 158, 159, 160, 175, 176
Biddle, B., 123
Bienvenu, M., 217, 231
Birdwhistell, R., 96, 124
Blake, R., 257, 265, 281
Blaylock, B., 160, 176
Block, H., 232
Blonston, G., 99, 124
Bordagaray-Sciolino, D., 168, 169, 176
Bostrom, R., 133, 148
Bradac, J., 79, 83, 90
Bradley, O., 89, 90
Breedlove, J., 160, 177
Brenton, M., 174, 176
Brown, B., 217, 232
Brunault, M., 126
Bryant, C., 133, 148
Buber, M., 28, 257
Buller, D., 149
Burgoon, J., 124, 149
Burgoon, M., 64, 88, 90
Burke, E., 244
Burke, R., 202
Burks, D., 17
Burns, D., 219, 231
Buscaglia, L., 231, 232
Buss, D., 159, 176
Byers, H., 124
Byers, P., 124

Byrne, D., 160, 176
Byrnes, D., 146, 149

C

Caldwell, M., 174, 176
Camden, C., 189, 190, 202
Campbell, C., 41
Campbell, D., 64
Candell, T., 92
Caplan, G., 16
Caraskadon, T., 232
Carifio, M., 126
Carlson, R., 17
Carroll, L., 68
Carson, R., 154, 176
Cash, T., 191, 202
Cather, W., 199
Chaikin, A., 163, 177, 186, 203
Chase, S., 90
Chelune, G., 185, 186, 198, 199, 202, 204
Childers, W., 149
Cissna, K., 237, 258
Civikly, J., 28, 42, 64, 113, 126, 191, 204
Clanton, G., 217, 232
Clark, V., 90
Clarke, F., 237, 257
Cleveland, B., 149
Cline, M., 63
Coakley, C., 129, 150
Cody, M., 92, 102, 103, 124, 126, 169, 176
Collins, J., 209
Condon, J., 63
Constantine, L., 217, 232
Cook, R., 90
Coon, D., 232, 257
Cooper, J., 160, 177
Corson, R., 124
Cory, C., 77, 90
Corzine, W., 217, 232
Cozby, P., 181, 196, 198, 199, 202
Craig, R., 87, 92
Crane, S., 223
Cronkhite, G., 62, 63

Acknowledgments continued from copyright page.

Love Poems for the Very Married by Lois Wyse (World Publishing Co.) Copyright © 1967 by Lois Wyse. Used by permission of Harper & Row, Publishers, Inc. **106** Excerpt from *Something Happened* by Joseph Heller. Copyright by Alfred A. Knopf, Inc. Used courtesy of the publisher. **107** Drawing by Modell; © 1983 The New Yorker Magazine, Inc. Used by permission. **108** Drawing by James Thurber. Copyright © 1943 James Thurber. Copyright © 1971 Helen W. Thurber and Rosemary T. Sauers. From *Men, Women, and Dogs*, published by Harcourt Brace Jovanovich. Used by permission. **115** Drawing by Bernard Schoenbaum; © 1983 The New Yorker Magazine, Inc. Used by permission. **118** Excerpt from "Decoding the Runner's Wardrobe" published in *Conformity and Conflict: Readings in Cultural Anthropology* by editors Spradley & McCurdy. Copyright Little, Brown and Company, Publishers. Used by permission. **119** Drawing by Richter; © 1968 The New Yorker Magazine, Inc. Used by permission. **133** "Peanuts" cartoon by Charles Schulz. © 1977. United Feature Syndicate, Inc. Used by permission. **137** Drawing by Saxon; © 1983 The New Yorker Magazine, Inc. Used by permission. **138** "At a Lecture—Only 12% Listen" from the *San Francisco Sunday Examiner and Chronicle*. Reprinted by permission. Courtesy of the San Francisco Examiner. **139** Poem "Duet" by Lenni Shender Goldstein. Used by permission of the poet. **139** "Momma" by Mell Lazarus. © 1977. Used courtesy of Mell Lazarus and New America Syndicate. **141** Excerpt from *The Best of Sydney J. Harris* by Sydney J. Harris. Copyright © 1957 by Sydney J. Harris. Reprinted by permission of Houghton Mifflin Company. **142** "Peanuts" cartoon by Charles Schulz. © 1978. United Feature Syndicate, Inc. Used by permission. **154** Drawing by Richter; © 1970 The New Yorker Magazine, Inc. Used by permission. **157** From *Notes to Myself* by Hugh Prather © 1970 Real People Press. Used courtesy of Real People Press. **159** "Peanuts" cartoon by Charles Schulz. © 1976. United Feature Syndicate, Inc. Used by permission. **164** Drawing by Saul Steinberg © 1965, Used by permission of artist and Julian Bach Literary Agency. **165** Chart, "Overview of Relational Stages" from *Interpersonal Communication and Human Relationships* by Mark L. Knapp. Copyright © 1984 by Allyn & Bacon. **168** Excerpt from *Leavetaking* by M. R. Feinberg, G. Feinberg, and J. J. Tarrant. Reprinted courtesy of the author, Mortimer R. Feinberg, Ph.D. **182** Thomas Wolfe, excerpted from *Look Homeward Angel*. Copyright 1929 Charles Scribner's Sons; copyright renewed © 1957 Edward C. Aswell, as administrator, C.T.A. of the Estate of Thomas Wolfe, and/or Fred W. Wolfe. Used by permission. Reprinted by permission of William Heinemann Limited. **183–185** Diagram, Johari Window, from *Group Processes: An Introduction to Group Dynamics* by Joseph Luft. © 1963 & 1970 by Joseph Luft. Used by permission of Mayfield Publishing Company. **187** Drawing by Ziegler; © 1983 The New Yorker Magazine, Inc. Used by permission. **189**

Excerpt from *The Best of Sydney J. Harris* by Sydney J. Harris. Copyright © 1957 by Sydney J. Harris. Reprinted by permission of Houghton Mifflin Company. **190** Chart from "White Lies in Interpersonal Communication: A Taxonomy and Preliminary Investigation of Social Motivations" by Carl Camden, Michael T. Motley, and Ann Wilson. *Western Journal of Speech Communication* 48 (Fall 1984): 309–325. Used by permission. **195** Drawing by Dana Fradon; © 1983 The New Yorker Magazine, Inc. Used by permission. **196** "Hands #1" from *Voice of the Hive* by Ric Masten. Published by Sunflower Ink, Palo Colorado, Carmel, CA 93923. **197** From "Mending Wall" by Robert Frost from *The Poetry of Robert Frost* edited by Edward Connery Lathem. Copyright 1930, 1939, © 1969 by Holt, Rinehart and Winston. Copyright © 1967 by Lesley Frost Ballantine. Reprinted by permission of Holt, Rinehart and Winston, Publishers, and by Jonathan Cape, Ltd. **200** Drawing by Stan Hunt; © 1982 The New Yorker Magazine Inc. Used by permission. **207** Drawing by Weber; © 1981 The New Yorker Magazine, Inc. Used by permission. **211** Drawing, "The Thinker," by Richard Stine from *Smile in a Mad Dog's I.* © 1974 by Richard Stine. Used by permission. **221** "Ziggy" cartoon by Tom Wilson. © 1974, Universal Press Syndicate. Reprinted with permission. All rights reserved. **222** "Peanuts" cartoon by Charles Schulz. © 1963. United Feature Syndicate, Inc. Reprinted with permission. **239** Diagram: "Progressive and Regressive Spiral Phases of a Marital Dyad" from *Dyadic Communication* 2nd Edition by William W. Wilmot. © 1979. Used by permission of Random House, Inc. **244** "Peanuts" cartoon by Charles Schulz. © 1965. United Feature Syndicate, Inc. Used by permission. **251** Drawing by Ross; © 1983 The New Yorker Magazine, Inc. Used by permission. **270** From *The Assertive Woman* © 1975 by Stanlee Phelps and Nancy Austin. Reproduced for Holt, Rinehart and Winston with permission from Impact Publishers, Inc., P.O. Box 1094, San Luis Obispo, CA 93406. Further reproduction prohibited. **272** Drawing by Bernard Schoenbaum; © 1983 The New Yorker Magazine, Inc. Used by permission. **278** "Hug O'War" from *Where the Sidewalk Ends: The Poems and Drawings of Shel Silverstein*. Copyright © 1974 by Shel Silverstein. By permission of Harper & Row, Publishers, Inc.